William Boy

William Boyce:
A Tercentenary Sourcebook and Compendium

By

Ian Bartlett
with Robert J. Bruce

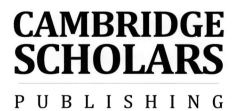

**CAMBRIDGE
SCHOLARS**

PUBLISHING

William Boyce: A Tercentenary Sourcebook and Compendium,
by Ian Bartlett with Robert J. Bruce

This book first published 2011. The present binding first published 2013.

Cambridge Scholars Publishing

12 Back Chapman Street, Newcastle upon Tyne, NE6 2XX, UK

British Library Cataloguing in Publication Data
A catalogue record for this book is available from the British Library

ISBN (10): 1-4438-4789-5, ISBN (13): 978-1-4438-4789-6

Portrait of William Boyce by Thomas Hudson (*c*1749), © Bodleian Library

TABLE OF CONTENTS

PREFACE

The almost total neglect of such a capable composer can only be a matter
of astonishment.
—William S. Newman

The avant-garde, experimental American composer, John Cage, was once
approached by a member of the audience after a performance of his 'silent'
piece, '4' 33'": "That was all very interesting" he said, "but couldn't anybody
have written it?" "Yes", was Cage's reply, "but nobody has!" Were I to be
asked a similar question about this book, my first response would be the
same as Cage's, but I would add that if there were ever to be a book about
Boyce, the ideal time to produce it would be now, in 2011, when the
tercentenary of the composer's birth is being celebrated.

My particular interest in the composer arose in the first place from pure
serendipity. In the early 1970s I had been looking for some music to edit
and study for the purposes of an academic dissertation. While perusing the
British Library Catalogue an entry caught my eye; it was for 'Solomon' by
William Boyce, a musician I knew little about, though I remembered
having once conducted an attractive anthem by him. It soon became
apparent that one of the most popular and significant compositions by an
Englishman in the whole of the eighteenth century still lay unexplored,
and for the most part, neglected.

Boyce played a leading role in English musical life throughout most of
his career. Having trained as a chorister at St. Paul's and served an
apprenticeship under Dr. Maurice Greene, Organist at the Cathedral, he
became a Composer at the Chapel Royal in 1736 and an Organist there in
1758, having already been appointed Master of the King's Music in 1755.
He also held a number of posts as Organist at parish churches in London
from 1734 to 1768. Boyce was also a highly respected and influential
teacher, at first giving instruction in harpsichord playing and later in
composition and theory. As a composer he produced a substantial output
of nearly 70 anthems, besides many secular, sacred, and court odes,
symphonies/overtures, trio sonatas, secular vocal music, organ voluntaries
and theatre music. For many years he conducted at the Three Choirs
Festival held annually at the Cathedrals of Worcester, Hereford and

Gloucester, and at the annual Festival for the benefit of the Sons of the Clergy at St. Paul's.

The first climactic point in Boyce's career came in July 1749 when he composed an ode for the Installation of the Duke of Newcastle as Chancellor of the University at Cambridge, was awarded his doctorate in music, and directed a mini-festival in which a number of his own large-scale choral works were performed. The second was in September 1761 when he wrote eight anthems for the Coronation of George III and directed the Coronation Service itself in Westminster Abbey. Finally, and perhaps most significant of all in relation to future developments in English musical culture, he edited and published his monumental and ground-breaking three-volume historical anthology of English church music, *Cathedral Music* (1760-73).

If Boyce had a rival for the leadership of English music during his lifetime it was Thomas Arne, his almost exact contemporary. Both men spent the whole of their careers labouring under the shadow of the great German composer Handel, who had settled in London about the time of their births. Arne, as a Catholic, inevitably worked entirely outside the established Anglican Church that was central to the development of Boyce's creative life. He wrote prolifically for the theatre, and made notable contributions to solo song, the secular ode and cantata, oratorio, orchestral music, the concerto and solo keyboard music. His significance in the history of English music has been duly recognized, for at least half-a-dozen books have been devoted to him in the last century. These include a pioneering study, *Dr. Arne and 'Rule Britannia'* (1912), by W.H. Cummings, a biography, *Dr Arne* (1938), by Hubert Langley, and four subsequent monographs on various aspects of his output. One of the purposes of the present volume has been to redress the balance somewhat in this regard, while at the same time addressing an evident lacuna in the literature on English music, specifically, a study of Boyce.

By the second half of the 19th century Boyce was generally known in this country only as the editor of *Cathedral Music*, and as a composer of anthems and the popular patriotic air, 'Heart(s) of oak', which later entered the canon as a 'national song'. However, by the turn of the century a number of arrangements based on movements from Boyce's trio sonatas and symphonies had begun to appear, and shortly afterwards articles about the composer by F.G. Edwards and later by H.C. Colles were published in the *Musical Times*. The first really significant breakthrough, however, occurred in 1928 when Constant Lambert, perceiving the qualities of Boyce's music, issued a complete edition of the *Eight Symphonys*. In 1938

Max Goberman recorded these works in New York, and eventually published a scholarly edition of them in 1964.

Perhaps the most telling aspect of the observation about Boyce quoted in the epigraph above is that it was made by an American pianist and musicologist of considerable international standing. His evaluation would not have been in any way partial, least of all could it have been tinged with chauvinism. Newman had come across Boyce's trio sonatas in the course of research for his seminal and magisterial book, *The Sonata in the Baroque Era* (1959). Yet, following in the footsteps of Lambert, a similar conclusion about Boyce had already been reached by the English composer, Gerald Finzi, who conducted a range of his works in the 1940s, and went on to edit a selection of his overtures for publication in Musica Britannica 13 (1957). Indeed, from the early 1950s a steady flow of critical editions of individual trio sonatas by Boyce had began to appear, and in 1960 both Arne and Boyce received unprecedented attention through performances and articles when the (assumed) 250th anniversary of their respective births was being celebrated.

Two of Boyce's previously unpublished anthems with orchestral accompaniment were printed in 1970, and about the same time his masque, *Peleus and Thetis*, was staged in London. But the next major steps towards Boyce's restitution were taken in 1979, the bicentenary of his death. A number of substantial articles on various aspects of the composer's life and work were published in periodicals. He was the subject of an extended talk on BBC Radio 3, who broadcast the serenata 'Solomon' for the first time, as well as the first performance in modern times of his short oratorio, 'David's Lamentation'. In 1982 the BBC also relayed the first modern revival of a substantial Ode to St. Cecilia, 'See famed Apollo and the nine'.

The most notable developments over recent decades have included the appearance of further university dissertations devoted to various aspects of Boyce's output, the publication of facsimile editions of his six-volume collection of vocal works, *Lyra Britannica,* the pastoral afterpiece, *The Shepherd's Lottery*, *Three Odes for Prince George*, the complete Trio Sonatas, and an edition of the serenata 'Solomon' in Musica Britannica 68 (1996). There has also been a considerable expansion in the range of Boyce's works available on CD, particularly with regard to the anthems, organ voluntaries, major choral works and theatre music.

This book has been strongly influenced by, but by no means closely modelled on, the documentary biographies devoted to Schubert, Handel and Mozart produced by O.E. Deutsch between 1913 and 1965. Such enterprises were characteristic of the positivistic musicology that prevailed in musical scholarship until the later decades of the 20th century, but is now, for a variety of reasons, much less in favour. Nevertheless, publications such as Deutsch's have proved to be of immense value to music historians as well as to scholars working in other humanities. They have also been of considerable interest to music lovers generally. So much so that the Handel volume (1955), is currently being revised and updated under the direction of Donald Burrows for publication in due course under the title *G.F. Handel: the Collected Documents.*

The fundamental aspiration of the present volume has been to record in detail, on the basis of contemporary evidence, the life of an English musician of the highest integrity, both as an artist and as a man. To this end the book brings together all sources relevant to Boyce's biography, his career, and the reception history of his music, supported whenever necessary by critical commentaries. The range of documents embraces letters to, from, and about the composer; materials relating to his Royal appointments and wider musical commitments; prefaces, title-pages and other details pertaining to his publications; advertisements for performances of his major works; assessments of his character, professional life and creative output in memoirs and histories; concert reports; poems and dedications in his honour; references to his activities in diaries and other literary sources; anecdotes revealing his personality as it manifested itself in his private life, and the subscriptions he made to musical and literary publications. I have also sought to explore Boyce's relations with the dramatists, poets, churchmen, and others with whom he collaborated. It is hoped that a clear and detailed picture of the contribution he made to the social and cultural life of Britain during his life-time will be discernible.

While most of the material included is inevitably 18th-century in origin, I have not hesitated to refer to post-1800 evidence when it is provided by witnesses whose lives overlapped with Boyce's, or when processes relevant to the dissemination of his music that began before 1800 continued into the next century. As far as possible I have also tried to avoid separating from their original sources literary references that help to establish the role played by Boyce's music in English social life. My concern has been on the one hand to place such quotations in their broader context, and on the other to reveal, for the pleasure of the reader, the distinctive and often engaging character of each writer's style.

It is hoped that the appearance of this volume will help to encourage in due course the writing of a conventional biography of Boyce, incorporating perhaps a critical evaluation of his music from a modern standpoint.

In conclusion, Robert Bruce's 'Catalogue of Works' constitutes the first comprehensive list of Boyce's musical output to have been published.

This book is dedicated with immense gratitude to my wife, Anne, who has borne my preoccupation with Boyce with remarkable stoicism over many years, and also to Robert Bruce's wife, Ann, who has suffered from the same syndrome.

—Ian Bartlett
Farningham, January 2011

ACKNOWLEDGEMENTS

I am much indebted to the many academic colleagues, librarians and friends who have given me assistance during this book's long period of gestation. First and foremost I would like to record my gratitude to Robert Bruce, formerly Senior Deputy Librarian at the Bodleian Library, Oxford, who has contributed the Catalogue of Works, the Boyce Bibliography and the Discography to this volume. Drawing on his extensive knowledge of the sources of Boyce's music, he has responded generously to numerous queries I have put to him over the last ten years. I have also appreciated greatly his willingness to engage in speculation and debate on a wide range of issues that have arisen in relation to Boyce's personal life, compositions and career.

Secondly, I owe a great deal to John Toner who has advised me in all matters relating to computer processes during the later stages of the preparation of this book. Like the late literary critic, Frank Kermode, I must confess to being "cheerfully but comprehensively baffled by computery". Not only did John give of his time unstintingly, but he also displayed remarkable forbearance in enabling me to overcome the numerous pitfalls lying in the path of an author preparing a sizable and in some respects complex manuscript for publication.

I must also thank the publishers, Cambridge Scholars Publishing, who have been consistently positive and encouraging. In taking on this project they were prepared to enter territory where others had feared to tread. I would particularly like to express my appreciation to Amanda Millar, my editor, who has steered the book through the processes of submission and publication with the utmost skill and sensitivity.

I am also very grateful to the following who have given me assistance, either by drawing attention to sources that might otherwise have been overlooked, or by responding to inquiries of one kind or another: Stephen Banfield, Julian Bartlett, George Biddlecombe, Donald Burrows, Richard Crewdson, Malcolm Davies, Harry Diack-Johnstone, Frank Dobbins, Joseph Hassan, Katharine Hogg, Kenneth James, J.S. Leedham-Smith, Rosemary Luckas, Frank Lynch, John McCabe, Philip Olleson, Andrew Pink, Benedict Sarnaker, Rosemary Southey, Roger Spikes, Ada Stewart, Colin Timms and David Wright.

In conclusion, I would like to record my gratitude for the always courteous and constructive service of librarians at the following institutions: The British Library, London, especially the staff in the Rare Books and Music Department, and the team at the Music Desk: Fiona McHenry, Christopher Scobie, Steve Cork and Clemens Gresser; the Bodleian Library, Oxford; Birmingham University Library; Cambridge University Library; Christ Church Cathedral Library, Dublin; Cecil Sharp House Library, London; City of Birmingham Reference Library; City of Liverpool Record Office; City of Westminster Archives Centre; Durham Cathedral Library; Fitzwilliam Museum, Cambridge, Department of Manuscripts and Printed Books; Freemasons Hall Library, London; the Foundling Museum, London; Glasgow University Library; Hereford Cathedral Library; Gloucester Cathedral Library; Gloucester City Music Library; Goldsmiths College London Library; Guildhall Library, London; Hereford Cathedral Library; Holborn Library Archives, London; John Rylands Library, University of Manchester; Kensington Central Library, London; King's College Cambridge, Rowe Music Library; King's College London Library; Lambeth Palace Library, London; Leeds Central Library; Liverpool Libraries and Information Services; the London Metropolitan Archive; London University Senate House Library; National Library of Wales, Aberystwyth; the Public Record Office, Kew; Reading University Library; Royal Academy of Music Library, London; Royal College of Music Library, London; the Society of Genealogists Library, London; St. Andrew's University Library, and the Worcester Record Office.

EDITORIAL NOTE

In the Documentary Biography full entries consist of a heading (in bold) followed by the reproduction of an original document (or an extract from one), an editorial commentary, and finally any foot-notes that may have been necessary. Where some entries are concerned the heading may be self-sufficient; in other cases only one or two of the subsequent sections may be required. If the precise source of a document is not explicit in the heading, it is fully identified at the start of the commentary. When the original document is known to have already been reproduced in later books or articles, the first known location of this reproduction is then acknowledged and placed in round brackets.

References in the commentaries or foot-notes to publications cited in the 'General Bibliography' are indicated as follows: for example, a reference to Winton Dean's *Handel's Dramatic Oratorios and Masques* (1959) will be abbreviated to 'Dean(1959)'. Similarly, references to works listed in the 'Boyce Bibliography', such as Roger Fiske's article on 'Boyce's Operas' published in the *Musical Times* 111 (1970), will be identified as 'Fiske *b*(1970)'. Whenever a work by Boyce cited in the Biography is not identified by its title, the relevant Bruce 'Catalogue of Works' number will be used; for example, the anthem, 'If we believe', will be called '*BC* 33'.

All original documents included in the Documentary Biography, whether complete or in part, are reproduced in a diplomatic transcription. Editorial interventions have been kept to a minimum, but when they are deemed to be desirable they are placed in square brackets. 18th-century usage with regard to capitalization is retained in the transcription of printed materials, but owing to the ambiguity inherent in many manuscript sources, modern practice in this area has been adopted.

With regard to monetary values in the 18th century, the pound was then worth 20 shillings, or 240 pence. One pound was represented as '1l', a shilling as '1s', and a penny as '1d'. The penny could be further divided into two halfpennies, or 4 farthings. A guinea was worth 21 shillings. Taking inflation into account, monetary values in the mid-18th century may be multiplied by *c*150 to arrive at the approximate modern equivalent.

Finally, it was in Boyce's lifetime, specifically in September 1752, that the Julian calendar of dates, 'old style', used in Britain previously, was replaced by the Gregorian system, 'new style', that remains in force today.

Up to that time the New Year had begun on 25 March, and dates between I January and 24 March were assigned to the previous year. Thus, the 20th of March, for example, would have been designated 'March 20, 1742-3'. In this book all such dates have been modernized, and that day would therefore be identified as '20 March 1743'.

ABBREVIATIONS

General Abbreviations

A.	Alto
addn(s)	additions
adv.	advertised
B.	Bass
BC	Bruce Catalogue
BMus	Bachelor of Music
cat.	catalogue
CG	Covent Garden Theatre
col.	column.
comp.	compiled
diss.	dissertation
DL	Drury Lane Theatre
DMA	Doctor of Musical Arts
doc(s).	document(s)
DPhil	Doctor of Philosophy
edn(s)	edition(s)
ibid.	ibidem (in the same place)
inc.	incomplete
intro.	introduction
loc. cit.	loco citato [in the place cited]
MA	Master of Arts
MMus	Master of Music
MPhil	Master of Philosophy
n.d.	no date of publication
n.p.	no place of publication
n(s).	footnote/endnote(s)
OKB	Ode for King's Birthday
ONY	Ode for New Year
op. cit.	opere citato [in the work cited]
PhD	Doctor of Philosophy
posth.	posthumous(ly)
pseud.	pseudonym
pubd	published
repr.	reprinted
rev(s).	revision(s); revised (by/for)
S.	Soprano
sic	thus

Sig.   Signor
s.n.   sine nomine [not named]
s.sh.f.   single sheet folio
T.   Tenor
trans.   transactions (of the)
t.s.   time-signature
unpubd   unpublished
WB   William Boyce

Book, Periodical and Newspaper Abbreviations

(Full citations of book titles will be found in the General Bibliography)

AR   *The Annual Register, or a View of the History, Politicks and Literature of the Year*
ABG   *Aris's Birmingham Gazette*
BDA   *A Biographical Dictionary of Actors, Actresses, Musicians, Dancers and Other Stage Personnel in London, 1660-1800*
BH(4)   The Blackwell History of Music, vol. 4, *The Eighteenth Century*
BM   *The British Magazine*
BurneyH   Burney: *A General History of Music*, 4 vols. (1776-89)
BWJ   *Berrow's Worcester Journal*
Deutsch   Deutsch: *Handel: A Documentary Biography*
DG   *The Daily Gazetteer*
DJ   *Dublin Journal*
EECM   Early English Church Music
EMP   *Early Music Performer*
FAM   *Fontes Artis Musicae*
GA   *General Advertiser*
GEP   *General Evening-Post*
GM   *Gentlemen's Magazine*
GDA   *Gazetteer and Daily Advertiser*
GNDA   *Gazetteer and New Daily Advertiser*
Grove   *A Dictionary of Music and Musicians,* 5 edns (1879-1954)
GSJ   *Galpin Society Journal*
HMM   *Harrop's Manchester Mercury*
HawkinsH   J. Hawkins: *A General History of the Science and Practice of Music,* 5 vols. (1776)
HWV   *Händel Werke Verzeichnis*
JOJ   *Jackson's Oxford Journal*
LB   Lyra Britannica
LDA   *London Daily Advertiser*
LDP   *London Daily Post*
LEP   *London Evening-Post*
LM   *The Lady's Magazine*

LM(2)	*The London Magazine*
LNJ	*Leicester and Nottingham Journal*
LS	The London Stage 1660-1800
MB	Musica Britannica
MC	*Morning Chronicle and London Advertiser*
ML	*Music & Letters*
MLE	Music for London Entertainment 1660-1800
MM	*Music and Musicians*
MMR	*Monthly Musical Record*
MO	*Musical Opinion*
MP	*The Morning Post*
MR	*Music Review*
MT	*Musical Times*
NCB	New Cheque Book, Chapel Royal
NG2	*The New Grove Dictionary of Music and Musicians,* 2nd edition (2001)
OCB	Old Cheque Book, Chapel Royal
ODNB	Oxford Dictionary of National Biography
PA	*Public Advertiser*
PRMA	*Proceedings of the Royal Musical Association*
Rem	*The Remembrancer*
RMARC	*Royal Musical Association Research Chronicle*
SJC	*St. James's Chronicle*
WEP	*Whitehall Evening-Post*
Z	Zimmerman Purcell Catalogue

Library Sigla

(Libraries in Great Britain are cited without their international sigla)

Abu	Aberystwyth, University College of Wales
Bu	Birmingham, University Library
Cfm	Cambridge, Fitzwilliam Museum
Ckc	Cambridge, King's College, Rowe Music Library
Cu	Cambridge, University Library
Ddhc	Dorchester, Dorset History Centre
Drc	Durham, Cathedral Library
GL	Gloucester, Cathedral Library
Glr	Gloucester, Record Office
Gu	Glasgow, University Library
H	Hereford, Cathedral Library
Lam	London, Royal Academy of Music Library
Lbl	London, British Library
Lcm	London, Royal College of Music Library
Lcr	London, Chapel Royal Archives

Lcs	London, Cecil Sharp House Library
Lec	Leeds, Leeds Central Library
Lfom	London, Foundling Museum
Lgc	London, Guildhall Library
Lhla	London, Holborn Library Archives
Lkc	London, King's College
Lkcl	London, Kensington Central Library
Llp	London, Lambeth Palace Library
Lma	London Metropolitan Archive
Lpro	Public Record Office, Kew
Lsg	London, Society of Genealogists.
Lwa	City of Westminster Archives Centre
Lvp	Liverpool, Libraries and Information Services
Mr	Manchester, John Rylands Library, Deansgate
Ob	Oxford, Bodleian Library
SA	St. Andrews, University Library
F: Pn	Bibliothèque Nationale de France
IRL: Dcc	Dublin, Christ Church Cathedral, Library
IRL: Dtc	Trinity College Library, University of Dublin
US: CA	Cambridge (MA), Harvard University Library
US: CAh	Chicago, Harvard University, Houghton Library
US: NH	New Haven (CT), Yale University Library
US: Nhub	New Haven (CT), Yale University, Beinecke Library
US: SM	San Marino (CA), Huntington Library
US: Wc	Washington, Library of Congress, Music Division
US: Ws	Washington, Folger Shakespeare Library

DOCUMENTARY BIOGRAPHY

PART ONE

THE EARLY YEARS, 1711-1739

From the *Register of Christnings within the Parish of St James Garlick-Hythe* [1708-46]

Lgc, MS9141. (Dawe *b*(1968), 803) Entry: "Boyes William Son of John & Elizabeth 11 Sept." [1711]. William Boyce was the fourth and last child of John and Elizabeth Boyce. His father was a cabinet-maker. At the time of his birth his parents resided in the Parish of St James Garlickhythe in the City of London. Their union in 1703 is recorded in the *Register of Marriages 1701-43* for the church of St Michael Paternoster Royall (*Lgc,* MS5145): "John Boys and Elizabeth Cordwell of the Parish of St Martins Vintry were married in the Parish Church of Michaell Royall the 28th day of March by lycons". [license] The two parishes had been united in 1670. Boyce's parents had moved to Maiden Lane (now Skinners' Lane, EC4) not long before William's birth. Ever since the publication of the 'Memoirs of Dr. Boyce' (Hawkins *b*(1788)), all biographers of Boyce had followed Hawkins in accepting that the composer had been born in 1710. Though Hawkins knew WB very well, the presumption had arisen simply on the basis of a deduction of 69 (his age at death according to his tombstone) from 1779, the year of his death. It was not until 1968, when Donovan Dawe published his researches into the history of the Boyce family, that it was revealed that his baptism had not taken place until September 1711. It was only from this time that writers on WB began to refer to the more or less certain date of his birth.

♣

Boyce is accepted into the Choir School at St. Paul's Cathedral *c*1719.

Details of Boyce's choristership are lacking since the relevant records of the Cathedral were destroyed in the Second World War. We do know, however, that his contemporary, John Alcock, arrived at St. Paul's in 1722 when he was about seven (Garrett(1974), 83). Boyce's father having soon observed his son's natural musicality, William probably entered St. Paul's *c*1719 when he was about eight. He remained there until 1727 when he became an articled pupil of Maurice Greene, then organist of the Cathedral. The Boyce family home at Joiners' Hall in Maiden Lane (now Skinners Lane) was conveniently situated near St. Paul's. WB was among the earliest generations of choristers to have worked in the inspiring surroundings of the then newly completed cathedral, designed by Christopher Wren to replace the original building devastated by the Great Fire of London in 1666. The new foundations were laid in 1675, but Wren's masterpiece as we know it today was not officially opened until 1711. During his seven-year apprenticeship, apart from pursuing his studies in composition and organ playing, WB undertook copying duties for Greene; indeed, he is known to have continued to assist in this role until at least 1736.

♣

From Royal College of Music, MS1189, 4 June 1726

N.B. This was given to me by Mr. Boyce when we were school-fellows and bed-fellows, under tuition of Mr. Charles King M.B. &c. J. Alcock, who imagines he cou'd not be above 14 years of age, when these pieces of music were compos'd.

(*Lcm*, MS1189, f. 5ᵛ) This manuscript presented to Alcock contains an anthem in Boyce's hand, 'Help me O Lord', which is the earliest of his finished works known to have survived. Boyce also copied into this source part of the anthem, 'Hosanna to the Son of David', by Orlando Gibbons. Alcock went on to become organist at Lichfield Cathedral in 1750 and was awarded a DMus (Oxon) in 1766. The anthems preserved here serve to illustrate on the one hand Boyce's early competence as a composer, and on the other, his youthful familiarity with some of the outstanding repertoire from the heritage of English church music. The seeds sewn at this early stage in his life ultimately led to his ground-breaking editorial achievement, the anthology of earlier English anthems, *Cathedral Music* (1760-73).

♣

Boyce's first published work is issued (c1730).

This was a solo song setting of an anonymous poem, 'The Herefordshire Winter: 'At Ross how altered is the scene''. It was first printed in a single sheet folio (*Lbl*, G.306(40)), and appeared later in the song collections, *The Agreeable Amusement* (1743-4), no. 83, and *The Vocal Enchantress* (1783), 138-9. In common with most songs of its period, it would have aimed to capture the large and growing domestic market for such pieces, and to achieve performances at the public pleasure gardens. Of the 79 individual solo songs Boyce is known to have composed, two are lost, 17 of the earliest survive only in manuscript, while the great majority were printed either in *Lyra Britannica* (1747-59), in anthologies, in s.sh.f, or as supplements in periodicals. The most popular among them were published on numerous occasions up to the end of the century. Two appeared in s.sh.f. only, namely 'O nightingale' (text: John Milton), publ. posth. (*Lbl*, G.310, (283)), and 'Why treat me still?' (John Lockman) in *Lbl*, G.313, (126).

♣

From the Vestry Minutes of St. Michael's, Cornhill, 20 June 1734

This Vestry was called for the choice of an organist in the room of M^r: Obadiah Shuttleworth deceased and upon the church wardens acquainting the Vestry that there were five candidates (viz:) Mr Froude Mr Kelway Mr Boyce Mr Young and Mr Worgan. It was agreed to that such election should be by ballotting by reducing the number of candidates names (each elector to put no more than one candidates name in the glass at one time) and the three who have the least votes to be sett aside and the two others to be ballotted for again and one of the two who shall have the majority to be organist. And upon the first securing them the majority fell upon M^r: Boyce and M^r: Kelway who were ballotted for again and the majority fell upon Mr Joseph Kelway who was accordingly declared Organist of this parish for the remaining part of the year at the usual sallery of 20^l:[£] p[er] annu[m].

Lgc, MS4072/2, 228. This was Boyce's first application for a post as a church organist. Froude was organist at St. Giles Cripplegate (1736-70). Young was either Anthony or Charles, who were brothers (see Dawe

(1983), 159-60). Charles was organist of All Hallows Barking by the Tower (1713-58); Anthony, was organist at St. Clement Danes from 1707 until at least 1743, and may have taught Thomas Arne from time to time c1730 (Nash(1977), 22). James Worgan was organist at St. Dunstan in the East (1738-53). Kelway, who later gained a reputation as a virtuoso keyboard player, resigned in June 1736, having successfully applied for a similar position at St. Martins-in-the-Fields. (Dawe, op. cit., 118). Kelway's departure offered WB a further opportunity to gain this post at St Michael's two years later. The salary was worth c£3,000 in modern currency.

♣

Boyce is appointed organist at the Oxford Chapel, Vere Street.

This was Boyce's first appointment as an organist. Having been pipped at the post by James Kelway for the organistship of St. Michael's Cornhill in June 1734, he seems to have found temporary consolation at the Oxford Chapel. This church opened in 1724, and survives to this day just off Cavendish Square, N.W. of Oxford Circus. It was built for the then growing population of Marybone by Edward Harley, 2nd Earl of Oxford, who commissioned a leading architect of the day, James Gibb, to design it[1] The fact that it was a proprietory rather than a parish church initially, probably explains why early records of its activities appear not to be extant.[2] However, we do know that the Harleys' daughter, Margaret, was married to William Bentinck on 11 June 1734,[3] and we may conjecture that Boyce played the organ at the ceremony. We know of Boyce's appointment through his friend and biographer Hawkins: "At the expiration of his Apprenticeship, he became organist of the chapel in *Vere Street* near *Cavendish Square*, called Oxford Chapel".[4] Only much later, in the mid-19th century, is any reference made to WB's resignation from this post. The well-informed music historian, Joseph Warren, then wrote: "In the year 1736, he quitted his employment at Oxford Chapel, the salary

---

[1] Gibb's other buildings included St. Martin's-in-the-Fields and the University Senate House at Cambridge, where WB was later to receive his doctorate.
[2] With the exception of a register of marriages (July 1736 to March 1754) preserved at *Lma*, X097/067.
[3] See Gower(1922), 2.
[4] Hawkins b(1788), i. If he is right, 1734 is confirmed as the year of Boyce's appointment to the Chapel.

whereof was but small."[5] It may be presumed that WB resigned in, or shortly after, June of that year. In that month he became organist at St. Michael's Cornhill at the second attempt, and he was also appointed a Composer of the Chapel Royal, a post that also involved some organ playing duties.

♣

John Walsh publishes *The British Musical Miscellany, or the Delightful Grove*, 2 vols. [1734].

These "celebrated English, and Scottish Songs, by the best Masters" include the earliest solo songs of Boyce to appear in a collection. Vol. 1 contains 'When Fanny blooming fair' (text: attrib. Thomas Phillips, but no composer identified); 'What tho' you cannot move her' (John Glanvill), 103, and 'Can nothing, nothing move her' (J. Glanvill), 122-3. Vol. 2 includes 'Silvia, the fair' (John Dryden), 89-90, 'I love! I doat!' (anon.), (*BC* 226), 109-10, and 'Come all ye youths' (Thomas Otway).

The attribution to Phillips of the poem set here by Boyce was reiterated in many subsequent editions of the song in the 1730s and 40s. However, from 1748 onwards the text gradually came to be widely acknowledged as the work of Lord Chesterfield. He had enjoyed a close relationship with Lady Frances ('Fanny') Shirley, a well-known society beauty universally recognised to be the inspiration for, and the subject of, this poem. It should be noted here in the context of the uncertain origin of the words that the autogr. MS of the song reveals that the original opening of the text received and set by Boyce read: 'When Cloe, blooming fair'.[6] A critical appraisal of the history of the song, and the case in favour of Chesterfield's authorship, has recently been published.[7] The music historian, Thomas Busby, later offered an assessment: "The elegant melody set to the song of Lord Chesterfield, 'When Fanny, blooming fair', was one of the first harbingers of Boyce's future eminence. It was remarkably distinct in its character, its features were beautiful, and perfectly its own" (Busby(1819), 2, 485). The poet Christopher Smart later paid tribute to the song by translating its text into Latin (Smart(1791), 86-9) and French (Williamson (1787), 4-6).

---

[5] Warren *b*(1849), 4.
[6] See *Lcm*, MS782, f.3ᵛ.
[7] See Bartlett *b*(2008).

♣

Boyce studies with Dr. J.C. Pepusch.

Having completed his apprenticeship under Greene in 1734, Boyce undertook further training with Pepusch, a German musician who had settled in London *c*1700. The latter earned a high reputation as composer, harpsichordist, viol player, musical director, and for his contributions to the production of the *Beggar's Opera* (1728), the most widely performed theatrical work of the century. Pepusch's greatest achievements, and those that were most long-lasting in their effects, however, lay in the influence he exerted within the Academy of Ancient Music, the inspiration he gave to a whole generation of English musicians with regard to the appreciation and performance of 'ancient', i.e. pre-18th-century, music, and last but not least, in the study of musical theory. As a later commentator put it: "[Boyce] became a constant attendant at the scientific lectures of the learned Dr. Pepusch, studying with deep attention the philosophical principles of music" Ayrton(1823), vol, 1, 159).

In addition to Boyce, Pepusch's students included the composers Bennett, Cooke, Howard, Keeble, Nares and Travers, probably the music historian Hawkins, and many others. The foundations were laid by these musicians, aided by the abiding popularity of Handel's church music and oratorios, for a new culture in which great music of the past took a central role in, indeed often took precedence over, contemporary works in the repertoire performed; thus over time a canon of 'classical music' gradually came to be established.

John Wesley summed up Pepusch's outlook with regard to the musical culture of the day in his *Journal* (entry for 13 June 1748): "I spent an hour or two with Dr. Pepusch. He asserted that the art of music is lost; that the ancients only understood its perfection; that it was revived a little in the reign of King Henry VIII by Tallis and his contemporaries; as also in the reign of Queen Elizabeth, who was a judge and patroness of it; that, after her reign it sunk for sixty or seventy years, till Purcell made some attempts to restore it; but that ever since the true, ancient art, depending on nature and mathematical principles, had gained no ground, the present masters having no fixed principles at all" (quoted in Scholes(1948), 1, 44). Later, in a letter dated 10 Jan. 1799 to A.F. Kollman, J.W. Callcott wrote: "You must have heard frequently of the great reputation Dr. Pepusch enjoyed in this country. He came over here with a great stock of learning derived from the pure sources of the last century. . . . He established a school which yet flourishes of which Dr. Boyce was one of the brightest ornaments" (quoted in Cook(1983), 324).

♣

John Walsh publishes the *British Musical Miscellany*, vol. 4 [1735].

Having included six Boyce songs in vols. 1 & 2 [1734] of this collection, Walsh added three more here: 'Of all the torments' (text: W. Walsh), 61-2, 'Would we attain the happiest state' (Anne Finch), 88, and 'The adieu to the Spring-Gardens at Vaux-Hall: 'The sun now darts" (John Lockman), 102-3. The last setting is not attributed to WB here.

♣

Boyce's sacred cantata, 'David's Lamentation over Saul and Jonathan', is performed in London (1736).

The title-page of the word-book for this piece reads: *David's* LAMENTATION | over | *Saul* and *Jonathan.* | A LYRIC POEM. | By Mr. *JOHN LOCKMAN* | Set to MUSIC by Mr *BOYCE.* | And performed in | The *Apollo-Society* April 16, 1736. [&c.] This was Boyce's first major composition. Lockman's text is based on the biblical account in II Samuel I of the deaths of Saul and Jonathan at the battle of Mount Gilboa, and the elegy which follows it. The appearance of such a work at this time should be seen against the background of the emerging genre of the dramatic oratorio in England following the performances of Handel's *Esther* in 1732. Lockman's poem, however, is not dramatic in character (there are no *dramatis personae*), but is essentially narrative and lyrical. Nevertheless, when Lockman amplified his text through the addition of five new airs for another setting by J.C. Smith performed in 1740, it was described as an 'oratorio'. Boyce's setting is for alto and tenor soloists, chorus and small orchestra. The autogr. score and related parts for the Apollo performance are preserved at *Ob*, MS.Mus.Sch.D.267, but when WB later adapted the work for performances in Dublin with local singers in mind, he transposed some of the airs upwards, and made sensitive changes to some of the instrumentation (see *Lcm*, MS91).

The Apollo Academy was a private society founded by Boyce's mentor, Maurice Greene, after the latter had withdrawn from the Academy of Ancient Music in the wake of the notorious 'Bononcini affair' of 1731. Meetings were held in the Apollo Room in the Devil's Tavern, Temple

Bar. The subsequent appearance of the text for *David's Lamentation* in the 'Miscellany of Lyric Poems, The Greatest Part written for, And performed in The *Academy* of Music, Held in the Apollo (1740)', suggests that the work remained in the repertoire there at least until that time and probably beyond. It was also performed at Windsor in 1737 (see *DA*, 18 Aug.) and in all likelihood at various times in Dublin during the early 1740s (see *DJ*, 29 Sept, 1744). Both Boyce's and Smith's settings may have received other performances in London as the following newspaper notice advertising Lockman's libretto(s) indicates: "David's Lamentation . . . set to Music by Dr. *Boyce* and performed by the Gentlemen of the King's Chapel, Set also by Mr. *J.C. Smith*; and performed by Mr. *Beard*, Mrs. *Arne*, &c, at Mr *Hickford's*.[8] The Fifth Edition. Price 6d"[9] (*Rem*, 1 Sept. 1750).

The first modern performance of *David's Lamentation* was broadcast by the BBC in 1979 (see Bartlett *b*(1979i)), and it was recorded on CD in 2000 (see Discography).

♣

From the Vestry Minutes of St. Michael Cornhill, 2 June 1736

A letter from M[r]: Joseph Kelway, Organist was produced and read, setting forth his having been elected Organist of St. Martins in the Fields and therefore would resign his place of Organist of this parish at Midsummer next And the church wardens acquainting the Vestry there are four candidates (viz.) M[r]: Boyce, M[r]: Cooke, M[r]: Young[10] and M[r]: Manwaring. It was proposed and agreed to that such election shall be by reducing the number of candidates to two by hands and afterwards to ballot for the two who shall have the majority of hands And he of the two who shall have the majority shall be Organist. Upon the question put and holding up of hands the majority fell upon M[r]: Boyce and M[r]: Young who were ballotted for and M[r]: Boyce having the majority was declared Organist of this parish for the remaining part of this year at the usuall Sallery of 20[l] p[er] annum.[11]

Lgc, MS4072/2, 237. Boyce had earlier applied for this post in June 1734 when Kelway was the successful candidate. Young had also been on the

---

[8] A well-known London concert venue.

[9] About £3.50 in modern currency.

[10] This applicant was either Anthony or Charles Young, both active organists in London at this time.

[11] In modern currency *c*£3,000.

short-list then, but Cooke and Manwaring were new applicants. Cooke was organist at St. Martin-in-the-Fields at this time, while Manwaring went on to become an organist at St. George Botolph from 1739-80.

♣

From the *Old Cheque Book* of the Chapel Royal, 21 June 1736

Whereas the Right Reverend the Lord Bishop of London, Dean of His Majesty's Chapels Royal, has appointed William Boyce to be Composer, and Jonathan Martin to be Organist of the said Chapels; And whereas the place of Organist has much more duty and attendance belonging to it than the place of Composer (both which were enjoy'd by M^r. Weldon lately deceas'd, during whose long indisposition the two places were jointly supply'd by the two persons aforesaid.) I the said William Boyce, do promise and agree, that so long as I shall continue in the place of Composer I will perform one third of the duty and attendance belonging to the Organist, provided that I am allow'd one third part of the travelling charges belonging to the place. And I Jonathan Martin promise to compose anthems or services for the use of His Majesty's Chapel, whenever required by the Subdean for the time being. In witness whereunto we have set our hands this twenty first day of June 1736.

William Boyce
Jona: Martin

Lcr, OCB, f.58^r. (Rimbault(1872), 51-2.) This entry serves to confirm that both Boyce and Martin had already deputised for Weldon as organists/composers for some time before their official appointments. The selection of Jonathan Martin to replace John Weldon as Organist was also recorded on 21 June in OCB, fol. 57^v. On the premature death of Martin in 1737, John Travers was admitted Organist in his place. No further reference to the special arrangement concerning Boyce and Martin occurs in the official records. In a list of members of the musical establishment at the Chapel Royal drawn up in 1742, WB is designated solely as a 'Composer'. It may be presumed, therefore, that until his much later appointment as Organist in 1758, WB continued to act, officially at least, only as a composer. The short-list of candidates for these appointments had been announced in the press the previous month: "The Candidates to succeed Mr. Weldon, in the Places of Organist and Composer to his Majesty [George II], are Mr. Kelway, Mr. Talbot Young, Mr. Robinson,

Mr. Boyce, and Mr. Martin" (*DG*, 15 May 1736.). Kelway, who had been organist of St. Michael Cornhill from 1734 until 1736 when WB replaced him, went on to St. Martin-in-the-Fields and subsequently established a national reputation as a virtuoso keyboard player. Young was organist at All Hallows Bread Street, and Robinson was organist at Westminster Abbey and two City churches. As for the successful candidates, Martin, who was only about 21 at this time, must have impressed most as an organist, even against the competition doubtless provided by Kelway, while Boyce clearly benefited from the reputation he had already gained as a composer.

♣

From the *Old Cheque Book,* 25 June 1736

M[r] John Weldon died May the 7th 1736, and by virtue of a Warrant from the Right Reverend Edmond Lord Bishop of London Dean of His Majesty's Chapels Royal I have sworn and admitted M[r] William Boyce into his place of Composer June 25th 1736.

Geo: Carleton Subdean

Lcr, OCB, f.57[v]. (Rimbault(1872), 51) This document records the completion of the formal processes for Boyce's appointment as a Composer to the Chapel Royal. The previous month the candidates for Weldon's post as Composer and Organist to his Majesty (George II) had been publicly announced.

♣

George Bickham publishes a collection of songs, *The Musical Entertainer,* 2 vols. (1737-39).

(Facs. edn: vol. 1, Cudworth(1965)) The 1st book includes four songs by Boyce: 'The ravished lover: 'When Fanny blooming fair" (text: attrib. 'Mr Philip'), no. 18;[12] 'The Rival or Desponding Lover: 'Of all the torments all the cares" (anon.), 19, 'Rural Beauty; or, Vauxhall Gardens: 'Flora, Goddess, sweetly blooming" (John Lockman), 21, and 'The adieu to the Spring-Gardens: 'The sun now darts" (J. Lockman), originally issued on

---

[12] The case for Lord Chesterfield's authorship of this poem is discussed in the commentary on Walsh's *British Musical Miscellany* (1734).

17 Aug. 1737, 49. This substantial collection was originally published in parts, each containing four airs, between January 1737 and December 1739. A 2nd edition appeared in 1740 (publ. C. Corbett) and a 3rd in 1765 (publ. J. Ryall). With its elegantly engraved songs, each of them accompanied by an illustrative vignette, *The Musical Entertainer* became the most highly regarded of all 18th-century song-books, and a model for other collections to emulate.

♣

Boyce is appointed conductor of the Meeting of the Three Choirs at Worcester (1737).

(Lysons(1812), 167). Information about the personnel involved and the repertoire performed in the Festival between its origin *c*1713 and 1752 is very scanty. It may be surmised, however, that Boyce continued to act as conductor for the then two-day meetings held successively each year at the cathedrals of Worcester, Hereford and Gloucester in late August or September at least up to 1755. His role as conductor was actually mentioned in the press at this point for the first time. Shortly after this, Boyce appears to have been succeeded by William Hayes, who is known to have conducted at Gloucester in 1757, 1760 and 1763. An interesting side-light is thrown on the social context of these meetings in a notice for the 1737 event due to be held on 14/15 September: "N.B. This Meeting is deferred a Week longer than the usual Time on account of several principal Performers being engag'd at Oxford Races" (*LEP*, 28 July).

Boyce's manner of directing large-scale musical forces was later described as "standing at a kind of desk among the performers, with a roll of paper in his hand, to beat the time through every movement" (Hawkins *b*(1788), vii). This practice was later confirmed by Samuel Wesley in a lecture given in London in 1827: "I remember that in the time of Dr. Boyce it was customary to mark the measure to the orchestra with a roll of parchment, or paper, in hand, and this usage is yet continued at St. Paul's Cathedral at the musical performances for the Sons of the Clergy" (quoted in *Grove 3,* vol. 1, 699). Wesley's observations would have dated from the 1770s when WB was still directing the Sons of the Clergy festivals. His method adumbrated the modern use of the baton by conductors, a practice which began to be adopted early in the 19th century.

♣

From the *Daily Advertiser*, 18 August 1737

To be perform'd at the Town-Hall in Windsor *For the Establishment and Benefit of a Fund for the Support of Widows and Orphans of the Gentlemen of the Choir of his Majesty's free Chapel of St. George in Windsor Castle.* A CONCERT of MUSICK, by the best Hands and Voices; this Day, being the 18th of August, consisting of A GRAND OVERTURE; David's Lamentation over Saul and Jonathan, Mr. Boyce. An Oratorio, Concerto, Mr. Festing, The spacious Firmament (from Addison) Set by Dr. Greene.[13] Solo on the German Flute, Augusti, Nuptial Song, Dr. Greene.[14] Violino Solo, Mr. Festing. Coronation Anthem, Mr. Handel. N.B. Tickets at 10s 6d[15] for both Concerts, to be had at Mr. Lee's, at Mr. Elford's, &c. in Windsor-Castle; and each Concert to begin at Five in the Evening.

This was the second of two concerts held for the benefit of the widows and orphans of the choir at Windsor. Both concerts were advertised in the *DA* (15 & 16 Aug.), the first of them taking place on the 16th. The second was advertised on the 17th and 18th. The Handel coronation anthem in the above programme would have been *Zadok the Priest*. It was specifically identified as the concluding item in the first concert which also featured Greene's oratorio *The Song of Deborah and Barak* (1732*)*, an anthem by Bononcini, and two violin solos played by Festing. This performance of Boyce's *David's Lamentation* is the first known to have taken place after its premiere at the Apollo Society of London in April 1736.

♣

Boyce subscribes to M.C. Festing's *Eight Concerto's in Seven Parts*, op. 5 (1739).

This is the first subscription Boyce is known to have made to a musical publication. Of the 154 subscribers for 166 copies of this edition a higher proportion than usual were musical societies, both in the provinces and in London. Many of their members were amateurs with limited technical ability who thrived on playing the tutti parts in concerti grossi for strings

---

[13] 'The spacious firmament on high', a sacred ode with words by Joseph Addison.
[14] The existence of this song has previously been overlooked in the literature on Greene.
[15] *c£*75 in modern currency.

such as these works are. Boyce himself went on to compose a number of such works, though none were published in his lifetime. At this point in his career he evidently felt sufficiently secure economically to begin to embark on the building of a substantial personal library. He subsequently acquired over sixty more musical publications by subscription. In 1755 WB also inherited Maurice Greene's musical library, so that when his magnificent collection came to be auctioned in April 1779, as many as 267 lots were advertised, and it took three days for the sale to be completed.

♣

John Simpson publishes *Calliope, or English Harmony* (1739).

Vol. I of this extensive collection of songs includes five of Boyce's early contributions to the genre: 'Come all ye youths', (text: Thomas Otway), 76; 'How wretched is a maiden's fate' (Thomas Phillips), 97; 'Of all the torments' (W. Walsh), 146; 'I love, I doat' (anon.), 185, (*BC* 226), and 'Silvia the fair' (John Dryden), 187.

♣

Boyce subscribes to Thomas Roseingrave's edition of keyboard sonatas by Domenico Scarlatti, *XLII Suites de Pièces* [1739].

Roseingrave's edition of Scarlatti sonatas was published by Benjamin Cooke in 2 vols., not long after a continental edition of 30 sonatas entitled *Essercizi per clavicembalo* had appeared in London *c*1738. In a note on the title-page Roseingrave writes: "I think the following Pieces for their Delicacy of Stile, and Masterly Composition, worthy the Attention of the Curious, which I have carefully revised & corrected from the Errors of the Press". These influential sonatas, with their virtuosic keyboard figuration and idiosyncratic harmony, attracted considerable interest from English composers and performers alike. Notable among the other 92 subscribers for 126 copies of this publication were Greene, Arne, Avison, Stanley and Pepusch. A reissue of Roseingrave's edition with an English title, *Forty two Suits of Lessons for the Harpsichord Composed by Sig^{rr}. Domenico Scarlatti*, appeared *c*1748. Boyce himself seems not to have been influenced by Scarlatti; indeed, he wrote no solo harpsichord music at all.

♣

Boyce subscribes to the 'Fund for the Support of Decayed Musicians and their Families'.

The formation of this charitable society is said to have been inspired initially by an incident in the life of the violinist and composer, Michael Festing. Sitting one day with two of his musical friends at a coffee house in the Haymarket, London, he happened to see the impoverished children of a well-known and recently deceased oboist, Kytch, driving asses along the street (see Matthews(1988), 1). With the co-operation of his companions, C.F. Weideman[16] and one of the Vincent brothers,[17] a formal meeting took place in April 1738 which ultimately led to a 'Declaration of Trust' for the Fund being drawn up on 28 August 1739. Prominent among the list of 230 subscribers were also Handel, Geminiani, Pepusch, Stanley, Kelway, Greene and William Hayes. In 1790 the Fund was granted a Royal Charter and re-designated 'The Royal Society of Musicians'. Flourishing to this day, the Society continues to offer financial support to musicians and their dependants who, for whatever reason, fall on hard times.

---

[16] Weideman was later appointed Assistant to Boyce as Master of the King's Music shortly after the accession of George III in 1761. He also gave the King flute lessons.

[17] There were a number of musicians from the Vincent family prominent at this time. Matthews suggests that the co-founder of the Society was probably Thomas Vincent the elder, a bassoonist, but a case may also be made for it being his brother Richard, an oboist and composer. Both names appear in the list of subscribers.

PART TWO

LIFE AND CAREER, 1740-1749

Boyce subscribes to Richard Bundy's *Sermons on several occasions, with a course of lectures on the church-catechism* (1740).

In the course of his duties at the Chapel Royal, Boyce probably became personally acquainted with Bundy who had died in 1739. In 1732 he had become Chaplain-in-Ordinary to George II, and was also Vicar of St. Brides, Fleet Street, not far from where Boyce lived. Bundy's reputation in the church at large must have been great, for this publication attracted over 1,200 subscribers, including members of the Royal Family.

♣

Boyce subscribes to Thomas Bisse's *A course of sermons on the Lord's Prayer preach'd at the rolls* (Oxford, 1740).

Boyce was the only prominent musician to acquire this volume. Bisse's reputation as a preacher must have been considerable for this publication attracted more than 700 subscribers, many of them from Oxford where Bisse was Chaplain of All Souls, as well as from clergy of the Church of England at large.

♣

The Apollo Academy of London issues a collective word-book (1740).

Title-page: A | MISCELLANY | OF LYRIC POEMS, | The Greatest Part written for, | And performed in | The *Academy* of MUSIC, | Held in the APOLLO. [line] | *Quem virum aut heroa lyra vel acri* | *Tibid sumes*

celebrare, Clio? | *Quem Deum?*[1] Hor. [line] | [Printer's ornament]||
LONDON: | Printed for the ACADEMY.

The Apollo was a private music Society set up by Greene and Festing
in 1731 after they had broken away from the Academy of Ancient Music.
This publication brought together the texts of a number of larger works by
Greene and Boyce performed at meetings of the Academy held between
1736 and 1740. They were Greene's oratorios *Jephtha* and the *Song of
Deborah and Barak*, Boyce's short oratorio, *David's Lamentation*, his two
Odes for St. Cecilia's Day, *The Charms of Harmony Display* and *See fam'd
Apollo,* and the masque *Peleus and Thetis*. The appearance of *Peleus* here
is of particular significance since it helps to date a work that otherwise
appears not to have emerged into the public domain until 1747.

♣

From the *Bibliothèque Britannique, ou Histoire des Ouvrages des Scavans de la Grande-Bretagne: Pour les Mois d'Avril, Mai et Juin, MDCCXL, xv/1,* (The Hague, 1740)

Mr. Lockman says,[2] that he will not speak about various English pieces set
to music by skilful composers, which have been performed less publicly
than the preceding ones.[3] Let us speak on his behalf. It is a question of
several works in different genres some of which are performed today in
public places where one pays for entry, but most of which have only been
performed until now (with some acclaim) in certain Societies or Musical
Academies; at these concerts one is only admitted either as a member, or
by means of tickets which members have a right to distribute to their
friends. I know two of these Societies & I do not know if there are any
more. One of these is commonly known as the Crown and Anchor:[4] The
Society has as its Concert Director Doctor Pepusch: it is famous, but I

---

[1] "What man or hero will you choose to celebrate in song on the lyre or flute, Clio?
What god?" The quotation is from the opening lines of Horace's Ode no. 12
(Book 1) in praise of Augustus, the first Roman Emperor. In classical mythology,
Clio was the muse of epic poetry and history.

[2] In his preface to *Rosalinda: a Musical Drama . . . to which is prefixed 'An
Enquiry into the Rise and Progress of Operas and Oratorios with some Reflections
on Lyric Poetry and Music'* (1740).

[3] The latter being the early English oratorios which followed in the wake of
Handel's *Esther* (1732).

[4] The Academy of Ancient Music which met at the Crown and Anchor Tavern.

cannot be certain that Mr. Lockman had it in mind. I do not know at all what pieces of which it may be said that they have been performed only by this Society. There is another that is very well known under the title it has taken as the Apollo Society. There has just been published, for the use of this society, a collection of pieces which have been set to music for its concerts,[5] & amongst these pieces there are two which are in the style of Mr. Lockman. The most recent is an Ode for St. Cecilia's Day for voices and instruments, and printed for the first time separately in 1739.[6] The music is by Mr. Boyce, one of the Composers of the King's Chapel. The other, set to music by the same, is entitled 'David's Lamentation over Saul & Jonathan', printed in 1736. I shall have occasion to say more about this piece in the article on *Oratorios* to which we shall now turn. [pp.60-62.]

. . . As one may observe, . . . it is not absolutely necessary for an oratorio to be a dramatic piece, nor even a piece in dialogue. *David's Lamentation over Saul and Jonathan* is called an oratorio without there being anything wrong about it; & at the same time it is neither dramatic nor a dialogue. It is properly what we would call in French a *Cantate Spirituelle,* with these two differences only: that it is not confined, as our cantatas seem to be,[7] to three or four recitatives interspersed with a similar number of airs; & that the poem begins with a chorus, which after inviting the poet to sing, sings with him at appropriate places. Note, moreover, that when I say *with him,* by this should be understood what appears to be the reading; for in performance it is not the same person who sings throughout the entirety of the action. Perhaps it would be too much for a single voice; perhaps also there must be more than one voice to satisfy the listeners. What is certain is that this piece (with new music by Mr. Smith)[8] is now performed by several voices, in Hickford's Room,[9] and it is at the same time that which had been performed with the music of Mr. Boyce; whether it be at the Apollo Society in 1736, or in a public concert that took place at Windsor in 1737. There is something of the dramatic in its execution. But the piece itself is not a dramatic work: what is true is that when it was printed for the concert of the Society in 1736, it was called a *Lyrical Poem.*[10] It has only appeared with the title of *oratorio* in other editions; and it must be

---

[5] *A Miscellany of Lyric Poems, the greatest Part written for, and performed in the Academy of Music, held in the Apollo* (1740).

[6] 'See fam'd Apollo'.

[7] i.e. French cantatas.

[8] Lockman provided five additional airs for J. C. Smith's setting.

[9] A number of performances were given there in 1740.

[10] In the *Miscellany of Lyric Poems* and in the press notices for the Hickford's Room performances.

acknowledged, moreover, that whatever right one has to give the title to poems which are not in a dramatic genre, it has been attached to those in that genre right from the start. At least that is what is indicated by the title of the piece, *Esther*, which I always consider to be the first to which the English have given the name *Oratorio*. The wording of the title is: ESTHER: *An Oratorio, or Sacred Drama*.[11]

I have thought these remarks necessary for those who do not otherwise know what English oratorio is. To know at present what has provided them with the name & the idea, & what is the origin of the thing itself, these are two questions on which I am content merely to provide a summary of what I find in Mr. Lockman's treatise [pp.64-66]. [transl.]

That Boyce's name, if not his music, was known in France at this time was entirely due to John Lockman's standing in that country. A prolific writer in his own language, he was also much admired for his renditions of French literary works into English. Having translated a number of books by Voltaire, the great French philosopher dubbed him 'l'illustre Lockman'.

♣

From *Faulkner's Dublin Journal*, 16-20 December 1740

Last Wednesday Evening at the Philoharmonic Society in Fishamble-Street, was performed, an Ode on Musick for St. Cecilia's Day, by the celebrated Mr. Lockman so eminently distinguished by his many curious Writings. The Musick set by Mr. Boyce Composer to his Majesty. It was allowed by several of the best Judges here, to be one of the grandest Performances that hath been heard.

(Bartlett *b*(1982), 760) John Lockman's extensive Ode for St. Cecilia, 'See fam'd Apollo and the nine', encouraged Boyce to produce the most ambitious and colourful of his works so far. The inclusion of its text in the Apollo Academy's *Miscellany of Lyric Poems* (1740) indicates a performance there by that time. This is confirmed by a French-language source which reviews Lockman's current works: "[His] most recent is an Ode for the Feast of St. Cecilia sung in a grand concert, and printed for the first time separately in 1739".[12] The appearance of the text in the Dublin Philharmonic

---

[11] The argument is rather convoluted here. In essence the writer seems to be saying that an oratorio does not of necessity have to be dramatic, just as Handel himself later demonstrated in *Messiah* (1742).

[12] *Bibliothèque Britannique* (La Hague, 1740), 61. See entry above. Copies of this word-book are preserved at *US*: WS and *US*: CA.

Society's *Collected Word Book* (1741) confirms a performance there too. The Ode was also scheduled for performance(s) in their 1744-5 season, and the availability of the word-book was still being advertised in 1748.[13] Boyce's autogr. and related parts for the London performances are preserved at *Ob*, MSMus.Sch.266, and the Dublin score, in which some of the airs for the alto (Joseph Ward) and the tenor (John Church) are upwardly transposed, is at *US: Wc*, MSML.96.3674. Boyce included the overture in his *8 Symphonys* (1760), no. 5. The overture to Part 2 of the ode has been edited by Finzi in MB 13 (1957). The first modern performance of the work was broadcast by the BBC on 22 November 1982 (see Bartlett *b*(1982)), and it has since been recorded on CD (see Discography).

Boyce had earlier written a St. Cecilia ode on a much smaller scale, 'The charms of harmony display' (*c*1738) with words by Peter Vidal, a little known cleric. This must also have been performed at the Apollo Society for its text also appears in the *Miscellany of Lyric Poems*. Boyce would have been fully aware of the earlier English tradition of paying homage to the patron saint of music through annual performances in London on 22 November of a Cecilian ode. He may also have been stimulated to try his hand at this genre by the great impact made by Handel's setting of Dryden's great ode of 1697 in the saint's honour, *Alexander's Feast*, in 1736. The autogr. score and related parts are preserved at *Ob*, MSMus.Sch.C.110. The overture has been edited by Finzi in MB 13, and the whole ode has recently been recorded on CD (see Discography).

A third ode, 'Gentle lyre, begin the strain', with a text by Walter Harte paraphrasing part of Pindar's 1st Pythian Ode,[14] also dates from *c*1740. It is not strictly speaking Cecilian, but its text is permeated by musical allusions. It does not appear in the Apollo *Miscellany*, but it is in the Dublin Philharmonic Society's list of works to be given in 1744-5. It was also performed at Cambridge in 1749 when Boyce took his doctorate there. The autogr. is at *Ob*, MS.Mus.Sch.C.112.

Boyce later composed another sacred ode to a fine text by Alexander Pope, 'Vital spark of heavenly flame'.[15] It is known to have been in the

---

[13] See *DJ*, 11 Oct. 1748. This notice refers to the works it contains being "performed at the Charitable Musical Society in Fishamble-street every Friday throughout that season".

[14] In Greek mythology, relating to the Priestess of Apollo (the god of music to whom Pindar was devoted) at Delphi. Harte's ode is also sometimes described as 'Pindaric', i.e. loose in structure and lyrical in character.

[15] For the full text see Butt(1963).

repertoire of the Academy of Ancient Music,[16] and has also been performed in modern times.

♣

The Philharmonic Society of Dublin publishes a collective word-book (1741).

Title-page: THE | TE DEUM, JUBILATE, | ANTHEMS, ODES, | ORATORIOS and SERENATAS, | as they are performed by | The PHILHARMONIC SOCIETY | in *DUBLIN,* | FOR THE | Improvement of CHURCH MUSICK, | AND THE | Further SUPPORT of MERCER's HOSPITAL. | (line) | Printed in the YEAR MDCCXLI.

IRL: Dtc, 190.u.151. This extensive and valuable collection brings together the texts of a large number of works by Handel, two by Percival, one by Bononcini, one by Greene, and two by Boyce being the Ode for St. Cecilia, 'See fam'd Apollo', and the serenata *Solomon.* This publication serves in particular to throw light on the history of these two most important early works of Boyce.

Since the Philharmonic Society was a private institution, by no means all of its concerts were advertised in the press. The first reference in the Dublin newspapers to performances of Boyce's *Solomon* and the Ode does not occur in fact until Dec. 1744. The evidence provided by a partially autogr. MS of *Solomon*, specifically prepared for Dublin, indicates that a performance almost certainly took place in the Philharmonic Society's 1742-3 season. Its apparently premature appearance in this word-book must have been due to the presence of Edward Moore, the author of its text, in Dublin at this time. WB's Ode, on the other hand, may well have entered the repertoire of the Society from its 1740-1 season.

♣

---

[16]   See Academy(1768), 186-7.

Boyce subscribes to John Alcock's *Six Suites of Easy Lessons for the Harpsichord or Spinnet, with a Trumpet Piece* (1741).

This was the first of a number of subscriptions Boyce made to publications by Alcock, a fellow boy chorister of his at St. Paul's. Alcock was organist at St. Andrew's, Plymouth when these suites were issued. 163 copies were sold to 144 subscribers, among them the leading musicians Chilcot, Kelway and Travers.

♣

Boyce subscribes to John Barker's *Twelve songs; Three for Two Voices; with Symphonies for the Violin, or German Flute* (Coventry, 1741).

Barker was Organist at Holy-Trinity-Church, Coventry. This publication gained considerable support, particularly from musical societies and individuals from the Midlands, attracting 348 subscribers for 380 copies. Boyce himself ordered six copies, but the only other prominent musicians to subscribe were William Hayes and Thomas Lowe.

♣

Two letters from Boyce to John Hawkins (November 1741)

I

Friday Even: Nov: 6th

S^r.

I am much oblig'd to you for the song you were so kind to favour me with on Tuesday last. I have already set it, and have endeavour'd to render the musick agreable to the words, which I confess in my opinion are as pretty as any thing of the kind I've yet met with. If the musick shou'd have the good luck to please you, as the words have done me, I shall be highly satisfied: if not, I desire you'll attribute the cause to my incapacity, and not want of inclination. I'm now in close waiting at St. James's, which will deprive me of an opportunity of seeing you, till the latter part of next week, when I shall take care to have a copy of the musick transcribed for you, and in the mean time, shall be much oblig'd, for an[y] information from you what day, time, and place will be ye most agreeable to you, after Thursday next, for a meeting to compare notes: which I desire you'd inform me of, by a line directed for William Boyce (my father's name being John) at Joyner's Hall in Thames Street near Dowgate. I am S^r (tho' without knowing who I'm obligated to) your much oblig'd humble servt:

W^m. Boyce

II

Friday Even: Nov:13th

S^r

I'm exceedingly sorry I can't have ye pleasure of waiting on you personally this ev'ning, by reason of an engagement which has been fix'd on this fortnight therefore can no ways wave it. However I've sent you the notes to your very agreeable words, and shall be always ready and willing to adapt musick to any thing you'll please to favour me with, and am, Sr Your most obed[t] humble serv[t]:

Wm Boyce

Ob, MSEng.Poetc.9, pp.2-4. (Scholes(1953), 261) The MS source of these letters contains copies of the originals made by Thomas Phillibrown. He included them in a substantial collection of contemporary literary works, articles, and letters compiled between 1740 and 1758, entitled *Miscellanies*. Among these are a number of poems by Hawkins. Eleven of these were used by John Stanley in his two sets of six cantatas (1742/1748). The text in question, 'In vain Philander at my feet', is quoted in full and described as "A song by M[r] John Hawkins set to musick by Mr. Boyce, organist to the King's Chappell at St. James's — 1741". The air was initially published in a s.sh.f. edition and subsequently appeared in a number of vocal collections and literary magazines.[17]

No records of Hawkins's communications to Boyce seem to have survived. However, this early collaboration between the two men led to a life-long friendship. Hawkins later subscribed to Boyce's *Cathedral Music* (1760-1773), while Boyce assisted Hawkins in the preparation of his

---

[17] See e.g., J. Simpson's 'Collection of of favourite English songs', *The Amphion*, Book 3, no. 27 [1745].

History of Music (1776) and set his elegiac poem, 'Hither ye sons of harmony', written in 1777 on the death of William Gostling. Even more significantly, Hawkins was eventually to write a substantial and frequently cited biography of Boyce in 1788, an account preceded only by the much more succinct entry on him in the *Universal Dictionary of Music* (1783).

♣

Letter from the 4th Earl of Shaftesbury to James Harris, 10 December 1741

Our friend Mr Percival tells me from a letter writt to him by Mr Debourg[18] dated Dublin November 25th that Handel arrived safe there the day before.[19] His cloaths & organ were not yet come[,] but notwithstanding the Speaker forced him to dinner the day he landed & the Master of the Rolls insisted on Handel's doing the same with him the day following. 'Tis thought he will get a considerable profit by his voyage. Some of the Irish people have behaved like true natives in severall respects towards Handel, which I have not time to speak of in this. One of these Irishisms was the asking Handel to accompany one Mr Bois's[20] (a disciple of Dr Green's here at London) new anthem lately [altered from 'newly'] sent them from England. The occasion being a public charity Handel has promis'd to accompany all his own music which they perform that day, but beg'd excuse for Mr Bois's. So they keep this curious piece[21] for the last. Debourg was enraged at this proposal & said his own playing should depend on their behaviour towards Handel. The town of Dublin in general are at present strong Handelians. Mr Percival says both the new orotorios [*sic*] especially the Messiah are far beyond Saul or any composition he ever made.

(Burrows & Dunhill (2002), 131) Handel's stand should not be misunderstood. He was clearly offended by the suggestion that he might also accompany Boyce's work, which was contrary to normal professional etiquette. His reaction certainly did not imply any disrespect for WB either personally or professionally.

♣

---

[18] Dubourg.

[19] Handel had arrived on 18 November.

[20] Boyce.

[21] In the sense of 'skilful' or 'ingenious'.

From *Faulkner's Dublin Journal,* 12 December 1741

Last Thursday was performed at the Round Church, for the Benefit of Mercer's Hospital, Divine Service after the Cathedral Manner, with the *Te Deum Jubilate* and one of the Coronation Anthems compos'd by Mr. Handel;[22] after which there was a most excellent Sermon, suited to the Occasion, preached by the Revd. Dean Owens, and after Sermon an Elegant and Grand Anthem composed on the Occasion, by Mr. Boyce, Composer to his Majesty, at the request of several well-wishers to the Charity; the Appearance was numerous, and it is hoped the Performance was so much to the Satisfaction of every Person who heard it, as to bescape the Favour of the Publick on the like Occasion.

(Deutsch(1955), 527) Given the close political, social and cultural ties between London and Dublin in the 18th century, and Boyce's by now well established reputation, it could have been no surprise that he was now invited to compose a work for Mercer's Hospital, Dublin, a charitable institution founded in 1734 for the those in poverty. The anthem he provided, 'Blessed is he that considereth the sick', was not only on a larger scale than any of its predecessors written for the Chapel Royal, but also his first with orchestral accompaniment.

'Blessed is he' remained in the repertoire at Dublin for some time. Four years later it was reported that "On Thursday last Cathedral Service, with Mr. Handel's Te Deum, Jubilate and Coronation Anthem, and Mr. Boyce's Anthem, were performed as usual at St. Michan's Church, for the Benefit of Mercer's Hospital", and this programme was repeated the following Thursday (see *DJ*, 10-14 Dec. 1745). In the first of these services "His Exellency the Lord Lieutenant favoured the Governors of the Hospital with his Presence".[23] Later still the hospital's board minutes for 3 Dec. 1757 record that "Mr Carre to be requested to order the Musical Books belonging to the Hospital to be bound & Dr. Boyce's Anthem composed for the Hospital to be copied".

Records of the programmes of the Meetings of the Three Choirs before 1751 are very scanty, but we know that 'Blessed is he' was performed at Worcester in 1743 and again in 1752. It was almost certainly done subsequently on other occasions when the advertised programmes refer merely to 'an anthem by Dr. Boyce'. The anthem certainly came into its own in the last decade of the century when it was included in six meetings

---

[22] Probably the 'Utrecht' Te Deum and Jubilate of 1713, and 'Zadok the Priest'.

[23] This post was held by Lord Chesterfield at that time. Appointed in 1744, he was resident in Dublin from August 1745 to April 1746.

between 1792 and 1799. Records of the programmes of the Festival of the Sons of the Clergy, held in London in the Spring each year, are also very defective before 1775, but it may well have been performed there from 1751-4, and it is clear from other evidence that it certainly took its place in the repertoire there too.[24] Moreover, its inclusion in the Nottingham Festival on 2 Sept. 1789 "As performed in St. Paul's Cathedral for the benefit of the Sons of the Clergy" (see Evans(1983), 70), suggests that it probably also made its mark outside the major venues. 'Blessed is he' was undoubtedly given an extended lease of life when it was at last published by Ashley in 1802, and again in 1849 when Novello issued an edition which provided an organ part in place of the orchestral accompaniment.[25]

Boyce took his text from Psalm 41 in the *Book of Common Prayer* and the biblical *Book of Job*. Being commissioned by a hospital, he modified the opening words of the psalm, 'Blessed is he that considereth the poor and needy', by replacing 'poor' with 'sick'. Subsequently, when the anthem was given at charities for alleviating poverty such as the Three Choirs or the Sons of the Clergy, Boyce appears to have reverted to the original form of his textual source. This background is reflected in Ashley's 1802 edition, where the title-page identifies the anthem as 'Blessed is he that considereth the poor', but the words of the opening chorus in the score itself are 'sick and needy'.

There are plentiful surviving contemporary MS sources for the anthem: a set of instrumental and vocal parts, *IRL: Dtc*, MS Mercer's Deposit 1-44; two full scores, *Lcm*, MS.783, and *Lbl*, Add.MS.28969 in London; a full score, *Ob*, MS.Mus.d.23, at Oxford; and an organ score, *H*, 30.B.vi, 111-139, at Hereford. Unfortunately, none of these MSS are in the composer's hand.[26] It is clear that various revisions were subsequently made to the original music, perhaps instigated by Boyce himself. As the Dublin parts reveal, the opening chorus was at first preceded by a short, slow orchestral introduction, but in the later *Lcm* MS, on which Ashley relied for his edition, it is replaced by a longer and more imposing French overture.

---

[24] Boyce himself conducted the Sons of the Clergy performances from 1755-78.

[25] See *W. Boyce:Services and Anthems* (1849), vol. 4, no. 56.

[26] The Novellos were mistaken in their belief, expressed in the *Lbl* MS on which they based their edition, that it was a Boyce autograph. This MS, however, does contain the signature 'W. Felton' written in pencil. This must be that of William Felton, an organist, composer, and vicar-choral at Hereford Cathedral, who also sometimes acted as a Steward at the Three Choirs Festival. The appearance of his name there, whether as its owner or as its copyist, would suggest that the MS, and hence the Novello edition, represents the form the anthem took when it was done at the Three Choirs.

Novello, on the other hand, basing his edition on the *Lbl* source, cut out the central tenor solo, 'I did weep', and replaced it with the then popular duet for tenor and bass, 'Here shall soft charity', from Boyce's sacred ode, 'Lo! On the thorny bed of care' (1774). Ashley published the latter as a supplement in the same volume. These MS sources, including the early parts preserved at Dublin, provide evidence that various cuts were made, particularly in the vocal solos in the central part of the work. Because of the 60 years that separated the composition of this work from its publication, the wide dispersal of its MS sources and the intricate relationships between them, its textual history has yet to be fully explored.

Alfred Novello, son of the publisher Vincent, wrote on a preliminary sheet of the *Lbl* MS which he edited: "Presented to me by the publisher [Vincent] of my edition of this beautiful and masterly composition". When Vincent in due course gave this MS to the British Museum he wrote: "I have now the pleasure of providing this extremely rare composition in score (which is the only known copy extant) for presentation to the Musical Library of the British Museum, as a tribute of respect to the memory of Dr. Boyce, who in my estimation, for purity of melody, solidity of harmony, and skilful refinement in the construction of his sterling counterpoint, was one of the best composers of the genuine English school". Nevertheless, in spite of its qualities, this anthem has so far been overlooked in modern times.

♣

Boyce subscribes to Charles Avison's *Two Concertos* (1742).

The first of these string concertos is "for an organ or harpsichord in eight parts", and the second "for violins in seven parts". This edition attracted 142 subscribers for 160 copies. Apart from his pioneering and stimulating *Essay on Musical Expression* (1753), the Newcastle-based Avison was greatly admired for his concerti grossi for strings, especially those based on keyboard sonatas by Domenico Scarlatti. Boyce's interest in this genre was evident from the five concertos for strings he himself composed, though none of them were published in his lifetime. Such works were the staple fare of many amateur orchestras at this time.

♣

From the *Daily Advertiser,* 7 August 1742

For the Benefit of Mr. ALLCOCK. AT the Castle Tavern in Pater-Noster-Row. On Wednesday next, the 11th instant, will be perform'd a CONCERT of Vocal and Instrumental MUSICK. The Vocal Part by Mr. Lowe,[27] and others. A New Concerto on the Bassoon by Mr. ALLCOCK, compos'd by Mr. BOYCE, To begin at Seven o'Clock. Note. There will be a BALL after the CONCERT is over. Tickets to be had at Mr. Johnson's, a Musick-Shop, in Cheapside, and at the Place of Performance, at Three Shillings each.[28]

This concerto for the bassoon is the only solo concerto Boyce is known to have composed. That he chose to feature the bassoon in this work serves to confirm a predilection for this instrument Boyce displayed in some of his orchestral music. Allcock gave another performance of the concerto on 5 March 1745[29] in Dublin where Boyce's music was held in high regard. The music for this work seems not to have survived.[30]

♣

John Walsh publishes *The British Orpheus,* vol. 2, [1742].

This 'Collection of favourite English songs never before publish'd' (adv. in *DA,* 18 Sept.) contains one song by Boyce: 'The Invocation to Neptune: 'Long detained by winds contrary'' (text: anon.). The poem, "written extempore at Calais", requests Neptune "to grant a favourable passage to a great lady returning to England". Vol. 4 in the same series (adv. in *DA,* 19 Feb. 1743) includes two more songs by WB: 'Cease, vainglorious swain' (text: anon.), 42, and 'On a bank' (J. Dryden), 45.

♣

---

[27] Thomas Lowe, a well known London tenor.

[28] In modern currency *c£*20, a price doubtless reflecting the charge for the ball as well as the concert.

[29] See *DJ,* 23-26 Feb..

[30] However, it has been suggested that Boyce's concerto may have exerted an influence on a bassoon concerto in Bb by Capel Bond in his *Six Concertos in Seven Parts* (1766); moreover, that WB's famous air and chorus, 'Softly rise, O southern breeze', from *Solomon* (1742), with its obbligato bassoon part, may have provided a model for the 1st movement of Capel's work (see P. Holman in the notes for a recording of Capel's concertos (Hyperion, CDA 66467 (1992)).

Boyce subscribes to Maurice Greene's *Forty Select Anthems in Score* (1743).

This substantial publication in two volumes was printed for the author, then Master of the King's Music, by John Walsh. It attracted 134 subscribers for 282 copies, a less than wholehearted national response that disappointed the composer. Dedicated to George II, it was published with the protection of the Royal Licence granted to Greene. Boyce appears in the subscribers' list as: *"Mr. William Boyce*, Composer to His Majesty's Chapel Royal, and Organist of St. Michael's in Cornhill". At the head of it is the King's son, Frederick, Prince of Wales. Other notable subscribers were Alcock, Nares, Stanley, Chilcot, Pepusch, the Italian composers Galuppi and Porpora, the Duke of Newcastle, later to become Prime Minister, and James Harris, a musical promoter and great admirer of Handel. In contrast, apart from a single exception, Boyce made no attempt to publish his own anthems. In deciding not to do so he was probably mindful of Greene's experience in this field. Publication of many of Boyce's anthems did eventually take place, but only after his death.

♣

Boyce subscribes to John Alcock's *Twelve English Songs* [1743].

Short title: *Twelve English Songs with a Recitative & Duet out of the Opera of Rosamund*. Alcock was at this time Organist of St. Lawrence's, Reading. In his youth Alcock had been a fellow chorister of Boyce at St. Paul's. Notwithstanding its composer's residence in the provinces, this volume attracted as many as 356 subscribers for 528 copies.

♣

John Newbery publishes *Universal Harmony* (1743-5).

This collection of songs, originally printed in parts, includes Boyce's setting of 'When Orpheus went down' (text: Samuel Lisle), 34, originally issued on 9 July 1743, along with two airs from *Solomon* (1742). An enlarged edition appeared in 1745 which added WB's 'Flora, Goddess, sweetly blooming' (John Lockman), 80.

♣

From the *Daily Advertiser,* 22 August 1743

For the Benefit of Mr. LOWE.[31] Low-Layton in Essex, this Day, being the 22d instant, will be perform'd a SERENATA, call'd SOLOMON. Set to Musick by Mr. BOYCE, Composer to his MAJESTY. With select Pieces of Musick by the best Masters, particularly, A Solo on the Violoncello by Mr. Cervetto, A Solo on the German Flute by Mr. Thumoth, And a Concerto on the Harpsichord by Mr. Henry Burgess. Tickets Five Shillings each. Note, In Consideration of Mr. Wenman allowing a Monday for Mr. Lowe's Benefit, he is obliged to pay the breakfasting out of each Ticket, and therefore humbly hopes no Gentlemen or Ladies will be offended at the Tickets being set at Five Shillings.[32] To begin exactly at Eleven o'Clock in the Morning. (&c.)

This concert held at Ruckholt House included the first public performance of the work which was soon to establish Boyce's name throughout the land. Ruckholt, an Elizabethan mansion, had been the country seat of the Hickes family until it was sold in 1720. In 1742 an enterprising musician, William Barton, leased it from the then owner, the Earl of Tylney, and established it as a public breakfasting house offering concerts in an amphitheatre on Mondays during the summer. The village of Leyton, only four miles north-east of London, was in easy reach by carriage for the more leisured classes from the metropolis. Such people at that time were inclined to regard Mondays as an extension of their weekends. Ruckholt was careful to offer good food as well as musical fare for "Proper Cooks are provided every Day in the Week and Plenty of Fish" (*DA*, 21 May 1744). Regular concerts continued to be held there each summer until 1751 when the house fell into disrepair. Due to the "general satisfaction" given by *Solomon*, and the "Desire of divers of the Nobility", it was given six performances at Ruckholt in the 1743 season, three in 1744, and two in 1745.[33]

The 'serenata' was a vocal genre of Italian origin, midway between a theatre piece and a concert item in that such works were often given with scenery and in costume but without stage action. They were also frequently written for celebratory occasions. In the case of Boyce's

---

[31] A fine tenor and actor who sang frequently at Ruckholt, and sometimes for Handel too. He later became the proprietor of Marybone Gardens.

[32] About £38 in modern currency. The normal charge at Ruckholt was two shillings.

[33] Details of these, and the upwards of 50 other 18th-century performances of the complete work identified by 1995, may be found in MB 68, 183-5.

Solomon, however, there is nothing to indicate that it was ever conceived as anything but a concert piece.

The text for *Solomon* was prepared by Edward Moore *c*1741 in Dublin where he was working in the linen trade. After his return to London in the mid-1740s Moore established himself as a prominent poet, dramatist and literary editor. He based this work on Samuel Croxall's popular paraphrase of the biblical 'Song of Solomon', first published in 1720. In adapting this poem, Moore created a well conceived libretto ideally suited to musical setting. In accordance with the nature of its biblical source, the work is freely erotic in character. The yearnings of the two lovers, 'He' and 'She', are expressed in a series of intimate solos and duets set against a pastoral background, interspersed with dramatic choruses, and accompanied by a full baroque orchestra.[34]

The early source material for *Solomon* indicates clearly that it had been given privately before the first public performance at Ruckholt. A libretto issued by the Apollo Academy in 1742 (copy at *Cu*) confirms that a performance took place probably in the Autumn of that year. The text of *Solomon* also appeared in the Philharmonic Society of Dublin's collective word-book of 1741. It must have been submitted in anticipation of a performance in due course, for Boyce did not complete his first autogr. MS of *Solomon* until March 1742. The score (*Lcm*, MS4109) is dated at the end in the composer's hand, and must have been used for the early Apollo performance(s). A later, partially autograph score (now at *US*: *Wc*, MSML96.B674(3)), was specifically prepared for Dublin and was almost certainly performed there sometime in the 1742-3 season. Finally, John Walsh published the work in full score by subscription in the Summer of 1743, and this was doubtless used for the Ruckholt performances. The title-page reads: SOLOMON. | A | SERENATA, | in SCORE, | Taken from the CANTICLES. | [line] | Set to MUSICK | By Mr. WILLIAM BOYCE, | Composer to HIS MAJESTY. | [line] | [ornament] | LONDON:| Printed and sold for the Author, by J. WALSH, in | Catharine-Street in the *Strand*. | M. DCC. XLIII. This first edition was a great success for it sold 290 copies to 270 subscribers, among whom were most of the leading musicians in the country, including Handel.

Solomon lays claim to being the most popular, widely performed and admired work by an English composer of the 18th-century. It is evident

---

[34] Ruckholt was evidently able to mount a good-sized orchestra when necessary, for a notice for one of the performances there in 1744 assures its potential audience that "The Band consists of eighteen of the principal Performers from both Theatres" (*DA*, 21 May}. The latter, of course, being the two patent theatres, Drury Lane and Covent Garden.

that it took a prominent place not only in concert halls, and theatres, but above all in domestic music making. The full score was re-issued by Walsh in 1760, his successor Hermond Wright printed it again *c*1790 and Harrison and Co. arranged it "For the Voice, Harpsichord, and Violin; with the *Chorusses in Score*" in 1785. Many of the airs and duets appeared regularly in song anthologies and ten of them were published separately, some at least five times. Performances of the complete work continued until the end of the century, and the sublime tenor air and chorus with obbligato bassoon, 'Softy rise, O southern breeze', even took its place in the final concert of the Academy of Ancient Music in 1848.

The English author, John Potter, wrote of this work: "[Boyce's] serenata of 'Solomon' is a great performance, a fine piece of composition! It has a number of beautiful strokes of genius; it is fine, it is elegant and sublime. It stares the *Italians* in the face, and asks them, with what justice they can claim the art of beautiful modulation alone? How delicate are the airs in it, how charming the melody! Can anything be more so? Really it is almost impossible!" (Potter(1762), 56) A modern edition has been published in MB 68 (1996), and the work is available on CD (see Discography).

♣

From the *General Advertiser*, 9 September 1743

At the particular Desire of several Persons of Distinction, on this Day, at the Castle Tavern in Pater-noster-row, will be perform'd a Serenata call'd SOLOMON; and several Solo's and Concerto's by eminent Masters: and Singing by Mr. LOWE and Mr BRETT Tickets may be had at Jacob's Coffee-house near Guildhall; the Ship Tavern at Temple-bar; and at the Place of Performance, at Five Shillings each.[35]

The first public performances of *Solomon* at Ruckholt House, Essex, in August 1743, were followed shortly by this London premiere. The work was given again at the Devil Tavern, Temple Bar in April 1744, at Drury Lane Theatre in March 1750, at the Great Room, Dean St. in March 1755, at Stoke Newington in Aug. 1759, and at Marybone Gardens in Aug. 1765 and Sept. 1767.[36] Five more performances have recently come to light, one at the Globe Tavern, Fleet St. in March 1744, and four at the concerts

---

[35] About £38 in modern currency.
[36] For further details see MB 68, Appendix II, 183-5.

of the Academy of Ancient Music on 6 and 13 Feb., and on 30 April and 7 May 1772.[37]

♣

From the *London Daily Post*, 15 September 1743

On the 7th & 8th Instant, was held at Worcester the Annual Meeting of the Choirs of Worcester, Gloucester and Hereford. Mr Purcell's, and Mr. Handel's Services were perform'd as usual; the Anthem was entirely new; the words suited to the Occasion, and set to Musick by Mr. Boyce. The Whole Performance was much admir'd; and the Collection for Charity amounted to more than 95 Pounds.[38]

This was one of the rare occasions before 1751 when any details of the music to be performed at the Three Choirs appeared in the press. The Boyce anthem could only have been the orchestrally accompanied 'Blessed is he' (*BC* 11), composed for Dublin in 1741. The work by Purcell would have been the *Te Deum and Jubilate in D* (1694), and by Handel his 'Utrecht' setting of the same texts (1713).

♣

Letter from the 4th Earl of Radnor to James Harris
[May 1744]

If you have the inclination to hear Mr. Boyce Solamon[39] this evening — I wish you would either dine with me at Mr Trenchards or cal upon me there — abought six or I wil cal upon you at any place you please to apoint, but if you should happen to be engaged, I shall in that case wait upon you at your lodgeing in Lincolns Inn sometime tomorrow morning. I am yrs etc etc   Radnor
P.S. Mr Trenchard lodges in Henrietta Street very near Tavistock Street. The musick is at ye Globe Tavern Fleet Street.

(Burrows & Dunhill (2002), 192-3) Until this letter by John Robartes was published, no other record of this London performance of *Solomon* (1742) had come to light. The growing popularity of *Solomon* at this time,

---

[37] Academy programmes preserved at *F: Pn*, Res.F.1507.

[38] About £14,000 in modern currency.

[39] The serenata *Solomon* (1742).

however, was reflected in a number of performances of the work given in the same month at Ruckholt House in Essex. James Harris's family home was in the Close at Salisbury. Here he was very active musically and organised the Salisbury Subscription Concerts and the annual Musical Festival there, while he pursued a life-long devotion to Handel. Moreover, in the same year (1744), he published an influential treatise, *Concerning Music, Painting and Poetry*. Harris's musical interests were evidently shared by his close friend, George Trenchard,[40] who lived at Lytchet Matravers in Dorset, about 25 miles from Salisbury. Like Harris, he evidently stayed in London from time to time. Among the many subscribers to *Solomon* on its publication in 1743 was *'The Musical Society at the* Globe *in Fleet-street'*. Radnor's abiding interest in music may be confirmed by his acting as a steward for the Festivals of the Sons of the Clergy in the 1770s.

♣

Boyce subscribes to Thomas Chilcot's *Twelve English Songs with their Symphonies* (1744).

Chilcot was mainly an instrumental composer, and these songs were his only published vocal works. Though he spent his whole life in Bath, Chilcot gained a national reputation. Consequently these instrumentally accompanied songs attracted orders for 347 copies from 278 subscribers. Prominent among them were Avison, Alcock, Stanley and Hawkins.

♣

Boyce subscribes to William Felton's *Six Concerto's for the Organ or Harpsichord with Instrumental Parts*, op. 1 [1744].

Felton was a distinguished keyboard player who pursued his career at Hereford, where he was a vicar-choral at the cathedral. Boyce may well have come into contact with him personally at meetings of the Three Choirs. Felton composed a number of other sets of concertos and suites for

---

[40] Trenchard was evidently an active buyer of music, since he (or perhaps his son of the same name) subscribed for two copies of Festing's *Six Solo's for a Violin and Thorough-Bass* (1747), a publication to which Boyce also subscribed.

the harpsichord. Notable among the other 161 subscribers for 195 copies were Handel, Pepusch, Stanley, Chilcot and Nares.

♣

Songs by Boyce are published in the *London Magazine: or Gentlemen's Monthly Intelligencer* (1744-52).

The first song to appear was 'No more shall meads be deck'd', (text: T. Carew), Sept. 1744, 459, followed by 'If you my wand'ring heart' (anon.), Aug. 1746, 417, 'How blest has my time been', (*s.n.* [Edward Moore], July 1747, 333-4, (*BC* 221), 'Come all ye young lovers', (*s.n.* [E. Moore], Oct. 1747, 446-7, 'Goddess of ease', (C. Smart), Jan. 1748, 34-5,[41] and 'To make the wife kind', (E. Moore), Oct. 1748, 472-3. Additionally, Boyce's setting of 'Ye mortals whom fancies and troubles perplex' from Garrick's *Lethe* was published in Jan. 1749, 36, four airs from *The Chaplet* (1749) in Feb.-May 1750, and one from *The Shepherd's Lottery* in March 1752, along with 'Come all ye youths', (*s.n.* [T. Otway] in April 1752, 185.

♣

Letter from John Lockman to James Harris, 15 September 1744

I do myself the pleasure to send you a large piece of music[42], & a cantata[43], both set by Mr Boyce, & never publish'd[44]. If, in your running them over, you shou'd approve of any part of them, they are very much at your service, to use them as you may think proper; for your agreable concert, or otherwise. I have perus'd, with great satisfaction, what you

---

[41] Boyce's setting here was one of the earliest publications of the poet's works. The composer later set four more poems by Smart, three as solo songs and one as a cantata. Smart, for his part, was subsequently to convey his admiration for Boyce in some of his writings.

[42] The Ode for St. Cecilia's Day, 'See famed Apollo and the Nine' (1739), text by Lockman.

[43] The sacred cantata, 'David's Lamentation over Saul and Jonathan' (1736), text also by Lockman.

[44] These early works remained unpublished in the 18th century and indeed remain so today. However, both have now been performed, broadcast and recorded in recent years (see Discography).

have writ on music, & its sister-arts; whence I imagin'd that some compositions of Mr Boyce woud not be a disagreeable present. I have two or three MSS airs more, by Mr Stanley & another hand, with which I will wait upon you myself.

(Burrows & Dunhill(2002), 199) Lockman was clearly aware of Harris's activities as a concert organizer at Salisbury and evidently hoped that Boyce's settings of his own works might be performed there, as they already had been in London and Dublin. Lockman had clearly already read Harris's recently published *Three Treatises . . . The second Concerning Music, Painting, and Poetry* (1744).

♣

From *Faulkner's Dublin Journal*, 29 Sept.-2 Oct. 1744

The Philharmonic Society will open their Performances with the celebrated Serenata call'd Solomon, on Wednesday the 10th Instant. Those Noblemen and Gentlemen who were Subscribers the last Year, and intend to continue this Season, are requested to send for their Tickets, by a Note directed to Mr. George Walsh Secretary to the said Society, at their Musick Room in Fishamble-street, where Attendance will be given on the 8th, 9th, and 10th Inst. from Ten in the Morning till Two o'Clock – N.B. The said Society propose to perform the following Entertainments this Season, viz. Esther, Athalia, Acis and Galatea, Israel in Egypt, and Alexander's Feast, composed by Mr. Handel, Solomon, Mr. Lockman's Ode on St. Cecilia's Day, David's Lamentation over Saul and Jonathan, and Mr. Hart's Pindaric Ode, composed by Mr. Boyce. [&c.]

(Bartlett *b*(1979), 296) The use of the epithet 'celebrated' in connection with *Solomon* in this notice suggests that members of the Philharmonic Society were probably familiar with it. Being a private society its activities were often not publicised. That *Solomon* had almost certainly already been performed in Dublin is indicated by the inclusion of its text in the collective word-book published by George Faulkner for the Society in 1741.[45] Moreover, a full score of the work prepared by Boyce specifically for Dublin is dated at the end in his hand "March 1741/2" [old style].[46] Thus it is likely to have been delivered and performed later in 1742. It is clear that Boyce had been asked to transpose upwards the male solo part in

---

[45] Copy at *IRL: Dtc*, 190.u.151.
[46] MS preserved at *US: Wc*, ML96.B674.

Solomon specifically at the request of the Dublin singer, John Church. He evidently liked to exploit the extreme upper register of his voice up to and including the Eb at the top of the treble clef.[47] Further performances of *Solomon* are known to have been given by the Society on 3 Dec. 1746 (*DJ*, 25-29 Nov.), 10 Dec. 1746 (*DJ*, 6-9 Dec.), 14 Dec. 1749 (*DJ*, 5-9 Dec.) and 4 Jan. 1750 (*DJ*, 26-30 Jan.). *Solomon* was also taken up by the Charitable Musical Society of Dublin who performed it at least six times between 1748 and 1753, and it was included in the group of his own works Boyce chose to conduct at Cambridge early in July 1749.

♣

John Walsh publishes the *Vocal Musical Mask* (1744).

This 'Collection of English songs never before printed' (adv. *DA*, 14 Dec. 1744) contains one song by each of the following: Boyce, 'Idleness: 'Goddess of ease'', (text: Christopher Smart), Handel, S. Howard, C.F. Weideman; and two by J.F. Lampe. Boyce's setting of Smart's poem was one of the earliest publications of the poet's works. Smart was subsequently to convey his admiration for Boyce in some of his writings.

♣

---

[47] It has been suggested, mainly on the basis of the use of the soprano and alto C clefs by WB for Church's part, that he was in fact an alto (see the review of MB 68 by Graydon Beekes in *Notes*, 2nd series, vol. 55, no. 3 (March, 1999), 738-41). However, Church was always designated a 'tenor', as for example when he sang for Handel in the first performance of *Messiah* in Dublin on 13 April 1742 alongside the alto, Joseph Ward (see Deutsch(1955), 545-6). Moreover, a number of prominent tenors who worked in London in the 18th century also exploited the falsetto range and colour in their voices. One of these, John Johnstone, also an Irish tenor, used "an extensive falsetto" (see Fiske(1973), 629). It was said of another, George Mattocks, that "we are often led to imagine that we are listening to the notes of a *Castrato*" (quoted in Fiske, op. cit., 634). Finally, Charles Incledon, the greatest English tenor of the late 18th-century was credited with "a voice of uncommon power, both in the natural and the falsetto. The former was from A to G, a compass of about 14 notes; the latter he could use from D to D, or F" (Fiske, ibid., 271). The emergence of tenors able and willing to sing up to top C in full voice did not occur in fact until the early 19th-century romantic period in opera.

George II grants Boyce a Royal License to publish his music (10 April 1745).

GEORGE the Second, by the Grace of God, King of Great Britain, France and Ireland, Defender of the Faith &c. To all to whom these Presents shall come, Greeting: Whereas *William Boyce,* one of the Composers of Our Chapels Royal, hath humbly represented unto Us, that he hath with great Study, Labour and Expence, composed several Works, consisting of Vocal and Instrumental Musick, in order to be printed and published, and hath therefore humbly besought Us, to grant him Our Royal Privilege and Licence for the sole Printing and Publishing thereof, for the Term of Fourteen Years: We being willing to give all due Encouragement to Works of this Nature, are graciously pleased to condescend to this Request; and We do therefore by these Presents, so far as may be agreeable to the Statute in that Behalf made and provided, grant unto the said *William Boyce,* his Executors, Administrators and Assigns, Our Licence for the sole Printing and Publishing the said Works, for the Term of Fourteen Years, to be computed from the Date hereof; strictly forbidding all our Subjects, within our Kingdom and Dominions, to reprint or abridge the same, either in the like or any other Volume or Volumes whatsoever; or to import, buy, vend, utter or distribute any Copies there of reprinted beyond the Seas, during the aforesaid Term of Fourteen Years, without the Consent or Approbation of the said *William Boyce,* his Heirs, Executors and Assigns, as they will answer the contrary at their Perils, whereof the Commissioners and other Officers of our Customs, the Master, Wardens and Company of Stationers, are to take Notice that due Obedience may be rendered to our Pleasure herein declared. Given at Our Court at St. James's the Tenth Day of April 1745 in the Eighteenth Year of Our Reign.

By His Majesty's Command
HOLLES NEWCASTLE

Lpro, SP/44/369, 403-4. The granting of a Royal Licence was a highly sought-after privilege which offered composers valuable protection against illegal reproduction of their works. Though there were no penalties laid down for breaches of the terms of the licences, there was evidently a general reluctance to flout the will and authority of the sovereign. The Licence was reproduced in all Boyce's major publications while it was in force, i.e. the first edition of the *Twelve Sonatas* (1747), the first five volumes of *Lyra Britannica* (1747-56), *The Shepherd's Lottery* (1751), and *The Chaplet* (2nd edn, *c*1755), but not in the Cambridge *Ode and Anthem* (1752), perhaps because these works lent themselves much less readily to casual appropriation. Significantly, after the Licence had expired in April

1759, many of WB's most popular songs now began to appear adapted to new words in pastiche stage works and other musical entertainments.

♣

Songs by Boyce are published in the *Gentlemen's Magazine* (1745-55).

The first song to appear in this distinguished and widely read periodical was 'Goddess of ease' (text: C. Smart) in *GM* 15, May 1745, 268-9. Two more were included later: 'When young and artless' (anon.), *GM* 24, June 1754, 283 (not attributed to WB here), and 'To Harriote all accomplished fair' (C. S[mart], *GM* 25, April 1755, 178.

♣

From the *General Advertiser,* 6 May 1745

The Drury Lane Theatre advertises a performance of the comedy *The Careless Husband*[48] coupled with Thomas Arne's opera *Rosamund*. With regard to *The Careless Husband* it is noted that there will be performed: "End of Act 1, A Cantata by Mr. Lowe, End of Act II A Dance by Mr. Muilment, End of Act III *Gentle Shepherd*[49] by Mrs. Arne, End of Act IV, A Dance by Signora Bettinc & others".

♣

John Walsh publishes *Harmonia Anglicana or English Harmony reviv'd,* vol. I [1745].

This 'Collection of the most favourite two, three and four part songs and dialogues' includes two two-part songs by Boyce: 'Since nature mankind for society fram'd (text: John Glanvill), 1-2, and 'How hard is the fortune' (Henry Carey), 18. In vol. 2 a duet from WB's *Solomon* (1742), 'Together let us range the fields', is included. This item became particularly popular towards the end of the century.

---

[48] A comedy by Colley Cibber (1705).

[49] The item referred to was almost certainly the soprano air, 'Tell me, lovely shepherd, where', from Part 1 of Boyce's serenata *Solomon* (1742). This was the most popular item from the work in the early years of its history.

♣

Boyce subscribes to John Travers's *Eighteen Canzonets for Two, and Three Voices* [*c*1745].

This volume, consisting mainly of settings of texts by Matthew Prior, was published by John Simpson for the author, and dedicated to Pepusch. Travers's career had much in common with that of Boyce. He had been apprenticed to Greene, went on to study with Pepusch, and gained an appointment as one of the organists of the Chapel Royal in 1737. The publication of these canzonets was well supported. A rare copy of this edition (*Ob*, Don.c.52) indicates that there were as many as 166 subscribers for 210 copies. Pepusch himself ordered six. In his dedication, Travers presents these works to him "as a publick Testimony of Gratitude" and offers him his "most sincere & hearty acknowledgements for your kind Instructions in the Science we profess". Simpson's music publishing business came to an end *c*1749, but a later edition of the *Eighteen Canzonets*, using the same plates but without the subscribers' list, was published by John Johnson *c*1754, and again *c*1770 by his wife, who succeeded to his business *c*1762. Various individual canzonets from this collection continued to be printed until the end of the century. On the death of Travers in 1758, WB succeeded him as one of the Organists of the Chapel Royal.

♣

T[homas] J[efferys] publishes *Amaryllis* in 2 vols. [1746].

This song collection was dedicated to Princess Augusta, eldest daughter of Frederick Prince of Wales. According to the title-page, the contents consisted of "such songs as are most esteemed for composition and delicacy, and sung at the public theatres or gardens". There are five settings by Boyce: in vol. 1: 'If you my wand'ring heart' (anon.), 15; 'No more shall meads' (text: T. Carew), 21; 'To sooth my heart' (anon.), 77; and in vol. 2: 'In vain, Philander' (John Hawkins), 9, and 'Goddess of ease' (Christopher Smart), 13. Four airs from WB's *Solomon* (1742) are also included in vol. 1: pp.6 and 66-67, and in vol. 2: 14-15 and 22-23 respectively.

♣

Boyce subscribes to Joseph Gibbs's *Eight Solos for a Violin with a Thorough Bass for the Harpsichord or Bass Violin* [1746].

These highly regarded sonatas were published for the author by Peter Thompson, and were dedicated to Sir Joseph Hankey, Alderman and Colonel of the blue Regiment of the City of London. 214 copies were ordered by 161 subscribers, many of them being musicians from Essex where Gibbs was active. Prominent in the list were Boyce, (who ordered two copies), and his close friend and colleague, Maurice Greene. Neither of them, however, contributed to the solo violin repertoire themselves. Much later, *c*1778, Gibbs wrote the first set of string quartets to be published by an English composer.

♣

From the *General Advertiser,* 10 March 1746

AT the Theatre-Royal in Covent-Garden, this Day, will be presented a Play, call'd The MERCHANT of Venice[50] . . . The Part of . . . Lorenzo, Mr. BEARD, with the usual songs in character, likewise the Song of Diana from Dryden's Secular Masque, set to Musick by Mr. BOYCE. [&c.]

This notice is of particular significance in that it provides the earliest known evidence for the existence of Boyce's setting of the *Secular Masque.* The 'Song of Diana', 'With horns and with hounds', was performed again twice shortly afterwards at CG in an 'entertainment of singing' by Beard incorporated into performances of *Much Ado about Nothing* (see *GA*, 12/13 March). The song subsequently gained wide popularity in its own right. When Walsh advertised his publication of WB's *Lyra Britannica*, he drew particular attention to its inclusion: "In this Collection is Inserted the Song of With Horns and with Hounds, sung by Mr. Beard at Ranelagh Gardens" *(GA,* 2 April 1747). The first public performance of the complete work was later advertised to take place at the Swan-Tavern in London on 9 April 1747, but it was at first postponed due to the unavailability of the solo singers, and later cancelled for unspecified reasons. John Beard went on to take many of the leading solo tenor roles in WB's works.

---

[50] Shakespeare's play.

♣

From the *General Advertiser,* 7 April 1746

For the Benefit of Mr. WOODWARD[51] AT the Theatre-Royal in Covent–Garden, this Day, will be reviv'd an Historical Play, call'd CYMBELINE, *King of* BRITAIN As written by Shakespeare. [&c.][52]

An invitation to Boyce from John Rich, the manager at CG, to set a dirge for his production of *Cymbeline* provided the composer with his first direct involvement in the London theatre world. With the masque *Peleus and Thetis* under his belt, and the serenata *Solomon* the talk of the town, Rich may well have been alert now to Boyce's potential as a theatre composer. As Charles Burney later put it, Rich's success as a man of the theatre was due to the fact that "he constantly possessed the favour of the public by his superior conduct, knowledge of Music, and intelligence as an actor" (*BurneyH,* 4, 667). At the same time, Rich may also have been prompted to offer Boyce this commission following the warm reception afforded to his 'Song of Diana' from the *Secular Masque* when John Beard had given three performances of this air at CG the previous month (see above).

Boyce's involvement in the production of *Cymbeline* is confirmed by a cast list for the first performance which again featured Beard: "Arviragus (with the dirge set new by Mr. Boyce) – Beard." (LS, 3, 1230). As a play, *Cymbeline* evidently exerted a limited appeal in the 18th century for it was only played twice in April 1746. It was subsequently revived in 1759 (7 performances) and in 1767-8 (10 performances). The dirge occurs when the supposedly dead Imogen, daughter of Cymbeline, King of Britain, is carried into the forest for a ritual funeral. The elegy is sung by Arrivagus and Guiderius (the latter part played by Henry Woodward), sons of Cymbeline. Shakespeare's original text at this point beginning 'Fear no more the heat of the sun', appears in a modified form in Boyce's score as 'Fear no more the scorching sun', following the common practice of the time to adapt plays in various ways to contemporary taste. The text used for the revival in 1759 was published by William Hawkins in *Cymbeline A Tragedy, altered from Shakespeare, as it is perform'd at the Theatre-Royal*

---

[51] Woodward, a distinguished and wide-ranging man of the theatre and a protégé of John Rich, was particularly admired as a comic actor. He worked for Rich at CG from 1741 to 1747 where the performances for his benefit were always well supported.

[52] In Shakespeare's original play, the dirge set by Boyce for this production occurs in Act IV, sc. ii.

in Covent Garden. The dirge takes place here at the end of Act III (pp.56-7) where Shakespeare's opening line in its original form is now reinstated. The music we are told is "set by Mr. Arne", so Boyce's music for the 1746 performances must have been set aside at this point. WB's autogr. score of the dirge is at *Ob*, MSMus.c.35, ff.2^v-4^r and bears the annotation "Covent Garden, 1746".

♣

John Simpson publishes *Calliope, or English Harmony*, vol. 2 [1746].

Like vol. 1 of *Calliope* (1739), its sequel also contains 200 songs, including a further six by Boyce: 'When Orpheus went down' (text: Samuel Lisle), 25; 'No more shall meads' (T. Carew), 26; 'In vain, Philander' (J. Hawkins), 90; 'If you my wand'ring heart' (anon.), 159; 'Venus to sooth my heart' (anon.), 175, and 'Goddess of ease' (C. Smart), 178. Three airs from *Solomon* (1743) are also reprinted here at 122, 124 and 132 respectively.

♣

John Walsh publishes Boyce's *Twelve Sonatas* (1747).

This initiative had been first signalled by Walsh early in the previous year when he announced: "*This Day is published*, PROPOSALS For *Printing* by SUBSCRIPTION, With His Majesty's *Royal Licence and Protection*, TWELVE SONATAS . . . By WILLIAM BOYCE" (*GA*, 10 April 1746). The cost for subscribers was to be half-a-guinea, but for purchasers after publication 15 shillings.[53] As promised, publication took place early the next year when subscribers were invited to send for their book[s] (*LEP*, 27-29 Jan. 1747) with title-page: *TWELVE* | SONATAS | FOR | Two VIOLINS; | With a Bass for the | VIOLONCELLO or HARPSICORD. | By | *WILLIAM BOYCE,* | Composer to His Majesty. [triple rule] | London, *Printed for the Author. & sold by* I Walsh. | *Musick Printer and Instrument Maker to his Majesty in* | *Catharine Street in the Strand. where may be had* | *By the same Author* | Solomon a Serenata *in* Score | MDCCXLVII.

---

[53] In modern terms *c*£75 and £110 respectively.

So well received were these works that less than two months later a second edition was announced (*GA*, 14 March 1747) and a further 'new edition' came out in 1751 (*GA*, 16 Jan.) using the original plates but erasing the date from the title-page and deleting the list of subscribers. WB left two MSS for these works, an early autogr. (*Lbl*, MSAdd.32160) and a later, partially autogr. score, used as a basis for the published text (*Ckc*, MS225).

In composing these trio sonatas Boyce drew inspiration from models provided by Purcell, Corelli and Handel. He was, however, writing at a time when such works were about to give way to the string quartet on the one hand, and other chamber ensemble genres involving composed keyboard parts rather than improvised continuo accompaniment. Nevertheless, the remarkable size of the initial subscribers' list, which identifies 487 purchasers for 631 sets,[54] in itself gives testimony to the public enthusiasm for these sonatas. Indeed, private devotees of chamber music evidently lost no time in trying out the music. In a letter dated as early as 10 February 1747 to James Harris from his brother Thomas, the latter reports: "We played over Boyce's sonatas one day at Sir W[yndham] Knatchbulls & I think you will like them very well" (Burrows & Dunhill (1998), 233). Twenty years or so later John Marsh, while living in Gosport, noted in his diary: "As to Mr Phillips concerts, Mr Wafer & I were sufficient of ourselves with the family, (if nobody else came) to play Corelli, Humphry[55] and Boyce's sonatas etc. w'ch we all enjoy'd & were even then glad to be thus left to ourselves & so escape Bach and Abel's symphonies" (Robins(1998), 49). The enduring popularity of these sonatas, especially among amateur players, may be illustrated by another private diary entry at the end of the century by James Harris who was then living at Chichester: "On the . . . Saturday after [October 21 1797] I had Target[56] to come for the evening & try some new trios of Pleyel & some old ones of Boyce belong'g to the Concert w'th John[57] and I" (Robins, op. cit., 654).

Charles Burney referred to the finale of Boyce's 1st sonata (though he does not identify it himself) in the course of a discussion of Handel's

---

[54] Prominent among them being Handel, Arne, Pepusch, Greene, Alcock and William Hayes. The ordering of multiple sets by the managers of the Covent Garden and Drury Lane theatres and by numerous musical societies indicate clearly that the trio sonatas were regularly performed by larger ensembles.

[55] John Humphries who had published a set of trio sonatas in 1734.

[56] The remarkably talented James Target was only ten at the time. He was later appointed Organist and Master of the Choristers at Chichester Cathedral in 1801.

[57] John was James Harris's son.

opera, *Flavio* (1723): "In an air for Mrs. Anastasia Robinson, in the same [2nd] act, *Con un vezzo*, there is an imitation carried on between the voice part and first violin, of which Dr. Boyce, one of the most honest of our composers, afterwards availed himself in a favourite movement of his sonatas. The opera had then so long been laid aside, that to draw from it incurred no danger of detection" (*BurneyH*, 4 (1789), 289). The writer inserts a footnote at this point: "In the examination of old operas, particularly those of Handel, we see the first idea and source of almost every movement and passage of our own composers['] productions, that were most in the favor of the public".[58]

Themes from the sonatas were sometimes borrowed and arranged by church musicians. For example, the popular 2nd movement 'March, Grave', from the 4th sonata was adapted for an elegy, 'View here the youth', preserved at *Lbl*, Add.MS.5337, ff. 85-6, and the same theme appears set to the words of a hymn, 'To thee my God', in Coombs's *Divine Amusement* (*c*1825). A 3-part setting by Thomas Sharp of the text, 'God is our refuge', published by John Page in *Divine Harmony* (1798), is based on the 3rd movement *Largo* from the 10th sonata. Boyce himself took the first and last movements of the 9th sonata to make an overture for his setting of Havard's 'Anniversary Ode' in 1756.

The first modern edition of a Boyce sonata, no. 3, was published by Augener in *c*1890. This was followed by 7 (Novello, 1909), 2 (Hinrichsen, ed. Murrill, 1951), and nos. 3, 4, 5, 6, 8, 9 and 12 (Hinrichsen, ed. Sadie, 1961-79). Finally, a facs. edn of the whole set, eds. P. Holman and C. Bartlett, was issued by King's Music (Godmanchester (1985)).

By way of homage to Boyce, movements from sonatas 1, 2, and 3 were utilised by Constant Lambert in his ballet, *The Prospect before us,* based entirely on music by WB, and first performed at Sadler's Wells Theatre in 1940 (see Cudworth(1958), 84-7). Additionally, John McCabe wrote an orchestral piece, *The Shadow of Light*, commissioned by the Royal Philharmonic Society for the bicentenary of Boyce's death in 1979, into which, amongst other things, he incorporated material from the 8th Sonata.

---

[58] It is difficult to comprehend Burney's comments on WB's sonata movement here for at least three reasons. (1) The connection between the thematic material in the two instances is tenuous (for a similar view see Sadie(1958), vol. 1, 141). (2) The borrowing of material by one composer from another was a common practice at the time, not least where Handel himself was concerned. (3) His remarks are at variance with views he expressed elsewhere, e.g., that Boyce "was one of the few of our church composers who neither pillaged nor servilely imitated [Handel]" (*BurneyH,* 3, 621).

A copy of the 2nd Sonata in F, arranged for harpsichord and in an unknown 18th-century hand, is preserved at *Abu*, NLWMS1934C. The adaptation involves the addition of ornaments in the 1st movement, the omission of the 2nd movement *Adagio*, and the deletion of the 2nd violin part from the 3rd and 4th movements.

WB probably wrote three other trio sonatas, in F and D major, and A minor, which were not published. They are preserved at *Cfm*, MU.MS.663, and were transcribed by an unknown hand who claims to have copied them "from a MS in the handwriting of S. Weeley Esqre.", (or perhaps 'S. Wesley'). In either case a direct link with Boyce may be established, for Samuel Wesley knew WB very well in his youth and admired him greatly, while Samuel Weeley, a Gentleman of the Chapel Royal, is known to have acted as a copyist for Boyce from time to time. The sonata in D was performed in a BBC Invitation Concert broadcast on BBC Radio 3 on 17 June 1982, and all three MS sonatas have now been recorded alongside the 12 published ones (see Discography).

♣

John Walsh publishes *Lyra Britannica* [1747].

(Facs. edn: Bruce *b*(1985)) This volume of vocal music by Boyce was advertised (*GA*, 30 March) the day before its publication with title-page: LYRA BRITANNICA: | *Being* | A Collection of | *Songs, Duets, and Cantatas* | *on* | *Various Subjects.* | Compos'd by | M$^{R.}$ BOYCE. [&c.] A later advertisement for LB (*GA*, 25 April), refers to the inclusion, for the first time in one of WB's publications, of His Majesty's Royal Licence, granted to Boyce on 10 April 1745. A measure of the success of this volume may be gauged by Walsh's subsequent decision to issue five similar collections under the same title. With the exception of the final book (1759), by which time the licence had expired, all of them incorporate a copy of the Royal Licence. This first volume contains three airs from the *Secular Masque* (*c*1746): 'With horns and with hounds', 'Thy sword within the scabbard keep', and 'Calms appear'; five independent songs, *BC* 224 (text: William Congreve), 236 (John Lockman), 243 (A. Cowley), 245, (anon.), 255 (W. Congreve), one duet, 176 ([H.] Carey), and a cantata (*BC* 180) with text by Christopher Smart, 177.

♣

From the *General Advertiser*, 7 April 1747

For the Benefit of Mr. JONES[59] AT the Swan-Tavern in Exchange-Alley, Cornhill, on Wednesday, April 29, will be performed DRYDEN's Secular Masque, Set to Musick by Mr. BOYCE With several Solos and Concertos on different Instruments. Some of the principal Singers being engag'd, occasion'd the putting off of the Concert. Tickets delivered for the 9th will be taken the 29th.

Evidence confirming that Boyce had already set Dryden's *Secular Masque* (1700) some time before March 1746 appeared when Covent Garden advertised performances by John Beard of the 'Song of Diana', an air from the work, on the 10th, 12th and 13th of that month. While one, or perhaps more, private performances may have taken place earlier, it is clear that the one planned for 9 April 1747, but postponed till the 29th due to the unavailability of some of the soloists, was intended to be its first public airing. In the event, and for reasons unknown, the performance scheduled for the 29th was also abandoned. A notice similar to that of 7 April above appeared in the *GA* on 22 April, but in the issues of 24, 27, 28 and 29 April the *Secular Masque* was dropped from the advertised programme in favour of Boyce's earlier masque, *Peleus and Thetis*. According to Burney it was "originally set by Dr. Boyce for Hickford's room, or the Castle concert, where, it was first performed, in still life",[60] and that "by the performance and friendly zeal of Mr. Beard, [it] was many times exhibited before it was wholly laid aside" (*BurneyH*, 3, 620). Documentary evidence for these performances is lacking, but we do know that the *Secular Masque* was performed publicly at Cambridge in July 1749 when Boyce was awarded his doctorate, on four occasions in the autumn of 1750 at Drury Lane, (see below), and at a concert advertised as 'Mr. Beard's Night' at the Long Room, Hampstead, on 30 Aug. 1762 (see *GDA*, 30 Aug.). WB published three of the airs from this work in *Lyra Britannica* (1747) and the overture in *Twelve Overtures*, no. 6 (1770).

The origin of the *Secular Masque* lay in an early-17th-century comedy, *The Pilgrim*, by John Fletcher, which was revived by John Vanbrugh and produced at DL on 29 April 1700. John Dryden wrote this new masque as an afterpiece for the play, and the music was composed by Daniel Purcell and Gottfried Finger. The poet adopted the term 'secular' with reference to its meaning as 'of a century', to describe a work which sets out to comment

---

[59] Jones, probably a member of the orchestra at Drury Lane, also appeared as a solo cellist on a number of other occasions about this time.

[60] That is, without scenery or action.

on the political history of Britain in the previous hundred years. While the plot is outwardly based on Roman mythology, Dryden's libretto is in fact a satirical allegory in which the character 'Mars' represents Charles II and his military preoccupations, 'Diana' the devoted huntress, the reign of James I, 'Venus' the court of Charles II, not least its courtesans, and 'Chronos' the reign of William and Mary, and the passing of time. Cross, the prompter at DL, reported on the reception of Garrick's revival of the *Pilgrim* on 30 Oct. 1750: "The play not much lik'd, and ye masque greatly disliked" (quoted in LS, IV, i, 217). This response may perhaps have been the consequence of a failure on the part of the audience to grasp the import of the libretto 50 years after its creation, rather than a lack of appreciation of the merits of Boyce's dramatic music. The play, with Boyce's masque, was repeated on 31 Oct. (when it "went off better") and 9 Nov.. Finally, the following night the masque was paired instead with Hoadly's popular comedy, *The Suspicious Husband.*

A libretto for the 1750 productions is preserved at *Lbl*, 841.c.23(b); a set of partly autogr. instrumental and vocal parts at *Ob,* MS.Mus.Sch.C107^a, and a score arranged for performance by male voices only at *Lcm*, MS.93. The latter would account for the tenor, John Beard, performing the popular 'Song of Diana', 'With horns and with hounds', even though it was originally written for a female voice.

♣

From the *General Advertiser,* 29 April 1747

BY DESIRE For the Benefit of Mr. JONES.[61] AT the Swan-Tavern in Exchange Alley in Cornhill, this Day, April 29, will be perform'd PELEUS and THETIS Wrote by Lord Lansdowne, and set to Musick by Mr. BOYCE Also Return O God of Hosts, and Honour and Arms, from the Oratorio of Sampson[62] With Several Solos and Concertos on the Violin, German Flute, and Hautboy, by the most eminent masters. With a solo on the VIOLONCELLO by Mr. JONES. Tickets to be had at Mr. Jones's House in Boswell-Court, in Devonshire street, and at the Place of

---

[61] Jones was probably a member of the orchestra at the Drury Lane Theatre where a performance of Boyce's *Solomon* (1742) on 28 March 1750 was also arranged for his benefit.

[62] Handel's *Samson.*

Performance, at 5s each.[63] Tickets delivered for the 9th will be taken this Day.

(Taylor (1953), 277) This concert brought into the public domain, apparently for the first time, Boyce's earliest venture into theatre music. According to his biographer, Hawkins, the masque *Peleus and Thetis* was composed much earlier. In the course of discussing the composer's activities in the mid 1730s he remarks that he "had it performed at the *Philharmonic Society* where it was received with the applause due to its merit".[64] A later commentator observed that "when performed at the Philharmonic Society, the piece was heard with equal pleasure and surprise. Under any circumstances, the form of genius and scientific proficiency evinced by the music of 'Peleus and Thetis' would have been worthy of eulogistic notice".[65] Further confirmation of the work's early origin is provided by the inclusion of its libretto in the *Miscellany of Lyric Poems*, issued by the Apollo Academy in 1740, which brought together the texts of the major works performed there since 1736. Boyce also included *Peleus* in the works he conducted at Cambridge in 1749 in a series of concerts connected with the Installation of the new University Chancellor, and the award of his doctorate.[66]

The origin of the libretto Boyce chose to set lies in a masque interpolated into George Granville's play, *The Jew of Venice*, an adaptation of Shakespeare's *Merchant of Venice*, first performed at Lincoln's Inn Fields Theatre in 1701. WB's text comes from an elaborated and improved 2nd edition of the original libretto published in 1713.[67] Drawn from Greek mythology, the action takes place on a mountain in the Caucasus where Prometheus is undergoing punishment by being chained to a rock and having his liver gnawed by an eagle. Peleus, the father of Achilles, though mortal, is permitted to marry a God. He is in love with Thetis, a sea nymph who is also coveted by Jupiter. Peleus consults Prometheus who persuades Jupiter (whose blustering introduces a comic element in the proceedings) to abandon his quest for Thetis in favour of his rival. WB may have been attracted to this subject by seeing Granville's play in London during the 1730s when it was performed on nine occasions; or

---

[63] c£38 in modern terms.

[64] Hawkins(1788), ii. The *Philharmonic* was a private musical society directed by Michael Festing, a distinguished violinist. It met at the Crown and Anchor Tavern in the Strand.

[65] (Busby(1825), vol. 3, 168.

[66] For details, see *Lcm*, XX.E.16.

[67] See Cholic(1995), 41-2. An independent libretto of the work dated 1745 is preserved at *US: SM*.

perhaps by hearing Handel's serenata, *Parnasso in Festa*, composed in celebration of the union of Princess Anne[68] and William Duke of Orange on 14 March 1734, which utilised the marriage of Peleus and Thetis as an allegory for the royal wedding.

WB's autogr. score and related parts are at *Ob*, MS.Mus.Sch.D.24. The overture has been edited by Finzi in MB 13 (1957), and the whole work successfully staged and recorded in modern times (see Discography). John McCabe included two themes from the overture in his orchestral work, 'The Shadow of Light', commissioned by the Royal Philharmonic Orchestra to mark the bi-centenary of WB's death in 1979.

♣

Boyce subscribes to Michael Festing's *Six Solo's for a Violin and Thorough-Bass,* op. 7 (1747).

Festing had been prominent in London musical life from the mid-1720s, particularly as a virtuoso violinist. Boyce would have known him from at least 1736 since, along with Boyce's teacher Greene, he had been a founder member of the Apollo Academy where Boyce's earlier large-scale choral works were first performed. Festing's prominence in English musical life encouraged orders for 281 copies from 254 subscribers, a fair number of them from Dublin, and from musical societies at large, including naturally the Apollo.

♣

Boyce subscribes to James Nares's *Eight setts of lessons for the harpsichord* (1747).

Having been a chorister at the Chapel Royal, Nares studied with Pepusch in London, as Boyce had done, before being appointed organist at York Minster in 1735. These Scarlatti-inspired works, incorporating abstract sonata movements, dances and fugues, attracted 151 subscribers for 168 copies. Among the many other prominent musicians who subscribed were Handel, de Fesch, Greene, William Hayes, Pepusch, Stanley and Travers.

♣

---

[68] Daughter of George II.

John Walsh publishes another volume of vocal music by Boyce, *Lyra Britannica*, II (1747).

(Facs. edn, Bruce *b*(1985)) Shortly after the evidently well received publication of LB in March 1747, a 2nd book was advertised (*GA*, 11 July) and published with title-page: LYRA BRITANNICA: | Book II | *Being* | a Collection of | *Songs, Duets, and Cantatas,* | *on* | *Various Subjects.* | Compos'd by | MR BOYCE. [&c.] This volume again contains a group of solo songs, *BC* 202 (text: anon.), 203 (anon.), (autogr. at *Lcm,* MS782, f.40), 218 (anon.), 221 (Edward Moore), 231 (anon.), one duet, 181 (John Glanvill), and a single cantata, 182 (anon.). Having set Moore's serenata *Solomon* in 1742, the above song was the first of five settings by Boyce of poems by him, the others being *BC* 204, 212, 222 and 258. WB also set a dialogue of Moore's, *BC* 179, and an orchestrally accompanied song for his tragedy, *The Gamester*, in 1753.

♣

Boyce subscribes to William Hayes's *Six cantatas set to musick* [1748].

Hayes was Professor of Music at Oxford when J. Simpson published these works for him. Among the 316 subscribers for 408 copies were many members of the Oxford music fraternity, the composers Chilcot, Lampe and Stanley, and the distinguished tenors, Beard and Lowe. In the same year, Hayes played a leading role in the building of the Holywell Music Room at Oxford which survives to this day as the oldest purpose-built concert hall in Europe.

♣

John Walsh publishes a further volume of vocal music by Boyce, *Lyra Britannica*, III (1748).

(Facs. edn, Bruce *b*(1985)) This volume, on a smaller scale than its predecessors, was advertised (*GA*, 9 Sept.) and published with title-page: LYRA BRITANNICA | Book 3^d. | A | CANTATA | AND | ENGLISH SONGS *Set to Musick by* | M^R. BOYCE | *in which is inserted the Songs of Johnny & Jenny.* | *To make the Wife kind, You Say you love* &c. | *Sung at* Vaux-hall, *and* Ranelagh Gardens. [&c.] The first item identified here is a dialogue, 'Let rake's for pleasure' (text, Edward Moore),[69] the second a solo song (also Moore)[70] and the third also a solo song (anon.). The other works included are the cantata, 'Blest in Maria's friendship', and the solo song 'Ah Chloe', both of them with anonymous texts.

♣

From the *Dublin Journal*, 1-4 October 1748

The Charitable Musical Society for the Relief of Prisoners, open their first Concert in their Hall in Fishamble-street on Friday next [7th], with their celebrated Oratorio[71] of SOLOMON they are to be assisted by several additional Voices, the best in this Kingdom, and by Mrs. Arne[72] who is immediately expected over, and propose to entertain their Subscribers frequently with Oratorio's [*sic*] and Entertainments of the like Kind during the Season.

An account of this concert appeared in the press shortly afterwards: "The celebrated Oratorio of SOLOMON was performed at the Musick-hall in Fishamble-street last Friday Evening, to a numerous and polite Audience with the greatest Applause: They were so delighted with the Elegance of its Composition and the judicious Manner in which it was executed that the Ladies of Quality and Gentlemen were unanimous in requesting it might be performed again next Friday, which Request was complied with. Mrs. Arne, who has been at Parkgate some Time, is expected over immediately, to join in the Concert of that Society. There will likewise be a Piece on the Organ by the best Performer in this Kingdom" (*DJ*, 8-11 Oct.). Notwithstanding the tendency of concert promoters to put the

---

[69] In the song book, *Polyhymnia* (1769), the caption to this piece reads: "This Dialogue is well set, and was greatly admired when first made public".

[70] In the same source, the caption reads: "Sung by Mr. Lowe at Vaux-Hall. Set by Dr. Boyce. This Song was pleasingly set, and received universal Applause when it was first made public".

[71] Although WB's *Solomon* was from its inception specifically designated a 'serenata', because of its title and the biblical origin of its text, it was sometimes described, as in this case, as an 'oratorio'. As a consequence, the assumption has been made that the work in question was Handel's *Solomon* (see Cummings(1912), 38). However, though Handel's oratorio was composed in May/June 1748, its premiere did not take place until 17 March 1749 in London. Prior to the arrival of Handel's work, '*Solomon*', was naturally taken to mean Boyce's serenata.

[72] Cecilia (née Young), a distinguished singer, was at this time married to Thomas Arne.

highest possible gloss on their enterprises, it seems evident that *Solomon* was still going down well in Dublin some six years after it first appeared there. In any case, a further performance of *Solomon* by the Charitable Musical Society was advertised for the 14th, and again that "On Friday next [16 Dec.] will be performed the celebrated Oratorio of SOLOMON, in which Mrs Arne (who was indisposed when it was perform'd before), will have a principal Part, on whose account this Entertainment is particularly requested" (*DJ*, 10-13 Dec.). Cecilia Arne had worked in Dublin from 1742 to 1744 and she returned there for the winter concert season of 1748-9.

The three known performances of *Solomon* that had taken place in Dublin prior to 1748 had been sponsored by the Philharmonic Society. Having taken up the work, the Charitable Musical Society went on to give further performances in 1750 (*DJ*, 17-20 Dec.), 1751 (*DJ*, 23-26 Feb.), 1752 (*DJ*, 9-12 Dec.) and 1753 (*DJ*, 20-23 Jan.). A later independent performance of *Solomon* in Dublin "for the benefit of Mr. Murphy"[73] took place in 1755 (*DJ*, 18-21 Jan.).

♣

From John Stafford Smith's *Commonplace Book*

The following anecdote came from Dr. Boyce. One day he & Dr Arne met. The conversation turn'd on music. D^r. Arne observed when he look'd at a new production of music, he 1st sought for the faults y^t he might enjoy the beauties with more satisfaction afterwards. D^r. Boyce replied, when <u>he</u> saw in any composition many instances of genius & judgement, he overlook'd y^e. faults entirely, believing y^e. parts wch. were less happy to be slighted wth. design, for reasons not always obvious.

Lbl, Add.MS34608, f. 10 (*c*1785-89). (Cudworth *b*(1960), 136) A shorter version of this encounter appears on f. 29^r of this MS. Smith, who had studied with Boyce, later published a more informative and lucid version of the anecdote in his *Musica Antiqua* [1812], ii, 11: "It happened, that Messrs. Boyce and Arne met one morning in Mr. Garrick's parlour, before they acquired academical degrees. Talking of music, Mr. Arne remarked that, when he took up a score, he looked for the faults in the first place, and, if they were numerous, he laid it aside. "You may be right", said Mr. Boyce, "although I differ from you; where I find many beauties, I wish to see no faults". If the latter account can be relied on, it may serve to

---

[73] A local organist and composer.

establish an approximate date for this exchange. Thomas Arne did not take his doctorate at Oxford until 1759, while Boyce received his at Cambridge in July 1749, thus a *terminus post quem* for their encounter may be postulated. Arne had collaborated with David Garrick in various theatrical enterprises from 1740 onwards, but Garrick did not commission work from WB until the revival of his play *Lethe* at Drury Lane in January 1749. A date for their meeting about this time would therefore seem the most plausible.

♣

From the *General Advertiser*, 2 January 1749

DRURY-LANE. *By His Majesty's Company of Comedians,* AT the Theatre Royal in Drury Lane, This Day, will be presented a Comedy, call'd The CONSCIOUS LOVERS.[74] . . . To which will be added a Dramatic Satire, call'd LETHE The PRINCIPAL Parts to be perform'd by Mr. GARRICK; Mr. Woodward, Mr.Yates, Mr. Beard, . . . And Mrs. CLIVE. [&c.]

Boyce was commissioned to write two songs for this production of David Garrick's popular afterpiece, *Lethe*. It had first been staged at DL in 1740 when two of the actors engaged above, John Beard and 'Kitty' Clive, had also taken part (notice in *LDP*, 15 April 1740). This revival took place in the wake of Garrick's appointment as manager at DL in 1747. The play went on to retain its place on the London stage into the late 1760s. The text was published in 1749 with title-page: LETHE. | A | DRAMATIC SATIRE. | By *DAVID GARRICK.* | As it is Performed at the | THEATRE-ROYAL in DRURY-LANE | By His Majesty's Servants. | THE SECOND EDITION. [&c.] Garrick must have been fully aware of Boyce's growing stature at this time. The actor had been in Dublin during the Spring of 1746, but on his return to London he acted at Covent Garden and must have become aware of the performances of Boyce's 'Song of Diana' there in March of that year, as well as the 'Dirge' commissioned by the manager, John Rich, for a production of *Cymbeline* a month later.

---

[74] A comedy by Sir Richard Steele, first performed in 1722. A reference to *Lethe* (see Schneider(1979), 340), may be taken to indicate that the play was revived on 27 Dec. 1748, but this entry signals only the appearance of a preliminary notice for the new production: "A Dramatic Satire call'd *Lethe*, is now in Rehearsal at the Theatre-Royal in Drury-Lane, and will be acted in a few Days".

Garrick introduced three songs into this version of *Lethe*. Both of the songs set by Boyce were written for John Beard in the character of 'Mercury'. The first, 'Ye mortals whom trouble and fancies perplex', occurs in the opening scene in a grove by the river Lethe (text, p.4). The second, 'Come mortals, come, come follow me' (with a chorus), occurs towards the end (text, pp.41-2). The third song, 'The card invites', was set by Thomas Arne. There are no references in the publicity for *Lethe* to the composers of these songs but Boyce later published both of his in *Lyra Britannica* IV (1754). 'Ye mortals' was evidently the more successful, for it appeared in at least five other publications up to 1770. Two of these, both of them s.sh.f. editions, have been dated *c*1750. They serve to suggest, therefore, that the new music by Boyce and Arne was almost certainly composed for the revival of *Lethe* in January 1749. Later in the century, Burney, in an oft-quoted remark, drew attention to the use made of both composers by Garrick in his early years as manager at DL: "Dr. Greene was now at the head of our cathedral Music, and the King's band. And Mr. Arne and Mr. Boyce were frequently concurrents at the theatres and in each other's way, particularly at Drury-lane. Arne was aspiring, and always regarded Handel as a tyrant and usurper, against whom he frequently rebelled, but with as little effect as Marsyas against Apollo"[75] (*BurneyH*, 3, 667). Arne wrote for the theatre throughout his career. Boyce on the other hand, having fulfilled his commission at CG in 1746, subsequently composed theatre music only spasmodically, and even then only for DL up to 1758. Boyce became 'Dr.' rather than 'Mr.' in July 1749. Burney must have had in mind, therefore, 1749 and the early 1750s when Boyce and Arne may have been seen as rival composers for the theatre.

♣

From the *Dublin Journal*, 4-7 February 1749

On Thursday next [9th] will be presented a Comedy called, The MERCHANT of VENICE. Written by Shakespear. . . . To which will be added a Masque, never exhibited before, called, The TEMPLE of PEACE

---

[75] The reference here is to the Greek myth in which a musical contest takes place between the satyr Marsyas and the god Apollo. The latter wins by reversing his lyre but continuing to play. Inevitably, Marsyas is quite unable to emulate this trick with his pipes. For daring to challenge him to such a duel, Apollo then flays his opponent.

occasioned by the present happy Peace established over Europe.[76] The character of Mars by Mr. Howard; Venus by Mrs. Storer, in which character she will introduce the Song of O Peace by Mr. Arne,[77] Cupid by Miss Pocklington, Peace by Mrs. Mozeen, with the Song of Rosey Chaplets by Signor Pasquali, Ceres by Mrs. Mynitt, first Attendant on Ceres by Mr. Dyer with the Song of Harvest Home,[78] the Words by Mr. Dryden the Musick by Mr. Purcel; Selenus by Mr. Morris, Pan by Mr. Sparks, Bacchus by Mr. Sullivan with the Song, Let the deep Bowl, by Mr. Handel,[79] the Part of Diana by Mrs. Lampe, with the Song, with Hounds and with Horn.[80] The whole adorned with new Scenes, Machines, Habits and other Decorations, particularly a grand View of the TEMPLE of PEACE.

Further performances of this production at the Smock-Alley Theatre, Dublin, took place on 15, 20 and 22 February, and 27 April. The music was arranged by Niccolo Pasquali who was active in Dublin 1748-52. A copy of the word-book issued for these performances is preserved in London (*Lbl*, 11775c. 85). Of the music for the masque, only the overture has survived.

♣

Boyce subscribes to John Johnson's publication of *A cantata and six songs set to musick by a gentleman of Oxford* [*c*1749].

Boyce appears in the list of subscribers to the edition as 'Mr. William Boyce', thus indicating a date of publication before July 1749 when he received his doctorate. The music is of fine quality and attracted 454 subscribers, including Greene, Stanley and other leading British musicians

---

[76] The British involvement in the War of the Austrian Succession (1743-48) had been pursued at great cost. The resolution of the issues involved that had been achieved at Aix-la-Chapelle, in particular the recognition by France of the legitimacy of the English Protestant succession, inspired general rejoicing throughout the kingdom. As part of the celebrations in London, George II commissioned Handel to compose his *Firework Music*.

[77] From the *Masque of Alfred*.

[78] From the semi-opera *King Arthur*.

[79] From the oratorio *Belshazzar*.

[80] The music used here must have been based on Boyce's very popular 'Song of Diana', 'With horns and with hounds', from the *Secular Masque* (*c*1746).

of the day. The work has not yet been attributed to any particular composer. A conceivable candidate would be William Hayes, who was in Oxford from 1735, had been Professor of Music in the University since 1741, and whose name is also in the list of subscribers. This speculation begs the question, of course, as to why he did not attach his name to this publication as he normally did.

♣

Boyce subscribes to Thomas Bowman's *A Collection of English Odes, Cantatas, Songs* (1749).

Little is known about Bowman's career except that he published a wide range of sacred and secular vocal music as well as a set of trio sonatas (1757). Notable among the other 181 subscribers were Alcock, Beard, de Fesch, Pepusch, Roseingrave and Hawkins.

♣

Boyce subscribes to John Hebden's *Six Concertos in seven Parts*, op. 2a, (*c*1749).

Hebden was a prominent cellist/bassoon player in London orchestras whom Boyce probably knew personally. Other than these well crafted concerti grossi he seems only to have published a set of flute sonatas. This publication was well supported for 162 copies were ordered by 145 subscribers, many of whom were prominent in London's musical life.

♣

From the *General Advertiser*, 1 July 1749

On Wednesday last saw near a hundred Vocal and Instrumental Performers set out for Cambridge. The Musick is compos'd, and to be conducted by Mr. William Boyce, Organist and Composer to his Majesty. A new Ode wrote by a Gentleman of Cambridge[81] and set by Mr. Boyce in honour of his Grace the Duke of Newcastle's being chose Chancellor, will be perform'd: the Vocal Parts by Miss Turner, Mr. Beard and the Gentlemen of the King's Chapel, the Choirs of St. Paul's, Westminster

---

[81] William Mason.

Abbey and Windsor and the Instrumental by several Hands from the Opera House.[82] [&c.] The Dinner ordered by the Duke of Newcastle, is for six hundred Persons, at Trinity Hall in Cambridge.

This public notice drew attention not only to the celebrations attendant on the forthcoming Installation of the Duke of Newcastle as the new Chancellor of the University, but over and beyond that, a virtual four-day festival devoted to the music of Boyce. During the period 1-4 July Boyce's Ode was performed at the Installation ceremony at Senate House, and the anthem, 'O be joyful' (*BC* 56), submitted to the University as his doctoral exercise, was sung at St. Mary's church. Four other major works, the ode, 'Gentle lyre begin the strain', the *Secular Masque*, *Peleus and Thetis* and *Solomon* were also publicly performed. Mason had written his ode in four days, and WB himself had only about ten days in which to set it, rehearse all six pieces, and make the necessary arrangements to get the performers to Cambridge.[83] The considerably costs incurred in this exercise were borne by the Duke of Newcastle himself. All the published librettos for these performances are now preserved at *Lcm*, XX.E.16(11-16). The eminent vocal soloists, John Beard and Molly Turner, were probably recruited with the two solo roles in *Solomon* (1742) particularly in mind. The latter was also well known as a harpsichordist.

The signal academic and musical honours paid to WB as a composer on this occasion had been matched previously in the 18th century only by the festival devoted to Handel at Oxford in July 1733 (though in this case the composer declined to accept the doctorate), and subsequently only by that offered to, and accepted by, Haydn at Oxford in July 1791.

♣

From the *Gentlemen's Magazine*, XIX, July 1749

Cambridge, July 1

This being the day appointed for the installation of his Grace the D. of *Newcastle,* Chancellor elect of this university, the Vice Chancellor, Heads of Houses, Proctors, Beadles and other Officers of this university, being assembled about 12 in the Senate-House, the Noblemen in their proper Habits; Doctors of the several Faculties in their Congregation–Robes; Batchelors of Divinity, Regent and Non–Regent Masters, and Batchelors

---

[82] Covent Garden Theatre.
[83] See Knight(1980), 46.

of Law and Physick, in their hoods and caps of velvet; and Non Graduated Fellow-Commoners, who are Batchelors of Arts, in their gowns, hoods, and square caps; Fellow Commoners, who are Batchelors of Arts, in their Batchelors gowns, hoods and square caps of velvet; and Non Graduated Fellow-Commoners, in their proper habits, caps, and bands: A deputation was sent to his Grace the Duke of *Newcastle,* Chancellor Elect, who resided at *Clare-Hall;* whence, preceded by the Beadles and several Doctors he came to the Senate-House, at the steps to which he was met by the Vice Chancellor, Dr *Chapman,* Master of *Magdalen-College,* who walked up the Senate-House at his Grace's left hand, when they ascended to the chair of state, his Grace standing at the left hand of the chair, the Vice-Chancellor on the right, the band of musick playing during the time a short overture: Which being ended, the Vice-Chancellor opened the ceremony with an elegant speech in *English*, wherein he expatiated on the honour done the University by so noble a person's accepting the place of their Chancellor and Protector, and of the great encouragement religion, literature and loyalty, had constantly found under his Majesty's mild and auspicious reign. This speech, which lasted about twenty minutes, was expressed with that beauty of diction and strength of elocution, that it charmed the whole audience, and received at its conclusion the universal applause due to its real merit. Then the Vice-Chancellor presented to his Grace the patent of office, which was read alone by the senior Proctor; he presented also to his Grace, the book of statutes, and then taking his Grace's right hand in his own, the senior Proctor administer'd to his Grace the oath of office. Then his Grace was seated by Mr Vice-chancellor in the chair of state, and thereby installed. Immediately Mr *Young* (of *Trinity*) Publick Orator to the University, addressed his Grace in a *Latin* Oration of about the same length as the former speech, and delivered it with that clearness, force and just propriety, as shewed the University had chosen for their Orator, one whom *Cicero*[84] would have been proud of for his pupil, if not fearful he should be eclipsed by him. Mr Orator having finished, his Grace arose, and in a very handsome speech returned his thanks to the University for the honour conferred on him, enlarged on the benefits arising from academical education in general, shewed how much religion, literature and loyalty, were advanced by the principles cultivated in the University, which had justly entitled them to the favour of his late and present Majesty whose mild and happy reigns were favourable to the culture of learning, arts and sciences, the glory of a nation, and companions to liberty. He concluded with a just encomium on the Vice-

---

[84] Distinguished Roman author of the 1st century B.C.

Chancellor and Mr Orator, who had so elegantly represented the sentiments of this learned and illustrious body. The words and musick[85] were extremely elegant, and well suited to the occasion. [&c.]

GM, XIX, 328-9. A very similar account of the Installation ceremony appeared in *WEP*, 4-6 July 1749, with an expanded peroration: "The Whole [Ceremony] concluded with an Ode by Mr. Mason, set to Musick by Mr. Boyce, and executed by a fine Band of Vocal and Instrumental Musick. The Words and Musick were extremely elegant, and well suited to the Occasion. The Procession went from the Senate-House to Trinity College, where a splendid and elegant Entertainment was provided for a most numerous and polite Company. . . . This Day his Grace the Chancellor went in State to St. Mary's and heard a Sermon preached by the Rev. Dr. Green, Professor of Divinity; which was highly applauded by the Whole Congregation. Last Night a grand Piece of Music was performed at the Senate-House, composed by Mr. Boyce, with which the Audience was highly delighted".[86] Some idea of the impact this event had on the town may be gauged from the following item published in London: "We hear from Cambridge that Part of the Ceremony and Entertainment on the Installation of his Grace the Duke of Newcastle, was put off till Yesterday; and that the Town was so full of Company, that the meanest Bed was not to be had for less than 7s. 6d. a Night"[87] (*WEP*, 1-4 July 1749). However, a rather less favourable view of the proceedings was conveyed in a later issue of the same journal: "We hear from Cambridge, that at the late grand solemnity, calculated to feed the Five Senses, at the Expence of a noble Duke, their tutelar Angel, the Concourse of all Sorts was so great, that little Order could be observed to gratify either. The small Senate House, and large Trinity-Hall, were insufficient for the Hearing of the Speeches of the noble University Latin Orator, and the English Vice Chancellor; Neither, by the Musick, Ear nor Taste could be gratified, by the great Confusion caused by such a Multitude, who (wanting an Oxford Theatre)[88] were rather penned up close for the Gratification of another Sense, and at last concluded, as usually Feasts are, by an ill cook'd, half cold Dinner, though in the high French Taste. It is

---

[85] Specifically the installation ode, 'Here all the active fires diffuse', written by William Mason, and set to music by WB.

[86] The anthem, 'O be joyful' (*BC* 56), submitted by WB for his DMus exercise.

[87] In modern terms c£55.

[88] The writer had in mind the more capacious Sheldonian Theatre at Oxford, built for the University by Christopher Wren in 1664-8.

expected that our Gazettes, and those of other foreign Countries, will be stuffed with this Ceremony as usual, *ad nauseam*" (*WEP*, 6-8 July 1749).

♣

An account of the Election and Installation of the Duke of Newcastle as Chancellor of Cambridge University, attrib. to Dr. William Richardson [July 1749]

The Duke of Somerset[89] died at Petworth 2ᵈ. Decʳ. 1748[.] Notice was received by me that day in Town which I immediately sent to Cambridge and which reach'd that place by 6 the next morning (the Vice Chancellor being in London with an address on the conclusion of the Peace)[.][90] On the 13ᵗʰ yᵉ Vice Chancellor notified the vacancy and appointed the next day for the Election when the Duke of Newcastle[91] was unanimously chosen by 190 votes. Then the orators Latin letter was read and agreed to desiring his acceptance of the office & a patent ordered to be prepared. It was put into the hands of Sʳ Thomas Brand to be illuminated (who was Illuminatʳ to the King as well as Gent Usher daily Waiter) who having finished it it was sealed & put into a silver-box gilt wᵗʰ the University Arms engraved thereon, on one side the Chancellors & Vice Chancellors on the other. It was long under consideration where the Installation shou'd be; at last about the beginning of June notice was given that it wou'd be at Cambridge on Saturday July 1. Several of the Duke's servants were sent down about a week before to make preparation for the Installation Dinner. The Duke himself came to the Earl of Godolphins on the Hills on Thursday June 29 & the next day came privately to the back of Clare Hall where he was to lodge about 7 o clock & was soon after waited upon by the Heads to congratulate him on his arrival. The next morning the University were met by eleven & a deputation of 4 Heads Dʳˢ. in Divinity one Dʳ of Law & one of Physick & Regents & Non Regents went from the Senate House where the Vice Chancellor preceeded by the 3 Beadles met him at the West Door & conducted him to the upper end giving him the right hand all the way but at last assumed it again. The Vice Chanc. then

---

[89] Charles Seymour, 6th Duke of Somerset, had been the previous Chancellor of the University.

[90] The Peace of Aix-La-Chapelle (1748) which brought to an end the War of the Austrian Succession.

[91] Thomas Pelham-Holles, a prominent politician who became Prime Minister in 1754-6.

made a long harangue in English full of flattery for half an hour presenting him with the Patent of Election & the Statutes fairly bound at the same time he resigned the Choir & Insignia & withdrew to an adjoining seat. The Orator then began his speech in Latin wherein he set forth the honour done the University by his Grace's accepting the Chancellorship and the many eminent good qualities conspicuous in him[,] the services he has done to his King & country from his very youth and the great room there was to hope that the University wo^d. flourish under him. The Orator as well as the Vice chancellor before him endeavoured to take off from the obloquy wch. might have been thrown upon the University for the late proceed^s of some of our youth & threw those irregularit^s on the licentiousness of the age in general. After the Orator had finished the Chancell^r in an English speech returned his thanks to the University for the honour they had done him & gave the strongest assurances of his endeavours to serve them. This finished a new ode (wrote on the occasion by M^r. Mason of Pembroke Hall set to musick by M^r. Boyce of the King's Chapel) was performed both vocally and instrumentally. Which done the procession began in the manner following[:] Fellow Commoners properly habited preceeded by the Yeoman Bedel . . . They thus proceeded till the Yeoman Bedel arrived at the stairs of Trin^y Coll Hall when (the Juniors stopping) the Chancellor Nobility D^{rs}. put on their common scarlet gowns. After a time the dinner being placed upon the table notice was given every one seated him as he pleased only at the Chancellors table more Heads sat than at any other; the Chancellor himself being seated in the middle of the upper table his face towards the Hall. Each table had a nobleman at the head of it. The Vice Chancellor[92] behaved scandalously letting himself down below the office of a common cryer to the no small concern of those who were friends to the University. On Sunday his Grace was twice at S^t. Maries & sat as Chancell. seats being erected near the rails in the chancel for such noblemen & D^{rs}. as the common seats would not hold. The Te Deum was vocally and instrumentally performed & an anthem in the morning & a new anthem in the afternoon composed by Mr Boyce.[93] On Monday the Duke officiated as Chancellor in the Senate House & admitted the following persons to degrees. . . . On Tuesday his Grace was also in the Senate House & saw the creation of the D^{rs}. in all Faculties when Mr Boyce before mentioned was created D^r in Musick by the Senr. Proctor. In the intervals of these two days the Duke visited every college in town & was met at the college gates by the respective Masters Fellows properly

---

[92] Dr. Chapman, Master of Magdalene College.
[93] The orchestrally accompanied anthem, 'O be joyful in God.'

habitted & by them regaled with wine & on Wednesday about 1 he left the University & went to Euston Hall in Suffolk the seat of his Grace the Duke of Grafton.[94]

Cu, UA.Misc.Collect.44, ff.1-3. This manuscript, in an unknown hand, is copied from an account known to have been written by Richardson.[95] It should be borne in mind perhaps that Richardson, Master of Emanuel College, had himself originally supported the candidature of Frederick Prince of Wales for the post of Chancellor, but the latter withdrew before the contest. This private account of the proceedings by an insider provides not only a personal, if in some respects jaundiced, view of the occasion, but also a glimpse into the processes that preceded the appointment of a new Chancellor.

♣

From the Vestry Minutes of Allhallows the Great and the Less, 28 July 1749

This day was held a Vestry for the United Parishes to elect an organist for the said United Parishes when D^r. W^m. Boyce was unanimously chosen with a salary of thirty pounds p[er] annum[96] to commence from Midsummer last, the salary to be paid equally between the United Parishes.

Lgc, MS819/2, 311. Allhallows, situated in Thames St., was the Parish Church for Joiners' Hall where Boyce stlll resided with his father. The two original churches, the Great, and the Less, were both destroyed in the Great Fire of 1666. The single church that replaced them, designed by Sir Christopher Wren and completed in 1683, was demolished in 1874. Boyce now held two parish appointments, at the above, and at St. Michael's, Cornhill, in addition to his post as a Composer at the Chapel Royal. Such pluralism was commonplace in the church at the time, not only where organists were concerned, but also amongst the clergy. Boyce would have made use of a deputy whenever necessary. Shortly before WB's formal appointment, Allhallows had announced that a "new organ, built by Mr Jordan, will be opened by Mr Boyce" (*GA*, 16 June 1749).

♣

---

[94] Augustus Henry FitzRoy, 3rd Duke of Grafton.
[95] Information kindly provided by Dr. E.S. Leedham-Green.
[96] In modern currency c£4,500.

Letter from Christopher Smart to Dr. Charles Burney

Market Downham   Norfolk
ye 29th of July 1749

My dear Charles

I have left your last unanswered so long that I am under some apprehension, lest it shou'd be now too late. You must know that I am situated within a mile of my Harriote[97] & love has robd friendship of her just dues; but you *know* the force of the passion too well to be angry of its effects. I condole with you heartily for the loss of your father,[98] who (I hope) has left behind the cole[99] which is the most effectual means of consolation. I am as much a stranger as you to what is going on at Vaux Hall,[100] for we are so wrapt up in our own smugness at this part of the kingdom, that we know little what's doing in the rest of the world. There was a great musical crash at Cambridge, which was greatly admired,[101] but I was not there, being much better pleased with hearing my Harriote on her spinnet & organ at her ancient mansion. — If you are still in the kingdom I beg the favour of an immediate line or two, but if you are not, I hope even the ocean will not, nay, he shall not cut off our correspondence & friendship —

Y^{rs} most inseparably   C. Smart

MS in *US: CAh.* (Lonsdale(1965/1986), 26) Smart had been acquainted with Burney from the mid-1740s and the latter's setting of Smart's poem, 'Lovely Harriote' (also set by Boyce about the same time), had been

---

[97] Harriote Pratt, with whom Smart had been in love for some years. She was the sister of Edward Pratt, a don at Caius College, who had earlier been a fellow student of Smart's at Cambridge.

[98] James Macburney had died the previous month.

[99] Cole (coal) i.e. money.

[100] The reference is to Vauxhall Gardens in London. Both men had a common interest in musical activities there since Burney had set Smart's poem, 'Lovely Harriote', the previous year, and it would almost certainly have entered the repertoire there.

[101] Smart is referring to the ceremonies associated with the Installation of the Duke of Newcastle as Chancellor of the University that had taken place at the beginning of July. WB had not only set the ode written by William Mason in celebration of the event, but had also composed and conducted the orchestral anthem, 'O be joyful' (*BC* 56), being the exercise submitted for his doctorate. He also directed performances of a number of his other major works while he was in Cambridge from 1-4 July. Harriote lived at Ryston Hall, Downham, situated only a mile or so from where Smart was staying at this time.

published the year before this letter was written. Altogether six of his letters to Burney, dating from the period 1749 to 1770, have survived (see Rizzo & Mahoney (1991).

♣

A letter from Thomas Gray[102] to Thomas Wharton,[103] 8 August 1749

My dear Wharton

I promised Dr. Keene[104] long since to give you an account of our magnificencies here[105] but the newspapers and he himself in person have got the start of my indolence, so that by this time you are well acquainted with all the events that adorned that week of wonders. Thus much I may venture to tell you, because as is probable nobody else has done it, that our friend Chappy's[106] zeal and eloquence, surpassed all powers of description. Vesuvio in an eruption was not more violent than his utterance, nor (since I am at my mountains) Pelion[107] with all its pine trees in a storm of wind more impetuous than his acting, and yet the senate-house still stands, and (I thank God) we are all safe and well at your service. I was ready to sink for him and scarce dared to look about me, when I was sure it was all over; but soon found I might have spared my confusion, for all people joined to applaud him; every thing was quite right; and I dare swear, not three people here but think him a model of oratory. For all the duke's little court came with a resolution to be pleased; and when the tone was once given, the university, who ever wait for the judgement of their betters, struck into it with an admirable harmony. For the rest of the performances they were (as usual) very ordinary. Every one, while it lasted, was very gay and very busy in the morning, and very owlish and very tipsey at night. I make no

---

[102] Gray was a Fellow of Peterhouse College, Cambridge, and a prolific poet, best known for his 'Elegy, wrote in a country church-yard'.

[103] A Cambridge contemporary of Gray's who had been a Fellow of Pembroke from 1739.

[104] A fellow academic of Gray's at the University who later became Bishop of Ely.

[105] Gray is referring to the ceremony to install the Duke of Newcastle as Chancellor of the University on 1 July for which Boyce composed the ode, and the celebrations that followed it.

[106] Dr Thomas Chapman, Master of Madgalene, and University Vice-Chancellor from 1748-9. It was he who led the campaign to appoint Newcastle as Chancellor.

[107] The references are to the volcano Vesuvius in Italy, and Mount Pelion in Greece.

exception from the Chancellor to Blewcoat. Mason's ode[108] was the only entertainment that had any tolerable elegance, and for my own part I think it (with some little abatement) uncommonly well on such an occasion. Pray let me know your sentiments, for doubtless you have seen it. The author of it grows apace in my good graces; he is very ingenious, with great good-nature and simplicity. A little vain, but in so harmless and so comical a way, that it does not offend one and all; a little ambitious, but withal so ignorant in the world and its ways, that this does not hurt him in one's opinion. So sincere and undisguised, that no mind with a spark of generosity would ever think of hurting him, he is so open to injury, but so indolent that if he cannot over come this habit, all his good qualities will signify nothing at all. After all I like him so well, I could wish you knew him. [&c.]

(Rhys(1912), 161-2) Apart from its assessment of the Mason/Boyce ode, this letter also offers a keen insight into the personality of the author of the ode's text.

♣

Songs by Boyce are published in the *Universal Magazine of Knowledge and Pleasure* (1749-52).

The first to appear was 'Tho' Chloe's out of fashion' (text; anon.) in Dec. 1749, 279-80, followed by 'In vain Philander' (J. Hawkins) in July 1751, 30-31, and 'If you my wand'ring heart' (anon.) in Sept. 1752, 126-7.

♣

From the *General Advertiser*, 2 December 1749

DRURY-LANE. By Desire *By His Majesty's Company of Comedians,* AT the Theatre-Royal in Drury-Lane, This Day, will be presented a Comedy, call'd The ALCHEMIST Written by BEN JOHNSON.[109] . . . To which will be added a New Musical Entertainment, in Two Interludes, call'd The CHAPLET. The Music Composed by Dr. BOYCE. The Principal Parts to

---

[108] 'Here all thy active fires diffuse', composed and directed by Boyce for the Installation ceremony.
[109] Play first performed in 1610.

be performed by Mr. BEARD, Master MATTOCKS, Miss NORRIS and Mrs. CLIVE. [&c.]

The origin of *The Chaplet* lies in the desire of David Garrick, after his appointment as manager at DL in 1747, to set about increasing the theatre's stock of attractive afterpieces. Garrick turned in this instance to Moses Mendez, a sociable, witty and wealthy stockbroker, who had in 1746 written a well-received comedy in two acts with six interpolated songs, *The Double Disappointment*, before approaching Boyce for the music. The resulting work was an immediate success. During its premiere the prompter for the theatre, Richard Cross, recorded in his diary: "Some gentlemen crowding behind ye scenes, ye audience resented it & ye farce was stop'd for half an hour — I drew lines with chalk but Miss Norris applying publicly to Capt. Johnson, desiring he would retire, he did, and ye farce went on with great applause".[110]

The great appeal of *The Chaplet* for contemporary audiences lay firstly in the deftly managed comedy of the pastoral plot with its attendant amorous intrigues, and secondly in the popular ballad style, as exploited in the *Beggar's Opera* (1728) and its many successors, which Boyce adopted in his settings of the airs. The central role is taken by the cynical shepherd Damon (Beard) who, though bent on avoiding marriage, pursues both the innocent shepherdess 'Laura' (Miss Norris), and the worldly-wise 'Pastora' (Mrs Clive), the latter having been rejected by her youthful lover 'Palaemon' (Mattocks). A happy outcome is arrived at when Damon finally offers his hand to Laura. All the solo songs, duets and trios, are linked by recitatives and set strophicly apart from one aria, 'How unhappy's the nymph', which is placed towards the end. Boyce contrives here to include a poignant, sophisticated minor key and through-composed lament for Laura, with an obbligato flute part, which plays its role in persuading Damon finally to accept, apparently with joy, the inevitability of marriage.

The libretto for the first production was "printed and sold by M. Cooper". John Walsh advertised a publication of the full score (*GA*, 4 Jan. 1750) with title-page 'THE | CHAPLET, a | Musical Entertainment | As it is performed at the Theatre Royal in Drury-Lane. | Compos'd by | Dr. Boyce'. [&c.] Walsh issued a 2nd edn (*c*1755) using the same plates while inserting a copy of Boyce's Royal Licence to print music. A copyist's MS

---

[110] Quoted in LS 4, 158. This incident is partly explained by the fact that at this time privileged members of theatre audiences were allowed to sit on the stage during performances. Cross evidently intervened to set limits as to their movements. A few days later Cross noted a payment of £40 "paid Dr. Boyce for the music for the Chaplet". This would have been worth *c*£6,000 today.

score, closely related to the published version is preserved at *Lbl*, RM.22.b.8. Since this source refers to the four leading singers identified above, it must be contemporary with the first production.

The Chaplet subsequently became one of the most popular and widely performed English afterpieces of the century. It received 31 performances in its first season, and 86 more in the 1750s. It reached Dublin early the following year[111] when it was given four performances and revived from time to time at least until 1759. It was produced in America at Philadelphia in 1767 and in New York in 1768,[112] and continued to be performed in London and the provinces until at least 1785. Selections from it were published in arrangements for 'German Flute or Violin' (*c*1770), and for 'Violin' (*c*1787). The piece was revived at the Arts Theatre Club in London in 1936, and has since been staged elsewhere in Britain and America. WB published the overture in *Eight Symphonys*, no. 3 (1760).

---

[111] See *DJ*, 10-13 Feb. 1750.
[112] See Loewenberg(1943), col. 212.

PART THREE

LIFE AND CAREER, 1750-1759

The Roman Father with music by Boyce is produced at Drury Lane Theatre on 24 February 1750.

A notice for the first performance announced: "DRURY-LANE. Never acted before. By His Majesty's Company of Comedians, AT the Theatre-Royal in Drury Lane, This Day will be presented a new Tragedy, called The ROMAN FATHER. The Principal Parts to be perform'd by Mr. GARRICK Mr. BARRY". [&c.] Richard Cross, the prompter at the theatre, recorded that William Whitehead's play "was received with extravagant applause" (LS, 4, 178). Nearly four decades later, in a memoir on the playwright, William Mason observed "This piece (which continues still to be what actors call a stock play) has been so frequently exhibited with applause, and has shewn so many actors and actresses to advantage, that it is almost unnecessary to say any thing more concerning it" (Mason(1788), 55). At DL it received 12 performances in its first season, and a further 11 up to 1765. It was later revived in 1776 and again in 1794. At Covent Garden it was first taken up in 1767 and went on to receive 30 performances between then and 1788. Boyce's music, commissioned by Garrick, was required at the beginning of Act IV, sc. ii. Although the music has not survived, it was clearly an integral part of the play and consisted of a chorus, 'Thus for freedom nobly won', with three solo verses for two youths and a virgin. The first published text of the *Roman Father* (London, 1750) establishes WB's authorship: "The Music composed by Dr. Boyce. The vocal parts by Mr. Beard Miss Norris Miss Cole". It seems almost certain that his music remained in use throughout the life of the play, at least at DL, if not also at CG. An advertisement for a revival at DL in November 1776 draws attention to "the grand triumphal entry of Publius [played by Barry] with the original music composed by Dr. Boyce" (PA, 18 Nov. 1776). Another notice, on 15 Nov. 1794, refers to "The Chorus of Youths and Virgins, composed by Boyce" (LS, 5, 1703). Whitehead was appointed Poet Laureate in 1758 on the death of Colley Cibber. Thus he provided WB, by then Master of the King's Music, with the texts for his settings of the court odes as from the Birthday Ode of that year. Whitehead included the full text of the *Roman Father* in his *Poems on Several Occasions* (1754).

♣

From the *General Advertiser,* 15 March 1750

DRURY LANE. *For the Benefit of Mrs.* CLIVE *By His Majesty's Company of Comedians, . . .* HAMLET To which will be added a Farce, never acted before call'd The REHEARSAL, *Or,* BAYES in PETTICOATS; The Musick composed by Dr. BOYCE. The Principal Parts to be performed by Mrs. Clive, Mr. Wood-Ward, Mr. Beard, Mr. Simpson, Mr. Cross, Mrs. Bennet, Miss Cole and Miss Norris. [&c.]

These performances were not only for 'Kitty' Clive's benefit, but they also introduced an afterpiece, 'The Rehearsal', written by her. She was best known as a brilliant comic actress and singer with a penchant for ballad opera.[1] Her light-hearted satirical play was based on an earlier piece of the same name by George Villiers (1671).[2] Act I involves discussions between a lady playwright, 'Mrs Hazard', and the male lead, 'Bayes', about a work which is to be rehearsed in Act II. A self-sufficient 'Pastoral Interlude' for which Boyce wrote the music is entitled 'Corydon and Miranda'. It involves a conventional amorous triangle in which Miranda (Miss Norris), who is in love with Corydon (Beard), is jealous of her rival, Marcella (Mrs Clive), who also covets Corydon. Marcello's suffering finally equals that of Miranda. When finally Corydon decides to abandon Marcello, her anguish proves to be as harrowing as Miranda's. Boyce's eloquent and sometimes impassioned music involves a series of orchestrally accompanied recitatives, arias, and a duet for the protagonists, with a concluding chorus.

After the premiere the prompter, Cross, noted in his diary: "A new farce partly singing, part speakg^g. Went off well".[3] Garrick staged the work three more times in 1750 but only revived it spasmodically on 14 occasions up to 1762. In the published text of Clive's play (Dublin, 1753), it is described as 'A Comedy in Two Acts', and the words of the songs (pp.

---

[1] She had played 'Polly' in the prototype of all ballad operas, *The Beggar's Opera*, in 1728.

[2] The original play remained in the repertoire of the London stage throughout the 18th century. Garrick himself often played 'Bayes' in this play.

[3] LS 4 (1), 182.

24-8) are attributed to 'a Gentleman'. The text here, however, differs in various respects from that set by Boyce in his autogr. score.[4] Boyce's setting of the interlude is available on CD (see Discography).

♣

Boyce sets a birthday ode, 'Strike, strike the lyre', for Prince George, performed on 24 May 1750.

(Facs. edn in Bruce(1989)) George William Frederick (1738-1820), Prince George's father, was the eldest son of Frederick Louis, Prince of Wales during the earlier part of the reign of King George II. Young George himself became Prince of Wales on the premature death of Frederick in March 1751, and subsequently acceded to the throne on the death of George II in October 1760. The text of the ode is by William Havard and is preserved in his hand *(US: Ws,* N.a.2, 159-60). It is headed: "Ode perform'd at Cliefden on the Birth-day of His present Majesty — then Prince of Wales". Havard's note, which clearly must have been written after George came to the throne in 1760, provides the only surviving evidence for the performance of this ode. Cliveden House, near Maidenhead, was Frederick's country-seat, where in August 1740 Thomas Arne's masque *Alfred* had been first performed. The evidence for dating the ode in 1750 (or perhaps 1749) is discussed in Bruce, op. cit., x. Boyce's ode was concluded, 'by desire', with a duet, 'Let Fred'rick and Augusta live',[5] based on a then still popular duet, 'Let Caesar and Urania live', from a welcome ode composed by Henry Purcell for James II in 1687. WB made some minor amendments to Purcell's score, while Havard appropriately updated the original text. The two singers who performed the ode are identified in WB's autogr. score (*Ob*, MS.Mus.Sch.D.264) as the soprano Mrs. Storer, and the tenor, John Beard.

♣

---

[4] At *Ob*, MS.Mus.c.3, ff. 44-69.
[5] Frederick's wife.

Boyce subscribes to William Bates's *Six Sonata's for two Violins with a Thorough Bass for the Harpsichord or Violoncello* [*c*1750].

Though not a composer of the first rank, Bates nevertheless wrote widely for the London theatres and pleasure gardens, besides publishing a set of concertos. There were 174 subscribers for 198 copies of these sonatas.

♣

Boyce subscribes to Elizabeth Turner's *Twelve Songs with Symphonies and a Thorough Bass for the Harpsicord* [1750].

Though by no means a leading figure in English musical life, Elizabeth clearly enjoyed a considerable reputation, for this publication attracted no fewer than 463 purchasers for 521 copies. She also composed two other substantial works and a number of separate solo songs. Prominent among the other subscribers were Beard, Stanley, Burney, Hawkins, John Rich and the Duke of Newcastle.

♣

From the *General Advertiser*, 11 August 1750

At the LONG-ROOM at Hampstead This Day will be perform'd the Annual CONCERT of Vocal and Instrumental MUSICK. The vocal parts by Mr BEARD Particularly a new Cantata set by Dr. Boyce, and sung with great Applause at Ranelagh. 1st Violin – Mr. Festing. A solo on the Violoncello by Signor Pasqualino, A Concerto on the Harpsichord by Mr Butler; A Concerto on the Trumpet by Mr Abingdon[6] And a Sonata by Mr. Festing, Mr. Froud,[7] and Signor Pasqualino. [&c.]

The particular cantata by Boyce performed here is not known, but it may well have been 'Blest in Maria's friendship'. This was the most recently published of Boyce's cantatas at the time, having appeared in *Lyra Britannica,* IV (Sept. 1748). Moreover, it was specifically set for a solo

---

[6] Probably James Abington.
[7] Charles Froud had been a competitor with Boyce for the post of organist at St. Michael's Cornhill in 1734.

tenor voice such as Beard's. This programme as a whole illustrates well the miscellaneous character of many public concerts at this period.

♣

From the *General Advertiser*, 1 October 1750

The Third Day. DRURY-LANE *By His Majesty's Company of Comedians.* AT the Theatre-Royal in Drury-Lane, This Day, will be revived a Play, call'd ROMEO and JULIET The Part of Romeo to be performed by Mr. GARRICK . . . And the Part of Juliet to be performed by Miss BELLAMY. With the additional Scene, representing The FUNERAL PROCESSION to the MONUMENT of the CAPULETS. The Vocal Parts by Mr. Beard, Mr. Reinhold, Mr. Wilder, Master Mattocks, Mrs Clive, Miss Norris, Mrs Mathews, &c. The Musick compos'd by Doctor BOYCE. Boxes 5s. Pit 3s. First Gallery 2s. Upper Gallery 1s. [&c.][8]

In providing music for the 'additional scene' in this production of *Romeo and Juliet*, Boyce found himself involved in one of the most notorious and well documented theatrical affairs of the century. The long-standing rivalry between the two patent theatres in London had come to a head in 1750 when Rich at Covent Garden, and Garrick at Drury Lane, opened their respective seasons not only on the same day, but also with the same play. On this occasion, Rich stole a march on Garrick by announcing *"An additional Scene*, will be introduced representing the *Funeral Procession* of Juliet, which will be accompanied by a Solemn Dirge, never performed before. The Music by Mr Arne".[9] This new scene was interpolated at the beginning of Act V. Arne set the new text, 'Ah! Hapless maid', conventionally enough for a three-part chorus with an interlude for a trio of soloists. However, the initial chorus is preceded by a short but effective introduction, scored for two 'muffled' trumpets and drum, and accompanied by a tolling bell.

Such was the response of the public to this theatrically effective dirge that Garrick felt compelled not only to retaliate immediately, but also to do so in kind. Within three days he had not only written a dirge of his own, but conveyed it to Boyce, who set it in time for it to be advertised, rehearsed and performed on 1 October. A contemporary commentator acclaimed Garrick's treatment of Shakespeare's play as a whole for having

---

[8] These ticket prices were equivalent to *c*£40, £25, £16 and £8 respectively in modern currency.
[9] See *GA*, 28 Oct. 1750.

made "the catastrophe, as it now stands, . . . the most affecting in the whole compass of drama".[10] The battle between the two companies raged for 12 nights before Rich capitulated by taking the play off, thereby allowing his rival to claim victory. The reason for his doing so, he said, was the indisposition of Mrs Cibber (his Juliet). As for Garrick, he contented himself for the moment with one further performance.

Garrick published his text in *Romeo and Juliet. A Tragedy. Written by Shakespeare.* [n.d.] The stage directions for Act V, sc. i are "*The inside of a Church. Enter the* Funeral Procession of Juliet, *in which the following Dirge is sung. Rise, rise! Heart-breaking sighs*" (p.61). It is evident from WB's setting of the dirge that even if he hadn't heard Arne's piece himself, he had been informed of its initial scoring. Boyce, however, began it starkly with the measured tolling of the bell alone, and he held back the entry of the trumpet until the second chorus. Garrick's text is more extended than Rich's, but WB's music gives no sign of its hurried composition. There are four choral refrains, separated by three poignant interludes, the first for Mrs Clive and Miss Norris supported by two boy sopranos, then an extended solo for Beard, and finally a trio for the two female soloists and Reinhold. The debate in the press that ensued focused entirely on the relative merits of the two productions as a whole, and the acting of Garrick as compared with Barry as Romeo, and of Mrs Cibber versus Miss Bellamy as Juliet. At no time did public discussion concern itself with the relative musical merits of the two dirges. Modern music historians, however, are unanimous in giving the palm to Boyce.

Garrick's version of the play with its interpolated dirge continued to be performed in London until the end of the century and beyond. WB's autogr. score is at *Ob*, MS.Mus.c.3, ff. 9-20. The dirge has now been recorded (see Discography).

♣

Boyce subscribes to Thomas Gladwin's *Eight Lessons for the Harpsichord or Organ* [1750].

Some of the lessons in this set are provided with a violin part. Gladwin was an early pioneer in England of this new genre of the 'accompanied keyboard sonata'. He had been employed as organist at Vauxhall Gardens from 1738, and was also the composer of many popular songs. There were only 83 subscribers, but they included John Beard and John Stanley.

---

[10] Murphy(1786), 2, 152-3.

♣

Boyce subscribes to Richard Carter's *Six Solos for the Use of young Practitioners on the Violin or Harpsichord* [1750].

Carter was active as a violinist and teacher in London. These sonatas were specifically written for his pupils, consequently perhaps limiting their appeal. Nevertheless, 147 copies were ordered by 118 subscribers, among them other leading musicians such as Defesch, Festing, Pepusch and Travers.

♣

From the *General Advertiser,* 4 April 1751

Last Night was solemnised the Funeral of Captain Thomas Coram, in the Chapel of the Foundling Hospital the Particulars of which are as follows: The Communion Table and the Governors Seats at the Upper End of the Chapel were cover'd with Mourning. At 6 o'Clock the Procession began; the Porter of the Hospital walk'd first; after him the Girls belonging to the Hospital two and two; the Boys two and two; the Matron; several Gentlemen belonging to St. Paul's Choir, as also Mr. Beard and four Choiristers two and two, all in Surplices; then a Person carrying a Velvet Cushion, with the Royal Charter of the Hospital laid thereon; the Corpse, the Pall of which was supported by Peter Burrell, Esq and two other Vice Presidents, . . . and another Governor; Taylor White, Esq the Treasurer, walk'd as Chief Mourner: He was followed by some of the Deceased's Relations, and a great Number of the Governors. As soon as the Corpse enter'd the Chapel, the Gentlemen began to sing the Burial Service which was composed by Dr. Boyce who played the same on a small Organ set on one side of the Chapel, and when the Minister had read all the Service, but the last Collect, the following Anthem, composed by Dr. Boyce, was sung by Mr. Mence and Mr. Savage, the Chorus Parts by the other Gentlemen.[11] *If we believe that* Jesus *died, and rose again.*[12] . . . The Clergyman then read the last Collect, after which the Corpse was carried down into the Vault, and laid under the Communion Table. The Inscription on the Coffin was, *Capt. Thomas Coram died 28 March* 1751, *Aged 85 Years.* The

---

[11] Boyce set the burial service specifically for this occasion, but the anthem had been composed in the mid-1740s.

[12] The full text of the anthem is reproduced at this point.

Galleries were fill'd with Gentlemen and Ladies all dress'd in Mourning and the great Decency and Order with which the whole was conducted, made a very awful Sight.

(Wagner(2004), 189-90) Thomas Coram was founding father of the institution in Holborn for whom Handel wrote his 'Foundling Hospital Anthem' in 1749. Handel also presented a small organ to the Chapel in 1750 and mounted annual performances of *Messiah* there in aid of the hospital until the end of his life, though J.C. Smith, then organist at the Hospital, deputised for him in 1755 and 1756. Coram's plans to establish a charitable institution in London for destitute or abandoned children were conceived on the basis of already established continental models of which he was well aware. Though his ideas provoked public resistance initially, he eventually succeeded in bringing his vision to fruition. The hospital was granted a Royal Charter in 1739 and first opened its doors in 1741 with William Hogarth and Sir Robert Walpole prominent among its extensive body of governors. The Chapel was not officially opened until 16 April 1753, though as early as October 1752 the Governors had agreed that Handel, Boyce and John Christopher Smith should be asked to assist with the music for the ceremony (Nichols & Wray(1935), 207).

The work of the hospital continues to this day at the Coram Family Centre in London, alongside the recently established Foundling Museum, where memorabilia and works of art associated with the hospital are now exhibited. The documentary records of the hospital are now preserved at *Lma*. Coram's achievements inspired Jamila Gavin's novel, *Coram Boy* (2000), and a dramatisation of the book by Helen Edmundson with music (indebted to Handel) by Adrian Sutton, was produced at the National Theatre in 2005.

♣

Boyce subscribes to John Marchant's *Puerilia: or, Amusements for the Young*, (1751).

This book only contains the texts of songs the author thought suitable for the use of young singers, along with a list of tunes that could be used with them. These are identified by the first line of the poems associated with them. Marchant almost certainly refers here to two of Boyce's well-known songs: 'How blest has my time been' (probably the tune to *BC* 221) and 'When Fanny blooming fair'. In view of the purposes of the book, it may seem surprising that the latter, a tune associated with an overtly erotic text, should have been recommended. Doubtless its popularity and its melodic appeal were the overriding factors.

♣

From the *General Evening Post,* 16-19 November 1751

At DRURY LANE THEATRE, This Evening is presented The *Revenge*[13] . . . To which is added, a New Musical Entertainment, called *The Shepherd's Lottery* (The Musick composed by Dr. Boyce). The principal Parts performed by Mr. Beard, Master Vernon, Mr. Wilder, Miss Norris, and Mrs Clive.

There can be no doubt about the motivation lying behind the creation of this second comic afterpiece by Boyce. In the light of the public enthusiasm generated by *The Chaplet* in 1749, it is clear that the Garrick/ Mendez/Boyce triumvirate were now bent on a repeat of that triumph. The original formula was indeed replicated here, but the outcome proved to be somewhat different. As a contemporary commentator noted: "This little Piece is in the same Stile of Writing with *The Chaplet*, another Piece of the same Author, but I do not think it quite equal to it. There are, however, several pretty Songs in it, and its musical Composition is very pleasing. It met with good success at first, but has not been often repeated, since the Season it made its Appearance in".[14] Notwithstanding the many qualities that the new piece shared with its predecessor, two factors in particular may have weighed against it. Firstly, the rather artificial and less engaging nature of its plot; and secondly, the simple fact that it was fighting on the same territory as its by now well established rival.

The libretto of *The Shepherd's Lottery* is based on an Arcadian convention that on May Day each year the shepherds should find their wives by the drawing of lots. Phillis (Miss Norris), and her young lover Thyrsis (Vernon), are fearful that they may lose each other after the lottery draw has taken place. Meanwhile, the more mature and worldly Daphne (Mrs Clive), who is indifferent as to the outcome of the lottery, arranges to meet Dorylas (Wilder) but purposefully lets him down. The disdainful Colin (Beard), a similar character to Damon in the earlier afterpiece, favouring love without marriage, disappoints Daphne by refusing to take part in the lottery. Finally, after she has prayed to Venus, Phillis is granted her heart's desire. As he did in *The Chaplet*, Boyce introduces here a single

[13] Tragedy by Edward Young (1721).
[14] Baker(1768), col. C H.

through-composed air, 'Goddess of the dimpling smile', with oboe obbligato, for Phillis's passionate appeal.

The word-book for this work was published by M. Cooper. Walsh advertised the publication of the full score with title-page: THE | SHEPHERD'S LOTTERY. | A | MUSICAL ENTERTAINMENT. | *As it is perform'd at the Theatre Royal* | in Drury Lane. | Compos'd by Dr. BOYCE (*GA*, 1 Jan. 1752). In contrast to *The Chaplet*, only one of the solo songs, Colin's 'To dear Amaryllis' in Act I, was published separately[15] but the music of twelve of the items appeared in *Apollo's Banquet*, vol. 1, [1754], being 'A Collection of Favourite Song Tunes . . . for the Improvement of Young Practitioners on the German Flute, Violin or Harpsichord'. An arrangement of the whole work for flute was also issued in 1787. In its first season *The Shepherd's Lottery* received 20 performances, but only two in 1753, and finally five in 1754. It was also given at the Three Choirs Festival in Sept. 1753. Boyce included the notably spirited and colourful overture in *Eight Symphonys*, no. 4, (1760).

♣

John Walsh publishes an Ode and an Anthem by Boyce [1752].

Title-page: An | *ODE* | Perform'd in the SENATE HOUSE at | *CAMBRIDGE,* | on the First of July, 1749, | *At the Installation of his Grace* | *The DUKE of NEWCASTLE,* | Chancellor of the University. | The Words by William Mason M.A. | *To which is added an* | *ANTHEM* | Perform'd y[e] following Day, at S[t]. Mary's Church, | being Commencement Sunday. | *The Musick by* | *D[r]. William Boyce.*

The following Dedication appears after the title-page: "To the most Noble THOMAS HOLLES *DUKE of NEWCASTLE,* Marquis and Earl of Clare, *Viscount Haughton, Baron Pelham of Laughton,* Knight of the most Noble Order of the Garter *Principal SECRETARY of STATE* and | Chancellor of the University of Cambridge. *The following ODE* and *ANTHEM* are with all due Humility, Inscribed by *His Grace's most Obliged most dutifull Servant William Boyce".*

This ode, 'Here thy active fires diffuse', was the only work of Boyce's in this genre published in his lifetime; similarly none of his anthems, apart from this one, were printed before his death. Both works were specifically

---

[15] In the *London Magazine,* March 1752, and again in the *Lady's Magazine,* June 1798.

written for Cambridge in 1749; the ode for the installation ceremony for the appointment of the Duke of Newcastle as Chancellor, and the anthem, 'O be joyful' (*BC* 56), being the exercise Boyce submitted for his doctorate at the University on that occasion. The autogr. score of the ode is at *Cu*, Nn.6.38., but WB's MS of the anthem has not survived.

♣

From the *General Advertiser,* 12 March 1752

For the Benefit of Mr. ARTHUR[16] *By the Company of Comedians,* AT the Theatre-Royal in Covent-Garden, This Day, will be presented a Comedy, call'd The CONSCIOUS LOVERS.[17] The Part of Young Bevil to be performed by Mr. BARRY; And the Part of Indiana to be performed by Mrs. CIBBER. With a new Song proper to the Play, set to Musick by Dr. Boyce, and sung by Mr. Lowe.[&c.]

Most of Boyce's theatre music was written for Garrick at Drury Lane. The song he provided for this production, however, was only the second, and indeed the last, that he wrote for Rich at Covent Garden. The history of the song is by no means straightforward.[18] Until relatively recently it was regarded as his swan-song to the theatre in *c*1759.[19] As he first conceived the play, Steele wrote a poem, 'From place to place forlorn I go', to be sung in Act II, sc. i, when 'Bevil' attends on 'Indiana' with whom he is in love. But in the first production an instrumental sonata was substituted for it since no suitable singer was apparently available. As Steele confesses in his Preface to the play: "I would willingly revive here a Song which was omitted for want of a Performer and design'd for the Entertainment of Indiana. . . . The Song is the Distress of a Love-sick Maid"[20] Steele's original song was in fact soon reinstated in performances of the play, for it was set at the time by Galliard, and also later by others. By 1752, Rich evidently wished to replace it with a new song, 'Does the languid soul complain' (anon.), and invited Boyce to set it. WB included the song in LB VI (1759). As for Steele's play, it stayed in the repertoire of both patent

---

[16] John Arthur was an actor, and later theatre manager, who performed regularly at CG from 1748-58.

[17] This highly successful play by Sir Richard Steele was first performed at Drury Lane in 1722.

[18] See Taylor *b*(1953), 280, McIntosh *b*(1979), 276-9, and NG1, 3, 142.

[19] For a detailed discussion of 'The song in *The Conscious Lovers*', see Bartlett, review of *The Shepherd's Lottery* (Bruce *b*(1990)), in *ML* 73 (1992), 158-61.

[20] Steele(1723), 5.

theatres until the end of the century, but how long WB's setting remained part of it is uncertain.

♣

From the *General Advertiser*, 25 May 1752

At Ranelagh-House this Day, will be performed a Rural Assembly, for celebrating His Royal Highness the Prince of Wales's Birth-Day.[21] The doors to be open'd at Five o'clock. Tea and Coffee at Six; the Concert begins at Seven; the Ode to be performed at Eight; Fireworks play'd off at Nine; as soon as over, the Wine and Sweetmeat Side boards will be open'd; the Ball Musick begins at Ten; the Sideboards to be shut up at Twelve o'Clock.

The ode advertised above, 'Another passing year is flown' (facs. edn, Bruce *b*(1989), autogr. score at *Ob*, MS.Mus.Sch.C.105), was composed by Boyce for Prince George's 14th birthday on Sunday 24 May. It was the last of three such works he composed in honour of the Prince. The text was published two days later with caption: "The following is the Ode performed at Ranelagh on Monday Evening last, on account of the Birth-Day of his Royal Highness, the Prince of Wales. The words by Mr. Havard, the Musick by Dr. Boyce" (*GA,* 27 May). Havard was a leading actor and author, and the distinguished vocal soloists were Mrs. Storer and John Beard. Unusually for such works, six further public performances of the ode were given at Ranelagh the following month. A typical notice for a concert at Ranelagh appeared three weeks or so later: "AT RANELAGH-HOUSE, This Day, will be A CONCERT of MUSICK. The Doors to be open'd at Five, the Musick to begin before Seven, Each Person paying two Shillings.[22] Tea and Coffee included. To be continued every Evening (Sundays excepted) till further Notice". However, on this occasion, and for the following five days, an additional sentence appeared: "This Evening will be performed the ODE, which was composed by Dr. Boyce, for his Royal Highness the Prince of Wales's Birth-day". (*GA,* 15, 16, 17, 18, 19 and 20 June).

♣

---

[21] The Prince who was to succeed to the throne as George III in 1760.
[22] About £15 in modern currency.

Boyce subscribes to Christopher Smart's *Poems on several occasions* (1752).

Boyce ordered two copies of this publication, one that attracted a large number of subscribers. WB had set an early poem by Smart in 1744 (see *BC* 219), the text of which is included in this book (pp.19-20). The text for WB's cantata, 'Long with undistinguish'd flame', published in *Lyra Britannica* (1747), also appears here (25-6). Subsequently, WB set three more poems by Smart in the mid-1750s (see *BC* 232, 252, and 265), the first of which was also taken from this collection (200-01). If WB held Smart in high regard, the feeling was reciprocated, for Smart acknowledged Boyce's stature in two of his later literary works, *The Hilliard*, vol. 1, (1753), and the *Universal Visiter* (Jan. 1756).

♣

From Berrow's *Worcester Journal,* 14 September 1752

THE MEETING OF THE THREE CHOIRS of Worcester, Gloucester, *and* Hereford, Will be held at *WORCESTER, On* Wednesday *and* Thursday *next,* the 20th and 21st of this Instant. On Wednesday will be perform'd at the Cathedral in the Morning, Purcel's TE DEUM and JUBILATE,[23] an ANTHEM by Dr. *Boyce*,[24] and Mr. *Handel's* celebrated CORONATION ANTHEM[25] and at the Town-Hall, in the Evening, A CONCERT of *Vocal* and *Instrumental* MUSICK. On *Thursday* will be perform'd, at the Cathedral, in the Morning, Mr. *Handel's* TE DEUM and JUBILATE,[26] a

---

[23] His setting in D written for St. Cecilia's Day in 1694. Purcell's work was regularly chosen to open the Three Choirs Festival programme each year until *c*1771. Its appearance in an edition by Boyce was first clearly identified in 1755 and the Boyce arrangement continued to be used fairly regularly up to 1784. From 1772 onwards, however, it was sometimes replaced by another *Te Deum and Jubilate* adapted to music "taken from the most eminent Italian composers". This arrangement was made by James Harris, but his name was not mentioned in association with the work until the Worcester Festival programme of 1800. In the same year it was published by Joseph Corfe in his miscellaneous collection, *Sacred Music.*

[24] 'Blessed is he' (*BC* 11), as performed at the Worcester meeting in 1743.

[25] *Zadok the Priest* was frequently referred to in this way.

[26] Almost certainly the 'Dettingen' Te Deum of 1743 with the 'Utrecht' Jubilate of 1713.

NEW ANTHEM by Dr. *Boyce*, and the same CORONATION ANTHEM; and at the Town-Hall, in the Evening, The *Oratorio* of SAMSON.

(Deutsch(1955), 726). Surviving evidence of what was performed at these Meetings from their origin *c*1715 is very scanty until 1751, when music by Purcell and Handel, and "an Anthem by Dr. Boyce" were advertised (*GEP*, 31 Aug.). The programme for 1752 is characteristic of the Festival throughout the second half of the 18th century. While Handel increasingly came to dominate the repertoire, Boyce's music continued to feature regularly until the end of the century. With few exceptions, at least one anthem by WB was advertised each year. As illustrated here, however, the works to be performed are often not clearly identified. On this occasion the 'new anthem' must have been the recently published and orchestrally accompanied, 'O be joyful' (*BC* 56), written for WB's doctorate at Cambridge in 1749. It was reported that festival attendance this year was "near a thousand each night" (*LEP*, 26 Sept.).

♣

A letter from David Garrick to William Mason (1752)

London
Oct^br 14th
Sir.
Dr Boyce shew'd me your most obliging letter, & since that I have had ye pleasure of seeing Mr Gray & of read^g y^e *faithful Shepherdess*. Tho I am much pleased with ye poetry, yet I am afraid it is not dramatical enough, to have a good effect upon the stage; when I have ye pleasure of seeing you in town I will give you the best reasons for my opinion that I can — You have desir'd, that I would freely give you my thoughts upon the affair, & I hope you will excuse me for so doing: I cannot say how much I am indebted to you for that part of Dr Boyce's letter which relates to me; I beg that I may see you when you come to London that I may thank you in person.

I am S^r Y^r most obedient humble servant
D: Garrick.

(Little & Kahrl(1963), 1, 189-90) The letter that Boyce passed on to Garrick was presumably written by Mason on behalf of Gray. It appears not to have survived. WB must have been in regular touch with Garrick at this time in connection with the theatre music he was composing for Drury Lane. Mason, a Fellow of Pembroke College, Cambridge, wrote the ode that Boyce set for the installation of the Duke of Newcastle as Chancellor of the University in July 1749. Thomas Gray, the distinguished poet, was a Fellow of Peterhouse, and a close friend of Mason's. His *Faithful Shepherdess*, an adaptation of John Fletcher's dramatic pastoral of *c*1610, was evidently rejected by Garrick, and indeed seems never to have been acted or published (Little & Kahrl, op. cit., 190).

♣

From the Parish Register of Christenings, Marriages and Deaths at All-Hallows the Great, Thames Street (1752)

Lgh, MS5161, f. 164. The burial of Boyce's father, John, is recorded on 19 November. Boyce's brother, also John, succeeded his father as Beadle at Joiners' Hall until he died prematurely in July 1755. Subsequent events would suggest that with the death of his father, WB now began to think about leaving the premises occupied by his family at Joiners' Hall.

♣

Boyce moves from his father's apartments at Joiners' Hall to Quality Court, Chancery Lane, London.

In reporting on his researches into Boyce's early biography, Donovan Dawe observed: "The date of William Boyce's departure from Joiners' Hall has not been established" (Dawe *b*(1968), 806). He goes on to refer to the Rate Books for Holborn (where the part of Chancery Lane occupied by Quality Court was situated) which he claimed did not show Boyce's name until 1755. However, local rates at this time were collected in two different categories, a 'scavenger rate',[27] and a 'poor rate'. Boyce's name does indeed appear for the first time in the scavenger rate book for 1755 (the books for 1753 and 1754 are not extant), but Dawe overlooked the poor rate books for 1753 and 1754 which do survive, and in both of which Boyce's name is recorded (*Lhla,* P/AH/RA/17). The rate for the year 1753 is set out in a preliminary statement referring to a council meeting held on 28 June. It seems clear therefore that WB moved to Chancery Lane early in 1753, i.e. not long after the death of his father in November 1752. Quality Court still exists towards the top of Chancery Lane, WC2, but no 18th-century houses have survived there.

---

[27] This rate covered the cost of employing men to clear rubbish from the streets.

♣

From Christopher Smart's *The Hilliard*, Book 1, (1753)

While in the vale perennial fountains flow,
And fragrant Zephyrs musically blow;
While the majestic sea from pole to pole,
In horrible magnificence shall roll,
While yonder glorious canopy on high,
Shall overhang the curtains of the sky,
While the gay seasons their due course shall run,
Ruled by the brilliant stars and golden sun,
While wit and fool antagonists shall be,
And sense and taste and nature shall agree,
While love shall live, and rapture shall rejoice,
Fed by the notes of Handel, Arne, and Boyce,
While with joint force o'er humour's droll domain,
Cervantes,[28] Fielding,[29] Lucian,[30] Swift[31] shall reign,
While thinking figures from the canvass start,
And Hogarth[32] is the Garrick[33] of his art
So long in flat stupidity's extreme,
Shall H'll[34] th' ARCH-DUNCE remain o'er every dunce supreme.

NOTES VARIORUM

Handel, Arne, and Boyce. The first of these gentlemen may be justly looked upon as the Milton of musick, and the talents of the two latter may not improperly be delineated by calling them the Drydens of their profession, as they not only touch the strings of love with exquisite art, but also, when they please, reach the truly sublime.

Smart(1753), 1, 43-4. (Williamson(1987), 4, 258-9.) Christopher Smart, author and poet, Fellow of Pembroke College, Cambridge, 1745-53, took a keen interest in music. He enjoyed life-long friendships with Charles

---

[28] The great 16th-century Spanish writer, author of *Don Quixote.*

[29] The contemporary English writer, author of the picaresque novel, *Tom Jones.*

[30] The classical rhetorician and humorist.

[31] Jonathan Swift, the recently deceased English satirist, and author of *Gulliver's Travels.*

[32] The great contemporary painter.

[33] The leading theatre director and actor of the age.

[34] The reference is to Sir John Hill – see commentary below.

Burney, the great historian of music, and William Mason, the Cambridge academic who provided Boyce with the text for his Cambridge Ode (July, 1749). The extract quoted above constitutes lines 241-59 from Smart's satirical epic poem, *The Hilliard*, which played its part in a literary war being waged at the time against the contemporary author, John Hill. It is clear that in Smart's estimation, Boyce and Arne had by now established themselves as the leading English composers of their generation. The admiration for Boyce explicit here is in keeping with a later encomium published anonymously in the *Universal Visiter* in 1756 that may with some confidence be attributed to Smart. Prior to the publication of these documents, Smart had been indebted to Boyce for setting an early poem of his, 'Goddess of Ease', as a song in 1744, and 'Long with undistinguish'd flame' as a cantata by 1747. Later, in the mid-1750s, WB composed three more airs to texts by Smart: 'To Florio', To Harriote', and 'When young and artless'.

♣

From the *Public Advertiser*, 7 February 1753

DRURY-LANE Never acted before. By His Majesty's Company of Comedians. AT the Theatre-Royal in Drury-Lane, This Day, will be presented a new Tragedy, call'd The GAMESTER. [&c.]

A vivid account of this first performance of Edward Moore's play[35] by an anonymous writer provides a context for the reception of the song Boyce provided for it: "Wednesday being the first day of the new Tragedy called *The Gamester,* the whole Corps of Cricticks assembled, at Half an Hour after Three o'Clock in Vinegar Yard, *vulgo dicto,*[36] Pissing Ally, when, notwithstanding the excessive Rawness of the Weather which it was apprehended would abate the Ardour of the Resolution, they made a most formidable appearance. They attacked the Door with incessant vigour, and about Four o'Clock the breach was made, which they entered in a prodigious Number, and in less than ten minutes, stormed the Pit, Sticks in Hand. This enterprise was achieved by dint of valour, there being but a very inconsiderable Part of it to be attributed to the Power of Money, as can be testified by all the Door Keepers. When the Troops had possessed

---

[35] By a cast which included not only David Garrick, but also Thomas Davies, a writer and bookseller as well, who was subsequently credited with having introduced Boswell to Johnson in his shop in 1763 (*BDA*, 4, 207).
[36] 'in common parlance'.

themselves of the Pit, they began the Operations usual upon such Occasions, such as Pelting the Footmen with Oranges, knocking out the Candles on the Stage, confounding the Musicians by calling for different tunes, &c. which they carried on in due form until the Performance began. During the Play they were tolerably silent, and upon the whole, expressed their Approbation. It was indeed observed by one Gentleman that the Sharper is made too consummate a villain which defeats the End of the Distraction proposed by this Piece. . . . As a Proof of the extreme Candour of a few in the Pit, a Song set by Dr. Boyce was denied a chance of being heard".[37]

The cool, if not hostile, response to the play initially was doubtless due to the exposure it gave to the consequences of gambling, a fashionable vice at the time. Nevertheless, the play went on to be performed 14 times before the end of the 1752-3 season at DL. It was revived in 1771 and continued to be staged from time to time until the end of the century. Boyce's song, 'When Damon languish'd at my feet', is scored for strings, oboe and continuo, and takes place in Act III where it is integral to the play itself: Mrs Beverley: "Prithee sooth me with the song thou sungst last night. It suits this change of fortune, and there's a melancholy in't that pleases me". Lucy: "I fear it hurts you madam — Your goodness too draws tears from me — But I'll dry 'em and obey you". Edward Moore's wife may have assisted him with the text of this song: "It has been said that Mr. Moore was assisted in his Gamester by his lady; but we are well assured that all the aid she gave him was in a song" (see *Parson's Select British Classics,* XXIV, (1794), 5-6). Boyce later published the song in LB, V (1756).

♣

Boyce subscribes to the *Works of the late Aaron Hill Esq.,* 4 vols. (1753-4).

The publication of this voluminous collection of letters and poems, along with an essay on acting, attracted over 1,500 subscribers. As well as the general public, the great and the good are well represented. In addition to being an immensely energetic and innovative character, Hill was well known as the librettist for Handel's *Rinaldo* (1711), the composer's first opera for the English theatre, and as the author of *Zara* (1736), a highly

---

[37] From a document in the Enthoven Theatre Collection, Victoria and Albert Museum, London, quoted in Taylor *b*(1953), 278-9.

successful adaptation for the London stage of Voltaire's tragedy, *Zaire* (1732). The only other musicians of note who subscribed were Greene and Beard.

♣

From the Dedication prefacing *A Second Collection of Favourite English Songs . . . Composed by L. C. A. Grenom Esq. Opera XIII*

To Dr Boyce

Sir,

As a musical performance naturally requires the protection of a musical Patron, I could think of no one so proper to address this Publication to, as D^r. Boyce, whose extensive Judgement in the Theory of this elegant Science, and whose pleasing originality of Taste in Composition, claim a first place in the list of musical Authors of the present Age. It is no flattery to say, that his productions have this singular merit, to be truly, and strictly his own, whereas most of our modern Composers, either from a barrenness of invention or a want of due application, endeavour to build a Fame on compiling only from the works of others. You will I hope excuse the freedom I here have taken, and consider it, as a sincere Testimonial of that Friendship, and Esteem, with which I am Sir, Your very obedient and oblig'd humble Servant.

Lew: A: Grenom

Rather than dedicating this publication to a member of the aristocracy or the Royal Family, as was common practice at the time, Grenom preferred to express genuine admiration for a fellow composer. This handsome volume published in oblong folio attracted well over four hundred subscribers, among them, naturally, Boyce himself. All of the pieces, mostly large-scale vocal solos, are orchestrally accompanied and were especially suited to performance at public concerts and the pleasure gardens. Some are taken from Grenom's oratorio, *The Prodigal Son*. It is of some significance that a contemporary musician should choose to stress WB's originality and independence. It was not until our own age that the suggestion was made that some of WB's anthems may have been no more than "adaptations of Restoration compositions" (see Fellowes(1941), 185). Setting aside the fact that not a few of the acknowledged masterpieces of

18th-century music incorporated ideas borrowed from other sources, such speculation about WB has proved to be without foundation.

♣

From an autograph letter of Charles Burney to Fulke Greville (July, 1753)

> BOYCE has the art, with holy rapture
> To lull asleep the Dean and Chapter —
> But wou'dst thou know them ev'ry one
> Go read with care friend Avison.[38]
> His flowery eloquence displays
> Their gifts from Orpheus[39] down to Hayes[40]
> In words w[ch] well the subject suit
> As breath'd thro' sweet Euterpe's[41] flute. [&c.]

US: NH, Osborn Collection, 101-7. (Ribeiro(1991), 12) Greville, a politician, was a patron of Burney. The latter would appear to have been unable to resist a witticism at Boyce's expense in this extract from an 'Epistle' in verse addressed to Greville, for it is clear from Burney's other writings that he held WB in high regard.

♣

From the *Public Advertiser,* 1 December 1753

DRURY-LANE. Never acted before. *By His Majesty's Company of Comedians.* AT the Theatre-Royal in Drury-Lane, This Day, will be presented a Tragedy, call'd BOADICIA. The principal Characters by Mr. GARRICK, . . . Mrs. CIBBER. With New Pieces of MUSIC between the Acts, adapted to the Play, And composed by Dr. BOYCE. [&c.]

Boyce's music for this play by Richard Glover, a writer and politician, is lost. Thanks to a star-studded cast, the play was initially well received and

---

[38] The reference is to Charles Avison and his *Essay on Musical Expression* (1752).

[39] In Greek mythology, the son of Calliope, the muse of epic poetry, who charmed wild beasts and natural objects through the power of his lyre.

[40] William Hayes, a leading composer, organist and singer who had become Professor of Music at Oxford in 1741.

[41] Muse of music.

given 10 consecutive performances, but it dropped out of the repertoire permanently after two more airings early in 1754.

♣

From the Minutes of the Joiners Company of the City of London, 4 December 1753

M^r. John Boyce the Beadle's Security Bond to the Comp^y. was at this Court executed by D^r. William Boyce the others security.

Lgc, MS8046/9. (Dawe(1968), 806) When Boyce's father, John, died in Nov. 1752, his son of the same name was elected from a short-list of seven to replace him as Beadle of the Joiners Company, and he was sworn in on 6 Feb. 1753 (Minutes for that date). He retained this post until his premature death in July 1755. In addition to the security provided by WB for his brother, a second security had been arranged with a William Godfrey (Minutes for 6 Nov. 1753).

♣

From a letter of James Harris to John Hawkins, 31 December 1753

. . . Old Tallis & Bird were admirable composers, to whom we may add Gibbons, Child & a few others, our own countrymen. Dr Green is, I am told, engaged in a most laudable design of giving us a correct edition of the works of these venerable artists, a design for which I much honour him, & which as the copies are faulty & much corrupted, can hardly be executed but by a skilful artist like himself.[42]

For the old Italian masters, concerning whom you enquire, I can give you no assistance myself, having little old music, except a volume of madrigals, & a piece or two of Carissime. The place, whence you are most likely to be furnished with every thing of that kind, is Christ Church Library in Oxford where all the fine musical collection of the celebrated Dean Aldrich is deposited. By proper application to the Dean & Chapter I make no doubt you may obtain liberty to have access to this collection, &

---

[42] Greene's work on this plan, based on a project first instigated by John Alcock, was cut short by his death in 1755. It was taken up and completed by Boyce in his publication, *Cathedral Music*, the first volume of which appeared in 1760.

if you thought any part worth transcribing, there are persons in Oxford well qualified for the undertaking.[43]

These old musicians seem to have been so fond of the scientific part of their art, & to have studied it so profoundly, that many of their compositions may be considered as so many musical theorems, requiring as much thought to comprehend the meaning of, as if they were mathematical ones. Thus was harmony in the beginning after a manner the sole object of musical artists. Melody at length crept in, softening the rigours of mere harmony, & rendring music in some degree an entertainment to the unlearned as well as learned. It may be said to have reached its perfection, when the perfections of harmony & melody came to be united. This age of perfection may be said to have commenced with Corelli & to have been carried on eminently by Handel & Geminiani, after these, by Martini,[44] Dr Green, Dr Boyce, Dr Hayes, Mr Stanley and a few others, such as Rameau among the French. But I fear we now live at the conclusion of this period, & that the days are hastening on, when harmony will be forgot, & melody alone cultivated. This I call the third & last & degenerate age of music, when it will hardly deserve the name of an art, being wholly bereft of all principles of science. Most of the Italian pieces of music (for compositions I cannot call them) which have been lately printed in England, fully answer this last character, & none more than the works of the celebrated Signor Giardino.[45] They may justly be called strains — inopes rerum nugæq[æ] canore.[46]

(Burrows & Dunhill(2002), 296) Besides being a keen amateur musician and concert organiser, Harris was also a prominent writer on music and the arts, and a great admirer of Handel. This letter clearly conveys his preference for the music of the 'ancients' and their successors, as opposed to that of the 'moderns'. Harris saw Handel as representing the culmination of a great musical tradition rooted in the past that was now under threat from a new generation of composers, later to be labelled 'pre-classical'. In writing to Hawkins in the terms that he did, he was probably well aware that his views would be sympathetically received.

---

[43] Hawkins's enquiry to Harris at this time indicates clearly that the former was already contemplating the writing of an unprecedented large-scale 'History of Music', an idea which finally came to fruition in 1776.

[44] Harris probably refers here to Giuseppe Sammartini, who spent much of his life in England, rather than his equally well-known younger brother, Giovanni Battista.

[45] The reference is to Felice Giardini, the Italian violinist and composer prominent in London's musical life at this time.

[46] The Latin quotation is from the *De Arte Poetica* of Horace (line 322) — "without sense, and musical trifles".

♣

A 'Pastoral Hymn' by Boyce is included in a *Set of new Psalms and Anthems* (1754).

Short title: A Set of New | Psalms and Anthems, | . . . and an | Introduction to Psalmody, | By William Knapp. | . . . The Sixth Edition | . . . To which is added | A Pastoral Hymn, by the late Joseph Addison, Esq; set to | Music by Dr. William Boyce, Composer to his Majesty's Chapel Royal.

Addison's text for the hymn, 'The Lord my pasture shall prepare', pp.208-10, was first published in the *Spectator,* 26 July 1712. The editor, Knapp, from Poole in Dorset, included many of his own settings in this volume. This hymn for two voices was reprinted in Novello's edition of Boyce's *Services and Anthems,* vol. 4 (1849), 140.

♣

Boyce composes a song to a text by Elizabeth Tollet.

The poem in question, 'Beneath my feet when Flora cast', appears in Tollet's collection, *Poems on Several Occasions* (1755), 132-3, with the caption "Set by Dr Boyce", but his music for it seems not to have survived.

♣

John Walsh publishes a further volume of vocal music by Boyce, *Lyra Britannica,* IV (1754).

(Facs. edn., Bruce *b*(1985)) This book was advertised (*WEP*, 19-21 March) and published with title-page: Numb: IV | LYRA BRITANNICA | A Collection of | ENGLISH SONGS | COMPOSED BY | DR BOYCE | *In which are inserted some Songs in LETHE.* [&c.]

David Garrick's satirical drama, *Lethe*, was first produced in 1740 and revived at Drury Lane on 2 Jan. 1749. The settings of the two songs from this play printed here, 'Come, mortals, come', and 'Ye mortals whom fancies and troubles perplex', were probably commissioned for this revival. The play continued to hold its place in the repertoire at DL for some years. The independent songs in this volume are *BC* 206 (text: A. Phillips), 235 (C. Smart), 242 (anon.), 269 (anon.) and 270 (C. Smart). The author of the words for this last song, 'When young and artless', was until recently not known (see Bruce *b*(1985), xv), but can now be identified as another setting of Smart by Boyce (see Williamson(1987), 4, 273).

♣

Henry Purcell publishes *The Muses Delight* (1754).

This "accurate collection of English and Italian songs, cantatas and duets" includes three songs by Boyce: 'Tho' Chloe's out of fashion' (text: anon.), 89; 'When Orpheus went down' (S. Lisle), 103, and 'Flora, Goddess, sweetly blooming' (J. Lockman), 124; plus a dialogue: 'Let rakes for pleasure' (anon.), 186, as well as four vocal numbers from *The Chaplet* (1749), 173, 174, 189 and 231. N.B. This Purcell was not Henry the composer.

♣

Boyce subscribes to Richard Langdon's *Ten songs and a cantata*, op.1 (1754).

Langdon had recently been appointed organist at Exeter Cathedral when he produced these songs. This was a highly successful publication which sold 381 copies to 296 subscribers, many of them prominent musicians. Langdon, who later moved to other cathedral posts, went on to publish more vocal music and a set of harpsichord pieces.

♣

From an edition of the song, 'Ye sacred Muses' (*c*1755)

A new Song

The words by a Gentleman on hearing a little Miss perform on the Harpsicord and German Flute. Set to Musick by Mr Richard Davies.

Ye sacred Muses now attend
Whilst I my ev'ry thought unbend
From Op'ras Plays and folly.
For sweeter Musick fills my Ear
And truer Beauty doth appear
In lovely pritty *Polly*.

Great Nature has been wond'rous kind
Who gave such Graces to the mind
Dear Charm for Mallencholly:
And as her Voice her Fingers too
Can equall Execution do.
Such Charm has pritty *Polly*.

In HANDEL's works she does rejoice
Tho' *ass* in *Chaplet* was by *Choice*
Design'd to make us jolly.
She said, a Song I never like
But when both words and Musick strike
So answered pritty *Polly*.

Amaz'd I stood such Witt to hear,
Such taste, such softness in each Air
That flow'd from pritty *Polly*:
And when the Flute I heard her touch,
By JOVE! The transport was too much
To hear, then pritty *Polly*
O! cease my pritty *Polly*.

A copy of this s.sh.f. is preserved at *Lbl*, G.316(46). Stanza 3 is reproduced in Deutsch(1955), 768. The author of the poem is not known but the 'little Miss' who inspired it was Marianne Davies. She gave her first public recital at the Great Room, Dean Street aged seven on 30 April 1751, when she sang and played the harpsichord and flute. She gave other concerts in London in the 1750s, and later became a noted performer on the glass harmonica, utilising the much-improved model of the instrument developed by Benjamin Franklin in 1761. The references in the 3rd verse are to Boyce's *The Chaplet* (1749) and the popular drinking song, 'Push about the brisk bowl', sung by John Beard in the first production. Its 1st stanza ends: "The lover who talks of his sufferings and smart, | Deserves to be reckon'd an Ass, an Ass, | deserves to be reckon'd an Ass". The composer of the song, Richard Davies, was also a flautist. He may well have been a relative of Marianne's, for in a notice for a later concert in the same venue (*PA*, 28 April 1756), 'Miss and Mr Davies' are billed together to contribute to the instrumental items in the programme.

♣

From the *Whitehall Evening-Post*, 22 March 1755

The Trustees of the Westminster Hospital or Infirmary, are desired to meet at the said Hospital on the 10th of April next, at Ten in the Forenoon, to proceed to St. Margaret's Church to hear the Anniversary Sermon, and after Divine Service to dine at the Sun Tavern in King Street, Westminster. In the course of the Service Mr. Handel's New Te Deum and Jubilate; an Anthem by Dr. Boyce, and Mr. Handel's Coronation Anthem, will be performed under the Direction of Dr. Boyce.[47] N.B. There will be a Rehearsal of the Musick at the Church on Tuesday the 8th of April next at Ten.

Founded in 1719, Westminster Hospital for the Sick and Needy was situated by the 1750s in James St.. Following the model provided by the long-established charity of the 'Sons of the Clergy', the hospital began to sponsor an 'Anniversary Sermon' associated with performances of choral and orchestrally accompanied sacred music. From the 1740s the programmes of music had invariably been dominated by Handel, usually with the addition of an anthem composed by the appointed conductor. The extent of the financial benefit of these events to the charities concerned may be illustrated by the collection taken for the Hospital in 1753 which amounted to no less than £305 (*PA*, 4 April).[48]

Boyce appears to have become involved with the Westminster Hospital celebrations when they began in 1753: "Yesterday was rehearsed at St. Margaret's Church, Westminster, to a numerous Audience, Mr. Handel's Grand Te Deum, the Coronation Anthem, and an Anthem of Dr. Boyce's, which met with great Applause, and it will be performed this Day at the same Church for the Benefit of the Westminster Infirmary" (*PA*, 3 April). The well-received Boyce anthem was almost certainly 'O be joyful' (*BC* 56), composed for Cambridge in 1749 and published in 1752.[49] No

---

[47] The Handel items were the 'Dettingen Te Deum' (1743) with the 'Utrecht Jubilate' (1713), and 'Zadok the Priest' composed for the Coronation of George II in 1727.

[48] In modern currency *c*£4,500.

[49] The only other possibility would have been the orchestrally accompanied, 'Blessed is he', written for Dublin in 1741.

newspaper references to such events at Westminster Hospital appear in 1754 and 1756, but they certainly took place annually from 1757 until at least 1777. In 1767 the music was specifically "under the Direction of Dr. Boyce", and it is probable that he continued in this role until 1769. In 1770 "an anthem by Dr. Howard" was advertised and it may be assumed that he took over the conducting at this time. Newspaper evidence suggests that he continued to do so at least until 1775 when the last reference to an anthem of his occurs. In 1762 the Boyce anthem was clearly identified as the one "performed at their Majesties Nuptuals" (*LC*, 22 April), i.e. 'The King shall rejoice' (*BC* 34). Two anthems by Boyce were programmed in 1763 and 1764, and so this would almost certainly have been one of them. The absence of references to such events in the press after 1777 would suggest that this tradition at Westminster Hospital died out about this time.

♣

From the *Public Advertiser,* 4 April 1755

THE REHEARSAL of the MUSICK for the FEAST of the SONS of the CLERGY will be at St. Paul's on Tuesday the 15th, and the Feast at Merchant Taylors Hall on Thursday the 17th Day of April. . . . The Overtures of Esther[50] Dr. Purcell's Grand Te Deum and Jubilate[51] a new Anthem by Dr. Boyce and Mr. Handel's Coronation Anthem[52] will be vocally and instrumentally performed. N.B. In order that the Choir may be kept as warm as possible, the West Doors only will be opened.[53] [&c.]

The new anthem by Boyce composed for this occasion was 'Lord, Thou hast been our refuge'. Later in the year the advertised programme for the Three Choirs Festival included "a new Anthem, composed for the last Meeting of the Corporation of the Sons of the Clergy at St. Paul's by Dr. Boyce" (*LEP*, 7 Aug. 1755). This Church of England charity, founded in 1655 and granted a charter by Charles II in 1675, was established in aid of "such of the Widdows and Children of loyall and Orthodox Clergymen who are poor and indigent" (Sanders (1956), 133). The society presented annual concerts and the feasts which followed them were held each Spring for fund-raising purposes. The extent of the success of this enterprise may

---

[50] Handel's oratorio of 1732.

[51] The Morning Service of 1694.

[52] 'Zadok the Priest' (1727).

[53] It was not unusual at this time for musical rehearsals such as this to be open to the public in order to increase the funds available for charitable purposes.

be gauged by the size of the collections made in 1754: at the rehearsal £224, at the concert £183, and £451 at the feast. With the addition of later benefactions, the final takings amounted to just over £900 (*WEP*, 23 May 1754).[54]

Most of the documentary records of the Charity prior to 1775 were destroyed by fire in 1838; thus we are reliant on newspaper advertisements and notices for information about its earlier activities. Boyce's name first appeared in programmes for 1751-4 when an unidentified "new anthem by Dr. Boyce" was announced (see e.g. *WEP*, 16 April 1751). This must have been one of the two orchestrally accompanied anthems, 'O be joyful' (*BC*, 56), composed for Cambridge in 1749, or 'Blessed is he' (*BC* 11), written for Dublin in 1741.

The composition of Boyce's 1755 anthem marked his appointment that year as conductor and organiser of the concert in succession to Maurice Greene. WB continued to carry out this duty until the end of his life. The above programme is typical of the repertoire chosen by the Stewards of the Corporation each year. Handel always dominated, with support from Purcell and whoever the current musical director might be. Purcell's 'Te Deum and Jubilate in D' (1694) had been a regular feature of the programmes early in the century, but in 1755 it was re-introduced in an arrangement by Boyce with fuller orchestration and some musical insertions of his own. Boyce's version appears regularly in programmes up to 1771, and thereafter occasionally up to 1794. As for 'Lord, Thou hast been our Refuge', it remained an almost invariable feature of the festival well into the 19th century. It was then observed that the fact that it was "still annually performed in St Paul's, is alone sufficient to transmit the name of Boyce to the latest posterity" (Ayrton *b*(1824), 194).

No autogr. MS of the anthem survives, but it was published eventually by Ashley in 1802 and by Novello (with organ accomp.) in 1849.[55] There is a modern edition by Bevan (Oxford, 1977) and it has been recorded (see Discography).

♣

From the *London Evening-Post,* 17-20 May, 1755

On Thursday last the Anniversary Sermon of the Middlesex Hospital was preached at St. Anne's Church, Westminster, by the Rev. Dr. Nichols,

---

[54] About £135,000 in modern currency.
[55] See *W. Boyce: Services and Anthems*, vol. 4, no. 57.

Master of the Temple, to a numerous and polite Audience, . . . when Mr. Handel's Te Deum and Coronation Anthem with an Anthem composed by Dr. Boyce[56] were vocally and instrumentally perform'd: The Musick was under the Direction of Dr. Boyce, and the Organ was play'd by Mr. Butler, to whom, with Mr. Beard,[57] the grateful Thanks of the Governors are due for their several Performances. After Divine Service the Right Hon. the Earl of Northumberland walked from the Church to the Ground appointed for erecting the new Building for the Middlesex Hospital in Marybone-Fields, . . . At the Place above-mentioned, . . . his Lordship . . . laid the First Stone of the Middlesex Hospital. His Lordship then return'd in the same Manner to the Great Concert Room in Dean-Street, where near 300 Persons dined together on this Occasion. [&c.]

Middlesex Hospital for the Sick and Lame, and lying-in Married Women, in Windmill St. off Tottenham-Court Road, was founded in 1745. Although notices in the press advertising an Anniversary Sermon to be given at St. Anne's Westminster and followed by a dinner to raise funds first appeared in March 1748, music was not mentioned until 1752: "Mr. Handell's [sic] new Te Deum and Coronation Anthem, with a new Anthem by Dr. Boyce, will be Vocally and Instrumentally performed" (LDA, 17 April). The Boyce anthem was almost certainly the orchestrally accompanied and recently published, 'O be joyful' (BC 56), composed for Cambridge in July 1749. The format of the programme is clearly derived from those adopted by this time for the long established Festival of the Sons of the Clergy. The same pieces were announced in 1753 (PA, 4 April), but no record of what took place in 1754, if anything, seems to have survived. The programme for 1755 as above was in most respects repeated in 1756, but on this occasion the music was "performed under the Direction of Dr. Boyce" (PA, 4 April). This is the only time when a conductor is mentioned, but WB may well have undertaken this role regularly from 1752 until 1758. From 1759 onwards the programmes of music associated with the anniversary celebrations seem to have been abandoned. Once the new hospital building had been completed in 1757, the drive to acquire additional income for the Charity through the annual musical celebration at St. Anne's may have been blunted. Notices relating to the Hospital in the early 1760s suggest that funds were now being raised

---

[56] The Handel works would have been the 'Utrecht' Te Deum (1743) and 'Zadok the Priest' (1727), and the Boyce anthem, 'O be Joyful' (see above comments).

[57] John Beard, the distinguished singer, who doubtless sang the tenor solo, 'Yea, like as a father pitieth his own children', in Boyce's anthem. He may also have helped to recruit some of his fellow singers to make up the chorus.

through firework displays in the pleasure gardens, and secular concerts in public music rooms.

♣

From *Berrow's Worcester Journal*, 7 August 1755

The ANNUAL MEETING OF THE THREE CHOIRS . . . *Will be held at* WORCESTER, *on* Wednesday *and* Thursday, *the 10th* and *11th Days of* September *next*. Mr. Handel's *New Te Deum and Jubilate*,[58] Mr. Purcell's *Te Deum and Jubilate* with Dr. Boyce's *Additions*,[59] with a *New Anthem* composed for the last Meeting of the Corporation of the Sons of the Clergy at St. Paul's by Dr. *Boyce*,[60] and Mr. Handel's *Coronation Anthem*,[61] will be performed in the Cathedral Church. *The Oratorio of Sampson* [*sic*] by Mr. Handel, and Dr. *Boyce's Solomon*[62] with several

---

[58] The 'Dettingen *Te Deum*' (1743) in D, probably with the 'Utrecht *Jubilate*' (1713) in the same key. Before 1743, Handel's *'Te Deum* and *Jubilate'* written to commemorate the 'Peace of Utrecht' had become well established in the English choral repertoire. However, following the composition of a 'new' *Te Deum* in celebration of the victory of the English over the French at the battle of Dettingen (27 June 1743) early in the 'War of the Austrian succession' (historically the last occasion on which an English monarch (George II) was to lead his troops into battle), the earlier *Te Deum* was invariably dropped in favour of the 1743 setting.

[59] Boyce's edition of Purcell's work for St. Cecilia's Day (1694) had been performed, probably for the first time, in April of the same year at the Festival of the Sons of the Clergy. It became an invariable feature of the opening concerts of the Three Choirs up to 1771. It remained in the Festival repertoire at least until 1784 but in some years it was replaced by a setting of similar texts based on music "taken from the most eminent Italian composers", Jommelli and Pergolesi in particular. The latter arrangement was made by James Harris of Salisbury, a prominent writer on music and the arts, and an ardent admirer of Handel. It was later published by Joseph Corfe in his collection, *Sacred Music dedicated . . . to the Right Hon. Earl of Malmesbury . . . Adapted to Some of the Greatest Italian and Other Foreign Composers . . . by the Late James Harris Esq.*, 2 vols. (London, 1800). The Boyce arrangement was sometimes dubiously credited with embodying his 'improvements' rather than merely his 'additions' or 'alterations'. It was also performed at other provincial Festivals, e.g. at Winchester in Sept. 1760 (see Pritchard & Reid(1970), 30), or at Oxford in July 1783 (Reid(1966), 8).

[60] 'Lord, Thou hast been our refuge' (April 1755).

[61] 'Zadok the Priest'.

[62] This is the first known performance of the serenata *Solomon* (1742) at the Three Choirs. It was also programmed at Hereford the following year, but was not taken up again until the Worcester Meetings of 1794 and 1797. The suggestion has been

other Pieces of Musick, will, in the Evenings of the said Days, be performed in *The Great Hall in the College of Worcester* which will be commodiously fitted up for the Purpose. . . . Care has been taken to engage the best Masters that could be procured. — *The Vocal Parts* (beside the Gentlemen of the Three Choirs) will be performed by Mr. BEARD, Mr. WASSE, Mr. DENHAM, Mr. BAILDON, Miss TURNER and Others. The *Instrumental Parts* by Mr. BROWN, Mr. MILLER, Mr. ADCOCK, Mr. MESSING &c. the Musick to be conducted by Dr. BOYCE.[63] [&c.]

(Deutsch(1955), 765)

♣

Boyce is requested to set the Birthday Ode for George II.

In the autumn of 1755, in his capacity as a composer at the Chapel Royal, Boyce was asked to provide the music for the royal ode written by the Poet Laureate to celebrate the birthday of George II. This was due to the illness of Maurice Greene, the incumbent Master of the King's Music, who would normally have been expected to fulfil this task. Boyce duly set Colley Cibber's ode, 'Pierian Sisters, hail the morn' (text in *PA*, 10 Nov.), arranged a public rehearsal, and conducted its performance on 10 November at St. James's Palace, the London residence of the royal family.

---

made, however, by E.F. Rimbault in his later edition of a book on the Three Choirs Festival by Lysons (1812), that an earlier performance of *Solomon* took place at Worcester. Rimbault quotes Lysons: "In 1743 he [Boyce] produced an anthem, then first composed for the occasion" and expresses his belief that the work in question was the serenata of *Solomon* (see Williams(1895), 32, n.2). While its title and the biblical source of its text (*The Song of Songs*) sometimes led to it being mistakenly designated an oratorio, it has never otherwise been described as an anthem. Furthermore, had it been so, it would undoubtedly have been performed in the Cathedral. As the above advertisement itself clearly indicates, a work such as *Solomon* would have been performed at the College Hall in the evening, not at the Cathedral in the morning. The anthem performed in 1743 was in fact 'Blessed is he', *BC* 11. This was not composed for the Three Choirs at all, but for Mercer's Hospital, Dublin in 1741.

[63] This was the first and last occasion since his appointment as conductor for the Meeting in 1737 that WB's work in that capacity was acknowledged in a press notice. It is known that William Hayes conducted at Gloucester in 1754 and 1757 (Boden(1992), 29). Since most of the advertisements for the Festivals from 1757 onwards identify the conductor(s) and WB's name is not amongst them, it would seem that he gave up directing the Three Choirs in 1756.

The origins of the court ode tradition inherited by Boyce lay in the period after the Restoration of the British monarchy in 1660. During this time odes celebrating occasions such as royal birthdays, the New Year, or the return to London of the monarch after fulfilling duties abroad (Welcome Songs) began to be composed. By no means all such works have survived, so it is difficult to gain a clear picture of the formal procedures in these matters before the early 18th century. From 1715 onwards, however, just after the accession of George II, a regular pattern came to be established. By this time welcome songs had dropped out of favour, but in normal circumstances the Poet Laureate was still expected to write an ode in praise of the monarch on the king's birthday and for the New Year. The Master of the King's Musick then set it and directed its performance. The musicians employed were the men and boys of the Chapel Royal choir and instrumentalists from the King's band. The texts of the ode were normally published in newspapers and periodicals when the names of participating vocal soloists were also sometimes included. All the original full scores and parts for WB's court odes are preserved at the Bodleian Library, Oxford. On the basis of the evidence provided by these parts, it has been calculated that the orchestral forces normally employed for the court odes amounted to about 20 string players and half-a-dozen or so wind/drum players (see Burrows(2005), 471).

The day before the event a public rehearsal of the new ode took place. In Boyce's time this was often held at a popular concert venue such as Hickford's Room in James Street. The performance itself invariably took place in the Great Council Chamber at St. James's Palace at 12 noon in the presence of the Royal Family, courtiers, government ministers, and foreign diplomats. Afterwards there was a reception at which congratulatory speeches were made, followed either by a family dinner or a State Banquet. The day finished with a ball beginning with a minuet in which the Royal Family themselves were expected to take part. As for the populace at large, both New Year's Day and the king's birthday were declared public holidays.

The 18th-century royal odes have generally received a bad press, and have never been revived, apart from a recent recording of one on CD (see Discography). However, Samuel Wesley, who evidently knew some of them, wrote of them in the late 1820s: "The variety of numbers employed in the construction of an ode is highly favourable to a composer of vivid imagination: and I well remember that the odes which Dr Boyce composed for the late King's birth day, and for the New Year altho' the poetry was frequently indifferent yet the continual alternation of cadence in the lines, engaged & preserved attention without inducing fatigue" (*Lbl*, Add.MS35,015, f. 49). For a critical assessment of WB's court odes that finds more merit in them than had previously been acknowledged, see Ford *b*(1990). The overture to this birthday ode was edited by Finzi in MB 13 (1957).

♣

A letter from Boyce to the Duke of Newcastle, 26 November 1755

My Lord

I intend myself the honor of waiting upon you, when you will please to give leave, to acquaint you with Doctor Greene's ill state of health, which is at present so far past a probability of cure, that it is thought he cannot live many more days,[64] and to beg your Grace's interest, that I may succeed him, as Master of his Majesty's Band of Musicians. — I am the more encouraged to ask this, from the favour shewn me upon a former application, when it was thought the Doctor would resign. — I set the last Birth-Day Ode for him,[65] am now setting that for the New-Years-Day[66] and have conducted all the performances during his illness.[67] The place is in the gift of the Duke of Grafton.[68]

I am My Lord, Your Grace[']s most devoted, and obedient humble servant William Boyce   Nov: 26th 1755

Lbl, Add.MS.32,861, f. 132. (Edwards(1901), 444) The Duke of Newcastle, Thomas Holles, would have known Boyce well, for the composer had set the ode for the Duke's installation as Chancellor of the University at Cambridge in July 1749. As for Boyce, he must have been aware that Newcastle was an ambitious politician who delighted in exercising to the full his powers of patronage. At the time Boyce wrote to him he was in fact serving as Prime Minister. Apart from the considerable prestige attached to the post of Master of the King's Music, there was also a substantial annual salary of £200 payable.[69] When Boyce himself died in 1779, no less a figure than Charles Burney was solicitous for the

---

[64] Greene died on 1 December.

[65] 'Pierian Sisters hail the morn', performed on 30 October 1755.

[66] 'Hail! Hail! Auspicious day'.

[67] Besides the two court odes mentioned these would have included conducting music for social events at court, and rehearsals and performances for the Festival of the Sons of the Clergy.

[68] In his capacity as Lord Chamberlain.

[69] Worth about £30,000 in modern currency.

appointment. Further to this, see the entry below. WB continued to carry out the duties he had already begun to undertake, but it was not until June 1757 that he was officially appointed to the post.

♣

A Letter from Charles Burney to Fulke Greville (1755)

King's Lynn
6 December 1755

Though I addressed a letter to you at Wilbury[70] some time since, I have not the least title to reproach you for taking y^r own time in answering it.

I have now a matter of great importance to myself to lay before you; & in wch I have the most pressing occasion for you[r] assistance. You must know that Dr Green is dead, & the place for wch I have so long languished is thereby become vacant.[71] You some time since were so kind to say you sh^d not scruple applying to Ld Holderness on my behalf, if Travers had died; sh^d you now think there w^d be any impropriety in *writing* to him for me, as I suppose you to be at Wilbury & unable to see him? If not, I sh^d think a line from you might be of service to me. As I suppose it natural for Dr Boyce to be advanced to Dr Green's place he being next to him in rank, either Boyce's place or Travers's w^d amply content me, as they will doubtless be removed. [&c.]

Lbl, Egerton MS3437, f. 303. (Ribeiro(1991), 21-2) Greville was an influential politician and author who had become a friend and patron of Burney's in the mid-1740s. This letter clearly reflects Burney's ambition to gain an appointment to the Chapel Royal, one he continued to harbour until 1779 when Boyce died. While Burney was seeking the support of Lord Holdness, even WB, already an established composer to the Chapel, felt sufficiently insecure to ask the Duke of Newcastle and David Garrick to endorse his claim to the Mastership. While WB was eventually to be satisfied, Burney was destined to remain a disappointed man in this particular aspiration.

♣

---

[70] Greville's country seat.

[71] Burney is referring to one of three vacancies which arose at the Chapel Royal following Greene's death. These were for a composer, an organist and the Mastership of the King's Music.

Boyce subscribes to Elizabeth Turner's *Collection of songs with symphonies and a thorough bass, with six lessons for the harpsichord* (1756).

Little is known about the origins or career of this composer, apart from the small body of music she published. She had certainly gained a reputation, for these musically impressive pieces attracted no fewer than 354 subscribers for 391 copies. Among the other subscribers were Handel, Beard, Stanley, Sir John Hawkins (at that time still Mr), William Hayes, and Lord Chesterfield no less (perhaps on behalf of his wife, who was rather more committed to music than he was).

♣

Boyce subscribes to Edward Moore's *Poems, Fables and Plays* (1756).

Boyce's collaboration with Moore had begun in 1742 when the latter submitted to him from Dublin, where he was then working, the words for his serenata *Solomon*. This subsequently became the composer's most popular and widely disseminated work, and Moore included its text in this publication (pp.203-11). This volume of collected works attracted 508 subscribers for 580 copies. It would naturally have appealed mostly to the literary and theatrical public, but in addition to WB, it was ordered by two other musicians, Thomas Lowe, a soloist in some of the early performances of *Solomon*, and John Hawkins, the music historian. Between 1747 and 1756, by which time Moore had settled in London, WB set four of his poems (one of them twice) as solo songs: *BC* 204, 212, 221, 222, and 258. He also set a dialogue of Moore's, *BC* 179, and a song, 'When Damon languished at my feet', for his play *The Gamester* (1753).

♣

Boyce sets Cibber's royal ode for New Year's Day 1756, 'Hail! 'Hail! Auspicious day', organises a public rehearsal, and conducts its performance at court.

Text in *LEP*, 30 Dec.-1 Jan. WB published the overture in *Eight Symphonys*, no. 1 (1760).

♣

From the *Public Advertiser,* 21 January 1756

By His Majesty's Company of Comedians. AT the Theatre Royal in Drury-Lane, This Day will be presented The WINTER'S TALE. A DRAMATIC PASTORAL in THREE ACTS. (From SHAKESPEARE) With proper Music, Songs, Dances, and Decorations. [&c.]

David Garrick's devotion to Shakespeare did not inhibit him from adapting the plays of his hero with a view to making them as accessible as possible to the theatre audiences of his day. In this case, he reduced the original four acts into three and focussed the plot more on the love element in the original play, as is suggested in the title-page of the word-book: FLORIZEL and PERDITA. | A | Dramatic Pastoral, | In three Acts. Alter'd from the WINTER'S TALE | of | SHAKESPEARE. . . . MDCCLVII. Garrick's revision was assessed by a contemporary critic as "a triumphant attempt at bringing a clear and regular fable out of the confusion of a *Winter's Tale,* the most irregular production of that eccentric poet".[72]

It is clear that Boyce was involved in providing some of the music for the new version, since his engaging setting of a trio, 'Get you hence for I must go', in Act II, sc. i, for the two shepherdesses, Mopsa (Mrs Vernon) and Dorca (Miss Young), and a shepherd (Beard), was inserted into volume V of WB's *Lyra Britannica,* only a month or so after the premiere. It is also clear that he composed 'The music for animating the statue of Hermoine' in Act III, sc. iv, for a partly autogr. score of it has survived.[73]

In the judgement of William Linley, Boyce may well have set other lyrics in this play. Linley was a son of Thomas Linley snr., a highly successful composer and director of concerts at Bath for many years, who had studied with Boyce in the 1750s. William, also an able composer and theatre music director, had in the late 1790s been appointed Composer at DL where he had easy access to the theatre's stock of music. In 1816 he published a collection of *Shakespeare's Dramatic Songs* in two volumes. Here, in addition to 'Get you hence', Linley attributed to Boyce two songs for Autolycus, 'When daffodils begin to peer' (Act I, sc. iii), and 'Will you buy any tape' (Act II, sc. i).[74] He had tracked down at the theatre settings of these songs in dilapidated anonymous MSS. Nevertheless, in considering the case for WB's authorship, he concluded: "Whether [these

---

[72] Murphy(1786), 2, 284-5.

[73] The music, for 2 oboes, strings and continuo, is at *Ob,* MS.Mus.d.14, ff. 12-14^v. The score itself was prepared by a copyist, but the title and another annotation are in Boyce's hand.

[74] See Linley(1816), 24 and 29.

songs] be his [Boyce's], the author has not been able *positively* to ascertain, but from the style of it he has not the slightest doubt about the matter".[75] 'Garrick presented the *Winter's Tale* 14 times in its first season and it was revived from time to time at DL up to 1789. 'Get you hence' and the 'Statue Music' have been recorded (see Discography).

♣

From the *Universal Visiter and Memorialist* (1756)

From Mr. Purcel, to *Dr.* Boyce
By Favour of Mr. *Bencraft*

Dear Sir,
While I remained on the face of the earth, I had no ambition equal to that of being acquainted with Corelli[76] since I have been in the regions of music and love, I have longed to have some correspondence with you. Mr. *Bencraft* will deliver you this. Your sonatas,[77] your *Solomon* your songs and above all your anthems *Corelli* (with whom I am now intimate) declares he should be proud to own. Go on, and let not music be any longer reckoned a *foreign* accomplishment. An ENGLISHMAN encouraged is invincible, as well in arts as in arms. BRITAIN STRIKE HOME![78] was (you know) of my setting; and were I disposed to reject that manly, alarming air, you should be the only man that I would permit to set it after me.

Yours, most sincerely,
H. PURCEL

[75] Linley, op. cit., Intro., 22.
[76] Arcangelo Corelli, the most universally admired Italian composer of the period before Boyce.
[77] The reference is to Boyce's 'Twelve Trio Sonatas' of 1747.
[78] The intended reference must be to 'Britons, strike home', a patriotic air for alto with chorus from Purcell's incidental music for *Bonduca, or the British Heroine* (1695). This was an adaptation of John Fletcher's tragedy *Bonduca* (c1612), which dramatizes the life of the ancient British warrior queen, Boadicea. John Walsh had recently reprinted the chorus section of this air in vol. 2 of his *Harmonia Anglicana* (1745), 78-9, and the complete air and chorus had earlier been included in Bickham's *Musical Entertainer*, vol. 2 (1740), 97-8.

Orpheus, Amphion, Timotheus, and *Corelli,*[79] desire their best respect. I had almost forgot to tell you that *Orpheus,* over a cup of nectar, drank your health in a bumper, and spoke these lines extempore:

> Orpheus, *with* Jason, won the golden fleece,
> *It is allowed:- - - so much, for tuneful* Greece.
> Corelli, SOUNDED SENSE in *ev'ry line*;
> Italia, *we acknowledge him divine:*
> *You justly claim'd the laureat* wreath *till now:*
> *But, learn, there is an* ENGLISHMAN! - - - and bow.

Universal Visiter (January, 1756), 24. (Facs. edn: Eddy(1979)). Published by Thomas Gardner, and edited by Richard Rolt and Christopher Smart, this monthly literary periodical, whose pages were graced by contributions from Samuel Johnson, David Garrick and Thomas Percy among others, survived for only one year (see Ferrero(1993)). The nature of the putative letter from the English composer Henry Purcell (*d.*1695) to Boyce is clarified earlier in the first issue (p.22) under the heading 'Bencraft's Intelligence': "Whereas Mr. *Bencraft,* the charitable founder of those alms-houses that bear his name, did, on his demise, declare his resolution of re-visiting his friends again within the space of thirty years, . . . PUBLIC NOTICE is hereby given, that the said Mr. *Bencraft* has proved, by some years, better than his word, and is now actually returned with a large packet of letters to all the most considerable and remarkable personages in the three kingdoms". Six other imaginary letters to distinguished contemporaries of a similar character were published in the first three issues, but none appeared subsequently. The author of these encomiums is not identified. A reasonable circumstantial case may be made, however, for attributing the authorship to Smart. The first signs of the serious mental illness that afflicted him for the rest of his life appeared early in 1756, and consequently the responsibility for producing the magazine fell largely to

---

[79] Corelli is placed alongside two heroic figures from ancient Greek mythology associated with music: Orpheus, who famously exercised magical powers through his lute; and Amphion, a son of Zeus, who charmed the stones in defence of Thebes with his lyre. Timotheus, a fictional character (though one based on an earlier Roman musician of the same name) had been introduced by Dryden into his second Cecilian ode, *Alexander's Feast, or The Power of Music,* which was set by Handel in 1736. In his poem Dryden assigns a central role to Timotheus as court musician to Alexander the Great. Timotheus's music-making exerts a pervasive influence at Alexander's court through its power to arouse or assuage the eponymous hero's passions.

Rolt. If Smart were the author, then the non-continuation of the series of letters after the March issue may well have been a consequence of this.

There are a number of reasons that may be adduced to account for Smart's admiration for Boyce. When the composer set his poem, 'Goddess of ease', at the beginning of Smart's career in 1744, and shortly before he became a Fellow of Pembroke College, Cambridge, the success of the song had brought him to the notice of the public at large for the first time. The case for Smart's authorship may also be reinforced by the evident admiration for Boyce embodied in his earlier satire, *The Hilliard* (1753).

Bencraft may have been entirely a figment of Smart's imagination, or perhaps one based on a real character. Research in relevant contemporary sources has failed to identify anyone of that name associated with the alms-houses of the time, at least not in London (see e.g., Besant(1902), Appendix III, 628-30). However, there was a contemporary actor, James Bencraft, who, given Smart's familiarity with the contemporary London theatrical scene, would have been well known to him, and whose character he may well have borrowed for the purposes of a literary conceit. A performance of *Hamlet* for Bencraft's benefit (and for that of a colleague, Mrs Baker) had taken place at Covent Garden in April 1755 (*PA,* 25 April 1755). After his death, which did not occur until 1765, a close colleague of his, William Havard, wrote of Bencraft and his well-known benevolent character: "A Person, who, in his lowest circumstance of Life, felt for Distress, & to the utmost of his Pow'r, relieved it" (quoted in BDA, 2, 28).

A supplementary song was attached to each of the twelve issues of the *Universal Visiter.* Three of these, all by anonymous poets, were set by Boyce: 'Again to the garden' (Feb.); 'Young Phyllis, one morning' (June) and 'Saw you Phoebe' (Aug.). The songs themselves were not paginated in the original monthly issues, but they were all included in the index to the publication of the complete periodical. Those by WB are listed in connection with pp.96, 284 and 384 respectively.

♣

Walsh publishes a further volume of vocal music by Boyce, *Lyra Britannica*, V (1756).

(Facs. edn (Bruce *b*(1985)) This was announced (*LEP*, 5-7 Feb.) and published with title-page: Numb:V LYRA BRITANNICA. | *A Collection of ENGLISH SONGS* | AND CANTATAS | COMPOS'D BY | *D^R. BOYCE.* [&c.] The volume includes items composed for two dramatic productions: the trio 'Get you hence, for I must go' from Garrick's *Florizel and Perdita* based on Shakespeare's *A Winter's Tale*, first performed at Drury Lane on 21 Jan. 1756, and a song, 'When Damon languish'd at my feet', written for Edward Moore's tragedy, *The Gamester*, first given at DL on 7 Feb. 1753. The independent songs included are *BC* 204 (text: E. Moore), 208 (Dr. Hill), 214 (George Coleman), 220 (George Lyttelton), 229 (Colley Cibber), 248 (anon.), 252 (anon.) and 248 (anon.), a drinking song. The last of these, 'Rail no more ye learned asses', was sometimes identified as the 'Bacchanalian song' as for example at DL in March 1759 when it was sung by John Beard at the end of Act III of Susannah Centlivre's witty and highly popular comedy, *The Busy Body* (1709), in which Garrick took the title role.[80] The tune of 'Rail no more' was also used again later in a political comic opera, *The Coach Driver*, where it was set to a verse in Act I, 'Curse such damn'd dull donnish drawling' (see *PA*, 18 Sept. 1766). The single cantata is *BC* 171 (Allan Ramsey), the text of which originally appeared under the title, 'A Scots Cantata', (see Cowgill & Holman(2007), 65).

♣

Extract from a letter of David Garrick to the Duke of Devonshire, 26 February 1756

I should not have troubled Your Grace so soon again, had not one part of ye last letter I had ye honor & pleasure to receive, requir'd an immediate answer — My wife had a very good opportunity ye last time she was at Chiswick, of telling her Lad^p that I had ventur'd to write to Y^r Grace in favor of Dr Boyce, & that I had receiv'd an answer, y^t would not oppose him — I thought this proper to be told as Y^r Lord^p hinted in y^r last; that letter & one I wrote upon a late melancholly occasion, (I think) may be all wch sh^d be own'd; tho her Lad^p will scarcely demand a confession, but whatever is thought right, we shall acquiesce in — there is such an unaccountable suspicion & jealousy in every word, action & look, that it behoves all persons concern'd to be extreamly wary[.] [&c.]

---

[80] On the same occasion at the end of Act V, Beard and Miss [Elizabeth] Young sang "A new Comic Dialogue, compos'd by Dr. Boyce, to be sung in Character" (*PA*, 29 March 1759). Bearing in mind that 'new' sometimes meant 'new to the venue' rather than 'recently composed' in contemporary usage, this item may have been 'Let rakes for pleasure' first published in LB, III (1748). When its text was later printed in a song book, *Polyhymnia* (1769), the caption read "This Dialogue is well set, and was greatly admired when first made public".

(Little & Kahrl(1963), I, 236). This letter is revealing of the kind of behind-the-scenes dealing that went on in the 18th century where appointments to high office were concerned. Although Boyce had been asked to take over Maurice Greene's duties as Master of the King's Music during the latter's illness in the Autumn of 1755, and after his death in December that year, he was not officially appointed to succeed him until June 1757. Meanwhile, he must have felt somewhat insecure. We know, for example, that Charles Burney had at this time been seeking political backing in his aspiration to a royal appointment.[81] In such circumstances it is entirely understandable that WB should approach the well-connected David Garrick, for whom he had done some very successful work, with a view to gaining support from the influential politician, William Cavendish, 4th Duke of Devonshire.

♣

From the *Public Advertiser,* 1 April 1756

DRURY-LANE For the Benefit of Mr. HAVARD,[82] AT the Theatre Royal in Drury-Lane, This Day April 1, will be presented a Play call'd ROMEO and JULIET. Romeo, by Mr. GARRICK; . . . Juliet, by Mrs CIBBER With the ADDITIONAL SCENE representing The FUNERAL PROCESSION. In Act I. A Masquerade Dance. After the Play will be performed a new Anniversary ODE, In Commemoration of SHAKESPEAR. Written by Mr. Havard; and set to Music by Dr. BOYCE. The Vocal Parts by Mr. Beard, Mr. Champness, &c. To which will be added a Farce call'd The ENGLISHMAN in PARIS.[83] . . . The Ode will be printed and given away at the Theatre.

The holograph MS of Boyce's setting of Havard's 'Anniversary Ode', 'Titles, and ermine fall behind', has a rare, if not unique, history. Until 1980 it had been preserved in Birmingham (*Bu*, MS5008, ff. 1-15), but in a defective state. It was lacking the initial folio and five inner leaves. At an auction at Sotheby's on 27 Nov. 1980, however, the missing inner folios were auctioned (Lot 217). Fortunately, they were acquired by the Barber Institute and subsequently reunited with the MS from which they had been taken. Finally, and most remarkably, the lost opening was identified in a copy of Charles Burney's *Account of the Musical Performances in*

---

[81] See his letter of 6 Dec. 1755 above.

[82] A respected actor and colleague of David Garrick's at DL, as well as an author.

[83] A popular farce by Samuel Foote (1753).

Westminster Abbey . . . in Commemoration of Handel (1785) which had been purchased by the Foundling Museum, London, in 2005. The missing first leaf had been inserted between pp.40-41 in the mid-19th-century.[84]

Another partly autograph score of the ode with related vocal and instrumental parts survives at *Ob*, MS.Mus.Sch.C.114.[a/b] The work is scored for 2 oboes, strings and continuo. A series of recitatives, solo airs and duets is concluded with a duet, 'Then Britain boast', in which the repeats are reinforced by a two-part chorus. The assignation of the solo roles to Beard (tenor) and Champness (bass) confirms that these materials are directly connected with the DL performance(s). It is also evident that Boyce used the first and last movements of his Trio Sonata no. 9 (1747) as an overture to this work.

The Ode was given again on 6 April, and Garrick continued to revive it in late March or early April each year up to 1760. With Garrick's devotion to Shakespeare in mind, it has been suggested that the anniversary being celebrated in the Ode was the bard's birthday on 23 April 1564. There can be little doubt, however, that it was in fact the anniversary of his signing the agreement to manage DL jointly with James Lacy on 9 April 1747 that he had in mind. The text was published in the *London Magazine*, March 1756, 144, and again in *SJC*, 3-5 Aug. 1769 at the time of Garrick's 'Shakespeare Jubilee' celebrations at Stratford. Havard suggested then that the Anniversary Ode might be included in the programme there, but Garrick did not take up the idea. Boyce's Ode did, however, enter the repertoire of the Academy of Ancient Music.[85] Finally, the Ode was revived at Birmingham University in 1982.

Boyce also set another Ode by Garrick, 'Arise, arise, immortal Shakespeare' (*c*1759). The autogr. score is at *Ob*, MS.Mus.d.14, ff.16-31, but no evidence of a performance has come to light; indeed, the MS gives the impression of being a long fragment rather than a finished work. Nevertheless, deploying an orchestra of two oboes, three trumpets and strings, WB gives vivid expression in places to the poetic eulogy and fervent patriotism of Garrick's verses. The initial bass aria, 'Arise, arise' is followed by two for soprano, 'In Fancy's glass' and 'Sweetest bard that ever sung'.[86] The insertion of a dance for Venus and the Graces is indicated here before a duet for the Goddess Minerva and Mars,'While Britains bow at

---

[84] For further details of this discovery and the earlier history of Boyce's MS, see Timms *b*(2006), [5-7].

[85] See Academy(1768), 183-6.

[86] This air was later included in Garrick's pantomime, *Harlequin's Invasion* (1759), and subsequently published in *Thalia* (*c*1767), a collection of six settings by various composers of texts by Garrick.

Shakespeare's shrine', is sung. The score ends with a duet with chorus, 'Hark. Hark, their glory', where the trumpets are deployed.

♣

Boyce subscribes to Thomas Chilcot's *Six concertos for the harpsichord accompanied with four violins, viola, violoncello, and bass-ripieno* (1756).

These works by the well-known 'Organist of Bath', were printed for him by John Johnson. The edition received a limited response, at least initially, for there were only 101 subscribers, but they included Greene, Avison and Stanley. Boyce retained the parts for these concertos until his death. In the sale catalogue for his library in April 1779 they appeared within Lot 72, though they lacked the harpsichord part.

♣

Boyce subscribes to John Alcock's 'The pious Soul's heavenly Exercise' [1756].

This collection of four-part settings of psalm tunes attracted 150 subscribers for 203 copies. The only other prominent musicians to support this publication were Philip Hayes and John Stanley.

♣

Boyce sets Cibber's ode for the king's birthday 1756, 'When Caesar's natal day', organises a public rehearsal, and conducts its performance at Court on 10 November.

Text in GM 26 (1756), 538). WB published the overture in Eight Symphonys, no. 2 (1760).

♣

From the *Public Advertiser,* 15 December 1756

Not acted these twenty Years. AT the Theatre-Royal in Drury-Lane, This Day will be reviv'd a Comedy, call'd AMPHITRYON Or, the TWO

SOCIAS. (With alterations.)[87] Jupiter by Mr. ROSS; Amphitrion, Mr. Havard; . . . In which will be introduc'd a new INTERLUDE of Singing and Dancing by Mr. Beard, Miss Young and others. . . . The Songs of the Interlude will be printed and delivered gratis at the Doors.

These songs were set by Boyce. The air, 'Away with the fables philosophers hold', sung by Beard in the role of 'Plutus', elicits a response, 'Plutus, vain is all your vaunting', sung by Miss Young in the part of 'Wit'. Finally, they come together in a duet based on the music of the first song, 'In vain would your jargon our senses bewitch'. WB's characteristically spirited music may have contributed to the success of this revival. His music probably continued to be used until 1769 when a performance of *Amphitryon* at DL was advertised "in which will be introduced an In[t]erlude of Singing and Dancing. The Music entirely new" (*PA*, 23 Nov. 1769). WB later published his song for 'Wit' in *Lyra Britannica*, VI, (1759). A contemporary score of the complete interlude in an unknown hand, entitled 'Dialogue in Amphitrion', is preserved at *DRc*, M205, 1-17. The text of the play with a preface by Hawkesworth entitled, *Amphitryon, Or, the Two Socias. A Comedy, alter'd from Dryden*, was published in 1756 (copy in *Lbl*, 11782.d.33(1)). The complete text of the interlude is on pp.45-7, towards the end of Act IV. In the preface, Hawkesworth explains the motivations lying behind his alterations to Dryden's play. His adaptation reached Dublin in 1758 when the opening to his preface was quoted in a press notice (see below).

♣

Boyce sets two Italian odes by G. G. Bottarelli published in London (1757).

Title-page: *Del Canzoniere* | d'Orazio | di | Giovan Gualberto *Bottarelli* | ODE XII. | *Messe in Musica d'piu rinomati* | Professori Inglesi. | *Dedicate* | Al Signor Guise | Luogatenente Generale dell' Armata *di* S.M.B. | Edizione Seconda | Non ante vulgatas per artes | verba loquor sociando chordis. | Orazio, Lib: IV. Ode: IX. Vei III. | LONDRA, MDCCLVII.

---

[87] This play by John Hawkesworth was based on Dryden's comedy of the same name, itself derived from a play by Molière. Dryden's work was first performed in 1690 with incidental music by Henry Purcell. It had gradually fallen out of favour in the 18th century but Hawkesworth's adaptation for his friend David Garrick, the manager at DL, gave it a new lease of life.

Among the 12 odes presented here Boyce set two da capo arias with continuo accompaniment: no. 5, 'Degli amor la madre altera' (29-30), and 10, 'Centra de canti amica' (48-9). The other composers represented in this volume are Thomas Arne, Willem de Fesch, John Worgan and Henry Heron. It was not uncommon for English composers to be invited to set Italian texts with a view to publication in London.

♣

Boyce sets Cibber's royal ode for New Year's Day 1757, 'While Britain in her monarch blest' (text in *GM* 27, 36), organises a public rehearsal, and conducts its performance at court.

♣

Boyce subscribes to Samuel Boyce's *Poems on several occasions* (1757).

The first works of Boyce the poet, had appeared in 1755. By the time this large-scale collection was published he had clearly established a wide following, for it attracted over 500 subscribers. Other leading musicians who supported it were the composers Thomas Arne, Defesch and Travers, and the tenors Beard and Lowe. Although a number of other composers set Samuel's texts, WB himself appears not to have done so. By the late 1750s he was doubtless fully occupied with his many other commitments, but curious perhaps about his namesake's work.

♣

Boyce subscribes to the publication of *The first fifty Psalms. Set to music by Benedetto Marcello, and adapted to the English Version by John Garth*, 12 vols. (1757).

This handsome and substantial publication, which includes an essay on Marcello's psalms by Avison, was supported by 119 subscribers for 130 sets. Given its inevitably high cost, it is not surprising that most of the subscribers were from the aristocracy or the higher ranks of the church. The only other leading musicians to invest in this edition, apart from Avison himself, were Stanley and Dupuis. These psalm settings, originally published in Venice (1724-6), were admired throughout Europe. Boyce was clearly interested in Marcello for he also owned two MS copies of his vocal duets.

♣

Boyce subscribes to Alessandro Scarlatti's *Thirty-six arietta's for a single voice* [*c*1757].

Alessandro (*d*. 1725), the father of the even more illustrious Domenico, was primarily a composer of operas and vocal music. This acquisition by Boyce reflects his abiding interest in the music of the older Italian schools. Many other leading London musicians were among the 110 subscribers for 165 copies of this volume.

♣

Warrant from the Lord Chamberlain to his Majesty's Treasurer on Boyce's appointment as Master of the King's Music

Whereas D^r. William Boyce is by my warrant sworn and admitted into the place and quality of Master of Music in Ordinary to his Majesty (in the room of D^r. Maurice Greene deceased) these are to pray and require you to take notice thereof and enter him into your books accordingly into the place of the said D^r. Maurice Green and to pay unto him the like wages and entertainment as the said D^r. Maurice Green formerly had and ought to receive by his Majesty's establishment to commence from the 2nd. day of December 1755. And for so doing this shall be your Warrant given under my hand this 27th. Day of June 1757 in the 31st. Year of his Majesty's reign.

                                                        Devonshire

To the Honble Charles Townsend Treasurer of his Majestys Chamber and to the Treasurer for the time being.

PRO LC3/58 (37). Although Boyce had taken over Greene's duties as Master of the King's Music in late 1755, he had to wait nearly two years to receive this formal confirmation of his appointment, and the warrant guaranteeing his annual salary of £200[88] (*Lpro*, LC2/24, f. 19). It has been

---

[88] In modern currency about £30,000.

suggested that this inordinate delay may have been due to the King's office being unduly distracted during this period by "political uncertainties both at home and abroad" (see Daub(1985), 178).

♣

From the *Public Advertiser,* 20 October 1757

Not acted these 14 Years. By His Majesty's Company of COMEDIANS. AT the Theatre-Royal in DRURY-LANE, This Day will be revived a Play, call'd THE TEMPEST As written by SHAKESPEAR. Prospero by Mr. MOSSOP, Hymen by Mr. Beard. With proper Decorations; particularly a grand Dance of Fantastic Spirits; and a Pastoral Dance proper to the Masque, by Mr. Delater, Sig. Giorgi, Signora Lucchi. . . . The words of the songs will be printed and delivered gratis at The Doors of the Theatre.

The Tempest had last been acted at DL in 1746, before Garrick had become manager. The music was provided by Arne. Wishing to revive the play in 1756, Garrick turned to J.C. Smith jnr. for the music. Having decided to make a new adaptation of the play the following year, Garrick now asked Boyce to write the music for the masque. It takes place in Act IV, sc. i, when Prospero gives his blessing to the marriage between his daughter Miranda and Ferdinand. Music is introduced at the point where Shakespeare in his original text indicated "They sing". The two characters in the masque are the Spirits, Ariel and Ceres, who are joined by Hymen, the mythological God of marriage. The masque consists of three songs linked by recitatives. Firstly 'Hither Hymen speed your way' for Ariel (sung by Miss Young at the first performance), then a duet for Hymen (Beard), and finally a duet for Ceres (Mrs Vernon) and Hymen, 'You sunburn'd sicklemen, of August weary'. The accompaniment is scored for strings, 2 flutes, 2 horns and continuo. The play was given 10 performances in its first season, and was revived at DL about 50 times up to 1776. WB's autogr. score is at *Ob*, MS.Mus.d.14, ff. 2-11. Another score made by a copyist is at *Lcm*, MS92, but the text and other annotations are in the hand of the composer.

♣

Boyce sets Cibber's ode for the king's birthday 1757, 'Rejoice ye Britons, hail the day!' (text in *LEP*, 8-10 Nov.), organises a public rehearsal, and conducts its performance at court on 10 November.

♣

Boyce sets the Ode for the New Year (1758).

Boyce's setting of Cibber's royal ode for New Year's Day, 'Behold the circle forms! Prepare!', was not performed on this occasion due to the court being in mourning following the death of Princess Elizabeth Caroline, George II's third daughter, on 28 December. Since Cibber had died on 11 December 1757 he must have written this ode, perhaps his last creative act, and passed it on to WB in good time. This allowed the court a comfortable period in which to seek another Poet Laureate, and for the new incumbent to write the next ode for the king's birthday in November 1758. Cibber's successor, William Whitehead, was in fact appointed on 19 December 1757. Normally when a completed royal ode was not performed for one reason or another at the time for which it was written, the Lord Chamberlain would give approval to its being performed on the next suitable occasion. The following year, however, Whitehead, though he had already produced his first royal ode for the king's birthday in October, was evidently so keen to make a mark in his new role that he wrote a new text for the New Year. He may well have been motivated by a desire to enhance the status of a genre that had been subjected to much satirical comment while Cibber was in office. Whitehead's new words were duly set by Boyce and performed on 1 January 1759. Nevertheless, at the same time, Cibber's discarded text was published in the press (*WEP*, Dec. 31-Jan. 3, 1758). Of the 43 royal odes that WB was eventually to compose, this was the only one that appears never to have been performed. The overture was edited by Finzi in MB 13 (1957).

♣

From the Vestry Minutes of Allhallows the Great and the Less, 5 January 1758

Ordered at the said Vestry the Sallery of D[r] Boyce the Organist be reduced to twenty pounds p[er] ann[um] from Lady [Day] next.[89] Ordered that Dr. Boyce have immediate notice of the above order and that he be at the same time requested to change Mr Bullbrick his deputy.

Lgh, MS 819/2, 369. Shaw(1991), 13. Despite the terms of these orders, and their implications, both Bullbrick and Boyce remained in their posts at Allhallows until March 1764. Notwithstanding Bullbrick's evident unpopularity with the church authorities, it would appear either that Boyce was loyal to his deputy, or he was rather negligent in taking appropriate action.

♣

From the *Public Advertiser,* 21 February 1758

By His Majesty's Company of COMEDIANS. AT the Theatre-Royal in DRURY-LANE, This Day will be presented a new Tragedy call'd AGIS. The principal Characters by Mr. GARRICK, Mr. MOSSOP, Mr. DAVIES, Mr. HOLLAND, Mrs. PRITCHARD, Mrs. YATES, and Mrs. CIBBER. The Vocal Parts by Mr. Beard, Mr. Champnes, Mr. Vernon, Mrs. Vernon, Miss Young, &c. The Music compos'd by Dr. Boyce. [&c.]

The Scottish playwright John Home's historical drama is concerned with events in the life of Agis, King of Sparta. Boyce was commissioned to set two substantial odes that are integral to the play. In Act III, 'A Chorus of Matrons and Virgins', 'Woes ap[p]roach till now unknown', incorporates airs for 'The Priest of Jupiter' sung by Champness, and 'Hercules' (Beard), and at the end of Act V, following the execution of Agis, the play culminates in a dirge, 'Mourn ye sons of Sparta, mourn', for 4-part chorus with solo interludes as in the earlier ode. A contemporary view of the work was that it was "performed with tolerable success being strongly supported . . . by the . . . advantages of very fine acting and two pompous, and solemn musical processions".[90] Public support waned, however, for after only 11 performances in its first season, and two more in 1760, Garrick

---

[89] Boyce was appointed at an annual salary of £30. In modern terms he suffered a reduction from c£4,500 to c£3,000.

[90] Baker(1782), II, 4-5.

decided to drop it. Home's play was published in *Agis: A Tragedy. As it was Acted at the Theatre-Royal in Drury-Lane* (1758).[91] The autogr. score is preserved at *Lcm*, MS807, ff. 15-42. The quality of WB's music was evidently recognised, for the odes were sometimes performed independently of the play at the Academy of Ancient Music.[92]

♣

Boyce subscribes to the publication of John Bennett's *Ten voluntaries for the organ or harpsichord* [1758].

Bennett was a well-known London organist. This volume was well supported by the organ playing fraternity nationally. 277 copies were ordered by 228 subscribers, among whom were leading figures such as Handel, Burney, Stanley, Travers and Nares. In addition to their fine craftsmanship, Bennett's voluntaries are notable for their unusually large scale and sometimes very florid passage work.

♣

From the Papers of the Lord Chancellor (1758)

These are to certify, whom it may concern, that by virtue of a Warrant from the Right Reverend Father in God, Thomas Lord Bishop of London, Dean of his Majestys Chapels Royal, I have addmitted, and sworn, D[r]. William Boyce into the place and office of Organist of his Majestys Chapels Royal in the room of M[r]. Travers deceased, and into all the privileges and advantages thereunto belonging. Given under my hand this twenty third day of June, in the year of our Lord 1758.

　　　　To commence July 1st. 1758　　　　　　F Allen. Subdean

Lpro, LC5/162(125). Allen also recorded Boyce's appointment in the Chapel Royal records, NCB, p.37. (Ashbee & Harley(2000), vol. 1, 227-8) Within the terms of his earlier appointment as a Composer to the Chapel Royal in 1736, WB had also been required to undertake some limited organ playing duties. His appointment as one of the organists at this stage in his career suggests that his powers had yet to decline significantly, as they appear to have done later when he was obliged to resign from his post

---

[91] The text of the 1st ode appears on pp.26-8, and the 2nd on pp.70-71.
[92] See Academy(1768), 180-3.

at St. Michael Cornhill in 1768. Jonathan Battishill is known to have sometimes acted for WB in his role as an organist at the Chapel Royal, at least until 1764 when the former was appointed organist at a Parish Church.

♣

From *Berrow's Worcester Journal*, 26 August 1758

[Three Choirs Festival] Upon Wednesday, August the 30th at the Cathedral . . . Purcell's Te Deum and Jubilate with Dr. Boyce's Alterations: An Anthem of Dr. Boyce's, 'O be joyful' &. Mr. Handel's Coronation Anthem. Upon Thursday, August the 31st, at the Cathedral . . . Mr. Handel's new Te Deum and Jubilate An Anthem of Dr. Boyce's, 'Lord thou hast been our Refuge': And the Coronation Anthem. Upon Wednesday, Thursday and Friday evenings, at the College-Hall — the Oratorios of Judas Maccabaeus, Alexander's Feast, and the Messiah. Care has been taken to engage the best Performers from London, and other Places. [&c.]

(Deutsch(1955), 806) No copy of the issue of *BWJ* from which Deutsch apparently quoted here survives in the Worcester Record Office today. Moreover, the dating of this issue must be regarded as dubious since *BWJ* was normally published weekly on Thursdays in the 18th century, and 26 August 1758 was in fact a Saturday. It may be assumed, nevertheless, that the copy of the notice quoted by Deutsch is authentic. It is significant for the inclusion for the first time in a Three Choirs Festival advertisement of precise references to the Boyce anthems to be performed that year. (The identification of 'Lord, Thou hast been our refuge' in the notices for the 1755 Festival was by deduction rather than direct reference to its title.) 'O be joyful' (1749) was only named again once (with regard to the 1760 Festival), and 'Lord, Thou hast been our refuge' was not mentioned again until 1791. Both these large-scale, orchestrally accompanied anthems, however, were almost certainly given many other performances at the Festival, even if they were not specifically identified in public notices.

♣

Boyce sets William Whitehead's ode for the king's birthday 1758, 'When Othbert left th'Italian plain', organises a public rehearsal, and conducts its performance at court on 10 November.

Text in *PA*, 11 Nov. Following the death in December 1757 of the previous Poet Laureate, Colley Cibber, the post was first offered to Thomas Gray, who declined it. Whitehead in his turn did accept the honour, and went on to provide Boyce with all the court ode texts until the latter's death. WB had already collaborated with Whitehead once before when he composed the music for his play, *The Roman Father* (DL, 24 Feb. 1750). Cibber's efforts in his role as royal poet had been widely derided, not least by Pope whose satirical barbs were particularly wounding. Whitehead's odes on the other hand gained wide respect. While his predecessor's verses had been overtly sycophantic in character, Whitehead moved the focus away from praise of the monarch towards giving emphasis to the ideal of patriotism. Moreover, his odes often gave expression to the widespread desire for peace at a time of conflict in Europe and growing unrest in the American colonies. The overture was edited by Finzi in MB 13 (1957) and has been recorded (see Discography under 'Theatre Music').

♣

From the *Dublin Journal*, 5-9 December 1758

The Comedy of AMPHITRYON, which is to be acted on Monday next at the New Theatre in Crow street, is supposed to be alter'd by Mr. Hawksworth [*sic*] the Ingenious Author of those Essays called The ADVENTURER[93] — "The Abilities of DRYDEN as a writer, are so generally and so justly acknowledged to be of the first Class, that it would be something worse than Impropriety to alter any of his Productions without assigning the Reason. — For the Alterations of his AMPHITRYON, indeed, the Reason is evident; for it is so tainted with the Profaneness and Immodesty of the Time in which he wrote, that the present Times, however selfish and corrupt, has too much Regard to external Decorum, to perm[i]t the Representation of it upon the Stage, without drawing a Veil, at least, over some Part of its Deformity. The principal Part of the Alterations, therefore, are made with a moral View;

---

[93] Hawkesworth edited and wrote for a literary journal, *The Adventurer*, which ran from 1752-54, in succession to Johnson's *Rambler*.

though some Inaccuracies, which were remark'd on the Examination, which these Alterations made necessary, are also removed. This Comedy, upon its Revival with the Alterations, was acted ten Nights successively, and many Times after in the Course of each Season since".[94]

John Hawkesworth's adaptation of *Amphitryon* had been first acted in London at Drury Lane on 15 Dec. 1756. Among the alterations Hawkesworth introduced was an interlude, 'The Contention of Wit and Wealth', which Boyce set to music. The above account of Hawkesworth's intentions is taken from the opening of his preface to the published text of the play (J. Payne, London (1756)). A second performance of *Amphitryon* was given on 28 December (*DJ*, 23-26 Dec.).

♣

Boyce composes an anthem for St. Margaret's Westminster (1758).

In 1758, Parliament made a grant of over £4,000 to St Margaret's, the official church of the Palace of Westminster, for renovations to the East End of the building. This involved the erection of new pews and other decorations, and above all, the installation of a magnificent new East Window. As has been recorded "in 1759 the 'beautified' church was re-opened, an anthem being composed for the occasion by Dr Boyce" (Bumpus(1923), 182). As its text may suggest, the anthem in question was 'I have surely built thee an house', and indeed the Church Accounts for 1759 record a payment of 10s, 9d[95] "to Dr Boyce for composing the anthem for the opening of the Church" (*Lwa*, E135 (1757-61). While no contemporary references to the occasion on which Boyce's anthem was performed seem to have survived, in the Vestry Minutes for 28 Dec. 1758 thanks are offered to "Dr Thomas Wilson for the excellent sermon preached on Sunday last [the 24th] re the repairs and beautification of the Church" (*Lwa*, E2421 (1755-71)). It may be supposed, particularly in view of its text, that this was when WB's anthem was performed, and if so that it had therefore been composed towards the end of 1758 rather than in 1759. WB's autogr. MS is preserved at *US: Wc*.

---

[94] The play did retain a place in the London repertoire until 1792, but the London revival of Dryden's play in 1756 opened with only six rather than the ten successive performances claimed.

[95] About £80 in modern currency.

♣

From 'Theatrical Music' by Thomas Wilkes in *A General View of the Stage* (1759)

In the compositions intended for the Stage the Poet and Musician ought to act entirely in concert; the words should be adapted to the Music, and the Music to the Words; that is, it should be noble, lively, bold, furious, graceful, tender, or even plaintive, according to the exigence of the situation, and of this Arne is always particularly careful; nor does Dr. Boyce seem to be less exact.

Wilkes(1759), 76. The ideas conveyed here reflect the widely held 18th-century idea that the primary purpose and aspiration of music was to give expression to the 'passions', no more so than when allied to a literary text. It is no surprise to find Thomas Arne, the most successful English composer for the stage of his time, being credited with success in maintaining these principles. At the same time it is significant that Wilkes also recognised Boyce's qualities as a theatrical composer, even though he exercised his artistry in these respects more prominently and consistently in his output for the church and the court.

♣

Boyce sets Whitehead's royal ode for New Year's Day 1759, 'Ye guardian powers' (text in AR (1758), 'Characters', 398-9), organises a public rehearsal, and conducts its performance at court.

♣

Boyce subscribes to Alessandro Besozzi's *Six solos for the German-flute, hautboy, or violin, with a thorough bass for the harpsichord* [c1759].

A virtuoso oboist, the Italian Besozzi pursued his career on the continent, where his output of chamber music was highly regarded. These galant-style sonatas, when published in London, were acquired by a wide range of prominent English musicians. There were 248 subscribers for 314 copies.

♣

Boyce marries Hannah Nixon in 1759.

Documentary evidence for Boyce's marriage to Hannah on 9 June of this year is preserved in London (*Lma*, X024/023). Prior to the discovery of this source, and the recognition of of its validity in relation to Boyce the composer, it has often been assumed that he married Hannah *c*1749 when her daughter Elizabeth was born. This seemed to have been given credence by Boyce when in his will he referred to his daughter's birth on 19 April 1749. This assumption about the marriage was until recently generally accepted. The marriage certificate referred to above, placing it much later, only came to light in 1968 (see Dawe *b*(1968)). Its authenticity, or rather its relevance to Boyce, was initially dismissed. It was at this stage suggested that "Future investigators should not be mislead by the marriage on June 9, 1759 at St Dunstan Stepney of William Boyce of St Andrew Holborn, the parish of Chancery Lane, 'gent.' to Hannah Nixon of Ratcliffe, spinster; if the 'spinster' is not enough to invalidate it, the signature of William Boyce in the register does not tally with the composer's" (Dawe, op. cit., 806-7). However, notwithstanding his initial scepticism about Boyce's signature, Dawe tacitly refuted his earlier position by accepting its validity as evidence for the composer's marriage in a later publication (see Dawe(1983), 81).

There seems to have been a long-standing, and perhaps understandable, reluctance to confront the fact that Hannah Boyce may have given birth to her first child before her marriage to Boyce. While Boyce clearly accepted Elizabeth as his daughter, whether he was her natural father or she was the outcome of an earlier liaison, either in or out of wedlock, will probably never be known. However, the fact that Boyce did not marry Hannah until ten years after Elizabeth's birth, would suggest that she was probably not his own flesh and blood. In fact, in spite of the above, Boyce's close friend and biographer got it more or less right when he wrote: "but being now arrived at great eminence in his profession, he [Boyce] went to reside in a house in *Quality Court, Chancery Lane,*[96] and soon after married" (Hawkins *b*(1788), vi).

♣

---

[96] In 1753.

John Walsh publishes a final volume of vocal music
by Boyce, *Lyra Britannica*, VI (1759).

(Facs. edn. Bruce *b*(1985)) This was advertised (*WEP*, 19-21 July) and
published with title-page: Numb: VI. | LYRA BRITANNICA. | *A
Collection of* | *ENGLISH SONGS* | AND CANTATAS | COMPOS'D BY |
DR BOYCE. [&c.] This is the only issue of LB that does not include a
copy of WB's Royal Licence to print music (1745) which had run out by
July 1759. The notice identified above also refers to the contents being
"New English songs . . . sung at the public gardens", though in keeping
with earlier issues of LB, this one also includes a cantata, *BC* 183. Its text
derives from an original Lapp, and later Latin, poem translated into
English and attributed to Ambrose Philips. It was finally published
anonymously in the *Spectator*, 30 April 1712, 366. There is also a
dialogue, *BC* 176 (anon.), and two songs originally composed for dramatic
productions: 'Plutus, vain is all your vaunting', extracted from a dialogue
in John Hawksworth's comedy, *Amphitryon* (based on a play by Dryden
first produced at DL on 15 Dec. 1756), and 'Does the languid soul
complain', from Richard Steele's comedy, *The Conscious Lovers*,
probably first performed at a production at CG on 12 March 1752 (*LS*, 4,
299). The independent songs included are: *BC* 205 (anon.), 216 (anon.),
239 (Gilbert Cooper), and 271 (anon.).

♣

From *Avis's Birmingham Gazette*, 1 October 1759

At the NEW THEATRE in BIRMINGHAM On Wednesday and Thursday
the 10th and 11th of October, WILL BE PERFORM'D THE ORATORIO
OF SOLOMON,[97] by Dr BOYCE Introduced by Mr. HANDEL's GRAND
CORONATION ANTHEM[98] And MILTON'S Celebrated *L'Allegro Il
Penseroso, ed il Moderato* Set to MUSICK by Mr. HANDEL. Between the
several ACTS will be A SOLO on the VIOLIN by Mr. PINTO A SOLO on
the BASSOON by Mr. MILLAR And a TRUMPET CONCERTO BY Mr.
ADCOCK. The principal VOCAL PARTS by Master CARPENTER,[99]
Messrs WASS PRICE MENCE SAVILLE BROWN, &c.&c.&c. After

---

[97] *Solomon* was sometimes assumed to be an oratorio rather than a serenata.

[98] 'Zadok the Priest'.

[99] This singer may have been Robert Carpenter, later an actor and singer, who
would then have been about 11.

each Night's Performance will be a BALL. No Pains or Expence will be spared to render the above Performance very compleat; many celebrated Performers from London, and the neighbouring Counties, are already engaged, so that the Performance will consist of an Organ, Kettle Drums, Trumpets, French Horns, Hautboys, four Bassoons, a Double Bass, four Violoncello's, four Tenors, sixteen Violins, a Harpsichord, six Solo Singers, and upwards of twenty-four Chorus Singers. As this Musical Entertainment will be greatly superior to any ever performed in this Country, so it will be attended with a far greater Expence than will be commonly imagined; wherefore, it's humbly hoped the Gentlemen and Ladies of this Town and Neighb[o]urhood, will heartily support it, which will be the only Means of procuring them so Noble a Performance another Year.

Shortly after these two performances it was reported: "The Musical Performance on Wednesday and Thursday last, at the New Theatre, met with the greatest Applause, from the most polite and brilliant Audiences that ever assembled there; to whom Mr. Hobbs begs Leave to return his Thanks for the Favours conferr'd on him, and shall think it his Duty to use his best Endeavours to entertain them another Year" (*ABG*, 15 Oct. 1759). While many 18th-century orchestras were undoubtedly modest in size compared with their modern counterparts, on the evidence of this notice, when circumstances were favourable to the creation of large ensembles, promoters and contemporary audiences were evidently far from averse to them. The vast forces later to be brought together for the Handel centenary concerts at Westminster Abbey in 1784 were clearly prefigured in these Birmingham concerts.

After the early public performances of *Solomon* at Ruckholt House and in London, the first performance outside the metropolis took place at Windsor in 1744. *Solomon* was subsequently done in the provinces at Hereford and Cambridge in 1749, Manchester in 1749 or earlier, Edinburgh in 1749 or later, Worcester in 1755, 1794 and 1797, Hereford again in 1756, at Bath in 1749 or earlier and in 1758, in Bristol (1759), Oxford in 1763, 1764 and *c*1790, and at Liverpool (1787).[100] Finally, more performances have recently come to light at Manchester in 1754 and 1755,[101] Edinburgh in 1757 and 1761,[102] York in 1769, and Sunderland and Durham in 1770.[103]

---

[100] For further details see MB 68 (1996), Appendix II, 183-5.

[101] See *HMM*, 13 Aug. 1754 and 25 March 1755 respectively.

[102] See Burchell(1996), 74.

[103] See Southey(2006), 132, 103 and 131 respectively.

♣

Boyce sets Whitehead's ode for the king's birthday 1759, 'Begin the song' (text in AR (1759), 'Characters', 448), organises a public rehearsal, and conducts its performance at court on 10 November.

♣

From the *Public Advertiser,* 31 December 1759

AT the Theatre Royal in Drury-Lane, This Day will be presented a Play call'd The LONDON MERCHANT;[104]. . . To which will be added HARLEQUIN'S INVASION A CHRISTMAS GAMBOL. After the Manner of the ITALIAN COMEDY. Harlequin by Mr. KING (Being the 1st Time of his appearing in that Character.) The other Characters by Mr. YATES . . . The Music composed by Dr. BOYCE. . . . The Songs will be printed and delivered at the Doors.

Not long before David Garrick produced his new pantomime, *Harlequin's Invasion* (based on an earlier pantomime, *Harlequin Student* (1741)), the British navy, under the command of admiral Edward Hawke, had inflicted a decisive defeat on the French at the battle of Quiberon Bay, off the coast of Britanny, on 20 November 1759. This victory in the course of the 'Seven Years' War' (1756-63), from which the French never recovered, takes its place among the most significant in the history of English naval warfare prior to the battle of Trafalgar in 1805. News of this event must have reached London in time for Garrick to write an appropriately stirring and patriotic song, 'Come cheer up my lads, 'tis to glory we steer' ('Heart of Oak').[105] Boyce set it in time for the opening night on 31 December, when it was inserted into the 3rd act. The song immediately made a great impact. It was published at least half-a-dozen times in the 1760s, and

---

[104] A tragedy (1731), subtitled *The History of George Barnwell*, by George Lille. It held the stage in the London theatres to the end of the century and beyond.

[105] The song is normally identified with reference to its refrain, 'Heart of oak are our ships, hearts of oak are our men', rather than its incipit, 'Come cheer up my lads'. The first phrase of the refrain clearly refers to the hardy nature of the wood used in the construction of the ships, while the second refers metaphorically to the resilience of the men of the navy. Strictly speaking then, the title of the song should be 'Heart of oak', but it became commonplace in Boyce's time and subsequently to call it, 'Hearts of oak'.

many times subsequently. Eventually, at the end of the 19th century, it achieved the status of a 'national song'. The contemporary response to this piece has been summed up by a modern historian who fails to acknowledge the indispensable role of Boyce in this matter: "Actor David Garrick thrilled London audiences with his recitation of his poem, 'Hearts of Oak', which became the Royal Navy's unofficial anthem" (Herman (2005), 290-91).

Harlequin's Invasion marked a turning-point in the development of English pantomime. Hitherto, the traditional clown-like figure of 'Harlequin' had been mimed, but Garrick now made him articulate. At the same time, his passion for Shakespeare became an integral part of a plot in which Harlequin invades Shakespeare's domain, 'Parnassus', though he is ultimately expelled from it. The work received 26 performances in its first season, and remained in the repertoire at DL until 1796. Boyce had also set two of the songs in the pantomime itself: in Act I, 'Sweetest bard that ever sung', which was "sung by Miss Young as one of the Muses to the Statue of Shakespeare",[106] and in Act III, 'Thrice happy the nation that Shakespeare has charm'd', for Mercury',[107] sung while the three Graces are dancing.

The singer, Samuel Champness, who sang 'Heart of Oak' on this occasion, gained a reputation for himself in the 1759-60 season at DL, not only for his performances of that number, but also of Boyce's 'Bacchanalian song', 'Rail no more ye learned asses' (see *BDA*, 3, 150). This characterisation of the song was confirmed when it was printed in a collection of song texts, *Polyhymnia* (1769), Song 146, with caption: "The Music . . . is set for a Bass Voice . . . in the 'Bacchanalian Stile'".

---

[106] Published in *Thalia, a Collection of Six Favourite Songs (Never before Published* (1767), pp.6-7, in a volume containing settings of six Garrick poems by various composers. This song was taken from WB's setting of Garrick's Ode, 'Arise, Immortal Shakespeare' (*c*1759).

[107] Published in a s.sh.f. (*c*1775), and in six other editions from 1760 onwards.

PART FOUR

LIFE AND CAREER, 1760-69

Boyce sets Whitehead's royal ode for New Year's Day 1760, 'Again the sun's revolving sphere', organises a public rehearsal, and conducts its performance at court.

Text in AR (1759), 'Characters', 225-7. The overture was edited by Finzi in MB 13 (1957).

♣

John Walsh publishes Boyce's *Eight Symphonys* (1760).

Title-page: EIGHT SYMPHONYS | *in Eight Parts.* | Six for Violins, Hoboys, or German Flutes. | *and* | Two for Violins, French Horns and Trumpets. | with a Bass for the | VIOLONCELLO and HARPSICHORD. | COMPOS'D BY | D^R. W^M BOYCE. | Opera Seconda. [&c.] Walsh advertised these symphonies in the press on the four days preceding their publication on 5 Jan. (see *GA*). It was common practice at this time, as in this case, to publish such music in parts rather than in score, on both practical and economic grounds.

Boyce lived in an age which had seen a gradual emergence of the modern independent symphony from its origins in the baroque, particularly the Italian operatic overture. By the 1760s the emergent concert symphony had become a well established genre throughout Europe. These symphonies of Boyce, however, reflect the past, since with one exception they originate in overtures written for choral or theatrical works in the previous 20 years. The overtures he drew on were as follows: for Symphony no. 1, that for the New Year Ode of 1756; for no. 2, the king's birthday ode for 1756; for no. 3, *The Chaplet* (1749); for no. 4, *The Shepherd's Lottery* (1751); for no. 5, the ode, 'See fam'd Apollo' (1739); for no. 6, *Solomon* (1742); for no. 7, the ode, 'Gentle lyre' (1740) and for no. 8 (the exception), an independent overture written for the Three Choirs Festival at Worcester.[1]

As is evident, Boyce did not order these works chronologically, but he divided them into two more or less homogeneous groups of four: the first modelled on the Italian style of overture in which the tempos of the three movements are ordered quick – slow – quick, and the second based on French baroque overture practice in which a slow introduction (often characterised by sharply dotted rhythms) is followed by a fugue and sometimes one or more dance movements.

These symphonies have become the best known and most widely appreciated works of Boyce in our own time.[2] They were first brought to public attention by Constant Lambert who arranged and published them (Oxford, 1928). Subsequently two critical editions have been issued, one by Goberman (Doblinger, 1964), and the other by Platt (Eulenburg, 1994). Furthermore, two modern British composers have paid tribute to Boyce and his symphonic music. In his score for a ballet with an 18th-century scenario, *The Prospect before us*, produced at Sadler's Wells Theatre in 1940, Lambert drew on music from the 2nd, 3rd, 4th, 5th and 7th of the Boyce symphonies.[3] In 1979, the bicentenary of Boyce's death, John McCabe was commissioned by the Royal Philharmonic Orchestra to write a work in honour of Boyce. He responded with a one-movement orchestral piece, *The Shadow of Light*, in which, amongst other things, he drew on themes from the 3rd, 5th and 7th symphonies.

Boyce also wrote four concerti grossi for strings, none of which was published in his life-time. Such works were particularly well suited to the activities of the numerous musical societies that flourished in 18th-century Britain. Three concertos are preserved in WB's hand at *Ob*,

---

[1] It has been suggested (see Abraham(1954), 215) that this work shows some affinities with Handel's Concerto Grosso op. 3, no. 2 (1734). This serves to indicate that Boyce may have written this piece (often called the 'Worcester Overture') at the time of his appointment as conductor at the Three Choirs in 1737, or shortly afterwards.

[2] The 1st symphony received perhaps the ultimate contemporary accolade when it was used as 'boarding music' by British Airways. Similarly, the gavotte finale of the 4th was once chosen by a captain of industry to keep him company during his lonely sojourn on BBC Radio's programme, 'Desert Island Discs'. All the symphonies are regularly performed and they have been recorded frequently (see Discography).

[3] For further details, see Cudworth(1958), 84-6. The ballet has been recorded on 'Tribute to Madame,' ASV Digital, WLS, 255. 2001.

MS.Mus.Sch.D.230[a], in Bb major,[4] D minor (incomplete), and E minor,[5] and one in B minor at *Lbl*, Add.MS.17836.[6]

♣

Dedication from a *Second Collection of Favourite English Songs* by Lewis Granom (*c*1760)

To D[r]. Boyce

Sir,

As a musical performance naturally requires the protection of a musical Patron, I could think of no one so proper to address this Publication to, as D[r]. Boyce, whose pleasing originality of Taste in Composition, claim a first place in the list of musical Authors of the present Age. It is no flattery to say, that his productions have this singular merit, to be truly, and strictly his own, whereas most of our modern Composers, either from a barrenness of invention or a want of due application, endeavour to build a Fame on compiling only from the works of others.[7] You will I hope excuse the freedom I here have taken, and consider it, as a sincere Testimonial of that friendship, and esteem, with which I am, Sir

Your very obedient and oblig'd humble Servant   Lew: C: A: Granom

Title-page: A Second Collection of | Favourite English SONGS, | With their Full Accompaniments. | COMPOSED BY | Lewis Christian Austin Granom Esq. | Opera XIII. | [Printer's ornament] | London; Printed for, & Sold by Thomas Bennett. [&c.] Boyce himself subscribed to this handsome and exceptionally successful publication which sold over 1,000 copies to more than 500 subscribers, among them the musicians Joseph Kelway, James Nares and John Beard, and numerous members of the aristocracy. Clearly, Granom was much in fashion at this time. Of the 40 songs included in this substantial edition, three are duets, and nine are taken from Granom's unpublished oratorio, 'The Prodigal Son'. All are

---

[4] Modern edns by Stevens (Heinrichsen, 1957) and Beechey (Eulenburg, 1973).

[5] Edn by Platt (Eulenburg, 1968).

[6] Edn by Stevens (Hinrichsen, 1953).

[7] Granom's testimony here is to be welcomed, for it is at variance with at least one contemporary implication to the contrary (see *BurneyH*, 3, 621).This subject is discussed further in the entry on WB's *Twelve Sonatas* (1747), and there has been a modern but still unsubstantiated suggestion that some of Boyce's anthems were "adaptations of Restoration compositions" (see Fellowes(1941), 185).

provided with accompaniments for string ensemble and basso continuo, with the addition of horns and flutes in a few cases.

♣

Boyce subscribes to Thomas Dupuis's *Six concertos for the organ or harpsichord* (1760).

Dupuis sang as a boy at the Chapel Royal in the early years of Boyce's career there. After Boyce's death in 1779 he was appointed organist and composer at the Chapel in his place. Prominent among the many leading musicians who appear among the 150 subscribers for 171 copies were Thomas Arne, William Hayes, Burney and Giardini.

♣

Boyce subscribes to William Felton's *Eight concertos for the organ or harpsichord,* op. 7 (1760).

Felton pursued his career in the provinces, but his works were widely performed, and Handel had subscribed to his *Six concertos*, op. 1 (1744). The only other leading musicians to appear in the list of 127 subscribers for this publication were Alcock, Beard and William Hayes.

♣

Boyce subscribes to Giorgio Antoniotto's *L'arte armonica or a treatise on the composition of musick*, 3 vols. (1760).

Boyce had been subscribing to the publication of musical works since 1739. This appears to have been the first, and indeed the only, occasion on which he invested in a contemporary theoretical work. Antoniotto had resided in London for about 20 years until the mid-1750s. This edition was a translation from the original Italian.

♣

Boyce subscribes to John Piper's *Life of Fanny Brown* (1760).

'John Piper' was a pseudonym for John Alcock, Boyce's friend and fellow chorister at St. Paul's in his youth. After holding posts as organist at various churches, Alcock had been appointed to Lichfield Cathedral in 1750. His temperament and outspokenness led to ongoing conflicts at the cathedral with both the clergy and the lay clerks. Alcock incorporated these polemical aspects of his personal life into the fabric of his novel, where he makes trenchant observations on the unsatisfactory musical conditions, questionable practices and slack moral standards then apparently prevalent in many provincial cathedrals. Boyce had already subscribed to a number of Alcock's earlier musical publications. On this occasion, apart from wishing to be supportive, he must have been more than a little curious, given his own wide experience of the church, to see how a musical colleague had treated such sensitive issues in a publicly available literary enterprise. In the event, WB is unlikely to have been disappointed, for the book is highly entertaining, rumbustious, and acute in its criticisms of contemporary social and ecclesiastical life. Word of the nature of the book's contents had probably spread in advance of publication, for it attracted 333 subscribers for 431 copies.

♣

The Preface to Boyce's *Cathedral Music,* vol. 1, 1760

My late worthy friend and master, Dr. MAURICE GREENE having designed to oblige the public with a correct collection of our old English Cathedral Music, I was induced to undertake this work from the general opinion of its extensive usefulness, and should the execution of it meet with a suitable encouragement from those for whom it is chiefly intended, my end will be fully answered.

The great and distinguished merit of our former Musical Writers has been universally allowed; but it has been also as universally complained of, that many gross errors have crept into their productions by the carelessness of copyists; my task therefore was to amend these errors, and to preserve their Music, as much as my ability would admit of, in its original purity. If I have not minutely executed this, I flatter myself no very capital inaccuracies will remain.

One advantage resulting from this publication, will be the conveying to our future composers for the church, these excellent specimens of what has hitherto been considered as the true style and standard of such compositions; and as this style in writing is at present but little studied, it is become necessary to publish some reputable models of it, lest it should be totally neglected and lost.

A further means of rendering this work still more useful would be for the superiors of our choirs in general to follow the laudable example some of them have set, by indulging their several choral members with these legible score-books to sing from: the reasons for the preference given to scores, rather than to single parts, for the use of performers, the late Dr. CROFT hath sufficiently explained in the preface before the printed anthems,[8] where he observes, "As to performers, every one who is but indifferently skilled in the art of singing, knows of what improving advantage it is, at one view, to see the disposition of the parts, and how they depend on one another, to observe the beauty of the composure, and to know upon the slightest view the exact point where every part takes place, either in observing the pauses or rests, or filling up the vacant spaces by joining properly in the harmony; and 'tis very obvious that their method of publishing music cannot but be most acceptable to the judicious and skilful, it being the only way whereby they can be capable at one view to find out the beauties, or discover the imperfections of any piece, which cannot in any wise be effected if the parts be kept separate".

I would just add this interesting remark, that as no person employed to copy church-music can afford to provide good paper, and write what is here contained in a page at the price these pages are sold for, which is less than seven farthings each, this must undoubtedly be the cheapest, and most eligible way of purchasing books for the above mentioned purpose.

Had my own profit been principally consulted, the work would not have received many of its present advantages; and if there should arise to me any further benefit than the reputation of perpetuating these valuable remains of my ingenious countrymen, it will be more than I expect.

WILLIAM BOYCE

The title-page of this handsome volume published in large folio is: Cathedral Music: | Being | *A COLLECTION in SCORE* | of the | *Most Valuable and Useful* Compositions | *FOR THAT SERVICE.* | By the | *Several English Masters of the last Two Hundred Years. The Whole Selected and Carefully Revised* | *By* DR WILLIAM BOYCE, | *Organist and Composer to the Royal Chapels, and* | *Master of his MAJESTY'S Band*

---

[8] The reference here is to Croft's *Musica Sacra, or Select Anthems in Score* (1724), in which he published 36 of his own anthems.

of Musicians. | VOLUME the FIRST | London: | Printed *for the* EDITOR. | M.DCC.LX.

Also included in the volume is an elaborate Dedication to George II, and biographical sketches of the composers represented in 'A succinct Account of the Several Authors'. *Cathedral Music* constitutes a significant landmark in the history of English church music, for it was the first historical collection of anthems and services to be published in full score. The impulse to undertake such a project was strong at this time in the circle of church musicians who had been influenced by Maurice Greene, Boyce's teacher at St. Paul's. The first manifestation of this occurred in 1752 when John Alcock, then Organist at Lichfield Cathedral, issued a notice: *"To all lovers of Cathedral Musick.* Having observed how incorrect the Services, &c. are at Cathedrals, and as I have now by me an exceeding valuable Collection of the choicest antient and modern Services, I propose publishing one every Quarter of a Year, completely in Score, and figured for the Organ". [&c.][9]

Not long afterwards an announcement appeared in the press indicating that Greene too was proposing to publish a similar collection; moreover, he indicated that he would give one or more copies *gratis* to all the cathedrals in England.[10] Greene had only been able to make this munificent offer as a result of the considerable wealth he had recently inherited. When Alcock heard of Greene's intentions he graciously withdrew his own project via an announcement in the press,[11] and generously passed on the materials he had collected in connection with his project to Greene. When the latter died in 1755, he left the whole of his library to Boyce who then of his own volition undertook the task of bringing the project to fruition.

It was not long before WB gave notice of "PROPOSALS *for* PRINTING, A CORRECT and COMPLETE BODY *of* CHURCH MUSIC". [&c.][12] Only four years later he had completed the 1st volume: "DR. BOYCE desires to inform his Friends, the Subscribers for the OLD CATHEDRAL MUSIC now publishing by him, that the First Volume is printing off, and will ready to deliver some Time in the ensuing Summer. This work, in which the best Compositions of our most reputable English Masters will be inserted, is to consist of three hundred Plates. The Price is

---

[9] *LEP*, 6-8 Aug. 1752. The complete notice is quoted in Johnstone *b*(1975), 29.

[10] See *LEP*, 7-10 April 1753. The announcement is reproduced in full in Johnstone, op. cit., 29-30.

[11] *LEP*, 29-31 March 1753.

[12] *WEP*, 23-5 Sept. 1756.

Six Guineas, to be paid at four equal Payments; the First at the time of subscribing, and the other three as the Volumes are delivered".[13] [&c.]

In the course of his researches for the purposes of *Cathedral Music* Boyce evidently visited Christ Church Oxford to inspect the extensive library of church music from the Renaissance period onwards collected by Henry Aldrich, formerly Dean of the College. While he was there WB compiled a 'Catalogue of Music', previously overlooked in studies of *Cathedral Music*.[14]

The national response to this labour of love on Boyce's part was bitterly disappointing to him, but nonetheless a true reflection of the general indifference to church music that prevailed at the time. Boyce dedicated his work to George II, but there were only 127 subscribers to the 1st volume who between them generated a total initial sale of 212 sets.[15] Notable among the initial list of subscribers were Burney and Hawkins, Alcock, Stanley, Nares, William Hayes and Overend, along with musicians and clerics from a range of Oxbridge Colleges, Cathedrals in England, Scotland and Ireland, as well as private individuals. There were few additional subscribers when the 2nd and 3rd volumes were published. When vol. 2 appeared in 1768 WB was clearly proud to place a new subscriber, 'THE KING' (now George III), at the head of the list. When the final volume appeared in 1773, WB had devoted 17 years to the project against a background of an already exceptionally busy professional life. The British public made at least partial amends for its initial failure fully to support Boyce's work when in 1788, nearly ten years after the composer's death, John Ashley published a 2nd edn of *Cathedral Music* which sold nearly 500 sets.

♣

[13] *PA*, 29 April 1760. For notice in full see Johnstone, ibid., 31. In modern currency the cost of the publication was *c*£900. Since the 3rd and last volume did not come out until 1773, the payments were eventually spread over at least 13 years. Undoubtedly, the cost must have been a deterrent to many potential individual subscribers, but that factor could not excuse the many Cathedral and Collegiate authorities who failed to support the project at its inception.
[14] *Och*, MS1200, 1. Philip Hayes wrote on a fly-leaf that he had found it among WB's papers after his death in 1779, and had arranged for it to be returned to the College.
[15] Preserved at Worcester Cathedral Library is a receipt (dated 28 July 1758) for a first payment of £11 & 6 pence (*c*£165 today) towards seven sets of *Cathedral Music* signed by the composer himself. A similar receipt for three sets signed by WB and dated 29 Sept. 1760 is at St. George's Chapel, Windsor (*WRch*, XVII.4.15).

Owing to the death of George II on 25 October 1760, no ode was required for the king's birthday this year.

♣

Boyce composes 'The souls of the righteous' for the funeral of George II on 11 November 1760.

The burial service took place in the Henry VII Chapel at Westminster. Though Boyce was now well established as Master of the King's Music, had Handel still been alive there can be little doubt that he would have been invited to write the anthem for the royal burial service on the basis of his extra-ordinary appointment as an additional 'Composer to the Chapel Royal'. This had been the case in 1737 for example, when the King's consort, Queen Caroline, had died. It was Handel rather than the incumbent Master of the King's Music, Maurice Greene, who was asked to provide the funeral anthem. This was Boyce's first major undertaking for the Royal Family apart from his regular duty to compose the bi-annual court odes.

Some idea of the background to the arrangements for the funeral may be gleaned from the following entry in the *New Cheque Book* of the Chapel Royal: "The 25th: October 1760 (between 7 and 8 o'clock in the morning) His Majesty King George the Second departed this life, at Kensington Palace. Prayers was continued (by the Household Chaplain) till the royal body was removed, which was on the 10th: November (in the evening) to the Princes Chamber. None of the Priests, Gentlemen, or Officers of the Vestry, had any orders to attend the funeral (as members of His Majesty's Chapel Royal) nor were they allowed to take any surplices out of the Chapel, except the boys who attended, at the request of the Master of the Band of Music (D[r]: Boyce) to the Master of the Children (D[r]: Nares) who was also answerable for the safety of the surplices. And D[r] Boyce sent a note and a messenger for the surplices, before the Serjeant wou'd let them be taken out of the Chapel. The officers of the Vestry had their travelling charges continued to and for the 10th: day of November, as they attended the whole time at Kensington [or] by their deputy's till the removal of the royal corpse. Notwithstanding his present Majesty[16] was at S[t]. James's Chapel on Sunday the 2[d]: November 1760" (*Lcr*, NCB, 155).[17]

---

[16] George III.
[17] Transcribed in Ashbey & Harley(2000), vol. 1, 318.

The circumstances of the composition of the anthem were recorded by Boyce himself in his autogr. score: "Note, Began this Anthem on Friday, Oct: 31st, 1760. Rehears'd it at Hickford's Room the Friday following" (*Ob*, MS.Mus.Sch.C.115a)). The original vocal and instrumental parts also survive with the score. They indicate that the work was performed by *c*31 singers accompanied by an orchestra of *c*33, which includes trumpets, horns, oboes, bassoons, strings and organ. A beautifully written score in another hand, but with the verbal text and other annotations by WB, is also preserved at *Lbl*, Egerton MS.2964. The words were published in *GM*, 30, (1760), 621. The anthem is known to have entered the repertoire of the Academy of Ancient Music.[18]

The instrumental 'Symphony' that introduces the first chorus was included by Finzi in MB 13 (1957), and the whole work was edited by J.R. Van Nice in 'Two Anthems for the Georgian Court', A-R Editions (1970).

♣

From a letter of Horace Walpole to George Montagu

Arlington Street
Nov. 13, 1760

Do you know, I had the curiosity to go to the burying t'other night; I had never seen a royal funeral,[19] nay, I walked as a rag of quality,[20] which I found would be, & so it was, the easiest way of seeing it. It is absolutely a noble sight. The Prince's Chamber,[21] hung with purple, & a quantity of silver lamps, the coffin under a canopy of purple velvet, & six vast chandeliers of silver on high stands had a very good effect. The Ambassador from Tripoli & his son were carried to see that chamber. The procession thro a line of footguards, every seventh man bearing a torch, the horse-guards lining the outside, their officers with drawn sabres & crape sashes, on horseback, the drums muffled, the fifes, bells tolling, & minute guns, all this was very solemn. But the charm was the entrance of the Abbey, where we were received by the Dean & Chapter in rich copes, the choir & almsmen all bearing torches; the whole Abbey so illuminated, that one saw it to greater advantage than by day; the tombs, long aisles, & fretted

---

[18] See Academy(1768), 63.

[19] George II's funeral, for which Boyce composed the anthem.

[20] The younger son of an Earl.

[21] Situated near the House of Peers.

roof, all appearing distinctly, & with the happiest chiaro scuro.[22] There wanted nothing but incence, & little chapels here & there with priests saying mass for the repose of the defunct — yet one could not complain of its not being catholic enough. I had been in dread of being coupled with some boy of ten years old — but the heralds were not very accurate, & I walked with George Grenville,[23] taller & older enough to keep me in countenance. When we came to the chapel of Henry 7th all solemnity & decorum ceased — no order was observed, people sat or stood where they coud or woud, the yeomen of the guard were crying out for help, oppressed by the immense weight of the coffin, the Bishop read sadly, & blundered in the prayers, the fine chapter, *Man that is born of a woman*,[24] was chanted not read, & the anthem,[25] besides being unmeasurably tedious, would have served as well for a nuptial. The real serious part was the figure of the Duke of Cumberland,[26] heightened by a thousand melancholy circumstances. He had a dark brown adonis,[27] & a cloak of black cloth with a train of five yards. Attending the funeral of a father, how little reason so ever he had to love him, could not be pleasant. His leg extremely bad, yet forced to stand upon it near two hours, his face bloated & distorted with his late paralytic stroke, which has affected too one of his eyes, & placed over the mouth of the vault, into which in all probability he must himself so soon descend — think how unpleasant a situation! He

---

[22] Black and white.

[23] A fellow politician of Walpole's who became Prime Minister in 1763-65.

[24] Job, XIV, i.

[25] Boyce's 'The Souls of the Righteous', a large-scale orchestrally-accompanied anthem. As a whole this letter is characteristic of its author's acute, witty and often acerbic observations on English society and art in his time. It also exemplifies his penchant for the character assassination of public figures, a personal trait that earned him notoriety. As to his curt dismissal of Boyce's anthem here, Walpole may be entitled to the view that it is not as vivid or as fully characterised as he might have wished, nor as masterful as Handel's funeral anthem for Queen Caroline in 1737, for example, but his likening of the work to a wedding anthem smacks of hyperbole. To illustrate the point, this anthem needs only to be compared with WB's 'The King shall rejoice' (*BC*, 34), written the following year for the wedding of George III.

[26] William, second surviving son of George II. Following the defeat by the French of the British army under William's command at the battle of Hastenbeck in June 1757 during the Seven Years' War, and his subsequent giving up of Hanover to the French at the convention of Kloster Zeven in September, he felt obliged to resign. The King said of him: "Here is my son, who has ruined me and disgraced himself!"

[27] A kind of wig.

bore it all with a firm & unaffected countenance. This grave scene was fully constrasted by the burlesque Duke of Newcastle[28] — he fell into a fit of crying the moment he came into the chapel, & flung himself back in a stall, the Archbishop hovering over him with a smelling bottle — but in two minutes his curiosity got the better of his hypocrisy & he ran about the chapel with his glass to spy who was or was not there, spying with one hand, & mopping his eyes with tother. Then returned the fear of catching cold, & the Duke of Cumberland, who was sinking with heat, felt himself weighed down, & turning round, found it was the Duke of Newcastle standing upon his train to avoid the chill of the marble. It was very theatric to look down into the vault, where the coffin lay, attended by mourners with lights. Clavering the groom of the bedchamber, refused to sit up with the body, & was dismissed by the King's order.

I have nothing more to tell you, but a very trifle, the King of Prussia[29] has totally defeated Marshal Daun.[30] This which would have been prodigious news a month ago, is nothing today; it only takes its turn among the questions, 'Who is to be groom of the bedchamber?' 'What is Sir T. Robinson[31] to have?' I have been to Leicester fields[32] to-day; the crowd was immoderate; I dont believe it will continue so. Good night.

$$Y^{rs} \text{ ever,} \qquad \text{H. W.}$$

Lbl, Add.MS70987, f. 242[r]–244[v]. (Lewis(1941), 9, 320-23) Montagu, a member of a well established aristocratic family who served as an MP for Northampton in the 1740s, had been a contemporary of Walpole's at Eton. Their life-long friendship thrived on common political interests and the acute sense of humour they shared. They maintained a regular correspondence from 1736-70.

♣

---

[28] Thomas Pelham Holles, a leading politician of the time, and Prime Minister from 1754-6.

[29] Friedrich II, 'Frederick the Great'.

[30] The Austrian Field Marshall had been defeated at Torgan in Saxony on 3 November.

[31] Probably Thomas Robinson, a rather unsuccessful politician.

[32] A popular area for public congregation, now Leicester Square.

Boyce's hymn,'Coulsden', is included in *A small Collection of Psalms* (1761).

Title-page: *A small Collection* | of | Psalms | To the Old Tunes, | s*ung* | *By the* Charity Children | of | *The City of Chichester.* Published | for General Use. | Printed by W. Faden (London, 1761). The text to the hymn, 'When rising from the bed of death', p.xxxviii, was first published without attribution in the *Spectator,* Vol. 7, No. 513, 18 Oct. 1712, 212-13.[33] It forms part of a letter entitled 'Thought in Sickness' submitted by an "excellent man in Holy Orders".

♣

Boyce sets Whitehead's royal ode for New Year's Day 'Still must the muse' (text in AR (1760), 'Characters', 218-20), organises a public rehearsal, and conducts its performance at court.

♣

Boyce subscribes to John Jones's *Lessons for the Harpsichord*, 2 vols. (1761).

Jones had succeeded Boyce's teacher, Greene, as organist of St. Paul's Cathedral in 1755. These technically demanding, Scarlatti-influenced works attracted nearly 300 subscribers.

♣

Boyce sets Whitehead's ode for the birthday of George III in 1761,'Twas at the nectar'd feast of Jove', organises a public rehearsal, and conducts its performance at court on 4 June.

Text in AR (1761), 'Characters', 220-1. WB published the overture to this work in *Twelve Overtures*, no. 8 (1770).

---

[33] In Faden's edition the page number is erroneously given as '151'.

♣

From *Jackson's Oxford Journal*, 15 August 1761

WORCESTER. August 13, 1761

THE MEETING of the Three CHOIRS will be held on *Wednesday* the 2d, *Thursday* the 3d, and *Friday* the 4th of September next. On *Wednesday* Morning the 2d, will be performed in the Cathedral Church, Mr PURCELL's *Te Deum* and *Jubilate* with Dr. BOYCE's Improvements, *Praise the Lord ye Servants*, a new Anthem, and Mr. HANDEL's Coronation Anthem. [&c.]

Boyce's Purcell arrangement had been regularly performed at the Three Choirs from at least 1755. The Handel work would have been 'Zadok the Priest'. Handel appears never to have set the words of the 'new anthem'. On the other hand, Boyce did compose an anthem to this text. The only other known setting of it from the period was by Blow (*d.* 1708) – hardly a recent work. The reference seems likely therefore to be to WB's setting. If it is, this notice serves to provide an approximate date for its composition not available from other sources. It should be noted here that anthems included in the repertoire at the Three Choirs were invariably orchestrally accompanied, and Boyce's 'Praise the Lord' (like Blow's), originally had an accompaniment for organ only. It was, however, by no means unknown in England at this time for anthems composed with organ accompaniment to be subsequently arranged for orchestral forces when they were available.

♣

Boyce composes 'The King shall rejoice', for the wedding of George III (8 September, 1761).

The marriage of the King to Princess Charlotte of Mecklebug-Strelitz was solemnized by the Archbishop of Canterbury, Thomas Secker. Two rehearsals of Boyce's anthem took place. The first was at Hickford's Room on 24 August.[34] The second was reported: "Yesterday the Anthem for His Majesty's Wedding was rehearsed in the Chapel Royal before many Persons of Distinction" (*PA*, 8 Sept.). The autogr. score of this orchestrally accompanied work was inscribed by Boyce: "An Anthem Performed on

---

[34] See *LM* 2, August 1761, 446. This account quotes the complete text of the anthem and the names of the soloists who took part.

the occasion of His Majesty King George the Third his Wedding with his Queen Charlotte, in the Royal Chapel at St. James's on Tuesday Sep[r] 8th, 1761" (*Ob*, MSMus.Sch.C.117[a]).[35] In fact, however, the ceremony took place at the 'German Chapel', i.e. Queen's Chapel, Marlborough Gate.[36]

On 12 August Dr. Secker had written to his Subdean:"Yesterday D[r] Boyce brought me the words of the wedding anthem by your direction which I presume you gave him in order to know my opinion of them. I think them very good: and do not see that any alteration is necessary. Yet, if it be not too late, I would propose to your consideration what follows". Secker goes on to propose reasoned changes to six of the verses Boyce had chosen, or been asked to set. Nevertheless his concluding paragraph reads: "If there be time, you will consider, whether any of these changes be improvements. If there be not, you will lay aside the thoughts of them".[37] The Archbishop was famed for his assiduous attention to duty, sometimes to the point of excess. We cannot be entirely certain whether or not WB had already started work on setting the anthem at this point, but the composer's response is clear from a letter the Archbishop sent him two days later: "These things, it is hoped, will not increase Dr Boyce's difficulties. As he hath represented, that the proposed alterations in the Wedding Anthem would, they are withdrawn & laid aside by his sincere friend".[38]

The scene at the wedding was described by Garter King of Arms: "Over the altar were the organ, and gallery for the the music and choir, the lower part of the walls being hung with crimson velvet, the upper part with tapestry, the floor covered with cloth, and the canopy of crimson velvet, and the Haut Pas[39] before the altar with silver tissue. The King and Queen sat under a canopy of crimson velvet laced and fringed with gold, and lined with silver tissue".[40]

The original vocal and instrumental parts are preserved with WB's score. They indicate that there was an orchestra of at least 30 players and a choir of about 20 (with one singer to a part). The anthem has been edited by J.R. Van Nice (A-R Editions, 1970).

♣

---

[35] For a full account of the background to this anthem (*BC* 35) and the nature of the work itself, see Range *b*(2006), 59-66.

[36] See Baldwin(1990), 81.

[37] Letter in Secker's hand but unsigned at *Llp*, MS.1130/1(35), ff. 75-6.

[38] *Llp*, MS.1130, vol. 1, 38. Quoted in Range, op. cit., 60.

[39] The high step.

[40] Quoted in Sheppard(1894), 2, 81.

From the *Public Advertiser,* 14 September 1761

Last Friday ended the Entertainment of the Spring Gardens, Vauxhall, when was performed to a crowded Audience, and with just Applause, by several Gentlemen of the King's Chapel, and Mr. Tyers's[41] vocal Performers, Dr. Boyce's Anthem, for the Nuptual's of their Majesties.[42] After the Anthem followed Mr. Lockman's Song (See Royal Charlotte come!) on the happy Arrival of the Queen,[43] sung by Mr. Lowe, the Gentlemen of the Chapel joining in the Chorus.[44]

♣

Boyce composes eight anthems for the Coronation of George III (Aug./Sept. 1761).

If Boyce's involvement with the ceremony connected with the Installation of the Duke of Newcastle as Chancellor of Cambridge University, and the musical performances related to the award of his Doctorate there in July 1749 represented a highpoint in his career, they have to take second place behind the contributions he made to the Coronation of the King on 22 September 1761. Undoubtedly, this was the culmination of his career. In undertaking the duties he did, he was fortunate to be able to collaborate closely with the then Archbishop of Canterbury, Dr. Thomas Secker, who was remarkably sedulous in carrying out his duties in that role. As one of his biographers has observed, "It was quite in accord with Secker's tastes that he should take a leading part in searching the precedent and settling the proper ceremonial to be followed at the King's coronation" (Rowden(1916), 278).

Some of the correspondence between the two men concerning preparations for the ceremony has survived. In a letter to Boyce of 14 August, unsigned and not in his own hand, (*Llp,* MS.1130/1(38), f. 80), Secker writes:

---

[41] The proprietor of Vauxhall Gardens from its inception in 1732.

[42] 'The King shall rejoice' (*BC* 34), sung at the royal wedding on 8 Sept..

[43] Charlotte, consort of George III.

[44] Lockman's text was set to the melody of the 'national anthem' as presented by Thomas Arne in his arrangement of 'God save the King' for Drury Lane Theatre in September 1745, which was warmly received. Lockman's song was published in a supplement to the *Universal Magazine of Knowledge and Pleasure,* XXIX, Dec. 1761, 381-2.

In the Coronation Service, the first anthem must not be omitted: for it will enliven the procession, and the service will not be longer for it. The fuller it is, and the more exactly it takes up the time of the Kings walking through the church the better.

His Majesty hath signified his pleasure, that the 4th anthem, *Zadok the Priest*, should be performed as it was set for the last Coronation: and that the other anthem should be as short, & have as little repetition in [it][45] as conveniently maybe.

In the 6th anthem,[46] the words, For kings shall be thy missing father, & queens thy missing mother, were peculiarly proper at the Revolution, when they were first used because the King and Queen were both sovereigns, & both were crowned together. They were not so suitable to the Coronation of Geo. 1 when there was no queen, or even of Geo. 2 when there was only a Queen Consort, whose coronation was not to begin till the King's was over and in whose Coronation these words come very silly; and for that reason amongst others, are better omitted before. It hath therefore been proposed, that the following words should be used instead of them: Behold a thing shall reign in righteousness: & princes shall rule in judgement. Is[aiah]. XXXII. 1. And his Majesty hath approved this alteration.

It seems requisite that the 6th anthem, since it follows immediately the principal act of the day, setting on the crown, should be accompanied with the other instruments, as well as the organ. And it needs not be much, if at all, the longer for that.[47]

These things, it is hoped, will not increase D[r] Boyce's difficulties. As he hath represented, that the proposed alterations in the wedding anthem would,[48] they are withdrawn & laid aside by

His sincere friend
Lambeth, Aug. 14. 1761

---

[45] 'them' in the original.

[46] 'Praise the Lord, O Jerusalem'.

[47] In the event, WB limited this anthem to three-and-a-half minutes.

[48] Boyce must have been under immense pressure at this time given that, apart from anything else, he was expected to compose eight new anthems. He made just one short cut. This involved using the opening chorus of the recently composed Royal Wedding anthem, 'The King shall rejoice', for one of the Coronation anthems. At the same time, he replaced the intimate solo items apt for a wedding, and the final chorus of the original anthem, with two new and imposing choral movements to different words. WB may well have finished the new version before he was confronted with the proposed amendments to words he had already set.

Boyce responded shortly afterwards to this letter of Secker's, (see *Llp*, MS1130/1(40)):

My very good Lord

I have received the honour of your commands, in relation to *Zadok* [,] the sixth anthem[49] and the length of the others, which orders, I will most punctually obey. Those anthems with the organ only, shall be as short as possible, and those with the other instruments as much so, as is consistent with the grandeurs of the solemnity; but were the words of these last to be run through without some repetition, the performance would appear rather mean than grand. When I have finished the Anthems, I will inform your Grace of the exact time each of them will require in the performance. [in *Llp* MS1130/1(77). See 'Catalogue of Works', Anthems, pp.293-5.] Your Lordship has greatly favoured me by with-drawing the proposed alterations for wedding anthem.

I most humbly propose it to your Grace, to give directions to the Dean & Chapter of Westminster that a proper Space may be reserved in the Isles, for the choir to perform the first anthem, otherwise, I am apprehensive, that the scaffolding to be erected within the Abbey, will be a great hindrance to the performers appointed for this particular occasion.

I am, with the most profound respect your
Grace's most dutiful humble servant
Monday Augst. 17th
William Boyce

My servant will wait to receive any orders your Grace may have for me.

Boyce later elaborated on the concern expressed in his last paragraph in a letter to the Lord Chamberlain: "Dr. Boyce most humbly begs leave to represent to his Grace the Lord Chamberlain, that the upper part of the A[l]tar at Westminster Abbey, as it now stands, will be in the middle of the gallery appointed for the music, which renders it impossible for the musicians to join in the performances as they ought to do, and will entirely spoil the composition.

The first grand musical performance in the Abbey, was at the Coronation of George the Second, and the late Mr. Handel, who composed the music, often lamented his not having that part of the Altar taken away, as he, and all the musicians concerned, expressed the bad effect it had by that obstruction. The D[ean] has been informed by the workmen in that

---

[49] The absence of a comma after '*Zadok*' (the 4th anthem) in WB's MS, suggests some confusion here, but the inserted comma removes the ambiguity.

brand of business, that it may be taken down & replaced at a small expence, and without damage to the work". (*Lpro*, LC2/32; quoted in Burrows(2005), 272-3). It should be observed here that WB himself may have been a participant in the 1727 Coronation for he could then have still been a chorister in the St. Paul's Choir.

In a note that may have been an addendum to his letter to Secker of 17 August, Boyce writes:

"All the anthems to be performed as directed. The second – fourth – eighth, & ninth[50] – to be set for voices & instruments – all the other anthems with the Te Deum, to be sung with voices alone accompanied with the organ.

The four anthems, for the voices & instruments, will be considerably the longest: those for the voices alone will be very short.

Note, the anthem *Zadok the Priest* cannot be more properly set than it has already been by M[r]. Handel.[51]

Note, at the sacrament, his Grace the Arch-bishop begins the Sentence of "Therefore with angels and arch-angels, and with all the company of heaven, we laud & magnify thy glorious name, evermore praising thee, and saying," — so far the Arch-bishop reads, then the choir begins, and sings Holy, holy, holy &c." (*Llp*, MS1130/1(66).

Finally, it is clear from a note in WB's hand dated 21 Sept. that he and the Archbishop were communicating with each other on details right up to the last minute: "D[r]. Boyce presents his most humble duty to his Grace, and shall be glad to know his pleasure concerning the Responses to the Ten Commandments, as likewise the Response after naming the Gospel, viz: *Glory be to God on high*, if his Grace would have these Responses sung by the choir accompanied by the organ?" (*Llp*, MS1130/1(65)

♣

---

[50] WB intended to refer here to the four anthems with orchestral accompaniment he was composing. He undoubtedly meant to cite here his anthem 'Praise the Lord O Jerusalem', no. 6, rather than 'Zadok', no. 4. Such slips may well have been symptomatic of the stress he must have been feeling at this time.

[51] Due to a misunderstanding on his part, Boyce originally thought he would be required to set the words of 'Zadok the Priest' for the Coronation. Having set his face against such an idea and consulted Secker, it was readily agreed by both parties that Boyce would set another text, and that Handel's inimitable anthem would be included in the programme as well (see Secker in *Llp*, MS1130/1, (81), p.4). Since then 'Zadok' has retained its place in every subsequent English Coronation ceremony.

Boyce directs the Music for the Coronation of George III (1761).

After about six weeks of intensive creative work on Boyce's part, and thorough research and planning by Archbishop Secker and his assistants, the Coronation took place at Westminster Abbey on September 22nd. A full rehearsal of the music to be performed took place at the Abbey at 11a.m. on the 19th to which members of the public were admitted by ticket (*PA*, 18 Sept.). A report of the event appeared in the press shortly afterwards: "The whole was judged to be the best composition as has been hitherto produced, and the execution of it by the performers so extremely just, as to merit that great applause which was universally expressed by the audience" (*Public Ledger*, 22 Sept.). After the Coronation itself, an assessment of the musical aspect of the ceremony was published: "The Anthems at the Coronation on Tuesday last were performed with the utmost Grandeur by upwards of three hundred Hands and Voices. The number of fine anthems was composed by Dr. Boyce, who very modestly introduced the inimitable Coronation Anthem ['Zadok the Priest'] composed by the late celebrated Handel". . . (*LEP*, 24 Sept.).

The very long and elaborate ceremony began with the singing of Boyce's anthem, 'I was glad' (with organ), while the King and his consort made their entrance to the Abbey. After the Recognition and the presentation of the King to his people by the Archbishop, 'The King shall rejoice' (*BC* 35) was performed with orchestral accompaniment The opening of the Communion Service, followed by the Sermon and a Declaration and Oath by the King, led to the anthem, 'Come, Holy Ghost' (with organ), before the Anointing of the King took place. Handel's orchestrally accompanied 'Zadok' then took its place in the scheme of things, and after some prayers, Boyce's 'Behold, O God our defender' (with organ).[52] After more ceremonial leading to the crowning of the King, the anthem, 'Praise the Lord, O Jerusalem' (with orchestra), was sung. Following the Benediction, the 'Te Deum' was sung to a setting by WB (*BC* 2). The enthronement of the King took place and led to a celebratory anthem with orchestra, 'The Lord is a sun and shield'. The Queen was then crowned and 'My heart is inditing' (with orchestra) was performed. In contrast to the pomp and circumstance of much of the earlier proceedings,

---

[52] Boyce seems to have judiciously, and also to good effect, placed the shortest and most modest of his anthems immediately after 'Zadok' in order to avoid an immediate juxtaposition of Handel's towering masterpiece with one of his own orchestrally accompanied anthems.

the service concluded with the taking of communion, and the singing of the final anthem, the ethereal 'Let my prayer come up', accompanied by the organ.[53]

Boyce's autogr. scores of the anthems for the Coronation are preserved at *Ob*, MSS.Mus.c. 11-12, along with the original vocal and instrumental parts. 'I was glad' has been edited by Bruce (Novello, 1979), and three of the orchestrally accompanied anthems, and one of those with organ, have been recorded (see Discography).

♣

An account of the Coronation of George III from the memoirs of William Hickey

The coronation of His present Majesty being fixed for the month of September, my father determined that all of his family should be present at the ceremony. He therefore engaged one of the nunneries as they are called, in Westminster Abbey for which he paid fifty guineas.[54] They are situated at the head of the great columns that support the roof, and command an admirable view of the whole interior of the building. Upon this occasion they were divided off by wooden partitions, each having a separate entrance with lock and key to the door, with each holding a dozen persons. Provisions, consisting of cold fowls, ham, tongues, different meat pies, wines and liquors of various sorts were sent in to the apartment the day before, and two servants were allowed to attend. Our party consisted of my father, mother, brother Joseph, sister Mary, myself, Mr. and Miss Isaacs, Miss Thomas, her brother (all Irish), my uncle and Aunt Boulton, and their eldest daughter. We all supped together in St. Albans Street on 21st September, and at midnight set off in my father's coach and my uncle's and Miss Thomas's chariot. At the end of Pall Mall the different lines of carriages, nearly filling the street, our progress was consequently tedious; yet the time was beguiled by the grandeur of the scene; such a multitude of carriages, with servants behind carrying flambeauxs, made a blaze of light equal to day, and had a fine effect.

Opposite the Horse Guards we were stopped exactly one hour without moving onward a single inch. As we approached near the Abbey, the difficulties increased, from mistakes of the coachmen, some of whom were going to the Hall, others to the Abbey, and getting into the wrong

---

[53] A detailed and comprehensive 'Order of Service' was printed, see *Llp*, 1083a.

[54] *c*£8,000 in today's money.

ranks. This created much confusion and running against each other, whereby glasses and panels were demolished without number, the noise of which, accompanied by the screeches of the terrified ladies, was at times truly terrific. It was past seven in the morning before we reached the Abbey, which having once entered, we proceeded to our box without further impediment, Dr. Markham having given us tickets which allowed our passing by a private staircase, and avoiding the immense crowd that was within. We found a hot and comfortable breakfast ready, which I enjoyed, and proved highly refreshing to us all; after which some of our party determined to take a nap in their chairs, whilst I, who was well acquainted with every creek and corner of the Abbey, amused myself running about the long gallery until noon, when notice being given that the procession had begun to move, I resumed my seat.

Exactly at one they entered the Abbey, and we had a capital view of the whole ceremony. Their Majesties, (the King having previously arrived), being crowned, the Archbishop of Canterbury.[55] mounted the pulpit to deliver the sermon; and, as many thousands were out of the possibility of hearing a single syllable, they took that opportunity to eat their meal when the general clattering of knives, forks, plates, and glasses that ensued, produced a most ridiculous effect, and a universal burst of laughter followed. The sermon being concluded, the anthem was sung by a numerous band of the first performers in the kingdom, and certainly was the finest thing I had ever heard.[56]

Thus I found myself in the very best place in the [Westminster] Hall, and within a few yards of their Majesties. I afterwards learned that this situation belonged to the Duke of Queensbury,[57] in right of some official post he held, they who occupied it being relations and friends of the Duchess. We were supplied abundantly with every kind of refreshment. Sitting perfectly at my ease, I saw the dinner, the ceremony of the champion, and every particular, and was at a loss to decide which I thought the most magnificent, the Abbey scene, or that of the Hall. About ten at night the whole was over, and I got home as fast as the crowd would

---

[55] Dr. Thomas Secker.

[56] Boyce wrote eight anthems for the Coronation, four of them with orchestra, but Handel's 'Zadok the priest' was also performed. It would be nice to think that Hickey may have been impressed as he evidently was by one of WB's anthems, but it must, inevitably, have been 'Zadok'. The anthem immediately following the sermon was 'Come Holy Ghost', a modest setting without orchestra, but 'Zadok' came next. The latter must indeed have been the one that made the greatest impact on Hickey.

[57] Charles Douglas, 3rd Duke of Queensberry [sic].

permit, highly delighted at all I had seen, but excessively fatigued, not having had any sleep the preceding night, and having been so actively employed the whole day. [&c.]

(Quenell(1960), 33-34) This account represents very much an unofficial, and highly personal view of the proceedings. Hickey was only about twelve years of age at the time of the Coronation, but his vivid and uninhibited diaries were not written up until 1808-9.

♣

Boyce sets Whitehead's royal ode for New Year's Day 1762, 'God of slaughter', arranges a public rehearsal, and conducts its performance at court.

Text in AR (1761), 'Characters', 215-16. WB published the overture to this ode in *Twelve Overtures,* no. 5 (1770).

♣

From the *Dublin Journal,* 19-22 January 1762

At the THEATRE ROYAL in CROW-STREET . . . ON Monday next [25th][58] will be presented a new English Burletta, called, MIDAS. The principal Characters by Mr. VERNON, Mr. CORRY Mr. MAHON . . . With new Dances and Decorations. The Prologue to be spoke by Mr. WOODWARD. Not acted this Season.

The libretto, commissioned by Lord Mornington, was by Kane O'Hara. Inspired by the burlesque comic operas (burlettas) performed by visiting Italian opera companies in Dublin during the 1750s, *Midas* was first performed privately at Lurgan, near Belfast, in 1760 (see Fiske(1986), 318-21). A mainly pastiche opera utilising British and French folk songs as well as contemporary airs, it was first conceived as a full-length opera and presented in that form when it was publicly performed in Dublin in 1762. It achieved considerable and long-lasting popularity when it was revived in 1764 as a two-act afterpiece. In its new guise it also came to London at Covent Garden in the same year (22 Feb. 1764), when it was enhanced by the addition of 'grand ballets' at the end of each act. *Midas*

---

[58] In Fiske(1986), 319, and NG2, 4, 160, the date is inadvertently given as 22 January.

subsequently remained in the repertoire at one or other of the London theatres well into the 19th century. A vocal score, incorporating all the material of the full-length version, was published by John Walsh in 1764 with title-page: MIDAS | A COMIC OPERA | *As it is perform'd at the* THEATRE ROYAL | In COVENT-GARDEN. [&c.] In Act I, p.11, the air, 'With fun my disgrace I'll parry', borrows the tune of 'Declare, my pretty maid' from Boyce's *The Chaplet* (1749).[59] The air in Act II, p.44, 'When fairies dance round on the grass', takes its tune (and some of the words as well) from the opening solo in the duet, 'When fairies dance', which concludes Part I of *The Shepherd's Lottery* (1751). In Act III, the rondo theme in the concluding dance (pp.66-7), is derived from the melody of the air, 'Dunce, I did but sham', from Part I of *The Chaplet.*

♣

From R.J.S. Stevens's unpublished *Recollections* (1802-1837)

When a young man, he [Jonathan Battishill] was for some time Deputy Organist for Dr. Boyce at the Chapel Royal. Being desirous for obtaining the approbation of this *great master,* he one day took a composition to Dr. Boyce, requesting his opinion upon it? Dr. Boyce was at first rather shy in criticizing it, but Battishill having waited upon him for the express purpose, Dr. Boyce at length looked at it with great attention, and corrected it in various places, at the same time giving him his reasons for such corrections. This afforded Battishill great satisfaction, as he justly inferred from the Doctor's taking the trouble to correct his compositions, that he must see merit in it, and be well inclined towards him. Boyce who was no doubt pleased in observing the genius of the young musician, returned him his composition with high commendations. Dr. Boyce then said to him, "Young man, will you have a glass of mountain wine?" - a common refreshment in the morning at this time. Battishill having readily accepted Dr. Boyce's offer, drank a glass of mountain: he then helped *himself* to a second glass, which Boyce thought rather extraordinary. He however said to him, "Young man, you had better eat some buiscuit with your wine" (and produced buiscuits). He began with the buiscuits, and in a short time had actually drunk up the whole quart of wine, and ate all the

---

[59] Fiske (op. cit., 608) refers to this song as 'Hang me if I'll marry'. This is in fact the last line of the first stanza in this strophic air, which is used as a memorable refrain in later verses.

buiscuits, tho' it was not later than one o'clock, at noon. Dr. Boyce would never speak to him. "By this one silly act", said Battishill, "I forfeited the esteem of the only man in the musical profession, whose friendship I had laboured for years to gain, and with whom I had assiduously endeavoured to be intimate. I never recovered the disappointment I experienced in consequence of this foolish action to the end of my life". This anecdote I had from Samuel Wesley, Battishill having told him the story.

(Trend(1932), 266) Battishill is known to have deputised for Boyce as an organist at the Chapel Royal for some years during his early career. WB had played a subsidiary role as an organist at the Chapel from the time of his initial appointment as a 'Composer to the Chapel Royal' in 1736. It seems probable, however, that Battishill assisted him during the period immediately following WB's formal appointment in June 1758 to one of the three posts of 'Organist to the Chapel Royal', when the former was in his early twenties.

♣

John Potter on Boyce: from his *Observations on the Present State of Music and Musicians* (1762)

I

Had the great Handel, Dr. *Boyce*, and several other ingenious professors, pursued things in that careless, negligent, superficial manner, which some of their contemporaries have done; their compositions would never have met with that universal applause and approbation they so deservedly have. [&c.] [p.9]

II

But in all this time, as I have before mention'd, the world has not been presented with a regular system of the theory part of music. Some have wrote on musical composition, musical proportion, and a few other particulars; yet these are not explain'd agreeable to the present establish'd methods of practice, and therefore are of but little use. . . . Such a laudable and praise-worthy scheme, would perpetuate the remembrance of every assistant with honour to the latest posterity. I could wish to see such a performance undertaken by the great Dr. *Boyce*, his Majesty's composer; but I fear he has not leisure time enough to do it;* however, should it be attempted by a person of inferior abilities, I would have it undergo his perusal and correction; and then the world would be sure, that it might be an universal standard to all. [&c.]

*   I am persuaded he would not omit any thing, that might improve the science or be of service to its practitioners, if the multiplicity of business did not take him off from it. For he is now obliging the world with a collection of cathedral music in score, being the works of several English masters, of the last two hundred years. The selecting and reviving them, must be a work of time; he has shewn a regard for the good of others in undertaking it. The generous spirit of disinterest, that breathes in his preface to the first volume deserves notice; and he seems of my opinion, that things are not studied, or attended to, so much as they should be; I shall quote a passage or two.[60] [p.15]

III

Whoever heard, and paid a proper attention to *the dead march in* Saul, *composed by* Mr. Handel, but thought he saw the funeral pile before him, moving with slow and solemn pace, nay, heard the very mourners weep? The music to several of the airs in Dr. *Boyce's Solomon,* is of this true descriptive character; we may almost understand what the subject of the poetry is, by the delicate expression of the music alone. [p.34]

IV

Dr. *Boyce*, is the greatest composer that this kingdom has to boast of; and no one ever came so near the great original [Handel] in powerful composition, as he has done: His justly admired anthems, are a convincing proof of this. In these, melody and harmony, taste and judgement, seem to contend with each other for superiority. . . . In all his music for the stage, he has shewn a fine genteel taste: in his accompaniments to his songs, he has expressed every thing that can be done by a variety of instruments, but never over-burdens the voice with rattling symphonies, so as to eclipse it, and render it insignificant; a thing too frequently done by most of our composers.* In short, he is a composer that seems to have every necessary qualification, to constitute greatness and perfection. He is the *glory* of the *English musicians,* and an *honour* to the *British nation.*

---

[60] Potter then quotes relevant passages from Boyce's Preface to vol. 1 of *Cathedral Music* (1760).

*   This is a very great error, and arises from a fondness to shew their abilities in the instrumental way; but it condemns their taste and judgement. The voice is the principal thing to be heard in the song, therefore no accompaniment should overpower it; nor any intervening symphony be too loud, for if so, the voice is not heard when it goes on again. [pp.55-6]

Potter was something of a polymath and in some respects a controversial figure. He published widely on a variety of topics, wrote prologues and epilogues for Garrick (with whom he later publicly quarrelled), and composed songs and cantatas for Vauxhall Gardens. In later life he qualified as a doctor and practised medicine. The *Observations* were based on a series of lectures on music he had given at Gresham College in 1761. As may be inferred from the extracts quoted, Potter was a great supporter of English music, and deprecated the dominance of Italian music in the culture of his time. He was the first writer to have given more than passing attention to Boyce's music.

♣

H. Roberts publishes *Clio and Euterpe or British Harmony*, vol. 3, (1762).

Vols. 1 and 2 of this extensive collection of English songs had appeared in 1758-9 but none by WB were included. The considerable representation of songs by Boyce in the 3rd book may be attributed to the running out in April 1759 of the composer's Royal Licence which had for the previous 14 years offered a degree of protection against the unsanctioned printing of his music. The independent songs by WB published here are: 'Tho' Chloe's out of fashion' (18-19); 'Rail no more ye learned asses' (76-7);[61] 'On thy banks, gentle Stour' (96); 'I look'd and I sighed' (105); 'Oft am I by the woman told' (134-5); 'The flame of love' (140-41); 'Near Thames' green banks' (156-7); 'You say you love' (166-7); 'Boast not mistaken swain' (169); 'When the nymphs were contending' (172-3); 'Let rakes for pleasure' [a dialogue] (177-8), and 'My Florio, wildest of his sex' (182-3). In addition, 14 airs by WB taken from *The Chaplet, The Shepherd's Lottery, The Secular Masque, Solomon, Harlequin's Invasion* and the incidental music for *Florizel and Perdita* are included. An air from

---

[61] Previously published in LB, V (1756), this was sometimes characterised as Boyce's 'Bacchanalian song'.

Boyce's *The Chaplet*, 'Contented all day' (124-5), is wrongly attributed to
Thomas Arne.

♣

Boyce sets Whitehead's ode for the king's birthday 1762, 'Go Flora, said the impatient Queen', organises a public rehearsal, and conducts its performance at court on 4 June.

Text in AR (1762), 'Characters', 216-7. WB published the overture in
Twelve Overtures, no. 1 (1770).

♣

From the *London Evening-Post*, 11 September 1762

LONDON. On Saturday morning their Majesties took an airing, and
returned about two-o'clock to St. James's. Sunday her Majesty was at the
chapel royal for the first time since her happy delivery of the Prince; at
which time the following Anthem was performed, composed by Dr. Boyce
on that occasion. ANTHEM 'O Give thanks unto the Lord, for he is
gracious'. [&c.]

The birth of George Augustus Frederick, Prince of Wales, and first child
of George III and his consort Queen Charlotte, had taken place on 12
August. George ultimately succeeded to the throne in 1820.

♣

From the *British Magazine* (1762)

Her Majesty was at the Chapel Royal for the first time since her happy
delivery of the Prince: at which time the following anthem, composed by
Dr. Boyce, was performed on that occasion. 'O give thanks unto the Lord,
for he is gracious'. [&c.]

BM, vol. 3, (1762), 501. Queen Charlotte, consort of George III, had given
birth to her first child, the future King, on 12 August. Due to her being
unwell, the Christening did not take place until 10 Sept., and this
celebratory service until Sunday the 12th. Not only was the full text of the

anthem published, but the solo singers in the performance were also identified.

♣

From the *Public Advertiser,* 8 December 1762

Never acted before. AT the Theatre Royal in Covent-Garden, This Day, will be performed a new Dramatic Opera, call'd LOVE IN A VILLAGE The MUSIC by HANDEL, BOYCE, ARNE, HOWARD, BAILDON, FESTING, GEMINIANI, GALLUPI, GIARDINI, PARADIES, AGUS. A new Overture composed by Mr. ABEL The principal Parts to be performed by Mr. BEARD, Mr. SHUTER, Mr. MATTOCKS, Mr. DYER, Mr. COLLINS, Mr. DUNSTALL, Miss BRENT and Miss HALLAM. With Dances incident to the Opera. [&c.]

This ground-breaking and influential pastiche opera by Thomas Arne was based on a reworking by Isaac Bickerstaffe of the text of an earlier, rather unsuccessful ballad opera, *The Village Opera* (1729), by Charles Johnson (libretto at *Lbl*, 1570/622.(6)). *Love in a Village* is a full-length comic opera. Though mainly based on borrowed material from composers of the early eighteenth century, it also includes five freshly composed airs by Arne and one by Samuel Howard. Walsh originally published separate scores for each of the three acts (1762-5) before producing a complete edition embracing all 62 vocal items with title-page: LOVE IN A VILLAGE. | A comic Opera | *As it is Perform'd at the THEATRE ROYAL in* | COVENT GARDEN. [&c.] [1763]. Item nos. 59 ('If ever I'm catched') and 62 ('Hence with cares'), were borrowed from Boyce's songs 'When Orpheus went down' (1740) and 'Rail no more ye learned Asses', published in *Lyra Britannica,* V, (1756). The work was an immediate hit, receiving 40 performances in its first season, and it was revived every year in London until the end of the century, and indeed beyond.

♣

Boyce sets Whitehead's royal ode for the New Year 1763, 'At length th'imperious Lord of war', arranges a public rehearsal, and conducts its performance at court.

Text in AR (1762), 'Characters', 222-3. WB published the overture to this work in *Twelve Overtures,* no. 3 (1770).

♣

From the *Reminiscences* of Samuel Wesley (1836-7)

Thomas Linley junior, brother of these [the three Linley sisters] . . . was a character of bright genius and extensive musical acquirements. He chose the violin as his instrument at an early age, upon which he soon became an eminent proficient and afterwards went to Italy where he pursued his studies and practice under the celebrated Nardini who was a pupil of the great Tartini. On his return to England he studied composition very diligently and successfully with the late luminous and worthy Doctor William Boyce, and became a bright ornament in the profession as a composer. [&c.]

Lbl, Add.27593, f. 85. Wesley was in error, as indeed in other matters too sometimes, in placing Linley's studies with Boyce after his stay in Italy. These occurred, in fact, between 1763 and the summer of 1768 when Linley left England for his three-year stay in Italy (Jenkins(1998), 58). Linley was brought to London to see Boyce each summer during this period after the completion of the concert-giving seasons at Bath organised by his father, Thomas Linley, snr.. A further reference to Boyce teaching Linley occurs in a collection of anecdotes compiled by R.J.S. Stevens that also contains a unique account of Boyce's daughter, Elizabeth: "Travelling from Brighton to London, Novr. 19th 1816, I had the pleasure of meeting Dr. Boyce's daughter in the stage coach. She was an intelligent chatty woman. She informed me that Thomas Linley Senior of Bath, and his son Thomas Linley Junior, both learned Counterpoint and Composition of Dr. Boyce. They used to attend him at Kensington Gore, when the Bath season was over".[62] Cudworth goes on to say: "In his Diary for the same date, Stevens calls her 'A daughter of Dr. Boyce' and adds that she was 'very communicative'. Unfortunately he makes no mention of the lady's probable age, nor does he give any more details of what she communicated to him". Boyce's daughter would have been 67 when Stevens met her, since we know from Boyce's will that she was born in 1749.

♣

---

[62] Quoted in a letter from Charles Cudworth, (*MT* 1510 (1968), 1118).

Boyce moves from Quality Court, Chancery Lane, to 3 Kensington Gore (1762-3).

None of the early biographers of Boyce, nor indeed their modern successors, offer a precise date for his change of residence. However, in Mortimer's *Universal Directory* of 1763, his address is given as 'Quality Court'.[63] Evidence from the rate books for Chancery Lane confirms that Boyce was still there in 1760, but no rate books are extant for 1761, nor are the poor rate books for 1762 and 1763. Both scavenger rate books for 1763 do survive, and the second one, dated at the end, '8 June', shows that WB's name was originally entered in its usual place but was subsequently crossed through.[64] In the Kensington rate books[65] WB's name does not occur until the second half of 1763 when it appears alongside that of a 'Lady Crofts'. He may have either rented his apartment from her, or shared the premises with her. In conclusion, WB would appear to have 'retired' from the heart of the bustling City of London to the then quiet and rural environs of Kensington, near what is now the Albert Hall and Kensington Gardens, some time between late 1762 and early 1763.

♣

Boyce agrees to participate in the composition of an oratorio, *Ruth*, for the Lock Hospital (1763).

Founded in 1746, this hospital in London was a charitable institution concerned with the treatment of venereal diseases. The trustees had invited three composers to share in the setting of this work, with a text by Thomas Haweis, the assistant Chaplain at the hospital, to be performed in the Chapel on 15 April (*PA*, 9 April). Act I was to be composed by Avison, Act II by Giardini, and Act III by Boyce. However, four days later it was announced that "Dr. Boyce, who kindly undertook to compose the music for the Third Part of the ORATORIO, being prevented by a serious Fit of Illness from executing it this Season, Mr. Avison being so obliging as to do it, that the Charity might not suffer, or the Public be disappointed" (*PA*, 13 April). The cause of WB's indisposition may well have been gout, from which he was a chronic sufferer. The highlighting of 'oratorio' in this

---

[63] Mortimer(1763), 32. The section on musicians is reproduced in *GSJ* 2 (1949), 27-31.
[64] *Lkla*, P/AH/RA/17 (1762), book 5, p.8.
[65] Preserved at *Lkcl*.

notice may have been with a view to catching the eye of the public at a time when there was particularly keen interest in that genre.

♣

From the *Public Advertiser,* 6 May 1763

LONDON. . . . Yesterday the Rev. Dr. Bentham Canon of Christ-Church, Oxford, preached before their Majesties, &c. at the Chapel Royal, St. James's. The Sword of State was carried to and from Chapel by Lord Hertford. When the following new Anthem, composed by Dr. Boyce, was performed. ANTHEM. The Lord is King be the people never so impatient.

This notice goes on to quote the complete text of the anthem. Thursday 5 May had been designated a day of general thanksgiving for the end of the Seven Years' War (1756-63). The Treaty of Paris between England, France, Portugal and Spain, which brought the war to an end, had been signed on 10 February, and was particularly advantageous to British interests.

♣

From the *Gentlemen's Magazine*, June 1763

A most magnificent temple and bridge, finely illuminated with about 4000 glass lamps was erected in the garden [of St. James's Park]. The painting on the front of the temple represented the king[66] giving peace to all parts of the earth, and at his majesty's feet were the trophies of the numerous conquests made by *Britain*, and beneath them were a group of figures representing Envy, Malice, Detraction, &c. tumbling headlong like the fallen angels in *Milton*.[67] In front of the temple was a magnificent orchestra with above fifty of the most eminent performers; but what is still more extraordinary is, that all this machinery, paintings, lights, &c. were designed and fixed under her majesty's[68] direction in so private a manner, that the first intimation his majesty had of this most elegant and affectionate mark of so amiable a princess, was the suddenly throwing

---

[66] George III.

[67] The reference is to the episode in Book 1 of *Paradise Lost* (1667) headed 'The Fallen Angels in the Burning Lake' (lines 283-313), in which Satan and his angels, thunderstruck and astonished, are flung into hell.

[68] George's consort, Charlotte Sophia of Mecklenburg-Strelitz.

back the window-shutters of her majesty's palace, when his majesty entered the apartments between nine and ten o'clock. What his majesty must have felt on receiving, and the Queen in presenting such a testimony of her love and respect, cannot be expressed nor conceived but by those whose lot it was to perceive it in a manner not to be expressed here. Most of the Royal Family were present and a cold supper of upwards of 100 dishes, with an illuminated desert, also was provided. An ode suitable to the happy occasion was written and set to musick by Dr *Boyce*, who conducted the *orchestra*. The voices were Mrs *Scott*, Miss *Brent*, and Mr *Beard*. A select band performed during the supper, assisted by some suitable vocal musick.

GM, 33, 300. The commission to David Mallet and Boyce to write this ode, 'See white-robed peace', may be seen to reflect a growing tendency after the demise of Handel in 1759 and the accession of George III in 1761 for the Royal Family to patronise indigenous rather than foreign talent in the service of the Crown. The performance of this special ode was partly conceived as a public celebration of the birthday of the king, additional to the essentially private birthday ode that had been given as usual at court on 4 June. At the same time it rejoiced in the recent signing of the 'First Treaty of Paris' by England, France, Spain and Portugal. This agreement had brought to an end the 'Seven Years' War', a complicated world-wide conflict that had been immensely draining on the national exchequer. Boyce's autogr. MS score (*Ob,* MS.Mus.Sch.C.118a) is inscribed: "An ODE, performed on the sixth of June 1763 before their Majesties, & the rest of the Royal Family, in the Gardens of the Queen's Palace, St. James's Park. Note the performance was in the ev'ning, and the garden was finely illuminated". [&c.] WB published the overture to this ode in *Twelve Overtures*, no. 4 (1770).

♣

Peter Welcker publishes six catches and a canon by Boyce in a Collection by Thomas Warren (1763).

Title-page: A COLLECTION of | Catches Canons and Glees | FOR *Three, four, five, six and nine Voices* | never before published | Selected by *Thomas Warren*. Warren went on to produce 32 volumes of such pieces more or less annually up to 1794. In addition to contemporary works he regularly included madrigals from the 16th and 17th centuries. Vol. 1 includes seven catches by WB: 'Tis thus' (1), 'A blooming youth' (11), 'Long live King George' (12), 'Glory be' (18), 'Allelujah' (20), "Mongst other roses' (26), and 'John Cooper' (27). Vol. 2 of Warren's collection, also issued in 1763, contains another setting by WB of 'Long live King George' (4). A note to this piece states: "The three lower parts in Canon three in one, the Upper part is added & the whole alter'd from the Original by DR Boyce". This arrangement is based on an anonymous canon published by John Playford in *Catch that catch can* (1667) and elsewhere, and is set to the text, 'Long live King Charles', to which WB added a free 4th voice and updated the royal reference.

♣

From 'A short account of the late Mr Thomas Linley, Junior' by Matthew Cooke (1812)

Mr Thomas Linley was the fourth son of Mr Thomas Linley of Bath,[69] and was born at Bath May the 7th. 1756 and gave such early, and strong passion for music, as determined his father to fix him in that profession, and accordingly the stripling studied the rudiments of music under his father (who was a strict disciplinarian) and was by the tuition of his parent, perfectly grounded in both theory and practice[.] The child's assiduity, and the rapid progress he made, called forth his father's approbation, and rewarded his anxiety[.] When young Thomas was seven years of age, his father took him to his friend Dr William Boyce,[70] Organist & Composer to his Majesty King George the 3^d who was so captivated by the child's genius, and disposition, that he agreed to instruct the youth for the tenure of 5 years. This proposal was readily agreed to, young Linley under his new master continued to make an astonishing progress, at the end of the aforesaid period, it was resolved to send master Tommy to Italy . . . [where] he studied under the eminent master Nardini and returned to England in the Spring of the year 1773.[71] [&c.]

---

[69] Linley snr. was well known as a composer and promoter of concerts at Bath for about 20 years from the mid-1750s, and as the father of a large family of talented musicians active in London and elsewhere throughout the late 18th- century.

[70] The elder Linley was personally well acquainted with Boyce since he himself had previously studied with him, probably in the mid-1750s. It would appear that Thomas jnr. was taken to London each year in the summer for an intensive period of lessons with WB after the season of concerts directed by his father in Bath had concluded.

[71] Thomas jnr. left England for Italy in the summer of 1768. The reappearance of his name in Bath concert notices early in 1772 (see MB 30, xv) suggests that he

Lbl, Egerton MS2492, fol. 2^r. Although Cooke's short biography was not written until 1812 when he was about 50, he appears to have enjoyed a close association with the Linley family during the earlier part of his career.

♣

Boyce sets Whitehead's ode for the king's birthday 1763, 'Common births, like common things' (text in AR (1763), 'Characters', 223-4), organises a public rehearsal, and conducts its performance at court on 4 June.

♣

1 January 1764 being a Sunday, by tradition no royal ode was required at court that day.

Nevertheless, both Whitehead and Boyce seem to have overlooked the fact that no ode needed to be prepared. Consequently an ode, 'Sacred to thee', was both written and set to music. The Lord Chamberlain gave his consent, however, to its being performed the following year. Other accounts do not serve to clarify the situation on this occasion. One public announcement reported: "There was a great Court at St. James's, to compliment their majesties on the new year, as usual, but no ode; an omission, which as there was no apparent reason for it, occasioned some surprise, considering how elegantly that custom used to be observed in times when there were neither the same materials for panegyric, nor the same genius to work them up" (AR, (1763), 'Chronicle', 45). Another observed: "There was a great Court at St. James's to compliment their majesties on the new year; but the ode was not performed as usual, and we hear is, for the present, discontinued" (*GM,* Jan. 1764, 42). The remarks in the *Annual Register* suggest that the artistic qualities of the Whitehead/Boyce royal odes were perhaps more appreciated now than was often the case earlier. Whatever misunderstandings may have arisen at this time, the court ode tradition continued normally as from the king's birthday in June 1764.

♣

---

may have concluded his studies with Nardini rather earlier than indicated here by Cooke.

Two poems on music by the Rev. Charles Wesley (*c*1764)

On Kelway's Sonatas

Kelway's sonatas who can bear?
They want both harmony and air;
Heavy they make the player's hand
And who their tricks can understand?
Kelway to the profound G —
Or B — compared, is but a ninny,
A dotard old (the moderns tell ye)
Mad after Handel and Corelli,
Spoilt by original disaster,
For Geminiani was his master,
And taught him, in his nature's ground
To gape for sense, as well as sound.

'Tis thus the leaders of our nation,
Smit with the music now in fashion,
Their absolute decisions deal,
And from the chair infallible,
And praise the fine, Italian taste,
Too fine, too exquisite to last.
Let Midas judge, and what will follow?
A whis[t]ling Pan excels Apollo,
A bag-pipe's sweeter than an organ,
A sowgelder[72] surpasses Worgan
And Kelway at the foot appears
Of connoiseurs — with asses ears!

On Modern Music

G —, B — and all
Their followers, great and small,
Have cut old music's throat,
And mangled every note;
Their superficial pains
Have dashed out all his brains;
And now we dote upon
A lifeless sceleton,

---

[72] One who operates on a female animal to destroy its power to reproduce.

The empty sound at most,
The squeak of music's ghost.

Mr, MSP at Misc., pp.5-6. (Lightwood (1937), 15, and Kimbrough & Beckerlegge, 3 (1992), 382-3). Wesley inscribed the first of these poems on a copy of Joseph Kelway's *Six Sonatas* (1764) for harpsichord, dedicated to Queen Charlotte, George III's consort. The background to both poems is the conflict in the mid-18th century between the supporters of the 'ancient music' of the Renaissance and Baroque periods, and those who favoured the 'moderns', who pioneered the emerging and ultimately triumphant 'galant' and later 'classical' styles. Charles Wesley and his two sons, Charles and Samuel, undoubtedly belonged to the former faction. In their edition of these poems, Kimborough and Beckerlegge identify 'G' as Giardini,[73] and 'B' as Boyce, while allowing for the possibility that 'B' might be J.C. Bach.[74] The seed for this misapprehension must lie in Lightwood who also took 'B' to stand for Boyce. There can be no question, however, that 'B' stands for 'Bach' (i.e. J.C. Bach) and not Boyce. The first poem must not divert the reader from the clear message being conveyed: Kelway and Boyce, both of whom were chosen by Wesley to be the principal music teachers for Samuel, and Kelway's teacher Geminiani,[75] represent the admired 'ancient' school who upheld traditional musical principles.[76] On the other hand, Bach and Giardini represent the progressive 'moderns' who threaten to undermine, if not replace them.

♣

From the Vestry Minutes of All Hallows the Great, 21 March 1764

At this Vestry it was unanimously *Agreed to that Dr Boyce Organist of the United Parish be dismissed* And that the Church Wardens are desired to let him know that it is also agreed at the same Vestry that the salary of the

---

[73] Felice Giardini, an Italian composer and violinist, who settled in London in 1751.

[74] Johann Christian Bach, the youngest son of Johann Sebastian, who worked in London from 1762.

[75] Francesco Geminiani, an Italian violinist and composer, who lived mainly in London from 1714.

[76] As did John Worgan, the composer and organist also mentioned in Wesley's first poem.

[future] organist be raised to thirty pounds p[er] year,[77] and it is *further agreed that no candidate be admitted to deliver his proposals for playing after Saturday next*, the 24 of March 1764 and not to be admitted after ten o'clock, and that Mr Bullbrick be not admitted to put in his proposals as a candidate.

Lgh, MS819/2, 408. Boyce had been requested not to use Bullbrick as a deputy as long ago as January 1758. This issue lay behind the reduction in WB's salary from £30 to £20 at that time. On the face of it, the church authorities seem to have been remarkably patient before taking decisive action to resolve the problem, whatever its nature may have been. It is impossible to determine whether WB acted, or failed to act, out of loyalty to Bullbrick, or simply did not give due diligence to the matter. He was succeeded by James Evance (*LEP*, 7 April).

♣

Boyce's son William is born at Kensington 25 March 1764.

Baptised at Hammersmith on 25 April, William jnr. arrived not long after his father had moved to 3 Kensington Gore. Boyce snr. would doubtless have been pleased had he lived long enough to see his son gain a place at Oxford, for he matriculated at Magdalen College on 27 January 1780 with a view to entering the priesthood. His satisfaction would have been relatively short-lived, however, for the younger Boyce did not complete his degree, and was eventually sent down. The College records reveal that on 17 Dec. 1783 "Guielmus Boyce, e Clericis, ob morum insolentium, concensu seniorum a Vice-Praesidente palam fuit expulsus".[78] Exactly what the offence was is not known, but his expulsion was later explained to be "on account of some little irregularities".[79]

William went on to make amends for this early setback, for he pursued a successful career as a double bass player and bass singer. His name appears in performers' lists in both capacities, not only in London but in many of the major provincial musical centres from the mid 1780s through to the second decade of the 19th century. In May 1792 he gained

---

[77] In current terms c£4,500 p.a., as the organist's salary had been until the unspecified problems arose in 1758.

[78] "William Boyce, one of the scholars, on account of his insolent behaviour, by the agreement of the academic staff, has been publicly expelled by the Vice-President".

[79] Ayrton(1824), 194.

acceptance as a member of the Royal Society of Musicians. His application was supported by John Ashley: "Gentlemen, I beg leave to recommend Mr. William Boyce, Musician, as a proper person to be a member of the Society; he has practised music for a livelihood for seven years, is employed at the Haymarket Theatre, at Covent Garden Theatre, at Ranelagh and at private concerts, has a wife, but no children, is in good health and aged twenty eight years, and not likely to become chargeable to the Society".[80] If this last point was true at that time, (he had inherited a third share in his father's wealth in 1779), it became even more so in 1808 when an organist, John Rice the younger, left him £7,000.[81] Boyce himself had become an organist at St. Matthew, Friday Street, from 1802 to 1812.[82] A surviving letter of Boyce's, written from his residence at Hungerford Wharf, Strand, London on 3 Dec. 1796 to a Rev. William Viner, indicates that the two men had met at Durham. Viner was evidently compiling a 'Biographical Chart' of early musicians, and Boyce passes on to him information he had acquired from J.S. Smith on the career of John Parsons, an organist at Westminster Abbey in the early 17th century.[83]

A further glimpse into the social life Boyce enjoyed as a travelling musician, giving evidence of a congenial and obliging personality, is provided in the diaries of the lawyer, John Marsh, a notable amateur composer, violinist and concert organiser. Marsh had evidently encountered problems in arranging some concerts at Abingdon in October 1798. He had approached a violinist from Gosport who was also "much improved on the double bass", but he had demanded a guinea and a half for each performance.[84] Marsh records: "Mr Boyce however the double bass player (son of the late D'r) and his wife coming for a few days before the first concert to stay at Mr Middleton's[85] thinking he wo'd have no objection to lend us his assistance in the orchestra, called to ask it & at the same time to pay my respects to him, but he not being at home, & Mr Middleton being too squemish to mention it to him, I thought no more of it 'till the concert night, when meeting with Mr Boyce in the lobby, at going in, I ventur'd to ask him to take the double bass, w'ch he most readily agreeing to, I put Mr Gear to fiddle, the expence of having whom we might have

---

[80]   See letter from Adrian Cruft (*MT* 109 (1968), 1019).

[81]   No less than a million pounds in present-day values.

[82]   BDA, 2, 268-9.

[83]   *Glr*, D2227/8. Notwithstanding its date, this letter had until recently been attributed at the library to Boyce the composer.

[84]   About £200 in modern currency.

[85]   A mutual friend of Marsh and Boyce.

saved for that night had it not been for Mr Middleton's over delicacy" (Robins(1998), 676).

Shortly after Boyce had taken up his organist post, he seems to have harboured further ambitions, for he made an approach to Charles Burney through J.W. Callcott, who had been a friend of his father, with a view to gaining an appointment at Canterbury Cathedral. In a letter to Callcott, written from Chelsea College on 14 Nov. 1803, Burney wrote: "'Though I have no doubt of the abilities of a candidate for Canterbury, recommended by so many eminent professors & worthy men; yet there seems something indelicate, & not quite correct, in my sighing [sic] a recommendation of a person whom I have not the pleasure of knowing even by sight, or of hearing him perform, even out of sight. There was no professor whom I was ever acquainted with that I loved, honoured, & respected, more than Mr Boyce's father, who signed my certificate for a degree at Oxford, & with whom I always lived upon terms of friendship; yet in point of rigorous probability, it does not seem perfectly right to say you know, what you do not know, except from hear-say. Yet I am so unwilling to put a negation upon solicitation of this kind, that if you, & the hon'ble gentleman you name, think it will be of any real use — I cannot refuse setting my name to what such men are certain of — that if Mr Boyce calls ab. noon on Thursday — I shall be at home to him only".[86]

At first glance this initiative on the part of Boyce may seem surprising in the light of his earlier career. However, such an opportunity was at least feasible at this time, for the organist at Canterbury, Samuel Porter, was about to retire. In the event, Porter was succeeded by Highmore Skeats whose appointment also involved duties as a lay clerk as well as organist, an arrangement probably devised to enhance his stipend. Had Boyce been appointed he would have been able to exercise his extensive experience as a singer as well as his only recently exploited skills as an organist. Moreover, his adolescent ambition to serve the church would at last have been realised.

Boyce stayed at St. Matthew's until October 1812 when the circumstances of his departure were recorded: "Mr. Boyce came to him [Mr. Chapman, the parish clerk] in the vestry and after giving him the receipt for his salary to Michaelmas said to him "Give my compliments to the churchwardens and tell them, I am much offended at the message that was sent to me and I give up my place from this day. There are three weeks since Michaelmas and the churchwardens may make an allowance if they please for that

---

[86] Letter preserved at *US: Nhub* in Osborn Collection. Information kindly supplied by Donald Burrows.

time" (quoted in Shaw(1994), 82). By now, of course, Boyce was very much a man of independent means. The cause of his irritation is not known.

Like his father, Boyce was a keen collector of musical scores; moreover, at his father's death he had retained items from the composer's own library when it went on sale in April 1779, including some autogr. manuscripts. After his own death in 1823, his library was put up for auction by W.P. Musgrave on 29-31 March 1824. Unfortunately, it is difficult to determine the precise contents of Boyce's library, as the sale also included "the Duplicates of a Professor, and the Libraries of a distinguished Amateur".

♣

From Thomas Busby's *Concert Room and Orchestra Anecdotes*, vol. 3, (1825)

Dr. Boyce, sensible of the congeniality between the young musician's talents [those of Thomas Battishill] and his own, cherished a partiality for his rising brother professor, and associated him with himself at the Chapel Royal, as his regular substitute at the organ, whenever his other avocations prevented his personal attendance. About the same time, Battishill formed an engagement with the manager of Covent Garden theatre, as the conductor of the band, and presided accordingly at the harpsichord. In that situation, he became acquainted with the merits, and charmed with the person, of Miss Davies,[87] the original *Madge*, in *Love in a Village*;[88] and a union ensued. Soon after the marriage, he was elected organist of the united parishes of St. Clement Eastcheap and St. Martin Ongar,[89] and also of Christ-Church, Newgate-street;[90] which appointment compelled the resignation of his engagement with Dr. Boyce.

(Busby(1825), 3, 70) Battishill had probably begun to assist Boyce shortly after the latter's appointment as one of the organists of the Chapel Royal in June 1758 He is more likely to have given up his role as a deputy to Boyce in 1764, when he was appointed to St. Clement's, rather than in 1767 when he took up a second post at Christ-Church. Later in his account of

---

[87] Elizabeth Davies, an actress and singer, who played the part of Margery.

[88] Thomas Arne's pastiche opera of of 1762 which included items by Boyce.

[89] In 1764.

[90] In 1767. Battishill's resignation had probably already taken place in 1764, if not before that.

Battishill, Busby records that "His dying request was, that he might lie in the vaults of St. Paul's cathedral; "And please place me", added he, "near that great man, Dr. Boyce" (Busby, op. cit, 74). In the event, when he died in 1801 his wish was fulfilled. Busby also observes that "[Battishill's] anthems are characterised by the learning and sober majesty of Boyce's last cathedral compositions;[91] and his choruses in *Almena*,[92] may be compared with those in the celebrated serenata[93] of his early friend and favourite master".

♣

Boyce sets Whitehead's ode for the king's birthday 1764, 'To wedded love, ye nations bow', organises a public rehearsal, and conducts it at court on 4 June.

That this ode was performed as normal this year is clear since it was announced that "At Noon the Ode, composed for his Majesty's Birth Day, was performed before their Majesties, &c. in the Great Council Chamber, St. James's" (*SJC*, 2-6 June). However, the text of this ode appears not to have been published in any of the newspapers as was the usual custom. Either this was an administrative oversight, or for some reason the formal celebration of the king's birthday was a low-key event this year. However, the place to be on this occasion seems to have been away from the palace, for it was reported that: "Among the rejoicings made in honour of his Majesty's birth-day, those made by Mr. Lowe,[94] proprietor of Marybone gardens, are worth mentioning. Early in the morning, St. George's ensign and a broad pendant was displayed, upon the top of a mast and a flag-staff sixty feet high, created for the purpose. About one o'clock at noon, Mr. G[J?]oseph Lowe, Engineer to the Hon. Artillery Company, fired three rounds from 21 pieces of cannon. After the first round their Majesties healths were drunk, and God save great George our King was sung by Mr. Lowe, Mrs. Vincent,[95] and Mrs. Lampe, jun., when upwards of fifty voices joined in chorus. After the second round, to his Royal Highness the Prince

---

[91] WB's last anthems were composed in the late 1760s.

[92] Battishill's *Almena,* an English opera, was produced at Drury Lane in 1765. The libretto was by Richard Rolt, and Michael Arne also composed some of the music.

[93] *Solomon* (1742).

[94] Thomas Lowe was a prominent tenor who had taken over the gardens in 1763.

[95] Isabella Vincent was also the soprano soloist in a performance of Boyce's *Solomon* (1742) at Marybone in 1767 (see *PA*, 12 Sept.).

of Wales:[96] the third to the rest of the Royal family. In the evening, about nine o'clock, a new Ode was performed in the garden to a numerous audience with great applause"[97] [&c.] (*LEP*, 5 June). WB published the overture to this work in *Twelve Overtures*, no. 10 (1770).

♣

From *Berrow's Worcester Journal*, 30 August 1764

THE MEETING of the THREE CHOIRS OF WORCESTER, GLOUCESTER, and HEREFORD will be holden here on Tuesday the 4th of September next. On Wednesday the 5th, at the College, will be performed PURCELL's TE DEUM and JUBILATE with Dr. Boyce's Additions; an Anthem by Dr. Boyce; to conclude with an Anthem performed at their Majesty's Coronation, composed by Dr. Boyce. In the Evening, at the College-Hall, the Oratorio of ATHALIA On Thursday the 6th, HANDEL's Grand TE DEUM, an Anthem by Dr. Boyce, and to conclude with another of the Coronation Anthems: In the Evening, at the College-Hall, ACIS and GALATEA with some select Pieces. On Friday Morning, at the College, MESSIAH; and in the Evening, at the College-Hall, a BALL. [&c.]

The programme for this Festival was unique in that it contained no less than four of Boyce's anthems. Following the death of Handel in 1759, it fell to Boyce in his capacity as Master of the King's Music, to compose the music for the Coronation of George III in September 1761. Of the eight anthems Boyce produced for the Coronation, four of them used orchestral accompaniment: 'My heart is inditing', 'Praise the Lord', 'The King shall rejoice' (*BC* 35) and 'The Lord is a sun'. Boyce would have selected two of these for the Three Choirs since full orchestral resources were available. Morning concerts at the Festival, essentially of 'sacred music', invariably took place in the Cathedral rather than the College Hall. That they were not located there on this occasion suggests that building repairs were being undertaken at the Cathedral at this time.

♣

---

[96] Later to be George IV.
[97] This ode, composed by George Berg, was performed with the singers mentioned above among the soloists. It was repeated every evening of that week (see *GNDA*, 4 June).

The royal ode for New Year's Day 1765, 'Sacred to Thee', was rehearsed in public and performed at court.

Text in AR (1764), 'Characters', 271-2. Boyce added a note in his autogr. MS of the score of this work (*Ob*, MSMus.Sch.D.315a): "This Ode was originally intended for the 1st of January 1764, but that happening on a Sunday, the Lord Chamberlain was pleased to consent that it should be performed on the first of January, 1765". WB published the overture to this work in *Twelve Overtures*, no. 7 (1770).

♣

Boyce teaches John Stafford Smith.

Smith, son of Martin Smith, organist at Gloucester Cathedral from 1739-81, came to London in 1761 to join the Chapel Royal as a chorister. "After some early instruction from his father he studied in London under Boyce" (*Harmonican* 11 (1833), 186), and went on to become a Gentleman of the Chapel Royal and later an Organist there. The strong influence WB exerted on him is evident not only from his success as a composer, but also from his pioneering activities as a historical musicologist.[98] Smith's studies in early music and musical theory led to two major publications: *A Collection of Songs* (1779), an edition of early 16th-century vocal music, and *Musica Antiqua*, a ground-breaking historical anthology of music ranging from Gregorian chant and medieval secular music, both English and continental, through to the early 18th century.

♣

Boyce subscribes to Christopher Smart's *Translation of the Psalms of David* (1765).

Boyce was one among nearly 800 subscribers to this edition, among whom were also the musicians Beard, Lowe, Stanley and Burney. Its attraction for the religious community was clearly considerable. Later, in October of the same year, John Walsh published *A Collection of Melodies for the Psalms* based on Smart's texts. Among the 45 settings by various composers, six were by Boyce.

---

[98] For an extensive account of Smith's career and musicological work, see Gramenz (1987).

♣

Boyce subscribes to Samuel Wise's *Six Lessons for the Harpsichord (c1765).*

Little is known about Wise, apart from the fact that he worked in Nottingham and also published *Six Concertos (c1770)* and *Three Anthems (c1780).* He was one of a number of English keyboard composers of his generation whose works show the influence of Domenico Scarlatti. A significant number of the 198 subscribers for 212 copies of this edition were from the Midlands.

♣

Boyce sets Whitehead's ode for the king's birthday 1765, 'Hail to the the rosy morn', organises a public rehearsal, and conducts it at court on 4 June.

Text in AR (1765), 'Characters', 272-3. WB published the overture to this work in *Twelve Overtures*, no. 2 (1770).

♣

John Walsh publishes *A Collection of Melodies for the Psalms* [1765].

Title-page: A | Collection of | Melodies | for the | Psalms of David, According to the Version of | Christopher Smart A.M.[99] | By the most Eminent Composers of | Church Music.

This publication was advertised in *PA,* 23 & 29 Oct., and again on 6 Nov. when Walsh highlighted Boyce's contribution to the volume. His settings are of 'The man is blest of God thro' Christ' (p.1), 'Lord, how my bosom-foes increase' (2), 'To the call of pressing need' (2-3), 'Weigh the

---

[99] Smart had entered Pembroke College, Cambridge, in 1739 and was elected Fellow in Philosophy in 1745. Although he retained this post until 1753, from 1749 onwards he spent less and less time in Cambridge. Notwithstanding his fine and considerable output of poems and translations, he is best known today perhaps as the author of the text set by Benjamin Britten in his cantata 'Rejoice in the Lamb'. WB also set three poems by Smart as solo songs: 'My Florio', 'To Harriote', and 'When young and artless'.

words of my profession' (3), 'How long O my God shall I plead?' (5), and 'Hosanna to the King' (30). Other composers represented in this collection of 45 hymns included Howard, Stanley, Cooke, Nares and Randall. Smart's version of the psalms, *A Translation of the Psalms of David,* to which Boyce subscribed, had been published earlier in the same year.

♣

From the *Public Advertiser,* 28 October 1765

AT THE Theatre Royal in Covent-Garden, This Day will be presented OTHELLO, MOOR of VENICE. . . . To which will be added a Pantomime Entertainment (not performed these six years) called The ROYAL CHACE; Or, HARLEQUIN SKELETON. [&c.]

The origins of the *Royal Chace* go back to the 1720s when John Rich produced the first of a long line of successful pantomimes, *Jupiter and Europa*, at Lincoln's-Inn-Fields Theatre on 23 March 1723. It continued to be performed from time to time up to 1728, though neither its author nor the composer(s) involved have been identified. Not long after taking over the management of the new Covent Garden Theatre in 1732, Rich presented a fresh version of the piece with text by Edward Phillips (word-book, *Lbl,* 11775.a.23) and music by J.E. Galliard entitled *The Royal Chace, or Merlin's Cave.* (CG, 23 Jan. 1736). In its new guise, Rich (stage name, 'Lun') played 'Jupiter' in the character of Harlequin, while John Beard, taking the part of a royal huntsman, made a big impression in the opening song, 'With early horn'. The pantomime remained in the theatre's repertoire until 1760.

Following Rich's death in 1761, it was Beard who took over the management at CG. He produced the pantomime in yet another manifestation involving further revisions (CG, 28 Oct. 1765). It was only at this point in the evolution of the work that Boyce's name became associated with it. Clues as to the nature of the alterations introduced by Beard are provided in two notices for slightly later performances. These refer respectively to a "new additional scene" (*PA,* 19 Oct. 1767), and "two additional scenes" (*PA,* 26 Oct. 1767). About the same time, instrumental arrangements of some of the music were published under the title, *The Comic Tunes in the Royal Chase (Lbl,* c.152.a.(3)). Among these is Galliard's 'The early Horn', the melody of which can be identified from separate publications of this well-known song. No composer is cited in *The Comic Tunes,* but there is no reason to believe that the rest of the music is not by Galliard too. However, in a contemporary collection of song texts, *Brent, or English Siren* (1765), the caption to an otherwise anonymous song, 'How pleasing we find the gay sports of the field' (no. 139), states "Sung by Mr. Beard, in the Royal Chace. Set by Dr. Boyce". The same poem appears along with similar captions in two other song anthologies: *The London Songster* (1767), no. 175, and *The Bull-Finch* [1769], no. 85. No copy of Boyce's setting of this song has, however, yet come to light.

After 1759 WB appears to have withdrawn from the theatre, but he may have been persuaded to compose one further short item for his friend Beard's new production. Not only had Beard been a close musical associate of his for many years, but he had also often sung Boyce's earlier and highly successful hunting song, 'The song of Diana: 'With horns and with hounds'' (from the *Secular Masque* (*c*1746)). While the possibility must remain that a pre-existent tune by Boyce was utilised for this song, the terminology quoted above, "set by Dr. Boyce", points to the possibility that he had been induced to make one final, albeit minor, contribution to English stage music. Finally, as if to illustrate the close thematic relationship between the scenario of the pantomime and Boyce's 'With horns and with hounds', a rare song sheet (date unknown) indicates that this earlier song of WB's was itself sometimes inserted into performances of *The Royal Chace*. It is headed "Diana. A favourite Song in the Royal Chace. Set by Dr. Boyce" (*Ob*, Harding, Mus.G.56 (2)).

♣

From the *Public Advertiser*, 6 December 1765

NEVER PERFORMED AT THE Theatre Royal in Covent-Garden. This Day will be presented a Musical Comedy of three Acts, called The SUMMER'S TALE. The Principal Parts to be performed by Mr. BEARD Mr. SHUTER Mr. MATTOCKS, Mr. DYER Mr. MORRIS Mr. DUNSTALL Mrs. VINCENT Mrs. MATTOCKS and Miss BRENT. . . . With Entertainments of Dancing, viz. End of Act I. A Grand Ballet called The GARLAND . . . End of Act II. A New Grand Ballet called The GALLANT SHEPHERDS. [&c.]

The production of this pastiche entertainment was inspired by the great success of Thomas Arne's *Love in a Village* (1762). The libretto (*Lbl*, 161.d.14) was by Richard Cumberland and the music was arranged by Samuel Arnold who included two freshly composed items of his own in a score which draws on the work of no less than 23 other mid-eighteenth-century composers. *The Summer's Tale* was given about a dozen times in its first two seasons, but only sporadically later. An attempt was made to revive it in an abridged form entitled, *Amelia*, at Drury Lane in December 1771, but it was dropped after only two performances. The vocal score containing 41 items was published by John Walsh in 1766 with title-page: THE | SUMMER'S TALE. | A Musical Comedy. | *As it is Perform'd at the THEATRE ROYAL in* | COVENT-GARDEN. *The Music by Abel Arne Arnold Boyce, . . . For the Harpsichord, Voice, German Flute, or Violin.* Walsh originally published the music in three separate volumes: Book I (Act 1) was advertised in the *PA* on 19 Dec. 1765, Book 2 (Act 2) on 6 Jan. 1766, and Book III (Act 3) on 29 Jan. 1766, and the complete score on 1 Feb. 1766. Walsh also published the airs in *The Summer's Tale Set for the German Flute, Hoboy, or Violin* (see *PA,* 13 Jan. 1766). Boyce is represented here by the tune of one of his most popular songs, 'If you my wand'ring heart' (*c*1746).

♣

No Royal Ode for the New Year is performed on 1 January 1766.

Owing to the death on 29 December 1765 of Prince Frederick William, the youngest son of George II aged only fifteen, the court was in mourning. In view of this the ode, 'When first the rude, o'er-peopled north', prepared for New Year's Day, was not performed. The Lord Chamberlain gave his consent to its being used instead the following year. Later in the month, however, a notice was published indicating that royal odes were sometimes performed on other occasions than the New Year or the king's birthday: "20 Jan. Being the day appointed for observing her majesty's birth-day, the ode composed for the new year, and postponed on account of the death of his R.H. Pr. *Frederick William*, was performed in the great council-chamber, St. James's, before their majesties, who received the compliments of the nobility, foreign ministers and gentry, on the occasion. The court was extremely brilliant, and a great number of the ladies were dressed in rich silks manufactured in *Spittle-Fields*, some of which, it is said, cost 36l per yard.[100] The Prince of *Wales*[101] and Bp of Osnaburg[102]

---

[100] In modern currency about £5,400.

[101] George Augustus Frederick, who much later, in 1820, was to succeed his father as king.

[102] Properly, Bishop of Osnabruck, in Germany. This nominal appointment was sometimes given to members of the English royal family as a consequence of George I's status, prior to his accession to the English throne, as Elector of

were at court. At night there was a ball which was opened by his R. H. the Duke of *York*,[103] and princess *Louisa Anne*;[104] minuets were danced till about 11, when their majesties withdrew, the country dances continued until past two, when the rest of the royal family and nobility retired" (*GM* 36, Feb. 1766, 102).

♣

From the *Gazetteer and New Daily Advertiser*, 19 April 1766

THE REHEARSAL of the MUSIC for the FEAST of the SONS of the CLERGY will be at St. Paul's Cathedral, on Tuesday the 22d, and the FEAST at Merchant Taylors Hall, on Thursday 24th of April. . . . The Music will consist of an Overture of GEMINIANI, HANDEL'S new Te Deum,[105] an Anthem composed by Dr. BOYCE, and Mr. HANDEL's grand Coronation Anthem.[106] [&c.]

The identity of the Boyce anthem advertised here was clarified shortly afterwards: "A new ANTHEM, composed by Dr. BOYCE, *Master of his Majesty's Band of Musicians,* which was performed at the Rehearsal this Day, is to be repeated on Thursday, before the Sons of the Clergy, at St. Paul's" (*LC*, 19-22 April). The full text of the anthem (*BC* 36), 'The King shall rejoice', is then reproduced. This was Boyce's third anthem with this title. As with his second setting, for the Coronation of George III in 1761, he retained the identity of the original 'Wedding Anthem' by keeping his setting of the opening chorus. He then went on to revise the text, and when necessary the music, taking into account its new context, in this case that of an anthem in aid of charity. Here, he also retained the original music of the 2nd movement (albeit in a transposed form) and the last, while composing fresh music for the new texts in the central movements. An incomplete autogr. score of this version survives at *Lcm*, MS585, ff. 44^v-64^v. A note on a fly-leaf in WB's hand confirms its first performance at St. Paul's on 22 April 1766.

Hanover. George III had secured this appointment for his second son, Frederick Augustus, in 1763 when he was only six months old, and he retained it until 1803.

[103] Edward Augustus, a younger brother of George III.

[104] A frail sister of George III, who died two years later aged only nineteen.

[105] This refers to the 'Dettingen Te Deum' (1743) rather than the 'old' 'Utrecht Te Deum' of 1713.

[106] 'Zadok the Priest'.

Boyce's first anthem for the charity, 'Lord, Thou hast been our refuge' (1755), became an almost invariable feature of the festival each year, but 'The King shall rejoice' replaced it in 1766 and 1767, and from 1768 to 1770 both anthems were included within the now traditional Handel-dominated programmes. 1777 was an exceptional year in that an all-Handel repertoire seems to have been adopted. In 1771 an additional rehearsal had taken place at St. George's, Hanover Square: "The Band was very large, and esteemed excellent, and gave the utmost satisfaction to a polite audience. It was conducted by Dr. Boyce; the instrumental parts were performed by upwards of 50 eminent Masters, led by Mr. Hay. . . . This extra-ordinary Rehearsal took place at the desire of several of the Nobility and Gentry, and the expences of it borne by a Clergyman of Richmond in Surry (*sic*), who sent a benefaction of 200l. for that purpose. Collection amounted to 140l. 16s.". (*LEP*, 9-11 May)[107]

Our knowledge of the activities of the society in the latter part of the century is much enhanced by the survival of the 'Festival Minutes Accounts, 1775-99' (*Lma*, A/FSC/1A). Boyce was succeeded by Samuel Howard as conductor for one year in 1779, but Philip Hayes then took over until 1796. An unidentified anthem by Hayes replaced Boyce's usual one in 1782, 1794 and 1796. However, WB's work was permanently re-instated from 1797, and one of the reasons for doing so was recorded: "Dr Boyce's anthem, composed for the Charity was sufficiently felt to answer its beneficial purpose" (Minute, 7 May 1799). Another Minute reveals an important social aspect of the event. It was evidently traditional for the Stewards to entertain the participating musicians at a local tavern the evening after the public rehearsal at St. Paul's: "and being returned to the house entertained at dinner D^R. Boyce, D^R. Howard, the Gentlemen of the three choirs,[108] & the other Gentlemen" (Minute, 7 May 1776).

♣

Boyce subscribes to Charles Lockhart's *Six Sonatas for the Harpsichord*, op. 1 [*c*1766].

Little is known of Lockhart, but he was organist at the Lock Hospital when these sonatas were published (rare copy at *Lcs*, MP30.4) and published a small amount of vocal music, hymns in particular, later in the

---

[107] In modern currency the benefaction was worth *c*£30,000 and the collection *c*£20,000.
[108] Those of St. Paul's, Westminster Abbey and the Chapel Royal.

century and beyond. The only other leading musician among the short list of 54 subscribers was Dupuis.

♣

Boyce sets Whitehead's ode for the king's birthday 1766, 'Hail to the man', organises a public rehearsal, and conducts its performance at court on 4 June.

Text published in AR (1766) in 'Characters', 257-8. WB published the overture in *Twelve Overtures,* no. 11 (1770).

♣

Boyce's setting of Whitehead's royal ode for New Year's Day 1767, 'When first the rude, o'er-peopled North', was publicly rehearsed, and performed at court on 1 January.

Text in AR (1766), 'Characters', 241-2. This ode had originally been prepared for 1 Jan. 1766. WB published the overture in *Twelve Overtures,* no. 12 (1770).

♣

A Boyce melody is borrowed in Andrew Barton's opera, *The Disappointment: or, the Force of Credulity* (1767).

This comic opera in the style of a ballad opera is credited with being the first dramatic work to have been written by an American for the professional stage. It was prepared for performance at the Southwark Theatre, Philadelphia on 20 April 1767. In the event, however, it was withdrawn at the last minute, due to its satirical treatment of some identifiable local personalities (see Graue & Layng(1976), vii). The libretto was published with title-page: THE DISAPPOINTMENT: | OR, THE | FORCE OF CREDULITY. | A NEW | American COMIC-OPERA, of Two ACTS. | *By* ANDREW BARTON, Esq; | . . . New York 1767 (preserved at *US*: *Wc*). 'Andrew Barton' is known to have been a pseudonym. Among a number of possible candidates for the authorship, the most convincing case has been made for Thomas Forrest (see Mays(1976), 10-12). A modern reconstruction of the score has been published (see Graue & Layng, op. cit.). The air in Act II, 'Now let us join hands', is set to the tune of Boyce's song, 'How blest has my time been' (*BC* 221). Apart from its publication in s.sh.f. editions, and in some later vocal collections, the song had been included in WB's *Lyra Britannica*, II (1747). Among the other contemporary English works to have reached America by this time were *The Beggar's Opera* (1728), which doubtless inspired *The Disappointment*, Thomas Arne's *The Masque of Alfred* (1740), and WB's *The Chaplet* (1749).

♣

Boyce subscribes to Richard Woodward's *Songs, Canons and Catches* (1767).

Woodward pursued his musical career in Dublin at the two cathedrals of Christ Church and St. Patrick's. Boyce may have known his father, also Richard, a London church musician who had settled in Dublin in 1751. Boyce's attention may also have been drawn to Woodward jnr. since one of the canons included in this collection, 'Let the words of my mouth', had won 1st prize at the Noblemen's and Gentlemen's Catch Club in London in 1764. This volume was dedicated to the Irish composer, Lord Mornington, and attracted 149 subscribers for 197 copies, though few of these were leading musicians.

♣

Boyce subscribes to Robert Hudson's *The Myrtle, A Collection of Songs*, book 3 (1767).

Robert Hudson was a vicar choral at St. Paul's and Gentleman of the Chapel Royal. He was a prolific composer of vocal music, and also a popular tenor who frequently appeared as a soloist at the London pleasure gardens where he doubtless performed some of Boyce's songs. WB would certainly have known Hudson personally. The initial public response to this edition was muted, for it attracted only 57 subscribers. The airs in this volume were specifically "sung at Ranelagh".

♣

Boyce sets Whitehead's ode for the king's birthday 1767, 'Friend to the poor' (text in AR (1767), 'Characters', 248), organises a public rehearsal, and conducts its performance at court on 4 June.

♣

Boyce sets Whitehead's royal ode for New Year's Day 1768, 'Let the voice of music breathe', organises a public rehearsal, and conducts its performance at court.

Text in AR (1767), 'Characters', 222-3. WB published the overture in *Twelve Overtures*, no. 9 (1770).

♣

Royal Dedication from *Cathedral Music,* vol. 2 (1768)

TO THE KING

May it please Your Majesty, THE FOLLOWING WORK, for which and himself the Editor humbly intreats your Protection, contains a complete Compilation of English Church Music from the principal productions of the several Writers, who have been esteemed excellent in that Species of Composition since the Reformation and of whom the Chief have had the Honour to serve in the CHAPELS of Your ROYAL PREDECESSORS.

Your Majesty's continued Goodness in cherishing the ARTS and SCIENCES naturally leads the Professors of them to solicit your Patronage; And none perhaps, in the whole Circle stands more in need, at present, of that POWERFUL RECOMMENDATION than the SUBLIMER Music; As it is but too apparent that even the Works of a Handel owe to it, in a great Measure, their Support.

That Your Majesty may long continue the Generous Patron of real Merit. That your Illustrious Example may have its just Weight; And that Providence may bestow upon YOU ABUNDANTLY it's [*sic*] choicest Blessings, whatever can dignify the Great or reward the Good, is the earnest Prayer of —

Your Majesty's Most Dutiful Subject and Servant
William Boyce

George III honoured Boyce by subscribing to *Cathedral Music* at this point. His predecessor, George II, had been close to death when vol. 1 was

published in 1760, but in any case he had failed to subscribe to it during
the previous four years when the opportunity to do so had existed. The
new king's support for the project reflected on the one hand his greater
commitment to music and the arts in particular, and on the other, his
positive support for the specifically English culture of his country.

♣

From James Boswell's *An Account of Corsica* (1768)

The Corsican peasants and soldiers were quite free and easy with me.
Numbers of them used to come and see me of a morning, and just go in
and out as they pleased. I did everything in my power to make them fond
of the British, and bad them hope for an alliance with us. They asked me a
thousand questions about my country, all which I chearfully answered as
well as I could.

One day they would needs hear me play upon my German flute. To
have told my honest natural visitants, Really gentlemen I play very ill, and
put on such airs as we do in our genteel companies, would have been
highly ridiculous. I therefore immediately complied with this request. I
gave them one or two Italian airs, and then some of our beautiful old Scots
tunes Gilderoy, the Lass of Patie's Mill, Corn riggs are Bonny. The
pathetick simplicity and pastoral gaiety of the Scots Musick, will always
please those who have the genuine feelings of nature. The Corsicans were
charmed with the specimens I gave them, though I may say that they were
very indifferently performed!

My good friends insisted also to have an English song from me. I
endeavoured to please them in this too, and was very lucky in that which
occurred to me. I sung them 'Hearts of oak are our ships, Hearts of oak are
our men'.[109] I translated it into Italian for them, and never did I see men so
delighted with a song as the Corsicans were with Hearts of oak. "Cuore di
querco["],[110] cried they, "bravo Inglese["].[111] It was quite a joyous riot. I

---

[109] Boswell is referring to the song by Boyce interpolated by David Garrick into
the first performance of his pantomime, *Harlequin's Invasion*, at Drury Lane on 31
December 1759. This song soon became universally popular throughout Great
Britain and lived on in the national consciousness well into the 20th century. The
initial text of the chorus of the song was originally 'Heart of oak are our ships',
referring to the quality of the wood used, rather than the plural 'Hearts of oak are
our men', from the next phrase. Boswell was by no means alone at the time in
adding an 's' to the title, as indeed did its author, a practice that became
commonplace and has persisted until our own time.

[110] 'Heart of oak'.

fancied myself to be a recruiting sea-officer. I fancied all my chorus of Corsicans abroad the British fleet.

Boswell(1768), 318-19. Boswell travelled to Corsica in 1765. In late October he interviewed the great Corsican hero, General Paoli, who was leading the Corsican resistance to the occupation of their country by the French and the Genoese. This incident occurred during Boswell's visit to Paoli and his supporters. Garrick, the author of the words of the song, read Boswell's book and wrote to him on 8 March 1768: " . . . I never was more flatter'd in my life – that you should chuse my hurly burly song of *"Hearts of Oak"*.

♣

From the Vestry Minutes of St. Michael Cornhill, 7 April 1768

The churchwardens reported to the Vestry that they had sent a letter to D^r. Boyce acquainting him that the playing of the organ did not give that satisfaction to the Parish which they had a right to expect and that they were determined to lay the matter before a General Vestry and that they had received a letter in answer thereto from D^r. Boyce which letter being produced and read and taken into proper consideration the Vestry were of the opinion that the letter from D^r. Boyce was intended as a resignation of the place of Organist to this Parish and therefore ordered that a letter should be directly sent to D^r. Boyce to inform him that they accepted it as such which was accordingly wrote and immediately sent to him and the place of Organist was declared vacant and directed to be advertised.

A motion was then made that it be referred to the Churchwardens to supply the Church with a person to play the organ till the election of a new Organist and the question being put it was carried in the affirmative.

Lgh, MSS819/2;4072/2, 367. Boyce's dismissal from his post at Allhallows in March 1764 had been connected with his apparent failure to deal with concerns at the church about the performance of his assistant. It would appear that WB's powers as an organist himself were now in sufficient decline to lead to dissatisfaction at St. Michael's.

♣

---

[111] "Well done the English".

Boyce sets Whitehead's ode for the king's birthday 1768, 'Prepare, prepare your songs of praise', and plans to conduct it at court on 4 June.

Text in AR (1768), 'Characters', 229-30. Circumstances intervened this year, however, and resulted in a postponement of the performance of the ode. A note in the manuscript of Boyce's score records that "This ode was not performed till the 23d of June, on the occasion of the death of the Princess Louisa Anne, the King's sister, who died in the preceding May" (*Ob*, MS.d.321ª). The overture was edited by Finzi in MB 13 (1957) and has been recorded (see Discography).

♣

1 January 1769 being a Sunday, no royal ode for the New Year was required.

♣

From the *Public Advertiser*, 14 January 1769

NEVER PERFORMED, AT THE Theatre Royal in Covent Garden, This Day will be presented A new comic Opera, called TOM JONES. The Characters by Mr. MATTOCKS, Mr. FOX, Mr. SHUTER. . . . End of Act II. A new Pantomime Dance called The GARDENERS. . . . To which will be added The COUNTRY WIFE.[112] [&c.]

The text for this pastiche opera was written by Joseph Reed (*Lbl*, 841.d.37(4)). It was apparently not based directly on Fielding's eponymous novel of 1749, but derived from a French libretto based on Fielding's book supplied by Antoine Poinsinet for Philidor's comic opera, *Tom Jones*, of 1765 (see Fiske(1986), 341). The music was taken from a range of 18th-century composers, particularly Thomas Arne and Samuel Arnold, one of whom was probably responsible for its selection and arrangement. A vocal score was published by Welcker with title-page: TOM JONES | *A COMIC OPERA* | as performed at the THEATRE ROYAL in | Covent Garden | the Musick by the most celebrated Authors | the Words by | JOSEPH REED [&c.] [1769]. Boyce is represented by one item. In Act III (54), the melody of the single stanza 'siciliana', 'Tell me,

---

[112] A highly successful comedy by Wycherly, first performed in 1675.

lovely charmer, why', is borrowed from the soprano air, 'Tell me lovely shepherd, where', the most widely admired number from the serenata *Solomon* (1742) in the mid-18th-century.

♣

From a letter of William Havard to David Garrick, 30 May 1769

. . . I give you joy, Sir, of your approaching Shakespearian Jubilee. The people of Stratford could not err in their choice of a President. — They had properly no other.

May I not be permitted, Sir, to be a walker in the cavalcade, and hold up the train of part of the ceremony? I have already written an Ode in honour of our great master, which you have formerly thought well of. Dr. Boyce has set it excellently to music; and voices, I should think, will not be wanting on this occasion; but you will determine all this yourself.

(Boaden(1831), I, 352.) Havard refers here to his ode in honour of Shakespeare, 'Titles and Ermine fall behind', first performed at Drury Lane on 1 April 1756 during Garrick's managership. Although Garrick wished to honour his revered Shakespeare at the Jubilee he was planning for Stratford later in the year, he evidently declined Havard's suggestion that he might repeat the earlier Havard/Boyce ode. In the event, Garrick chose to declaim a new dedication ode of his own at the Jubilee.

♣

Boyce sets Whitehead's ode for the king's birthday 1769, 'Patron of arts! At length by thee', organises a public rehearsal, and conducts a performance at court on 4 June.

Text in AR (1769), 'Characters', 231-2. The overture was edited by Finzi in MB 13 (1957).

♣

Boyce subscribes to John Knox's *An Historical Journal of the campaigns in North America for the years 1757, 1758, 1759, and 1760*, 2 vols. (1769).

Boyce is known to have subscribed to the publication of nearly 70 works in his life-time. Most of them were musical, and a few literary or religious; this was the only historical book he invested in, albeit one concerned only with contemporary political and military events. Among the 250 or so subscribers were many military men and citizens of Ireland, where Knox himself resided. Boyce was the only prominent musician among them.

♣

Boyce subscribes to Philip Hayes's *Six Concertos . . . for the organ, harpsichord or forte-piano* (1769).

Professor of Music at Oxford (1777-99), Hayes was a friend of Boyce who went on to edit two pioneering sets of his anthems (1780/1790). These were the first English keyboard concertos to specify the possibility of performance on the newly emerging fortepiano. As he explains in his preface, Hayes added a solo harpsichord sonata at the end by way of compensation for a delay in publication. This was a highly successful enterprise for 447 copies were sold to 373 subscribers, notable among them being Alcock, Stanley, Dupuis, Nares and Hayes's father, William.

♣

Boyce subscribes to Capel Bond's *Six Anthems in Score* (1769).

After serving his musical apprenticeship at Gloucester, Bond pursued a notable career as an organist at Coventry. With wide support from the Midlands, this publication attracted 218 subscribers for 321 copies. The only other prominent musician to subscribe was Philip Hayes. Boyce's attention may have been drawn to Bond by the success of his *Six Concertos* (1766). It has been suggested that the concerto for bassoon in this set may have been influenced by the striking solo bassoon obbligato in WB's vocal duet, 'Softly rise', in *Solomon* (1742).[113]

---

[113] See NG2, 3, 850.

PART FIVE

LIFE AND CAREER, 1770-1779

Boyce sets Whitehead's royal ode for New Year's Day 1770, 'Forward, Janus, turn thine eyes', organises a public rehearsal, and conducts its performance at court.

Text in AR (1769), 'Characters', 201. The overture was edited by Finzi in MB 13 (1957).

♣

Boyce publishes a set of twelve overtures (1770).

Title-page: *TWELVE* | OVERTURES | *IN* | Seven, Nine, Ten, *and* Twelve Parts, | *FOR* | *Violins, Hautboys, Flutes, Horns,* | *TRUMPETS, and DRUMS,* | *A Tenor, Violoncello or Bassoon.* | and a figured Bass for the HARPSICORD: | *BY* | WILLIAM BOYCE, | *Master of his Majesty's Band of Musicians, &c.* | LONDON MDCCLXX.

Following the precedent he had set in publishing his *Eight Symphonys* in 1760, Boyce also brought together overtures from earlier works to make up this collection. Most of them were taken from court odes composed in the 1760s, and two were taken from other earlier compositions. The original sources are as follows: no. 1 from the KBO for 1762; no. 2 from KBO 1765; no. 3 from NYO 1763; no. 4 from the Ode 'See white-robed peace' (1763); no. 5 from NYO 1762; no. 6 from the *Secular Masque* (*c*1745); no. 7 from NYO 1765; no. 8 from KBO 1761; no. 9 from NYO 1768; no. 10 from KBO 1764; no. 11 from KBO 1766, and no. 12 from NYO 1767. As was the case when he published his *Symphonys*, Boyce imposes an order on his selections. Here, each of the odd-numbered works begins with a French overture and ends with a characteristically lively minuet in 3/8.

There can be no doubt that these late baroque style overtures of Boyce would have seemed anachronistic to concert audiences in the 1770s, who were now familiar with, and responsive to, the newly emergent early classical style. The latter was now the dominating force in the programmes of the fashionable concerts promoted in London by the two leading immigrant German composers then resident in London, J.C. Bach and C.F. Abel. As a consequence there was little or no demand now for overtures such as Boyce's. He did his best, however, by continuing to advertise their availability at £1 11s 6d a set[1] (see *GNDA*, 14 Feb., and *PA*, 23 Feb. 1771).

When WB's library was auctioned in April 1779 lot 261 offered "A most valuable Set of Plates[2] of Overtures, in twelve Parts, composed by Dr. Will. Boyce, which have never been publicly sold; also thirty copies of the above Work. — For the Purchase of which, the Gentlemen in the Trade of Music-selling are humbly requested to attend, as they can never have a better Opportunity of getting a Work of Credit into their Possession". This item was purchased by Marmaduke Overend, a former pupil, and fellow music theorist of WB's, who paid £11 11s for it.[3]

The Overtures were edited by Platt (Oxford, 1970-2), and have since been widely performed and recorded (see Discography).

♣

John Johnston publishes Boyce's edition of the music for Shakespeare's *Macbeth* [1770].

Title-page: The Original | Songs Airs & Chorusses | which were introduced in the TRAGEDY of | MACBETH | in Score | Composed by | MATTHEW LOCK | Chapel Organist to Queen Catharine[4] Consort to King Charles II. | Revised & Corrected | by | D^r. Boyce, | Dedicated to | DAVID GARRICK Esqr | John Johnston [n.d.].

Locke contributed music for a staging of *Macbeth* in 1664, and his name continued to be associated with that work throughout the 18th

---

[1] In modern currency c£230.

[2] The pewter plates prepared by the printers from which the multiple printed copies of the music were generated.

[3] See Bruce & Johnstone *b*(2010), 164. Setting aside what value, if any, the plates may have had at this time, Overend acquired each set of overtures at a quarter of the price asked by Boyce in 1770.

[4] Catharine of Braganza had married Charles II in 1662.

century. However, modern research has established that the music Boyce arranged was mainly composed by Richard Leveridge[5] for a production of the play at Drury Lane on 21 Nov. 1702 (see Fiske(1964), 116). The role of this music in the performance history of *Macbeth* may be indicated by the following contemporary assessment: "Locke's excellent music had given the managers an opportunity of adding a variety of songs and dances suitable, in some measure, to the play, but more agreeable to the then taste of the audience, who were pleased with the comic dress which the actors gave to the witches, contrary, in the opinion of every person of taste, to the original design of the author" (Davies(1781), 121-2). In Burney's view the music's "rude and wild excellence cannot be surpassed" (*BurneyH*, 4, 185). Since Boyce dedicated his edition to Garrick, it may be assumed that it was commissioned by him for performances of the play given at DL in the 1760s. Garrick kept *Macbeth* in the repertoire there from 1763 until his retirement in 1776, but WB's edition must have continued in general use at least until the end of the century, for it was reprinted in *c*1780 and *c*1803. The date of the first edition has erroneously been given as 1750 (see Dent(1928), 129). WB's score has been reproduced in Baldwin & Wilson(1997).

♣

Boyce subscribes to Richard Langdon's *Twelve Songs and two Cantatas*, op. 4 [1770].

Langdon was organist at Exeter Cathedral (1753-77), after which he moved on to similar posts in the provinces. He had previously published a set of harpsichord sonatas, and a number of other vocal collections, to one of which Boyce had subscribed in 1754. These pieces, which are provided with light orchestral accompaniments, sold 220 copies to 164 subscribers, among whom were also Thomas Arne, Hawkins, Giardini, Stanley, Dupuis, and William and Philip Hayes.

♣

Boyce subscribes to Handel's *Jephtha* (1770).

This was the first of four editions of Handel oratorios published 'in score' by William Randall that Boyce acquired in the last decade of his life. It

---

[5] Also a distinguished and long-lived bass singer.

attracted 158 subscribers for 195 copies. The later editions were of *Israel in Egypt* (1771), *Saul* (1773) and *Joshua* (1774). Given Boyce's great admiration for Handel, they may have been purchased simply for the personal pleasure they gave him, but they may also have had practical uses where his conducting activities were concerned. Given that he acquired *Israel in Egypt* in 1771, it was probably about that time that he made his arrangement with organ accompaniment of an extract from that work, *Moses and the Children of Israel*, published eventually by John Page in 1800.

♣

Boyce subscribes to Edward Miller's *Elegies, Songs, and an Ode*, op. 4 (*c*1770).

After studying with Burney in London, Miller took an active part in the musical life of Doncaster and East Anglia in the late 18th century. He published a wide range of vocal and instrumental music from *c*1755, which may have attracted Boyce's interest. Miller later published a large volume of simple settings of the 'Psalms of David' (1790). This seems to have broken all records for musical publications at the time for it attracted as many as 3,420 subscribers, among them George III and Queen Charlotte, and two other members of the Royal family.

♣

Boyce sets Whitehead's ode for the king's birthday 1770, 'Discord hence! The torch resign', organises a public rehearsal, and conducts its performance at court on 4 June.

Text in AR, (1770), 'Characters', 224-5. The overture was edited by Finzi in MB 13 (1957).

♣

A Letter from Boyce to a friend at Gloucester

Sir

As it possibly may have escaped your knowledge that I was flattered with the expectation of tasting your venison the last season, on account of my supplying the meeting at Gloucester with my music; so in [*sic*] behalf of myself & friends I now take the liberty of acquainting you that I still consider you as my debtor on that score.

M^r. Isaac informs me that my worthy friend M^r. Blackwell repeatedly promised him to remind you of this, but my not hearing either from him or you obliges me to trouble you with this, who am   Sir   your most obedient

Kensington Gore   humble servant

near London   W^m. Boyce

August 14,^th 1770 —

Lcm, MS8949. This document has only recently come to light, having previously been in private ownership. It is distinctive among the small number of surviving letters by Boyce in being concerned with personal rather than professional matters. "The meeting at Gloucester" clearly refers to the Three Choirs Festival held there in the late summer of 1769 when two Boyce anthems and his arrangement of Purcell's 'Te Deum in D' had been programmed. Though he gave up conducting at the Festival in the mid-1750s, this letter suggests that Boyce may have continued to attend later meetings. Since it was written a few weeks before the 1770 Festival at Worcester was due to take place, it would appear that he was looking forward to the possibility of enjoying the gastronomic feast evidently offered by his (unknown) friend in the company of their mutual acquaintances, one of whom, Elias Isaac, was the organist at Worcester Cathedral. The tone of friendly banter adopted by Boyce here provides a rare glimpse into the composer's personality as projected in his social life, even if his thoughts are expressed in the rather formal style characteristic of the times.

♣

Boyce sets Whitehead's royal ode for New Year's Day 1771, 'Again returns the circl'ing year', organises a public rehearsal, and conducts its performance at court.

Text in AR (1770), 'Characters', 218-9. The overture was edited by Finzi in MB 13 (1957).

♣

From the *Reminiscences* of Samuel Wesley (1736-7)

My brother Charles had two most able instructors in playing and composition. — Mr Joseph Kelway who was Harpsichord Master to the

late Queen Charlotte,[6] was his constant and attentive assistant, who entirely perfected him on the above instrument. He was an admirable player, and Organist of S[t]. Martin[7] and composed a charming set of Lessons for the Harpsichord.[8] — he was pupil to the famous Geminiani and wrote much in his style. — My brother learned Scarlatti's Music[9] of him of which he was very fond, and he was Kelway's favourite scholar.*
— And the late D[r]. William Boyce who was Organist and Composer to his Majesty, instructed him in composition for several years,[10] by which he was rendered a thorough proficient in the scientific branch of music, and became himself an excellent composer. I shall speak more largely of Dr. B. when I come to my own life.

*   Kelway said "It is of the utmost importance to a learner to hear the best music: if any one would learn to play well, let him hear Charles".

Lbl, Add.MS27593, f. 30.

♣

From the unpublished *Reminiscences* of Samuel Wesley (1836-7)

There is an instance of silly obstinacy in my musical biography which I have cause to regret. I have before noticed that my brother Charles had the advantage of studying the Science of Harmony under the late excellent D[r] Boyce, and I might have had all the same exercises to peruse and digest with my brother, which opportunity I neglected and even rejected.

Lbl, Add.MS27593, f. 130. It should be noted here that in spite of this confession of Samuel's, Charles's subsequent career as a composer was, probably for reasons of temperament and lack of application, much less productive and successful than his own.

---

[6] Consort of King George III.

[7] St. Martin's-in-the-Fields.

[8] Wesley is referring to Kelway's *Six Sonatas* published in 1764.

[9] That of Domenico Scarlatti. His often flamboyant and sometimes idiosyncratic harpsichord sonatas had became well known in England from 1739 when a volume of 30 sonatas was published in London under the title *Essercizi per Gravicembalo.* Thomas Roseingrave produced an expanded collection of Scarlatti sonatas, *XLII Suites de Pièces pour le Claveçin*, shortly afterwards.

[10] From *c*1771 when the Wesleys, though based in Bristol, also acquired a house in London.

♣

Boyce sets Whitehead's ode for the king's birthday 1771, 'Long did the churlish East detain', organises a public rehearsal, and conducts its performance at court on 4 June.

Text in AR (1771),'Characters', 233-4. The overture was edited by Finzi in MB 13 (1957).

♣

Boyce subscribes to Thomas Morley's *A Plain and Easy Introduction to Practical Music* (1771).

This reprint of Morley's famous treatise of 1597 undertaken by William Randall, who had taken over the music publishing business of John Walsh in 1766, attracted 236 subscribers for 331 copies. Randall's timely initiative may be seen in the context of the growing interest in 'ancient music' characteristic of English musical culture throughout the 18th century. Prominent among the many leading musicians who subscribed to this edition was one of Boyce's pupils, the musical prodigy, 'Master Charles Wesley of Bristol', then only 13 years of age.

♣

Boyce subscribes to John Alcock's *Six and Twenty select Anthems* (1771).

This was the fifth occasion on which Boyce had chosen to support a musical publication by Alcock, his former fellow boy chorister at St. Paul's. The handsome and substantial folio volume, with an informative preface, was dedicated to the then Archbishop of Canterbury, Frederick Cornwallis, formerly Bishop of Lichfield, where Alcock had been organist from 1750. The composer wrote an informative preface that provided a detailed background to the composition of his anthems. Only 143 copies were ordered by 79 subscribers, but among these were also Burney, William and Philip Hayes, and Stanley.

♣

Boyce sets Whitehead's royal ode for New Year's Day 1772, 'At length the fleeting year is o'er', organises a public rehearsal, and conducts its performance at court.

Text in AR (1771), 'Characters', 205. The overture was published by Finzi in MB 13 (1757) and has been recorded (see Discography).

♣

Thomas Chapman publishes two hymns by Boyce in the *Young Gentlemen and Ladies Musical Companion* (1772).

Though the imprint is dated 1772, the dedication to the pupils of St. Martin's School in Hungerford Market, Strand, is dated 'March the 1st. 1773'. WB's setting of 'The Lord does them support that fall', followed by an 'Hallelujah hymn', XCVII, appears on pp.128-9. In 1774 Chapman re-issued his collection with a supplement that included another hymn by WB, 'The Lord my pasture shall prepare', on p.23.

♣

Boyce sets Whitehead's ode for the king's birthday 1772, 'From scenes of death and deep distress', organises a public rehearsal, and conducts its performance at court on 4 June.

Text in AR (1772), 'Characters', 218-9. On this occasion we know that the ode was initially rehearsed at the Turk's Head tavern in Greek St., Soho, on 29 May, and publicly rehearsed at Hickford's Great Room on 2 June (*LEP*, 2 June). The overture was edited by Finzi in MB 13 (1957).

♣

Boyce sets Whitehead's royal ode for New Year's Day 1773, 'Wrapt in the stole of sable grain' (text in AR 'Characters', 238-9), organises a public rehearsal, and conducts its performance at court.

♣

Boyce subscribes to William Jackson's *Eight Sonatas*, op. 10 (*c*1773).

Jackson, an energetic and multi-talented figure, spent most of his life in Exeter. In order to distinguish himself from a contemporary Oxford musician of the same name he designated himself 'Jackson of Exeter'. Appointed organist of the cathedral there in 1777, he produced a substantial amount of vocal music, including a successful comic opera, but only a few instrumental works. His reputation clearly extended far beyond his home town, for 246 copies were ordered by 206 subscribers. Among them were the Germans J.C. Bach and C.F. Abel, the two most fashionable composers of the time in England, both of whom were then working in London. These sonatas are for harpsichord and string quartet.

♣

Boyce subscribes to J.E. Galliard's *Morning Hymn* (1773).

This work was based on Galliard's *Hymn of Adam and Eve* (1728), a setting of an extract from Milton's *Paradise Lost* for two vocal soloists and strings. Benjamin Cooke, organist of Westminster Abbey, added for this edition an overture, further orchestral accompaniments, and chorusses to create a cantata-like work. It is dedicated to the Academy of Ancient Music of which Galliard was a founder-member in 1726, and to which Cooke belonged. The latter must have collaborated regularly with Boyce in choral activities. 174 copies were ordered by 149 subscribers, notable among them being Hawkins, Stanley, and William and Philip Hayes.

♣

Boyce's Foreword to *Cathedral Music,* vol. 3, (1773)

When I first under took this Work, I had not sufficiently considered the length of time necessary to complete it, which occasioned my proposing to deliver the Volumes much sooner than it was possible for me to effect. However, I hope it will appear by the execution that this has been the single instance in which I have not fully performed my engagement.

It may easily be discovered in the perusal of this collection, that the pieces which were composed between the Reformation and Restoration are in a more grave style than those written since; a gravity in Church Music having been particularly ordered by Authority in the reign of Queen

Elizabeth, with intent to distinguish it from every other Species, calculated for secular purposes; but on the return of King Charles the Second from his long exile in Foreign Countries, when a lighter kind of Church Music prevailed, and which better suited the gay disposition of that Monarch and his Court, the Musicians of the Chapel found it their interest to deviate in some measure from the former plan, by adding a variety and liveliness, especially in their Anthems, which had not been customary before. Yet, notwithstanding this alteration of Style, they still reserved a solemnity and learning in their Compositions which have rendered them lasting monuments of ingenuity and expression.

Nor have the more early writers been wanting in their expression, although it is not so particularly marked, for their music being generally full, and composed of many parts, they seem to have aimed at giving to each of these an equal degree of sweetness, as may be conjectured from the elegance and purity of the several melodies; and, it must be confessed, that their skill in the joining and intermixing of them in the formation of harmony, are indubitable testament of their indefatigable application, and eminent abilities. The Anthems of TALLIS TYE BIRD and GIBBONS, with the Morning Service of FARRANT &c, abound with admirable examples of this kind of art & expression.

Had I not been under a restriction by the last Will and Testament of the late Dr. MAURICE GREENE I should have inserted some valuable pieces of his, particularly his Services, a very learned and judicious composition, and highly deserving of presentation: There are also three ancient Services by NATHANIEL PATRICK, ADRIAN BATTEN, and ALBERTUS BRIAN with Two by the late Mr. CHARLES KING Almoner, and Vicar Choral of the Cathedral Church of St. Paul, London the one in the key of F faut,[11] the other in B flat, which I would willingly have found room for, could it have been done without omitting what appeared to me to claim the preference.

I am truly sensible how much I owe to the goodness of Providence in granting me health & perseverance to labour through this very difficult, and tedious business, and it will be a most grateful reflection to me hereafter, that I have been enabled to do justice to these excellent productions of my Countrymen, by conveying them to Posterity in a more respectful and accurate manner than hath yet been experienced in any other musical publication whatever.

I cannot finally quit this undertaking without acknowledging my obligation to those members of our Choirs who have kindly assisted me

---

[11] A solmisation term indicating the key of F major.

with copies to forward it, and in particular to my worthy Friends the Rev. Mr. WILLIAM GOSTLING of Canterbury Cathedral, Mr JAMES KENT, Organist of the Cathedral and College at Winchester, Dr. WILLIAM HAYES Music Professor in the University of Oxford, and Dr. SAMUEL HOWARD of London, they all having been materially useful in the progress of the work, more especially the last-mentioned, who by his friendly zeal and assistance left nothing undone in his power, to lesson my trouble in it, and to render the task easy & agreeable to me.

William Boyce

Boyce's decision to add a Foreword to this final volume of *Cathedral Music* reflected not only his desire to publicly apologise for the delay in completing this demanding project, thirteen years after the issue of the first volume, but also the immensity of the task he undertook in the light of the many other duties he had to fulfil as a composer and organist. Samuel Wesley later wrote of *Cathedral Music*: "Our worthy countryman, and musical ornament, Dr William Boyce, has brought together a brilliant phalanx of harmonic perfection in his invaluable collection of church music, where we have the refulgent names of Byrde, Tallis, Orlando Gibbons, Farrant, Blow, Purcell, Wise, Weldon, Clark, Humphries etc. all of whom are abundant proofs of England having produced genius of the most solid and permanent texture" *(Lbl*, Add.MS27593, f. 118).

♣

Boyce sets Whitehead's ode for the king's birthday 1773, 'Born for millions are the Kings' (text in AR (1773), 'Characters', 247-8), organises a public rehearsal, and conducts its performance at court on 4 June.

♣

Boyce subscribes to William Randall's edition of James Kent's *Twelve Anthems* (1773).

After holding posts as organist at Finedon, Northants, and Trinity College Cambridge, Kent had been appointed to Winchester Cathedral in 1738. As a composer, he limited himself to church music. This publication sold as many as 343 copies to 246 subscribers, among them the composers

Alcock, Stanley, William and Philip Hayes, and Nares. Kent assisted
Boyce when he was working on *Cathedral Music* (1760-73).

♣

Boyce subscribes to Richard Eastcott's *Six Sonatas for the Harpsichord or Piano Forte* (1773).

Eastcott published very little, but these sonatas sold 260 copies to 223
subscribers. Notable among them were Abel and J.C. Bach, the two
fashionable emigrant German composers who dominated musical life in
London at the time. In his self-effacing preface, Eastcott writes that he was
"relying on the sincerity of a few friends who have promised to give me a
favourable reception". They did not let him down, for there were many
orders from Exeter and the West Country where he worked.

♣

Boyce sets Whitehead's royal ode for New Year's Day 1774, 'Pass but a few short fleeting years', organises a public rehearsal, and conducts its performance at court.

Text in AR (1773), 'Characters', 217-8. This is the only court ode of
Boyce's that has so far been performed in modern times (see Discography).

♣

From the *Journal* of the Rev. Charles Wesley (1774)

Dr. Boyce came several times to my house to hear him; [his son Charles]
gave him some of his own music, asked if the king had heard him, and
expressed much surprise when he told him no.[12] My brother the Rev. John
Wesley,[13] enriched him with an inestimable present of Dr. Boyce's three

---

[12] Boyce clearly had in mind here the eight-year-old child prodigy Mozart, and his
elder sister, Nannerl, who had been received at court by George III and Queen
Charlotte on 27 April 1764. Accompanied by their father, Leopold, the Mozarts
had only recently arrived in London. Their performances for the Royal family were
not only greatly enjoyed but also inspired a generous reward of 24 guineas (in
modern currency c£4,000). However, the following year, Charles's similarly gifted
younger brother, Samuel, was indeed invited to meet the King.
[13] The founder of Methodism.

volumes of cathedral music.[14] Several have offered to teach him, but as I waited & deferred his instruction in the practical part till I could get the very best instructor for him so I kept him back from the theory. The only man to teach him that & sacred music he believes to be Dr. Boyce.

Mr, DDCW10/2, appendix 2, 7. (Jackson(1849), 333) Wesley eventually selected the keyboard virtuoso, Joseph Kelway, to teach his son the harpsichord and organ.

♣

A poem of the Rev. Charles Wesley presented to Boyce on behalf of Samuel Wesley (*c*1774).

TO DR. BOYCE

The humble petition
Of a rhiming musician,[15]
(A petition of natural right)
Undeniably shews
That, wherever he goes,
Church-music is all his delight.

That he never can rest,
Till enrich'd with the best,
His talent aright he employs,
And claims for his own,
As true harmony's son,
The collection of good Dr. Boyce.[16]

Three volumes of yours,
Which his prayer procures
Will afford him examples enough,
And save poet Sam

[14] The third and final volume had been published the previous year.

[15] As the poem subsequently makes clear, the 'rhiming musician' is Charles Wesley's second son, Samuel Wesley snr. had selected Boyce to teach his elder son, Charles, harmony, composition and theory. The composer soon became a close friend of the family.

[16] The collection refers to the three volumes of Boyce's *Cathedral Music*, the last of which was published in 1773. We know from Charles's *Journal* that his brother, John, had recently presented Boyce's *Cathedral Music* to Samuel's older brother, Charles.

(Your petitioner's name)
From a deluge of musical stuff.

So good Doctor, if now
This suit you allow,
And make him as rich as a king,
Taken into your CHOIR,
To his ORGAN and LYRE,
Your petitioner will ever shall — Sing!

(Lightwood(1937), 22-3) Charles Wesley snr., brother of John, the founder of Methodism, was famed for his hymns. At the same time he was a prolific writer of poetry, much of it not only inspired by his religious convictions, but by his family life, as in the above. Here he conveys on behalf of his precociously gifted son, Samuel, his wish to possess a set of Boyce's *Cathedral Music*. An element of sibling rivalry may have been involved here for Samuel's older brother, Charles jnr., had only recently been presented with *Cathedral Music* by his uncle, John Wesley.

♣

Songs by Boyce are published in the *New Musical and Universal Magazine*, 3 vols. [1774].

This collection, "consisting of the most favourite songs, airs &c. as performed at all public places", includes Boyce's two-part drinking song, 'Since nature mankind for society framed', in vol. 1, 53-5, and in vol. 2 an air from *The Chaplet* (1749), 68-9, a three-part catch, 'A blooming youth', 77, and a solo song, 'On thy banks', 130-31.

♣

Boyce's sets Whitehead's ode for the king's birthday 1774, 'Hark! or does the Muse's ear' (text in AR (1774), 'Characters', 226-7), organises a public rehearsal, and conducts its performance at court on 4 June.

♣

Boyce subscribes to Thomas Brown jnr.'s *A Collection of Songs and a Cantata* (1774).

Brown was a London organist with few compositions to his credit. These songs, his only major publication, attracted only 96 subscribers for 118 copies. The only other leading musicians to subscribe were Philip Hayes and James Nares.

♣

From the *Leicester and Nottingham Journal*, 3 September 1774

LEICESTER INFIRMARY The New ORGAN in St. MARTIN'S CHURCH will be open'd on Wednesday the 21st of SEPTEMBER;[17] when in the course of DIVINE SERVICE will be perform'd an OVERTURE; HANDEL'S GRAND DETTINGEN TE DEUM JUBILATE, and CORONATION ANTHEM. — The annual SERMON will be preached by the Rev. Mr. BURNABY of GREENWICH. In the Evening will be a CONCERT. — The first Act will consist of an ODE, written on the occasion By JOSEPH CRADDOCK, Esq; Set to Music, by Dr. BOYCE, Composer to his MAJESTY, in which Miss DAVIES the First FEMALE SINGER will perform. — The second Act will consist of an OVERTURE, SOLO'S, — AIR'S and CONCERTO'S. — AND ON Thursday Morning the 22nd of September, will be perform'd the SACRED ORATORIO of JEPHTHA. Signr. GIARDINI will lead the BAND which will be remarkably full, and consist of the most EMINENT PERFORMERS. [&c.]

The Infirmary at Leicester had opened in 1771. The primary purpose of the two events advertised here was to raise funds for the hospital. The driving force behind these initiatives was the remarkable John Montague, 4th Earl of Sandwich, whose country seat, Hinchinbrooke House, near Huntingdon, was not far from Leicester. Sandwich, was a prominent politician and reforming First Lord of the Admiralty, the founder of the Concerts of Antient Music in 1776, a leading promoter of the Handel Commemoration Concerts at Westminster Abbey in 1784, friend of Garrick, and a keen amateur drummer. The author of the ode set by Boyce, Joseph Cradock, had been a High Sheriff of Leicester, was an inveterate

---

[17] The organ was made by Snetzler, the finest organ builder working in England at the time, and the distinguished organist was Joah Bates who organised the Handel concerts in 1784, and also happened to be Private Secretary to Lord Sandwich.

theatre-goer, and an author who was himself a leading patron of the Leicester concerts.

A review of the ode and its rendition appeared shortly in the press: "The words and music were well adapted to each other and the effect upon the hearts of all the hearers was very visible in their countenances, and spoke more in its commendation than all that can be wrote upon the subject, in short the performance was excellent" (J.B. Nichols in Cradock (1828), xxv). Much later, details of the work and its performance were published: "The following Ode was written for the occasion by Mr. Cradock, set to music by by Dr. Boyce, Composer to his Majesty, and ably conducted by his friend Mr Howard.[18] Air (Mr Norris)[19] 'Lo! On a thorny bed of care' — Chorus 'Deplore his fate' — Recit (Miss Davis)[20] — Air 'Think not in vain' — Duet (Norris and Champness)[21] 'Here shall soft Charity repair' — Recit (accomp) Davis 'Why lingers then the generous flame?' — Full chorus 'To hail the work'". Lord Sandwich himself played the drums and his characteristic performance made an indelible impression on a 14-year old member of the audience: "On seeing Lord Sandwich beat the kettle-drums, I took station as near to him as I could. The grandeur of the sound, added to the display he made in flourishing his ruffles and drum strokes, mightily pleased me. The loudest sounds first arrest the attention: I was riveted to the spot, and was so captivated by his Lordship's performances that for a time I heard nothing else" (Gardiner(1838), 1, 5). The concert Gardiner heard was repeated at Hitchinbrook the following day.

Finally, Cradock himself gave an account of the early performance history of the work: "[It] was again introduced at Hinchinbrook at Christmas, and the Bravura air[22] was executed by Miss Ray,[23] It was likewise performed in Lent at Covent Garden Theatre, under the care of

---

[18] Dr. Samuel Howard, a long-standing friend and colleague of Boyce's.

[19] Thomas Norris, a leading tenor.

[20] Cecilia Davies, a much admired soprano in London and on the continent where she was dubbed 'Inglesina prima donna'.

[21] Samuel Champness, a well-known bass.

[22] 'Why lingers then the generous flame'.

[23] Martha Ray was a brilliant young soprano whom Sandwich met when she was only seventeen. She became his mistress and bore him nine children, five of whom survived. She was eventually shot in London in 1779 by a rival suitor for her affections. Martha usually sang in performances promoted by Sandwich, but she was unavailable for the Leicester performances and arranged for Miss Davies to deputise for her.

Mr. Linley, after Alexander's Feast;[24] but the score has never been printed. The duet of 'Here shall soft Charity repair,' has been repeated at St Paul's and indeed is now admitted after an introductory line of recitative from Scripture, into almost all the Cathedrals. Mr. Braham and Mr. Bartleman, from their own celebrity, have greatly contributed to make it so popular" (Cradock(1828), 123). The popularity of WB's duet continued well into the 19th century at the Three Choirs Festival too, for in 1811 one of the concerts "opened with Dr. Boyce's beautiful and appropriate duet of 'Here shall soft charity repair" (Williams(1895), 259). When it was published by Bland and Weller in 1804, the title-page also refers to performances "by Mr Harrison and Mr Bartleman at the Antient Concerts".

The libretto published for the Leicester performance is preserved at *Lfom*, Acc.No.1423. The complete ode was edited and published by W.H. Cummings in 1908. Boyce's autogr. score on which Cummings based his edition is now at *US: Wc*. Another contemporary score is at *Lcm*, MS784. This was evidently used for performances at the Concerts of Antient Music. Attached to it is a list of parts which indicates that provision was made for an orchestra of at least 28 players, and a chorus of at least 23 in performances by the Society.

♣

From the *Reminiscences* of Samuel Wesley (1836-7)

Dr Boyce came to my father's house[25] [in late 1774], and said to him "Sir, I hear you have got an English Mozart in your house.[26] Young Linley[27] tells me wonderful things of him". I had then scrawled down the oratorio of Ruth:[28] the Doctor looked over it and seemed highly pleased: he said, "These airs are some of the prettiest I have seen: this boy writes by nature as good a bass as I can by skill & study. There is no man in England has

---

[24] Cradock's memory seems to be at fault here, for Thomas Linley (sen.) worked at Drury Lane, and the concert including WB's Ode and Handel's *Alexander's Feast* took place there on 19 March 1779 (see *PA* 19 March).

[25] Samuel was the second son of the Rev. Charles Wesley, hymn-writer and poet, and brother of John, the founder of Methodism.

[26] Boyce clearly had in mind Mozart's visit to London with his father Leopold in 1764-5 when his precocious musical abilities made a great impact.

[27] Thomas, the musically gifted son of Thomas Linley snr., who had been a pupil of Boyce.

[28] Samuel's MS of *Ruth* (now preserved at *Lbl*, Add.MS34997) was completed on 26 October 1774 when he was only eight years old.

two such sons".[29] — He told my father to let me run on my own way without check of rules, or masters. — Whenever the Doctor came, I used to run to him, with my song, sonata, or what not, and he examined them with great patience.

I sent my oratorio of Ruth to him as a present, and he honoured me with the following note: "Doctor Boyce's compliments & thanks to his very ingenious brother composer; M[r] S.W., and is very much pleased and obliged by the possession of the oratorio of Ruth, which he shall preserve with the utmost care, as the most curious product of his musical library" (*Lbl,* Add.MS27593, ff. 32[r]-33[v]). Samuel's father wrote an earlier account of this event in his *Journal* (repr. in Kassler & Olleson(2001), 99). The latter had also been quoted in an article about Samuel's career published by George Hogarth in the *Musical Herald* 2, no. 3, 19 Dec. 1846, 13-14.

♣

Boyce subscribes to Joseph Ganthony's *An Anthem for Christmas-Day* (1774).

This extended work was written for Cripplegate School in London where Ganthony taught. He also published some other small-scale vocal pieces. Despite the composer's modest profile, this publication was remarkably successful, for it sold 236 copies to 204 subscribers, notable among them being Thomas Arne and Samuel Howard.

♣

The Royal Ode for the New Year 1775

1 January 1775 being a Sunday, neither the Poet Laureate nor Boyce would have expected to have to produce a New Year Ode for the court this year. However, the following notice appeared in the *MC*, 2 Jan., 1775: "It was thought that New Year's Day would have been kept at Court this day, and an Ode was composed and set to music, to be performed as usual; but Their Majesties received the compliments of the Nobility and Gentry yesterday, without giving them the annual entertainment of new music" (quoted in McGuiness(1971), 59). No documentary evidence has so far

---

[29] Samuel's elder brother was Charles jnr. who, unlike Samuel, was formally taught by Boyce.

come to light to explain this anomaly. If an ode was composed at all, it
was almost certainly the one performed on New Year's Day 1776.

♣

An account by Samuel Wesley of a visit to King George III in 1775

The king called for any pieces he chose, and was surprised I had them in
my memory. His Majesty ordered the Queen's page to bring Dr. Boyce's
Church Music[30] which he asked me to perform. The Duke of
Mecklenburg, the Queen's brother, arrived, and said to the King, "What is
dat?" "What, what?" said the King, "Do not you know? Any school boy
could inform you. It is, 'Lord, have mercy upon us' the response to the
commandments! I found his Majesty partial to a response of Dr. Child,[31]
who in the reign of Charles I, had been organist at Bristol Cathedral".

(Stevenson(1876), 454) The precocious Samuel was about nine at the time
of this visit.

♣

From Joel Collier's *Musical Travels through England*, 3rd edn (1775)

Here [Liverpool] I instantly went to pay my respects to Mr. *Cable*, who
had formerly commanded a ship in the African slave-trade, but had long
quitted that inhuman employment, and given himself up entirely to the
cultivation of music. I found him sitting in a pleasant summer-house,
which he had created on the top of a decayed elm, and with infinite taste
fitted up in imitation of a ship's cabbin. Here he was solacing himself with
a pipe and a bowl of grog. He very civilly invited me to sit down, and
when I had presented my recommendation letter to him, he put it into his
pocket, and said, he would overhaul it at his leisure, though I afterward
found that the Captain had never the advantage of learning to read or
write. After having emptied two bowls in the most amicable manner, the
captain very civilly proposed to me to sing, which I instantly complied

---

[30] The request was for WB's edition of *Cathedral Music* (1760-73), a set of which
the Wesley family already possessed by this time.

[31] This response comes from the 'Kyrie eleison' of Child's Service in E minor,
edited by Boyce in *Cathedral Music*, vol. 1, 155-6.

with, and began tuning up, *Let not age thy bloom ensnare*, &c.[32] but was much surprized to hear him roar out, before I had finished the first line, that "d[amn] his eyes, he did not like that palaver, but wanted to hear *Hearts of Oak*,[33] or something that was jolly". I, very submissively excused myself as never having learnt that air, and he, accepting my apology, told me, as I could not sing, I might have a bout with my fiddle, as he supposed I knew how to scrape that. Though this behaviour was very opposite to that softness which the love of music generally inspires, and made me envy the good fortune of my great master, who in his travels had always performed to princes and elections; yet not chusing to exasperate my host who was a middle-sized, broad-shouldered man, with bow-legs, and a fist like a shoulder of mutton, I took up my violoncello, and began an overture which I thought capable of disarming the greatest ruggedness of temper. Full twenty minutes I continued playing without interruption, congratulating myself upon the conquest I had gained over the captain's ferocity, and reflecting with admiration upon the amazing power of sound, which could thus silence the jarring passions, and soften the roughest dispositions. "O why", said I to myself, "is not the great Dr. here,[34] to share in the triumphs of his pupil?" Saying this, I venture to steal a glance at a pierglass,[35] that was opposite to me, in order to adjust my attitude, when, with the utmost surprize and indignation, I beheld the captain, whom I thought enraptured by my skill, fast asleep, and nodding in his elbow chair. I confess, I was scarcely able to contain my fury at this affront, but thinking it inconsistent with my character to express my feelings in any other than a musical way; I sang with great vehemence – *I rage – I burn – despair – despair.*[36] – *To arms, to arms, your silver trumpets sound*[37] – and touching my violoncello in the rudest manner, I awoke such sounds of horror and anguish; I made the strings so responsive to the agitation of my mind, that the captain started up precipitately from his seat, overset the bowl of liquor, and blasting my eyes, asked me what I meant by making such a caterwauling? There was something so terrific in

---

[32] The reference here is to the air, 'Let not age thy bloom ensnare', from "a favorite cantata sung by Mrs Weichsell at Vauxhall" by Tommaso Giordani (1773).

[33] Boyce's popular setting of David Garrick's patriotic song of December 1759.

[34] It may be presumed that the reference is to Dr. Burney, one of the butts of Collier's satire.

[35] A tall mirror, often placed over a chimney-piece or between two windows.

[36] The quotation is from the giant Polythemus's 1st recitative in Handel's *Acis and Galatea*, part II.

[37] These words are from the dramatic chorus of Persians in Act 2 of Handel's oratorio, *Belshazzar's Feast*.

his looks and gestures, that I could not resist the impulse I experienced, to pacify him by my apologies. These he kindly received, and we cemented our reconciliation by another bowl of grog; after which the captain felt himself in such good humour, that he insisted upon my giving him my impartial opinion upon his own musical acquirements, and ringing the bell, ordered his *Gom-gom* to be brought in. This instrument was a wooden bow, the ends of which were confined by a dried and hollow gut, into which the captain blew, scraping upon it at the same time with an old fiddle–stick, stamping upon the ground, and roaring out, Ho! ho! with such a force of lungs, and extension of voice, that at length, unable to bear the horrid discord any longer, I begged him to desist. He then told me that he had acquired the knowledge of this instrument during the course of several voyages to the coast of Africa, and that his proficiency was allowed to be so great, that the king of *Benin*[38] had offered to make him his prime minister, provided he would have continued at his court, and that he had secretly received proposals of marriage from a princess of *Monopatapa.*[39] "But", added he, "I loved old England so well that I did not chuse to stay with their black majesties, and having made a very pretty fortune, retired hither, where I live very happily, and amuse myself every afternoon with my favourite instrument". – He then asked me with a very self-sufficient smile, or rather grin, if I did not prefer it to an overgrown fiddle, and all the Italian whimsies, and tweedle–dums, that people played upon in these days? – I thought myself and my profession so much insulted by this impertinent discourse, that I could not help telling him with a contemptuous smile, that the music was adapted to the musician, that it might do very well for sea-faring people, but to cultivated ears it was absolutely barbarous; and therefore I advised him to confine his exhibitions to his negro princes and princesses, and never again attempt to perform before any person possessed of the least brilliancy of finger. Saying this, I took up my violoncello, that by the execution of a most masterly *capriccio,* I might convince him of his ignorance, and my own skill. But scarce had I touched the chords before this unmannerly tarpaulin burst into the most reproachful language. He called me a lousy rascal; a squeaking son of a b[itc]h; a lubberly gut-scraper; and not contented with this contumelious treatment, when I attempted to vindicate my character, he knocked me down at one blow, and after this unprecedented outrage, ordered two black slaves to bring him a rope, and swore he would keel-

---

[38] A primitive country in Southern Nigeria involved in trading with Britain in minerals and slaves at this time.
[39] An area in south-east Africa ruled by a negro chief and held from the 16th century by Portugal (now Zimbabwe).

haul me. In vain did I remonstrate against this inhuman treatment, in sounds which might have "melted rocks, and softened things inanimate to pity"; I was dragged to a large horse-pound, in the middle of which was a kind of Indian canoe, under which I was three times successively drawn by two ropes, while the captain stood on the bank, shaking his sides with laughter, and playing a war-like measure with his *gom-gom.* Having undergone this savage operation, I was thrust headlong into the street, my teeth chattering, and my whole body shivering with cold and affright; and the captain muttering out the most barbarous jests on my condition, threw my violoncello after me, and shut the door. In this distressed situation did I wander about the town, hooted at by the boys, and exciting the derision of the vulgar; till at length a very decent woman, who lives at the sign of the French horn, (to which circumstances I principally ascribe her humanity) kindly invited me in, and after drying myself at her fire, and drinking a quartern of gin, to prevent my catching cold, I slept very comfortably that night upon a flock bed, and set out early the next morning for Chester.

(Collier(1775), 49-57) It is now generally accepted that Joel Collier was a pseudonym for John Bicknell the elder, a lawyer and writer (see Lonsdale(1965), 156-7). In an appendix to his book (p.15), 'Collier' readily admits to "the imitating, as exactly as possible, the three greatest works which the present age has given birth to; the letters of a late noble Earl to his *dear boy;* the Musical Tour to the Continent; and the much admired *Tour thro' Sicily and Malta*".[40] Collier's satire proved to be highly successful and was reissued five times between 1775 and 1818. That the Burneys were irritated by Bicknell's satire, however, is evident from the *Memoirs* of Frances, Charles Burney's daughter, who described it as "ludicrous parody . . . though executed with burlesque humour, whether urged or not by malevolence, was never reprinted; and obtained but the laughter of a moment, without making the shadow of an impression to the disadvantage of the tourist" (D'Arblay(1832), 159-60).

♣

---

[40] The references are respectively to Lord Chesterfield's *Letters to his Son* (1774), Charles Burney's *The Present State of Music in France and Italy, or the Journal of a Tour through those Countries* (1771), and James Boswell's *An Account of Corsica. The Journal of a Tour* (1768), see above, pp.184-5.

Boyce sets Whitehead's ode for the king's birthday 1775, 'Ye powers who rule o'er states and kings', organises a public rehearsal, and conducts its performance at court on 4 June.

Text in AR (1775), 'Characters', 194-5. The overture was edited by Finzi in MB 13 (1957).

♣

Longman & Broderip publish Thomas Warren's *A Collection of Vocal Harmony consisting of Catches Canons and Glees . . . vol. 13 (c1775).*

The text of a glee by Boyce, 'Elegy: 'Genius, genius of harmony" (anon.), was written "In memory of the R^t. Honble. Alexander late Earl of Eglington a great Encourager of this Species of Music". It appears on pp.221-8. Eglinton, the 10th Earl, had died in 1769.

♣

Boyce draws up his will on 24 June 1775.

In the Name of God. Amen.

William Boyce of the Parish of Kensington in the County of Middlesex being at this present time in perfect health of Body and Sound mind do make my last Will and Testament in manner following First and principally I Assign my Soul to Almighty God trusting for salvation through the Merits of my dear Redeemer Jesus Christ And my Body I commit to the Earth to be buried at the discretion of my two Joint Executrixes hereinafter named but not untill Seven days and Nights are fully expired after my decease And as to such worldly Estate and Effects with which it has pleased God to bless me I give and dispose of the same as follows Item I do hereby nominate and Appoint my present wife Hannah Boyce and my only Daughter Elizabeth Boyce begotten of the Body of my said wife Hannah Boyce Joint Executrixes of this my last Will and Testament and Joint Trustees and Governesses of the Estate and person of my Son hereinafter named during his Minority and till the time he attains to the full age of Twenty one years Item I give and bequeath unto my said wife Hannah and to my said Daughter Elizabeth in trust to be disposed of in manner herein after specified all my personal Estate including my Debts of every kind Government Stock and Securities plate Jewels Rings China Pictures Household Goods Wearing Apparel Laces Linen of every denomination for personal wear as well as for the Bed Table and other uses my Music printed and in Manuscript of my own composition and of the various other Authors my Musical Instruments Engraved Music plates with my printed Books of every sort and whatever else may be omitted in the above enumeration of my property to be and to remain at their joint disposal and in manner following after all my just Debts are paid out of the said Estate Item I give and bequeath unto my said wife Hannah Boyce one third part of the whole of my personal Estate to become and to remain from the time of my decease her sole property and for her use for ever Item I give and bequeath unto my said Daughter Elizabeth Boyce begotten of the Body of my said Wife Hannah and born on the Twenty ninth day of April 1749 old Stile one other third part of the whole of my personal Estate to become and to remain from the time of my decease her sole property and for her use for ever Item I give and bequeath unto my Son William Boyce begotten of the Body of my said Wife Hannah Boyce and born on the Twenty fifth day of March 1764 New Stile the third and last remaining third part of the three equal Divisions of the whole of my personal Estate to be disposed of and appropriated for his sole use in the maintenance and Education of him during his Minority at the discretion of my joint Executrixes the whole of the sums so expounded for his use to be accounted for by his said Mother and Sister and the remaining part whether more or less to be paid to him when he attains to his full age of Twenty one years Item in case of the decease of my said Son William Boyce during his Minority I give and bequeath that Third part of the whole of my personal Estate before bequeathed to my said Son William to my said Wife Hannah Boyce and my said Daughter Elizabeth Boyce to be equally divided between them share and share alike to become from the time of my said Son William his decease their property for ever Item in case of the decease of both my said Executrixes during the Minority of my said Son William Boyce I do hereby nominate and Appoint my Brother in Law James Wyndham Taylor of Salisbury Court ffleet Street London and my own Sister Elizabeth Wyndham his wife of the same place Joint Executor and Executrix of this my last Will and Testament and Joint Trustees and Guardians of the person and Estate of my said Son William Boyce during his Minority and till the time he attains to his full age of Twenty one years And now I hereby revoke all former Wills by me heretofore made and so declare this to be my last Will and Testament wrote with my own hand on this Sheet of common writing paper containing four pages In witness whereof I have hereunto set my hand and Seal This Twenty fourth day of June in the year of Our Lord One thousand Seven hundred and Seventy five William Boyce.

Signed Sealed published and declared by the said William Boyce as and for his last Will and Testament in the presence of us who in his presence and at his request have set our names as subscribing Witnesses thereto.

19th February 1779

Lpro, Prob II/1049.3603. Boyce's will was in due course proven on 20 Feb. 1779. The witnesses were the Rev. John Gibbons from the Parish of St. Andrew Holborn, and Thomas Barrow, a distinguished countertenor from the Parish of St. Martins-in-the-Fields, who was a lay-clerk at the Chapel Royal and Westminster Abbey, and who must frequently have sung under Boyce's direction. Given the success of WB's career, and the relatively high income he is known to have enjoyed from various sources, one would expect his estate to have been of some significance. Yet his widow, Hannah, pleaded poverty after her husband's death.[41] There are two features of the will in particular that bear on these matters. Firstly, that WB had considerable investments in 'Government Stocks and Securities'. Secondly, that it was clearly his intention that the third part of his estate left to his son William (aged 14 at the time of WB's death) was intended to cover the cost of his maintenance and education during his minority, thus relieving Hannah of direct financial responsibility for such matters.

♣

Boyce sets Whitehead's royal ode for New Year's Day 1776, 'On the white rocks which guard her coast', organises a public rehearsal, and conducts its performance at court.

Text in AR (1775), 'Characters', 202. This work may have been composed originally for 1 January 1775.

♣

---

[41] See the commentary below on Hannah's letter to the Dean of Gloucester Cathedral of 24 August 1779 where the issues surrounding Boyce's finances are discussed in some detail.

Two extracts from Sir John Hawkins, *A General History of the Science and Practice of Music* (1776)

I

In the state of affluence to which Dr Greene was raised by this event,[42] he meditated on the corruptions of our church-music, occasioned by the multiplication of copies, & the ignorance & carelessness of transcribers; and resolved to correct, & also secure against such injuries for the future; accordingly he began with collating a great number of copies of services & anthems, & reducing them into score. By the year 1755, he had made a considerable progress in the work; but his health failing him, he made his will, and remitted the further prosecution of it to one that had been his disciple, his friend Dr. William Boyce, who, in a manner worthy of himself, completed the work, and thereby gave to the public a collection that has not its fellow in the world.[43]

II

It remains now that due acknowledgement be made of the assistance which the author has been favoured and honoured in the course of this work; but as this cannot be done without an enumeration of names, for which he has obtained no permission, he is necessitated to declare his sense of the obligation in general terms, with this exception, that having need of assistance in the correction of the music plates, he was in sundry instances eased of that trouble by the kind offices of one, who is both an honour to his profession and his country, Dr. William Boyce, and of deciphering as it were, and rendering in modern characters the composition of greatest antiquity amongst those which he found it necessary to insert, by the learning and ingenuity of Dr. Cooke of Westminster Abbey, Mr. Marmaduke Overend organist of Isleworth in Middlesex, and Mr. John Stafford Smith, of the royal chapel.

---

[42] The inheritance by Greene in 1752 of his family's extensive estates in Essex which made him a man of considerable wealth.

[43] In his will Greene left Boyce the contents of his library, and hence his work in progress on the projected historical collection of anthems entitled *Cathedral Music*. He did not, however, stipulate that Boyce should complete the project. Boyce took on this immense task entirely of his own volition, notwithstanding his numerous other professional responsibilities.

Extract I, from Hawkins (2nd edn, 2, 910); extract II, from the Preface, vol. 1, xiii. In view of Boyce's standing, and the close personal and professional relationship that existed between him and Hawkins, the fact that these two passages embrace the only references made to WB in the whole of the *History* may, on the face of it, be more than a little surprising. So much so that the question has been raised as to whether the two men may have quarrelled.[44] However, the explanation, evidently overlooked by Scholes, was simply that Hawkins when he planned the *History* had made a policy decision to exclude living composers from his purview.[45]

♣

From the *Westminster Magazine*, March 1776

'On the Witches, Fairies, and Aerial Beings in Shakespeare.'
This poem [Lyric Ode] is said to be written by a young gentleman of Oxford,[46] and has many strokes of genius and imagination in it. The music, we hear, is composed by Mr Linley Jnr. who has (since his return from Italy) been a student under that most excellent musician Dr Boyce. This composition must be allowed to be an extraordinary effort of genius in so young a man. . . . From the general and sincere applause with which the Ode was received, we may venture to pronounce, that if Mr Linley Jnr. pursues his studies, he will one day stand foremost in the list of modern composers.

The work in question is now better known as the *Shakespeare Ode*.[47] WB is known to have taught the younger Linley from 1763 to 1768 (see Cooke, *Lbl*, MS Egerton 2492), when the latter left for Italy where he studied for some years under Nardini. Unless the writer of the *Westminster Magazine* review was misinformed, Linley appears to have resumed his studies with WB in the early 1770s. The younger Linley's highly promising career was tragically cut short by a boating accident in 1778.

♣

---

[44] See Scholes(1948), 144-6.
[45] See *HawkinsH*, 2nd edn, 2, 917.
[46] The author of the lyric ode was French Laurence, who was only nineteen at the time. He went on to become a distinguished lawyer and politician.
[47] Modern edn in MB 30 (1970/1985).

Boyce sets Whitehead's ode for the king's birthday 1776, 'Ye Western gales, whose genial breath' (text in AR (1776), 'Characters', 203), organises a public rehearsal, and conducts its performance at court on 4 June.

♣

Boyce subscribes to Charles Burney's *General History of Music*, 4 vols. (1776-89).

The first volume of Burney's *History* was published more or less simultaneously with the pioneering *History of Music* by Sir John Hawkins. While Boyce was much closer to Hawkins socially, and also with regard to musical and cultural outlook, there was nevertheless considerable mutual respect between him and Burney. Moreover, WB must have been keen to compare the long-awaited works of the two great rival historians. Burney's *History* (not completed until 1789) proved remarkably successful with 856 purchasers for well over a 1,000 copies. The subscribers' list, headed by six representatives of royalty, includes not only a wide cross-section of English musical society, but also leading intellectuals such as Diderot, David Garrick, Samuel Johnson (not usually noted for his enthusiasm for music), Horace Walpole, along with some distinguished continental musicians such as C.P.E. Bach, Galuppi, Farinelli, Jommelli and Piccini.

♣

From the *Journal* of the Rev. Charles Wesley (late 1776)

On our coming to town this last time he [his son Samuel Wesley] sent Dr Boyce the last anthem he had made. The D[r] thought, from its correctness, that Charles [Samuel's older brother] must have helped in it: but Charles assured him that he never assisted him, otherwise than by telling him, if he asked, whether such or such a passage were good harmony. And the Doctor was so scrupulous, that when Charles shew'd him an improper note, he would not suffer it to be altered.

Mr, DDCW10/2, 12. (Barrington(1781), 297) The Wesleys were normally resident in Bristol, but came to London fairly frequently. Samuel was ten at this time and Charles nine years older. While Boyce had regularly been engaged to teach Charles, his musical relations with Samuel were entirely informal.

♣

Boyce sets Whitehead's royal ode for New Year's Day 1777, 'Again imperial Winter's sway', organises a public rehearsal, and conducts its performance at court.

Text in AR (1776), 'Characters', 196. The overture was edited by Finzi in MB 13 (1957).

♣

From the *Journal* of the Rev. Charles Wesley (1777)

Charles [Wesley's older son] has now been some years under Dr. Boyce's tuition, learning composition. He retains the most grateful veneration for his old master, Mr Kelway, & played to him, while he was able to hear him, every week. Under two such teachers as Mr. Kelway and Dr. Boyce, he believes he has the two greatest masters of music in Christendom. Dr. Boyce and he seem equally satisfied. I hope he has caught some of both his masters' temper and skill: a more modest man than Dr. Boyce I have never known. I never heard him speak a vain or ill-natured word, either to exalt himself or depreciate another!

(Jackson(1849), 335) Joseph Kelway was a virtuoso keyboard player who had been preferred to Boyce in the election for the post of organist at St. Michael's Cornhill in 1734. We owe much of our limited knowledge of Boyce the man to the writings of Wesley and his younger son, Samuel.

♣

From the *Anecdotes* of Laetitia Matilda Hawkins (1822)

If Lady Hawkins [Laetitia's mother]was inclined to take an airing, she would drive in the carriage when it went to fetch Sir John home from some friend's house; and he was always glad of the company. She never showed impatience at being kept waiting, nor did she allow a hint to be given him that his carriage was at the door. I have sat with her till past eleven o'clock at Dr. Boyce's gate in Kensington Gore. My mother only laughed when he at last appeared, and listened to his account of what had happened; but the next time he called out from one room to another, "My dear, have you a mind for a ride this evening?" she answered laughingly, "Yes, but not to Dr. Boyce's if you please!"

Hawkins(1822), 283. (Skrine(1926), 17) Laetitia was the daughter of John and Sydney (née Storer) Hawkins, who had married in 1753. Hawkins, magistrate, author and music historian, had maintained a close personal and professional relationship with Boyce from the early 1740s. Such events as the above would have taken place in or after 1763 when Boyce had moved to Kensington.

♣

Obituary from the *Gentleman's Magazine*, March 1777

At his house in the Mint Yard, Canterbury, in the 82d year of his age, the Rev. William Gostling, M.A. fifty years Minor Canon of that Cathedral, and Vicar of Stone, in the Isle of Oxney, twenty-four. His amiable, communicative, benevolent disposition, justly endeared him to his numerous friends and acquaintance, and, amidst the infirmities of age and disease, and a long and hopeless confinement to his room, he retained to the last his natural chearfulness and good-humour. Of his taste and knowledge as an Antiquary, he has left one specimen in his *Walk in and about Canterbury*, 1774, of which the public will be glad to hear that a second improved edition is in the press, with additional plates, and will now be published for the benefit of the author's daughter. [&c.]

GM, xlvii, 147-8. Gostling, was the son of John, the great bass singer whose long career had straddled the 17th and 18th centuries. Gostling jnr. had accumulated an extensive collection of scores of earlier English music, both printed and manuscript, As a result he had been of assistance to both Boyce, when he was working on *Cathedral Music* (1760-73), and also Hawkins with regard to his *History of Music* (1776). Hawkins, in his turn, assisted the Gostling family after William's death by preparing the catalogue for the sale of his valuable library. He also wrote an elegy, '*A Monumental Inscription to the Memory of Mr. Gostling*', beginning 'Hither ye sons of harmony repair', which Boyce agreed to set to music. Apart from the last four court odes, this was his final composition. Hawkins refers to Gostling's devotion to early music in the lines: "Him shall his much lov'd Bird with rapture great / And Blow and Purcell hold in converse sweet". Hawkins's daughter, Laetitia, later wrote of this work: "Dr. Boyce had previously, with great good-nature, set to music my father's elegiac lines on the death of Mr. Gostling of Canterbury, and when performed as Dr. Cooke[48] took care to have done, at Westminster, they were so gratifying to every feeling of a writer, that it would hardly be termed vanity to wish to try again" (Hawkins(1822), 229). Further on the text is quoted in full (Hawkins, op. cit., 262). Boyce produced a restrained and dignified setting for SATB choir and organ continuo. The autogr. score is preserved at *Nypl*, Drexel 4248. For a modern edition, with an introduction by B.H. Davis, see Baldwin(1973).

♣

Two extracts from 'The Trial of Midas the Second— or Congress of Musicians', by Charles Burney

I

As Rome endanger'd by a Foe, or Traytor;
Among her chiefs elected a Dictator:
To judge this self-elected judge, the choice,
Almost unanimously, fell on Boyce:
A man whose Probity was bias proof,
And Music, like his Manners, bold and rough,
In both, tho' new refinem^t he withstood,
His heart and Harmony were sound and Good;
The Pris'ner's Friend he seemed in former days,
Before he had disgrac'd him with his Praise.[49]

II

Learn hence, Ye Scribes! The world can never brook
At once a hated man, and worthless Book,
Uncommon as your deeds and fell Intent.
O Midas! now must be your punishment!
To rid the World at once of such a name,

---

[48] Benjamin Cooke was well acquainted with both Hawkins and Boyce, and in common with WB had been a pupil of Pepusch. He had been organist of Westminster Abbey since 1757.

[49] The implication here that Boyce and Hawkins had fallen out led one commentator to consider whether they may indeed have done so (see Scholes(1953), 144-6). What motive Burney may have had for hinting at such a rift can only be a matter of speculation, for there is not a shred of evidence from any other source to suggest anything other than that they remained close friends until Boyce's death.

> And choke the Trumpet harsh of Evil Fame,
> To both I now consign a dirty Niche
> Deep in the darkest part of loath'd Fleet-Ditch!

Autogr. at *Mr*, Eng. MS.648; copy at *US: NH*, Osborn Collection, 36.14. The background to this extensive satirical poem, in which Boyce appears as an allegorical figure, lies in Burney's deeply felt rivalry with Sir John Hawkins with respect to their respective magisterial and pioneering Histories of Music. Both men had independently embarked on their researches *c*1760. Burney eventually issued the first of his four volumes early in 1776, though the last did not appear until 1789, while by the end of 1776 Hawkins had published all five of his. It is evident from the start that Burney had taken offence at certain remarks Hawkins made in his preface about the latter's first volume. Moreover, as a trained and active professional musician with intellectual aspirations, Burney seems to have regarded Hawkins, in his eyes a mere music-loving lawyer and antiquarian, as an unqualified upstart in his territory. To make matters worse, a deep chasm existed between their respective attitudes to the musical culture of their age. While Hawkins took the view that the art of music had culminated in the late Renaissance, and with some notable exceptions such as Purcell and Handel, had entered into a gradual decline, Burney was inclined to disparage early music, much of which he regarded as 'Gothic', and tended to see the progressive and fashionable music of his time as part of a process of refinement towards a state of perfection.

Hawkins is represented in Burney's poem by the mythological figure of King Midas who, when called upon to adjudicate between the music of the rustic pipes of Pan[50] and the heavenly lyre of Apollo,[51] chose the former. As a punishment he was given asses' ears. In Canto I a clamorous crowd of indignant music-lovers confronts Apollo with the demand that Midas should be punished for his failure to recognise the virtues of their favourite composers, but Apollo indignantly insists that they should try him themselves. In Cantos 2 and 3 the crowd finally elects Boyce to be the judge (see Extract I) and in the course of the trial 'Science', 'Taste' and 'Wit' appear for the prosecution, and a 'psalmodist' and an 'antiquarian' appear for the defence. While Boyce is concerned to be fair in his summing up, as may have been anticipated, the final verdict is that Midas is 'guilty'. The sentence he imposes is that an effigy of 'Hawkins' along with the five volumes of his *History* should be dumped in a ditch (see Extract II).

---

[50] The Greek god of the countryside.
[51] The Greek and Roman sun-god, and patron of music and poetry.

Burney appears never to have attempted to publish the poem, but he must have gained satisfaction from circulating it amongst his friends. Psychologically, in the process of writing the poem perhaps he purged himself of much of the personal bitterness and antagonism he felt, rightly or wrongly, towards his rival.

Burney's poem and its background have been assessed, and further extracts from it quoted, in Roberts(1933), 304-12, Scholes(1948), 1, 297-8, Scholes(1953), 139-48, Lonsdale(1965), 189-208, and Davis(1973), 150-1.

♣

From the Rev. Charles Wesley's *Journal* (1777)

At the rehearsal at St. Paul's[52] Dr Boyce met his [Charles Wesley jnr,'s] brother Sam; & shewing him to Dr H.[53] told him "This boy will soon surpass you all". Shortly after he came to see us, took up a Jubilate wch Sam had lately wrote, & commended it as one of Charles's. When we told him whose it was, he declared that he could find no fault in it, adding, "There was not another boy upon earth who could have composed this", and concluding with "I never met wth that person who owes so much to nature as Sam. He is come among us, dropt from heaven".

Mr, DDCW10/2, Appendix 1, 13-14. (Jackson(1849), 1, 298) Samuel was about 11 at this time, and Charles 20. Two years or so earlier Wesley snr. had recorded that "On our coming to town this last time,[54] he [Samuel] sent to Dr. Boyce the last anthem he had made. The Doctor thought, from the correctness, that Charles must have helped him in it; but Charles assured him that he never assisted him, otherwise than by telling him, if he asked, whether such or such a passage were good harmony; and the Doctor was scrupulous, that when Charles showed him an improper note he would not suffice it to be altered".[55] While WB had regularly been engaged to teach Charles, his musical relations with Samuel were very friendly but entirely informal.

♣

---

[52] Probably for the Festival of the Sons of the Clergy held on 13 May that year.
[53] Almost certainly Samuel Howard.
[54] From Bristol.
[55] *Mr*, op. cit., 12. (Barrington(1781), 297).

Boyce subscribes to Handel's *Thirteen Celebrated Italian Duets* (1777)

Boyce's acquisition of these duets at this late stage in his life bears testimony to the composer's ongoing admiration for his great contemporary. In spite of the continuing dominance of Handel's music in England after his death, there were only 109 subscribers for this edition. The generally enthusiastic public response to publications of vocal music of all kinds at this time was doubtless blunted in this instance by the retention of the original Italian texts.

♣

Boyce sets Whitehead's ode for the king's birthday 1777, 'Driven out from Heav'n's etherial domes' (text in AR (1777), 'Characters', 197), organises a public rehearsal, and conducts its performance on 4 June.

♣

Two Letters from Boyce to Marmaduke Overend (1777-8)

I

Dear Sir

By my not hearing from you I conclude that Monday next will not be a convenient day for our intended visit: I shall expect the favour of a line, if 'tis to be on Thursday, which will fix this business.

I have here sent the only ratio I would wish to have added to what is already in the diagramma[56] you took with you on Thursday:

The numbers are at a great distance from the highest of those now in the paper, & should be placed at the very top of all. The highest number to be over the duples[57] from 3072 — The number is 393216 — The other to be over the quintuples[58] 3125 — the number is 390625 — This ratio takes from two enharmonics [and] produces the Semitone Minor.[59]

---

[56] In modern terms, the musical scale.
[57] Concerning mathematical ratios involving twos.
[58] Concerning ratios involving fives.
[59] In the pre-equal temperament tuning systems that Boyce was familiar with, and which lie at the heart of his mathematical calculations, the enharmonic genus, as

As to the Pythagorean Comma,[60] I have met with it, but as it can be of no use on the present plan, I shall not think of putting it in this draught. Here are included all that are sufficient to demonstrate the musica[l] intervals in use, & even more than are essentially necessary for that purpose.

My compliments, with those of my family attend you, your sister, &c, &c, and believe me to be with sincerity

Your friend & obliged humble serv[t.]

Saturday Aug[st]. 30th. 1777.   W[m]. Boyce

II

Dear Sir

Yours I have this morning, & must now ask pardon for putting you to the expence of postage for this, as indeed the intelligence it contains is hardly worth it: I sent to you by the last night's post, informing you of my having found out the ratios wanted, and by yours of this morning I find that they exactly correspond with your account of them. I made a small mistake in numbering of them. There are four of the first ratio, six of the second (I said 5 only) and two of the third: And you have not been clear of mistakes, for your first ratio, is not one that we wanted! You have taken cb[flat] & a##[double sharp] instead of a#[sharp] & cb[flat] — which (you truly observe) is 3 commas & 2 schismas,[61] but how could such a distance interfere without interruption in our account of the octave intervals! A little consideration must have set you right in this matter.

I must leave these kind of enquiries for the present, as I have some business coming on which will engage the greatest part of my time. However I shall hope to see you, and am Dear Sir

Your most obed[t.] humble servant

Oct: 8th 1778.   W[m]. Boyce

---

opposed to the diatonic or chromatic, involves intervals smaller than a semitone. The semitone minor arises when a natural note passes to its sharp.

[60] The term 'comma' here refers to the discrepancy between a mathematically perfect musical interval and one which, for reasons to do with the nature of musical acoustics, only approximates to it. Specifically, the 'Pythagorean comma' identifies the difference between the frequency of the note produced by creating an interval of seven perfect octaves from any given pitch, as compared with reaching the same note via twelve intervals of a perfect 5th; in mathematical terms, $(2/1)^7 = 128$, but $(3/2)^{12} = 129.75$.

[61] A term used with reference to even smaller acoustical discrepancies than the comma.

Ob, MS.Don.c.136. Overend was a former pupil of Boyce's. A letter by him replying to the second communication above is preserved at *Lbl*, Add.33965, f. 17, along with a further response by Boyce. Both documents contain abstruse calculations of intervals in the tuning systems prevailing at the time, such as 'just intonation', or 'mean tone temperament'. These were gradually superseded in the second half of the 18th century by our modern 'equal temperament'. With the general adoption of the latter, the complex issues raised by the existence of the Pythagorean comma were at last resolved. This final solution involved the adoption of a compromise in which all perfect 5ths are slightly flattened in order to resolve the conflict inherent in nature's acoustical system.

Boyce's interest in such matters was undoubtedly kindled by the studies he undertook with Dr. Johann Pepusch in the mid 1730s. While he did not pursue his own researches in the field until the early 1760s, at his death he left an extensive but unfinished document of 186 folios entitled 'Harmonics, or an attempt to explain the principles on which the science of music is founded' (*Ob*, MS.Don.c.136). Boyce's objective was not only to explore the mathematical basis of the science of music, but also to relate acoustical principles to harmonic practices in musical composition. Shortly after WB's death Overend acquired his teacher's treatise from Hannah Boyce. In due course he advertised a series of lectures he proposed to give in London "founded on the Knowledge and Observations of the late Dr. WILLIAM BOYCE" (*PA,* 10 March 1781), and shortly afterwards he published 'A brief Account of, and Introduction to, Eight Lectures in the Science of Music'. In 1784 Overend announced his intention to publish Boyce's *Harmonics*, but this bold and perhaps unrealistic ambition was not realised.

Laetitia Hawkins later provided a colourful account of Overend: "the scientific organist of Isleworth, who gave theoretic lectures on music in London, in delivery of which he turned his back on his auditors, pointing with a rod to immense sheets covered with diamonds and series of figures that defied numeration. He spoke very unintelligibly at all times; and in this execution, his head being very much thrown back, when progressions led him to the top of his chart, those who listened to him lost still more than usual of what he said: added to which, he was sometimes *un peu embrouille*[62] by having mistaken one incalculable total for another, and being therefore under the necessity of beginning again" (Hawkins(1822), 12).

---

[62] 'rather perplexed'.

After Overend's death in 1790 WB's MS was acquired by the composer J.W. Callcott. In the latter's 'Commonplace book' (preserved at *Lbl*, Add.MS.27687) a section is devoted to 'General outlines of a system of music founded chiefly on the theoretic MS of Dr. Boyce'. Callcott intended to draw on and develop some of the theoretical ideas of Boyce and his successors in a musical dictionary, but illness prevented him bringing this plan to fruition. He eventually deposited WB's treatise at the Royal Institution in London in 1807 where it became available for public study. Among those that consulted it was John Farey, a leading geologist, writer, and keen amateur musician, who made use of the theoretical work of Boyce and his successors in the musical calculations he published in his own articles. It is possible to identify an English school of musical theorists stemming not only from Pepusch[63] but also including others working independently and outside his sphere of influence, which sustained itself into the 19th century.[64]

♣

Boyce's setting of Whitehead's royal ode for New Year's Day 1778, 'When rival nations great in arms', (text in AR (1777), 'Characters', 192), organises a public rehearsal, and conducts its performance at court.

♣

Charles Wesley jnr. dedicates a set of string quartets [1778] to Boyce.

These works by Boyce's pupil, composed in 1776, were published by John Johnson with title-page: Six | QUARTETTO's | *for two Violins* | a Tenor and Violoncello. | *Dedicated to* Dr BOYCE. | by | *Charles Wesley* [&c.], copy in *Lbl*, h.2830.(10). Samuel Wesley later wrote of them: "they were of of a very pleasing cast and wrought with the most correct adherence to the best established rules of sound counterpoint and pure harmony".

---

[63] Sir John Hawkins, who may himself have studied with Pepusch, later expressed reservations about the latter's commitment to theory for he commented on "his numerous arithmetrical calculations of ratios, of which he appears to have been too fond" (*HawkinsH* (2nd edn, 1875, 908).

[64] For a comprehensive survey of the English school of musical theorists, see Kassler(1979). The entry on Boyce is on pp.110-11.

Charles complimented Boyce by basing the 'Tempo di Minuetto' finale of his 1st quartet on the opening 4 bars of the finale from WB's overture to the King's Birthday Ode for 1765 (see *BH* 4, 235). A modern edn by Finzi of Wesley's quartet no. 5 was published in 'Easy Quartets' (Heinrichsen, 1953).

♣

From the *Reminiscences* of Samuel Wesley (1836-7)

Doctor William Boyce greatly regretted his not having had the Advantage and good fortune of studying under so great and accomplished a Musician [as J.S. Bach].

Lbl, Add.MS27593, f. 175. Wesley's recollections of the past were not always entirely reliable when he came to write the *Reminiscences* towards the end of his life. It is entirely feasible, however, that he transmitted accurately here Boyce's reaction when he became aware of Bach and some of his music. The so-called 'Bach revival', referring to the growing awareness in England of Bach's works and their greatness, took place largely after WB's death, but the green shoots were appearing before that time. Peter Welcker had published six of Bach's violin sonatas in 1773, and even more significantly, Boyce's friend and admirer, Sir John Hawkins, had not only given a brief account of Bach in his *History of Music* (1776),[65] but also included by way of illustration the theme and two variations from Bach's 'Goldberg Variations' (*BWV* 988), thus amply demonstrating Bach's unique mastery of contrapuntal processes.[66] Given Boyce's background and musical outlook, he would surely have appreciated that as much as anybody.

♣

Boyce lends his name to Anton Bemetzrieder's *Music made Easy to every Capacity* (1778).

This music tutor consisted of "practical Lessons for the Harpsichord, laid down in a new Method. . . . The whole translated, and adapted to the Use

---

[65] See *HawkinsH* (1776), 5, 254-8.

[66] For a survey of the evidence relevant to J.S. Bach and his music in England prior to WB's death in 1779, see Yo Tomita in Kassler(2004), pp.3-7.

of the English Student by Gifford Barnard, MA. Perused and approved of by Doctor Boyce and Doctor Howard".

(Jones(2000), 232) Bemetzrieder had been 'Musick Master to the Queen of France'. This treatise had been first published in French under the title *Leçons de claveçin, et principes d'harmonie* (Paris, 1771). It was reproduced in *Oeuvres complètes de Diderot*, ed. J. Assezat, xii (Paris, 1876).[67] Having already enjoyed great success as a theorist and teacher in Paris, Bemetzrieder moved to London in 1781 where he continued his career until his death about 1809. He was friendly with Diderot, who not only wrote the preface to this publication, but also collaborated with him in various other ways. Doubtless potential sales of this tutor in England were enhanced by the endorsement provided by Boyce and Howard, especially given WB's reputation as a theorist. A year after WB's death the exact terms of his endorsement were revealed when the contents of a card by him to the publisher, Elizabeth Randall, were published in another advertisement for the treatise: "Dr. Boyce's compliments and with this returns the third part of the Musical Treatise, which he finds equally useful and entertaining; with the foregoing, he thinks there is little doubt to make of its reception. When the public are in possession of it, its utility and agreeableness must necessarily recommend it" (*MP*, 2 Feb. 1780).

♣

From the *Anecdotes* by Laetitia Hawkins (1822)

My father's intercourse with Dr. Boyce began early, and during the printing of his 'History of Music'[68] was very frequent. In the first year of their intimacy,[69] my father had written words which he set, and the last coalition of this kind was his setting, in a very grand style, the lines before mentioned on Mr. Gostling of Canterbury[70] which shall be inserted in their proper place.[71] Dr. Boyce had laboured hard in the duties of his profession, and had achieved a task, which I should have supposed would have been a fortune to those who inherited his property, — the compilation of his

---

[67] For a discussion of problems of dating concerning the English translation see Sarah McCleave, 'The Mackworth Collection: a Social and Bibliographical Resource', in Jones, op. cit., 213-33.

[68] *c*1776.

[69] 1741.

[70] 'Hither ye sons of harmony' (1777).

[71] The complete text of this work is reproduced on p.242.

magnificent volumes of Cathedral-Music. On his death my father
interested himself most warmly in the disposal of the plates for the benefit
of his family. *I* never was more astonished, nor did I ever see my father
more indignant, than when he was offered by one of the principal music-
sellers in London, the value of the pewter only![72]

On subsequent application to Mr. Ashley,[73] father of the celebrated
performer of that name,[74] he immediately offered one hundred guineas,[75]
which, though compared with *my* expectation small, yet set against the
previous offer, was such as was chearfully accepted.

Hawkins(1822), 243-4. (Scholes(1953), 145-6)

♣

Boyce subscribes to James Nares's *Twenty Anthems* in Score (1778).

This was the last work to which Boyce subscribed before his death early in
1779. He had previously invested in this composer's *Lessons for the
Harpsichord* (1747). WB must have known him well by this time, for
Nares had become a colleague when he was appointed an organist and
composer at the Chapel Royal in 1756. Dedicated to George III, this
substantial publication was well supported by Cathedrals and Chapels
throughout Britain and Ireland, and by many leading musicians. There
were 144 subscribers for 262 copies.

♣

---

[72] Laetitia was the daughter of Sir John Hawkins.

[73] John Ashley later published a 2nd edition of Boyce's *Cathedral Music* in 1788
using these plates, and to which he prefixed *Memoirs of Dr. William Boyce* by
Hawkins.

[74] The reference here is probably to Ashley's son, Charles, one of the leading
cellists of his time in London.

[75] In modern currency c£11,500.

Boyce sets Whitehead's ode for the king's birthday 1778, 'Arm'd with her native force' (text in AR (1778), 'Characters', 193), organises a public rehearsal, and conducts its performance at court on 4 June.

♣

Boyce sets Whitehead's royal ode for New Year's Day 1779, 'To arms, to arms ye sons of might', organises a public rehearsal, and conducts its performance at court.

Text in AR (1778), 'Characters', 169. This royal ode was the last of 44 such works that Boyce composed in his capacity as Master of the King's Music. His death took place little more than a month later. An indication of Boyce's growing frailty at this time lies in his decision not to compose an overture for this ode, but to use instead the overture to his first court ode, composed in October 1755.

♣

Ode on the Death of Dr. Boyce by the Rev. Charles Wesley (1779)

Father of harmony, farewell!
Farewell for a few fleeting years!
Translated from the mournful vale!
Jehovah's flaming ministers
Have borne thee to thy place above,
Where all is harmony and love.

Thy generous, good, and upright heart,
That sighed for a celestial lyre,
Was tuned on earth to bear a part
Symphonious with that warbling choir
Where Handel strikes the golden strings,
And plausive angels clap their wings.

Handel, and all the tuneful train,
Who well employed their art divine
To announce the great Messiah's reign,
In joyous acclamation join;

And springing from their azure seat,
With shouts their new-born brother meet.

Thy brow a radiant circle wears,
Thy hand a seraph's harp receives,
And, singing with the morning stars,
Thy soul in endless rapture lives,
And hymns, on the eternal throne,
Jehovah and his conquering Son.

(Jackson(1849), 2, 410) Wesley's son, Samuel, refers to this elegiac ode in his *Reminiscences* (1836-7): "Upon the death of his revered master D[r] Boyce, my dear father composed a very fine elegiac ode which my brother [Charles] set to music in a delightful style: it contains several interesting airs, and three splendid and highly wrought choruses. It is much to be regretted that it has remained unpublished, and I am sorry to add that I am unable to announce in whose hands the manuscript original is now to be found". (*Lbl*, Add.MS27593, f. 31) Charles's ode was performed at one of the Wesley family's concerts on 30 March 1780 (see (Olleson(2003), 23). The original MS of the poem seems not to have survived.

♣

From the *Lady's Magazine,* February 1779

On Tuesday, Feb. 16, the remains of Dr. William Boyce, late organist and composer of his majesty's chapel royal, and master of his majesty's band of music, were interred in the vault under St. Paul's cathedral.[76] The procession began from Kensington, and the corpse was carried into the cathedral attended by his son, a youth of about fifteen years of age[77] (and several other mourners) at the south door, and went down the south aisle, and then turned round into the grand aisle, where it was received by the Rev. Dr. Wilson and Dr. Douglas, Residentiaries,[78] and the gentlemen and choiristers of the choirs of the king's chapel St. Paul's and Westminster abbey with many other gentlemen, professors of music, all in surplices. The procession from thence began two and two, the gentlemen of the choirs singing the first verse of the burial service without the organ; and

---

[76] Boyce had died on Sunday 7 February.
[77] William Boyce jnr.
[78] Canons of the cathedral.

when it came under the dome, the organ struck up, and the voices sang to it the three verses of the said service; and the body being put upon tressels in the choir, and the attendants being got into their seats, the Rev. Mr. Wight, senior minor canon, began the daily service, in the course of which the 39th and 90th psalms were chanted to solemn music. The first lesson was read by Mr. Hayes and the second by Mr. Gibbons. Before the prayer for the king, an anthem composed by the deceased, beginning, *If we believe that Jesus died and rose again,* was sung by Mr. Dine and Mr. Soper and the chorus by the gentlemen and choiristers. After this, the reader proceeded to the end of the morning service. The body was then taken up by the bearers, and carried down into the vault, and deposited under the brass grate, which is in the centre of the church. Whilst this was doing, the residentiaries, the gentlemen of the choirs &c. walked from the choir, and formed a circle in the middle of the church, round the above brass grate, and when the corps was placed in the vault underneath the brass grate, the choirs began singing, the organ playing at the same time the four verses in the burial service, *Man that is born of a woman hath &c.*[79] Which done Mr. Wight proceeded with the prayers, committing the body to the ground, whilst a person with a shovel scattered some dust through the brass grate upon the coffin. The voices and organ then performed the verse, *I heard a voice from heaven &c.*, and then the reader went on with the prayers to the end of the burial service. The sound of so many voices singing directly in the centre under the cupola of the church, and the organ not being at too great a distance, had a most pleasing effect, and struck the audience with the utmost awe in this solemn service; and it may be truly said, that there was the utmost decency and regularity in the management of it.

The late Dr. Boyce was greatly esteemed by his acquaintance as a private man, as well as for his great merit in the musical world. It was intended by his friends to have buried him in a private manner; but some of the minor canons of St. Paul's thought it would be a great pity that he should go to his grave without some mark of regard to his remains; they therefore applied to the Dean and Chapter, who very readily consented to his public funeral, and waved their fees; and their design being communicated to the gentlemen of the other choirs, they all most heartily joined, and promised their attendance. The mourners were the son of the

---

[79] It is clear from another account that this was from Henry Purcell's setting of the Burial Service (Z, 27, *c*1680), see *MC*, 18 Feb. 1779.

deceased, the Rev. Mr. Gibbons, and the Rev. Hitchcock, Dr. Howard, Dr. Cooke and Dr. Hayes, Mr. Linley and Mr. Depuis.[80]

Dr. Boyce was 69 years of age,[81] was a choirister in St. Paul's cathedral under Mr. Charles King was afterwards apprentice to Dr. Maurice Greene – became organist of the earl of Oxford's chapel in Bond-street, as he was afterwards of St. Michael's Cornhill, and Allhallows Thames-street. In June, 1736, he was sworn composer in ordinary to his majesty's chapel royal. In July, 1749, was admitted Dr. in Music in the university of Cambridge, at the time of the Installation of the Duke of Newcastle as chancellor of that university. In April, 1757, on the death of Dr. Greene, was appointed, by the Duke of Devonshire master of the king's band of music; and in June, 1758, sworn organist of the chapel royal, in the room of Mr. John Travers. On the death of Dr. Greene, in 1757,[82] he conducted the music for the Sons of the Clergy at St. Paul's, as he has repeatedly done from that to the present time. He published, at a great expence to himself, three volumes of cathedral music being a collection in score of the most valuable compositions for that service, by the several English masters, of the last two hundred years, which was designed to have been published by Dr. Greene; and in this Dr. Boyce was assisted by the late Dr. Hayes, of Oxford,[83] and Dr. Howard who was one of the mourners at his funeral.

LM 10, (Feb. 1779), 94-6. (Edwards *b*(1901), July, 447) The latter reproduces this account in a slightly abbreviated form that omits the 2nd paragraph. Edwards took as his source for Boyce's obituary a version of the same notice that appeared in *MC* on 18 Feb. 1779. An even more detailed account of the funeral service as planned survives in the Minutes taken at a meeting of the choir of St. Paul's held the day before the event (*Lgh*, MS22, 298). This was transcribed in John Pridden's *Topographical*

---

[80] Apart from Boyce's son and the two clerics, the other mourners were all musical friends and colleagues of the composer. The last three were Philip Hayes, Thomas Linley snr. and Thomas Dupuis respectively.

[81] The assertion that WB died at 69 appeared on his tombstone as well. It subsequently led to the common belief that he was therefore born in 1710. Evidence of his baptism in September 1711 eventually came to light (see Dawe *b*(1968), 803), since when it has been generally accepted, on good grounds, that he was born shortly before his baptism, and hence died at 68. Even if WB himself was not vague as to his own date of birth, he may well have mentioned to some of his acquaintances that he was in his 69th year.

[82] Greene had in fact died in December 1755, by which time Boyce had already succeeded him as conductor of the annual Sons of the Clergy festival.

[83] William Hayes.

Collections for the history of St. Paul's and is reproduced in Wilson(1996), 293-4. Sir John Hawkins evidently drew on the *LM* article in his description of the funeral in his *Memoirs of Dr. William Boyce* (see Hawkins *b*(1788), x). The final two paragraphs of the above constitute the first, albeit brief, published biography of the composer. *The Gentlemen's Magazine* also printed a short notice of the funeral (*GM* 49, Feb. 1779, 103). Its conclusion reads: "The sound of so many voices in the centre of the church, accompanied by the organ, produced a very uncommon effect, and struck the audience with a pleasing reverential concern, not easy to be conceived or expressed. Some account of the deceased shall be given in a future Magazine". The intention conveyed in its last sentence, however, seems never to have been carried out.

♣

From Samuel Wesley's *Reminiscences* (1836-7)

Dr. Boyce was among the best composers and learned musicians of his day: the odes which he annually produced for the New Year and the King's Birth Day are demonstrative evidence of this; and the simple anthem which he composed for the Sons of the Clergy, and which is yearly performed at St. Paul's Cathedral had he written nothing else, would have immortalized him.[84]

His musical criticisms were always of the most acute, judicious and valuable kind. — When it was objected to Handel that he sometimes took the thoughts of others; the Doctor said, "What does he take? he takes pebbles, and converts them into diamonds".[85]

Lbl, Add.MS27593, ff. 35-36.

---

[84] The orchestrally accompanied anthem composed for the Feast of the Sons of the Clergy in 1755. It was eventually published by John Ashley in 1802. A copy of this edition (*Lbl*, H.1081.c), formerly owned by Samuel's older brother Charles, a pupil of Boyce, is inscribed in his hand: "This anthem is a most excellent composition, I think not inferior to Handel or Purcel".

[85] This anecdote was quoted in a rather different form by William Linley jnr. in the preface to his *Eight Glees*: "Again speaking of the same wonderful genius [Handel] as a plagiary, another of these worthy scrutinizers observed to Dr. Boyce that he had stolen many of his best subjects from Habbermans: "What then", replied the honest Doctor", he found them *pebbles*, but he left them *diamonds"* (Linley(1832), 3). Habbermans (or rather 'Habermann') was a Bohemian composer and a contemporary of Handel's.

♣

From the *New Cheque Book* of the Chapel Royal,
24 March 1779

March 24th. Thomas Saunders Dupuis by virtue of a Warrant from the
Right Reverend Robert Lord Bishop of London, Dean of his Majesty's
Chapel Royal, was sworn and admitted into the place of Organist of His
Majesty's Chapel Royal in the room of Doctor William Boyce deceased,
this twenty fourth day of March 1779.
Witness   Anselm Bayly   Subdean   W[m] Dickes   Clerk of the Check

Lcr, NCB, 45. (Ashbee & Harley(2000), 235-6.) On the same day, Bayly
also recorded the appointment of Dupuis to replace WB as a Composer at
the Chapel Royal.

♣

From the *Morning Post and Daily Advertiser*,
13 April 1779

Sales by Auction By Mess CHRISTIE and ANSELL At their Great Room,
in Pall-Mall, on To-morrow the 14th of April and the following day, A
Large and most valuable Collection of MUSIC by the most scarce authors,
containing scores of masses, mottets, antifonie, madrigals, &c. of Orlando
Lassus Clauda le Jeum [*sic*] Stradella Lotti Scarlatti Pergolese Bononcini
Handel Colona Pachebel [*sic*] Porpora, &c. Many of which have the parts
wrote out for performance immediately. Also scores of Corelli Geminiani
Purcell Crofts, [*sic*] Blow, and many unpublished score[s] of modern
authors, collected by Dr WILLIAM BOYCE, Deceased, Late Master of
his Majesty's Band of Musicians, Organist and Composer to the Chapels
Royal, amongst which are many of his own scores in his hand writing.
Also Dr. Green's scores of Birth Day and New Years Odes, with the parts;
like-wise the plates of Dr. Boyce's Overtures, and thirty perfect copies. To
be viewed to the sale. Catalogues may then be had of Mess. Christie and
Ansell as above.

The advertisement for the sale was placed first on 31 March and was
repeated on six occasions before 13 April. The sentence starting "Also Dr.
Green's" did not appear until 13 April. The auction was originally planned

to take place over two days (see above) but the final advertisement on 15 April gave notice of a third day's sale on the 16th.

The sale catalogue was published with title-page as follows: A | CATALOGUE | OF THE | Truly Valuable and Curious | LIBRARY OF MUSIC, | Late in the Possession of | DR. WILLIAM BOYCE, | Organist and Composer to his Majesty, | And Master of his Majesty's Band of Musicians, | Deceased; | Consisting of all DR. GREEN'S Curious and | Valuable Manuscripts, with the greatest Variety | of Excellent Compositions for the CHURCH | CHAMBER, and the THEATRE, ever yet offer'd | to Sale. | Also various other Articles specified in the | Catalogue, equally Good | WHICH WILL BE SOLD BY AUCTION, | By Mess. *Christie* and *Ansell,* | At their Great Room, PALL MALL | On WEDNESDAY, APRIL 14. 1779, and | The Two following Days. | To be viewed *Tuesday* preceding, and to the Sale, | which will begin each Day at 12 o'Clock. | CATALOGUES may be had as above.

Copies of the catalogue are preserved at *LEc*, 781.973304763, at *Lfom*, 2986, and *Lkc*, Marsden Add.05Book(9). Boyce's extensive library consisted not only of items he had acquired himself, but also the contents of the library of Maurice Greene which he had inherited at the latter's death in 1755. Greene's library itself also contained materials collected by John Alcock, for he too had planned to publish an anthology of early English anthems in score. When he heard of Greene's project, however, he gave up his scheme and passed on relevant sources to him.

While there was inevitably much 18th-century material in Boyce's collection, it was notable for the richness of its 16th- and 17th-century holdings. Apart from a number of items that did not belong to Boyce, including some musical instruments, the core of the sale was his wide-ranging library of scores and parts, both printed and manuscript, along with treatises on music. As one might expect, the collection was particularly strong in English music and Handel. The foreign material reveals a strong leaning towards the Italian rather than the French Schools, while German music is represented by only a handful of items. Notable among the 35 buyers active at the auction were Sir John Hawkins, John Stanley, Philip Hayes, John Ashley, Marmaduke Overend and Frederick Nicolay, who was present in order to acquire music on behalf of George III and/or Queen Charlotte. The 19 lots purchased for the Royal family are now in the Royal Music Collection at the British Library (see King(1963), 124-6). The total proceeds amounted to £270 12s. Allowing for Christie's

commission, the Boyce family must have benefited from an injection of
c£220 into the family coffers.[86]

For a diplomatic transcription of the catalogue annotated by the
auctioneers themselves during the sale, along with notes on the purchasers,
the prices paid, and the current location of each item as far as is currently
known, see Bruce & Johnstone *b*(2010).

♣

A letter from Hannah Boyce to the Dean of Gloucester Cathedral, 24 August 1779

Reverend Sir,

Not having the honor to be personally known to you, I take the liberty
in this manner to submit to your consideration the enclos'd proposal, at the
same time informing you, that I am the widow of the person mentioned in
it.

I am sensible that my presumption in thus troubling a dignitary of the
Church, and a stranger, stands in need of an apology, and I trust that the
reasons I here offer will be construed.

The work mentioned in the Proposal, is a Collection of Anthems of my
late husband, and for the most part selected by himself for publication in
his life time as being in his judgement the best of the many, which,
according to the duty of his appointment, he composed for the service of
the Royal Chapel, and it is the honor and favor of a subscription of the
Chapter over which you so worthily preside, that I now solicit.

Of the merits of my husband as a professor of his art, it becomes not
me to speak, but as a proof of his zeal for the honor of God, and of Divine
Service, I may be allowed to say, that at the expence of many years labor
and study, and not without pecuniary loss, and injury to his family, he
revised and published a collection of cathedral music in three volumes,
and has thereby preserved from corruption and oblivion a very great
number of the most valuable composition's [*sic*] that our national Church
is possessed of. And it is yet remembered that besides conducting for
many years gratis the performance at St. Pauls for the Corporation of the
Sons of the Clergy, he added to the solemnity and variety thereof, by

---

[86] In modern currency worth about £33,000.

sundry anthems of his own composition, adapted to the purpose of that benevolent institution.[87]

If these considerations should fail to excuse the presumption of this address, or I should be deceiv'd in my hopes that the merit and utility of the work will recommend it to the favor and protection of the several cathedral and collegiate foundations in this realm, there is yet another, which I flatter myself will have its weight with the reverend body of your church. I am a widow with two children in circumstances so narrow as to render me dependant for their support, on the bounty of those whom respect for the memory of a deceased artist, or compassion for his distressed family, may move to favor the proposed publication.

I am with great respect and submission

Your humble suppliant
Hannah Boyce.

Kensington Gore
August 24.th 1779

GL, D936X126. This letter is annotated "The Chapter agree to subscribe for one sett". The address and signature at the end appear to have been written by Hannah Boyce, but the rest of the letter is in another hand. The handbill embodying the 'proposal' that was evidently attached to the letter is also preserved at Gloucester: "LONDON, *May* 13. 1779. | PROPOSALS | FOR PRINTING BY SUBSCRIPTION | *(from the Author's Originals)* | One Folio Volume of CHURCH-MUSIC, in Score, | Composed for the Royal Chapels, | By the late Dr. WILLIAM BOYCE, | Organist and Composer to His Majesty, &c. | I. The work will be correctly Engraven, and printed on a | good Paper. | II. Each Subscriber to pay half a Guinea at the time of | subscribing, and half a Guinea[88] more upon the delivery of | the Book. | SUBSCRIPTIONS are received for the Widow and Family, at Messrs *Randal's Catherine Street, Strand*; *Longman* and *Broderip, Cheapside, London*; *Mathews* at *Oxford*, *Wyne* at *Cambridge*, and of the Author's Friends, who will be furnish'd with proper Receipts". Neither in this handbill, nor in Hannah Boyce's letter, is the name of WB's self-effacing friend, Philip Hayes, the editor of this volume, *15 Anthems by Dr Boyce*, mentioned. The list of subscribers in the published edition

---

[87] In contrast it should be noted here that after her husband's death Hannah submitted a bill for three guineas each year to the Stewards of the Feast of the Sons of the Clergy for the use of her husband's anthem, 'Lord, Thou hast been our refuge' (Pearce(1928), 239).

[88] A guinea would now be worth *c*£160.

confirms that the Dean and Chapter of Gloucester Cathedral eventually ordered six sets.

Whether or not Hannah was entirely justified in pleading financial insecurity after the death of her husband, this letter, whoever may have composed it, gives eloquent expression as to how she seems to have felt. In the circumstances, since Hayes states on the title-page of his edition that it was published "for the Author's Widow and Family", it seems clear that he was concerned to ameliorate the family's financial situation, as well as to make more accessible to the church at large his former friend's anthems. There can be no doubt that the Boyce family's economic position had now radically changed. While WB must have been the most highly paid musician in the country, apart from the virtuoso singing stars of the operatic world, Hannah and her son and daughter had to confront an immediate loss of income into the family's coffers. Moreover, at this point William jnr. was only fifteen, and about to go up to Oxford for three years (1780-82), so substantial fees and living expenses needed to be allowed for. On the other hand, Hannah was shortly to be relieved of responsibility for her daughter. Evidence has recently come to light showing that she married in 1782: "Marriages: Saturday [17 Aug.] at Fulham. Andrew Fenn, Esq. of Brooke-Green, Hammersmith, to Miss Boyce, of Kensington Gore, daughter of the late Dr. William Boyce" (*WEP*, 17 Aug. 1782).

Furthermore, the rate-books for the Boyce property show that Hannah was able to remain there until 1788.[89] Her whereabouts after that have not been traced, but since Hayes published a 2nd volume of Boyce anthems in 1790, *A Collection of Anthems*, "for the author's Widow", she must have lived on at least until that time.

At this point the hitherto unanswered question about the Boyce finances must be broached: Was the family in fact wealthy all the time? A number of significant facts bear on this. Firstly, when Boyce's extensive library was auctioned by Christie and Ansell in April 1779, two months after the composer's death, the total proceeds were over £270.[90] Even allowing for the auctioneer's commission, the sum paid to Boyce's estate must have been well in excess of £30,000 in today's currency, and under the terms of Boyce's will a third of this would have gone to Hannah. Moreover, since Elizabeth and WB jnr. also received a similar share, the latter may well have been in effect financially independent while he was at Oxford. Indeed, under the terms of Boyce's will WB jnr.'s third part of his estate was specifically "to be disposed of and appropriated for his sole use

---

[89] Rate-books preserved at *Lkcl*.

[90] Bruce & Johnstone *b*(2010), 115.

in the maintenance and education of him during his minority." Even more telling, is the fact that at the time of his death WB held an investment of £500 in 4¼ % Consolidated Annuities worth upwards of £75,000 in today's money.[91] Finally, Hannah was also selling single items of her husband's legacy that had not been put in the sale, such as his 'Harmonic Treatise' in MS which was bought by Marmaduke Overend for 50 guineas (see Kassler(1979), 110).[92]

   With regard to the subsequent history of the Boyce family, it is clear that Elizabeth's husband, Andrew Fenn, was also probably wealthy, for their unmarried daughter Caroline left a large inheritance. It was reported in 1849 that "Miss CAROLINE ELIZA FENN, who is lately deceased, has bequeathed a legacy of £1,000, 3¼ per cent stock, to the Royal Society of Musicians. She was for many years a life subscriber to the institution; and, in addition to the legacy above-named, she has left other equally munificent donations to various charities. The lady was a granddaughter of the celebrated Dr. Boyce, the musical composer".[93] Since William jnr. also died childless, the line of the Boyce family descending from the composer appears to have died out at this point.

---

[91] See Richard Crewdson in Burrows(2008), 25-29. The evidence adduced in the article cited here is limited to identifying the owner of these annuities as one 'William Boyce', of whom there were a number in the public domain at the time, including a surgeon, a military man, and an inveterate criminal, and not necessarily the composer. While the similar investment identified as part of WB's estate in his will does not entirely clinch the matter, it is in fact put beyond doubt by the the Bank of England document, dated 6 May 1779, which authorised the claim made by Hannah and Elizabeth Boyce of Kensington Gore for the release of these funds under the terms of their father's will. The entry also reveals that WB made this investment in 1762. See *Lsg*, Bank of England Wills 1777-81, Book 30, Reg. No. 4882.
[92] In modern currency *c*£8,000.
[93] See *MT* 58 (1849), 133.

PART SIX

THE LEGACY FROM 1780

Letter from James Harris to John Henry Jacob, 9 May 1780

There is a pleasing airy burletta[1] of Bertoni's to be perform'd this night. The Saturday's serious opera is the Rinaldo of Sacchini, quite superlative throughout, and, if it has fault, too good for common English ears, that long for *Heart of Oak* and *The Early Horn*.[2] Bach's 2nd concert[3] is crowded, from the reputation of Miss Harrup — Crosdile & Cervetto are both (as usual) marvellous, & both play there. Tomorrow is the last concert.

Burrows & Dunhill(2000), 1052. For Harris, as well as many other Englishmen of his time, Boyce's 'Heart of Oak' had already become a symbol of Englishness, not only from a musical point of view, but in particular as an expression of political and military nationalism.

♣

From the *Reminiscences* of Samuel Wesley (1736-7)

The late D[r]. William Boyce was among the best of English church Composers: he annually provided an Ode for the New Year and for the King's Birth Day which were always performed at St. James's — His anthem 'Lord, thou hast been our refuge' composed for the Sons of the

---

[1] A light, especially Italian, opera.
[2] Two of the most popular songs of the age, the first by Boyce and the second by J.E. Galliard from his pantomime, *The Royal Chace*, of 1736.
[3] The reference is to J.C. Bach, the youngest son of J.S., active in London at the time both as composer and concert promoter.

Clergy is an immortal production, and a set of 12 anthems[4] published after his decease are specimens of the most consummate ability. — One of them, 'If we believe that Jesus died' was performed at his funeral, in St Paul's Cathedral, where he was buried amid the tears & lamentations of the numerous friends who felt an irreparable loss of one of the best of men.

Lbl, Add.MS27593, f. 74^v. 'If we believe' was later chosen to be sung at Wesley's own funeral, but whether in the event it actually was is not certain (see Olleson(2003), 216).

♣

A volume of church music by Boyce is edited and published by Philip Hayes (1780).

[PREFACE]

AGREEABLE to what the Proposals promised,[5] a Volume of my late worthy friend Dr. *Boyce*'s Compositions for the Church ventures into the World, which it is humbly hoped will in all respects answer the Expectations of those who have honoured it with their generous Patronage and support.

The several pieces made choice of are calculated for general use: many of them are not only well known, but have even received distinguished marks of Royal Favour, and Universal Approbation.

If the present undertaking should meet with a favourable reception, a second Volume will probably take place in the course of a few years; as there still remains ample Materials for a work, in no respect dissimilar to the present.

---

[4] *A Collection of Anthems and a Short Service* (1790), edited by Philip Hayes. This volume does indeed contain 12 anthems. However, 'If we believe' is not one of them, for Hayes included that work in his first collection of Boyce anthems, *Fifteen Anthems* (1780). By the time Wesley came to write his *Reminiscencies* at the end of his life he was prone to some confusion and inaccuracy.

[5] Hayes had advertised his project early in the summer of 1779. The cost of the volume would be a guinea (*c*£160 today), and it would be "correctly engraven, and printed on good paper" (*MP*, 9 June 1779).

I have carefully adhered to whatever was intended by the Author, and endeavoured to approve myself a faithful Editor of this his work.[6]

Nov. 1780   PHIL HAYES.

Title-page: FIFTEEN ANTHEMS, | *together with a* | *TE DEUM, and JUBILATE,* | IN SCORE | For 1, 2, 3, 4, & 5 Voices, | *COMPOSED FOR THE* | Royal Chapels, | BY | *William Boyce, Mus.Doc.* | *late ORGANIST and COMPOSER to* | His Majesty, | AND | *Master of his Majesty's* | BAND OF MUSICIANS | LONDON: | *Printed for the Author's Widow and Family.* | MDCCLXXX.

This enterprise on the part of Hayes achieved considerable success, for it attracted a distinguished list of 167 subscribers for 295 copies, among them most of the country's Cathedral and Collegiate foundations. Notable among the individual purchasers was Frederick Nicolay who acted for George III and Queen Charlotte in acquiring music for the Royal Library. A letter written to the Dean and Chapter of Gloucester Cathedral by Hannah, Boyce's widow, in the summer of 1779, eventually elicited an order for six copies. At Boyce's death in 1779 his daughter, Elizabeth, was 29, and his son William only 14. Hannah evidently felt at this point that her financial position was insecure. Apart from making up for the fact that only one of WB's anthems had been published in his lifetime, 'O be Joyful', *BC* 56, Hayes was also evidently concerned to raise funds to assist the composer's family. The contents of the volume are: *BC* 1, 8, 15 (MS at *Ob* dated 1745), 18, 33, 46, 55, 59, 60, 61, 66, 68, 69, 72, 73 and 76.

Charles Burney later made an astute assessment of Boyce as a composer for the church: "Dr. Boyce, with all due reverence for the abilities of Handel, was one of the few of our church composers who neither pillaged nor servilely imitated him. There is an original & sterling merit in his productions, founded as much on the study of our own old masters, as on the best models of other countries, that gives to all his works a peculiar stamp & character of his own, for strength, clearness, and facility, without any mixture of styles, or extraneous & heterogeneous ornaments" (*BurneyH*, 3, 620).

Detailed critical reviews of individual musical works were not common in 18th-century publications. However, John Marsh, an amateur musician and avid concert organiser, commented on one of the anthems selected by Hayes. It was one of the texts Marsh chose to set in his *Six*

---

[6] Asserted here is an important principal, one that has by no means always been observed in the past, but is now fundamental to modern ideals of editing.

Anthems (1797). In common with a number of his contemporaries, he was particularly concerned with the issue of word-setting in church music. In his preface he writes: "As to the Anthem, 'By the Water of Babylon', the author is well aware of the presumption he may be accused of in selecting these words, after they have been so beautifully set by Dr. Boyce. He however begs leave to observe that tho' the Music of the latter is such as needs not the feeble praise of an Amateur to recommend it, yet in the matter of expressing the words with propriety, he cannot help thinking that the Doctor has a little mistaken the idea in one or two parts, particularly in the verse *'Sing in one of the songs of Sion'*; here he has introduced some pleasing melody and fine singing, not considering that the words are sarcastic and uttered by a jeering multitude. But the greatest objection perhaps to Dr. Boyce's Anthem, is its concluding with the imprecation, *'Yea happy shall he be that rewardeth thee, as thou hast served us'*, tho' he stops short of the cruel idea in the following verse.[7] . . . The verse, *'If I forget thee'* etc. is so beautifully and expressively set by Dr. Boyce, that the Author of this collection could not help imitating the same style of setting them, which he has humbly endeavoured to do, only varying the melody. . . . As any kind of comparison between a feeble attempt of an Amateur, and a celebrated classical work, must require an apology, the Author must be understood to relate solely to the expression of the words, or subject, of the poem, and in no regard whatever to the Music, exclusively as such" (Marsh(1797), 3-4).

♣

Programme for a concert given at the New Rooms, Tottenham-Street on 23 April 1781

Act I

5th Ov.	Martini[8]
Song and Chorus. Softly rise (*Solomon*)	Dr Boyce
Song. Consider fond Shepherd (*Acis and Galatea*)	Handel
1st Concerto, op. 7	Geminiani
Scene in King Arthur	Purcell
Recit. And Song. Sweet Bird (*L'Allegro il Penseroso*)	Handel

---

[7] Quoted in Robins(1998), 383, n. 25.
[8] Probably Giuseppe Sammartini rather than his brother, Giovanni Battista.

Act II

Chorus. Gird on thy Sword (*Saul*)	Handel
9th Grand Concerto	Handel
Duet. What's sweeter than the new blown Rose (*Joseph*)	Handel
Dixit Dominus	Handel

Lbl, 11784.e.1. The collection from which the above sample is taken brings together the surviving programmes of concerts held between 1780 and 1800 promoted by 'The Concerts of Ancient Music', an important London society founded in 1776. Its primary concern was to preserve and revive music composed 20 years or more earlier. As this programme would suggest, the repertoire was dominated by Handel. The works by Boyce chosen give a good indication of those suitable for public concerts that remained especially popular after his death. The Boyce item included here appears at least 14 times. Other extracts selected from *Solomon* were 'As the rich Apple' (three times); 'Balmy Sweetness' (twice); and 'Together let us once range the Fields' (twice). In addition, the 'Worcester Overture' (Symphonys, op. 2, no. 8) is listed twice, 'Calms appear' from the *Secular Ode*, twice; the 'Cambridge Anthem', 'O be Joyful', once, and the duet, 'Here shall soft Charity' from the 'Leicester Ode', once. In the 1788 season the society attracted about 400 subscribers, and the orchestra normally available for their concerts consisted of more than 30 players.

♣

Songs by Boyce are published in the *Lady's Magazine* (1782).

Boyce was favoured this year by the appearance in this periodical of three of his independent songs: 'When the nymphs' (text anon.), Aug., 'Boast not mistaken swain' (A. Phillips) Sept., and 'When young and artless' (C. Smart), as a supplement. His setting of 'Come mortals' from Garrick's play *Lethe*, also appeared in the June issue.

♣

From the *Universal Dictionary of Music* (1783)

BOYCE, DR. WILLIAM. This gentleman, who had the honour of being chapel-master and organist to his late and present Majesty, was the son of Mr. William Boyce a joiner & cabinet maker. He received his first instruction in music at St. Paul's cathedral under the tuition of Mr. Charles King, M.B. and was afterwards bound apprentice to Dr. Greene who had not long cultivated the talents of his promising pupil, before he became evidently jealous of his growing fame.[9] This jealousy, though it might probably for a time retard Mr. Boyce's improvement, did not deprive him of the esteem and confidence of his master; who, at his death, not only left him in possession of all his original manuscripts, but entreated to his care the collection of Anthems which he was preparing to print in score, and which was completed and published by Dr. Boyce about ten years ago, in a stile of superior elegance and accuracy.[10] Notwithstanding the merit of the several pieces contained in the work to which we allude, it had not a very rapid or extensive sale; and Dr. Boyce is known to have been a considerable loser by the undertaking.

In 1757, he was appointed by the Duke of Devonshire to succeed Dr. Greene deceased, as master of the King's band,[11] and organist of the Royal Chapel, on the death of Mr. Travers in June 1758. In consequence of these preferments, he found it necessary to resign his engagements in the latter department, at St. Peter's, Cornhill,[12] and at All Hallows Thames Street, after fulfilling them with equal credit to himself, and satisfaction to the respective parishes.[13] He was also Weldon's successor as composer to his Majesty; so that three honourable employments in the musical department, which used to be separate, were for the first time united in his person.[14] The degree of doctor in music was conferred on Mr. Boyce at St. Mary's Church, Cambridge, on the second day of July 1749 at the instance of his friend and liberal patron the Duke of Newcastle chancellor of that university, and prime-minister.

---

[9] There is no evidence from any other source that Greene's relationship with Boyce was ever anything but cordial, or that the older man was in any way discomforted by his pupil's increasing reputation.

[10] *Cathedral Music* (1760-73).

[11] Boyce had acted in this capacity from December 1755, when Greene had died.

[12] Busby should have said, 'St. Michael's, Cornhill'.

[13] Boyce did not resign from St. Michael's until 1768, and was indeed dismissed from Allhallows in 1764.

[14] In fact, Maurice Greene had also held the posts of Organist and Composer at the Chapel Royal, alongside his Mastership of the King's Band.

On the death of Dr. Greene in 1757[15] Dr. Boyce conducted the music for the Sons of the Clergy at St. Paul's; which he continued to direct till the gout put a final period to his days, on the 7th of February 1779. He had long been occasionally subject to that painful disorder; and, previous to his dissolution, had been confined to his apartment for a considerable time. Dr. Boyce was buried with great solemnity in one of the vaults of St. Paul's cathedral; his funeral being attended by the singers of the choirs, and many other eminent lovers of the science, willing to pay the last sad duties to a person whom they justly considered as one of it's[*sic*] principal improvers and ornaments. On his tomb is the following inscription: WILLIAM BOYCE, M.D. | Organist, Composer, And | Master of the Band of Music, | To Their MAJESTIES | KING GEORGE II AND III. | Died February the 7th, 1779, Aged 69. | Happy in his Compositions, Much Happier | In a constant Flow of Harmony, | Through every Scene of Life, | Relative or Domestic; | THE HUSBAND, FATHER, FRIEND!

Dr. Boyce's merit as a composer, though universally admitted, is in our opinion, greatly superior to general estimation. His style possesses all that richness of harmony which constitutes the chief merit of ancient music, without it's [*sic*] heaviness; and is, besides, replete with the graces of modern compositions, whilst it is free from the imputation of levity. He may, indeed, in this respect, be said to occupy the medium between Handel and Arne both of whom he rivals in most of their beauties. Many of his valuable productions are as yet only to be seen in manuscripts; which, when published, will at once confirm the idea already entertained of his taste and judgement, and prove him to have attained a much greater depth of musical knowledge than has been generally supposed even by his warmest admirers.

As a man, he was justly esteemed for every domestic and social virtue: the Duke of Newcastle has already been mentioned as one of his warmest patrons: nor did he experience less friendship from the Devonshire and other noble families. It is a trite remark, that a man's temper may be read in his countenance; but to this general rule Dr. Boyce was an undoubted exception. Whoever looks on his portrait will readily pronounce him to have been a person of an austere and morose disposition, but in this judgement he will be greatly mistaken. Possibly, the outlines of his features might be hardened by the disappointments and infirmities which he experienced towards the close of his life: certain however it is, from the concurring testimonies of all who shared his intimacy, that the Doctor was

---

[15] In 1755.

a man of uncommon affability of manners, and that ill-nature had no share in his composition.

His modesty was not less conspicuous than his benevolence; of which the following instance is selected from a variety of others, which, if related, would do him equal honour. At the Coronation of his present Majesty, the composition of an Anthem in honour of that solemnity fell to Dr. Boyce, as organist of the Chapel; and the words 'Zadok the Priest' &c. were pitched upon for this purpose. The Doctor, however, declined the task; alledging, that as Mr. Handel had composed a Coronation Anthem to the same words, it would be presumption in him to take up the subject. His Majesty was graciously pleased to acquiesce in this apology; and the Coronation Anthem, as set by Handel, was accordingly performed, instead of a new composition.

[At this point Busby prints a select list of Boyce's compositions, both published and in manuscript. The last of these is the anthem, 'Lord, Thou hast been our Refuge'. He describes it as "An Instrumental Anthem composed for the Anniversary Meeting, at St. Paul's Cathedral, of the Stewards to the charity in favour of the Sons of the Clergy. This excellent production is now printing by subscription for Mr. William Boyce son of the Doctor; and will, no doubt, be highly acceptable to all admirers of genuine cathedral music".][16]

Busby concludes: "It may not be improper to mention, that, of the above pieces, the Ode on St. Cecilia's Day (words by Mr. Lockman) and the Serenata of Solomon, have been frequently performed in the Philharmonic Society established at Dublin for the Improvement of Church-music; and so great is the veneration in which Dr. Boyce is held by the members of this society, that even Handel himself is hardly thought his superior in the composition of sacred music".

This account was the first attempt in the 18th century to provide an independent biographical sketch of Boyce's career. It was followed only by the much more detailed and subsequently influential *Memoirs of Dr William Boyce* by Sir John Hawkins (see Hawkins *b*(1788)). Busby's article was, however, distinctive in providing a select list of the composer's compositions, both printed and in manuscript. This was not superseded until much later when Joseph Warren published a more substantial work-list in the preface to his edition of Boyce's *Cathedral Music* (1849).

---

[16] In the event, this anthem did not appear in print until 1802, when it was published by John Ashley. The young WB jnr.'s enterprise evidently failed to gain sufficient support at this stage.

♣

Songs by Boyce are published in Joseph Ritson's *Select Collection of English Songs*, vol. 3 (1783).

Vol. 1 of this publication contains an extensive essay on 'The Origin and Progress of National Song', while vol. 2 is concerned only with the texts to the songs. The following settings by Boyce appear in vol. 3 classified under 'Love-Songs': 'Of all the torments' (text: W. Walsh), XLV, and 'I love, I dote' (T. Otway), LIV. Other songs included in 'Airs to the Songs in Vol. II' are: 'In vain, Philander' (J. Hawkins) [no song number], and 'Bid me when forty winters more' (J. Hill), X, 'Rail no more, ye learned asses' (anon.), XXXI, and in 'Airs Part III, 'Goddess of ease" (C. Smart), XVII, and 'When Orpheus went down', (S. Lisle), XLI. Two popular airs from WB's *The Chaplet* (1749) were also reprinted here.

♣

A set of organ voluntaries by Boyce is published (*c*1785).

Title-page: Ten | VOLUNTARIES for the | *ORGAN or HARPSICHORD* | Composed by the late | Dr *William Boyce.* | Price 5^{s}.[17] | *London, printed for S. A. & P. Thompson N^O 75, St. Paul's Church Yard.*

Boyce must have improvised or played from score innumerable voluntaries during his long career as a church organist. Such pieces were invariably played before and after services, and sometimes during them too. WB evidently adopted the format established by John Stanley in his voluntaries published between 1748 and 1754, in which a slow introductory movement leads into a lively fugue or an 'allegro' featuring the trumpet or cornet stop. In these posthumously published pieces by Boyce, five end with a solo stop movement, there are four fugues (a 'double fugue' in no. 10), and no. 2 concludes with a 'moderato'. No manuscript sources for these pieces would appear to have survived.

Longman and Broderip had earlier published an anthology of *Ten Select Voluntaries* (*c*1780) in which Boyce's name appears on the title-page as one of the featured composers. Not all the pieces are assigned to a specific composer within the volume. However, Boyce's name does not appear there, but in a copy preserved at the British Library (*Lbl*, e.1089.d), WB's name was entered at some stage in pencil above no. 9 in A minor.

---

[17] *c*£38 in modern currency.

Since its style is not incompatible with that of Boyce, and indeed it has some affinities with the 9th voluntary in his published volume, it seems reasonable to attribute it to him.

A further collection, *Twelve voluntaries for the organ or harpsichord composed by the late Dr. Greene,* published by J. Bland [*c*1779], has also been credited to Boyce. The reason for this apparent anomaly lies in the discovery of the printer's MS score for this edition into which a hand-written note had been inserted: "Supposed by Dr. Greene, falsely. Composed by Dr. Boyce & his own MS. J.S. Smith, 1788".[18] Consequently, when these pieces were edited by Peter Williams he entitled the volume *Twelve Voluntaries for Organ by William Boyce or Maurice Greene.*[19] As a pupil of WB, Smith might be expected to have recognised his own teacher's hand, but a modern scholar who has examined a microfilm of the MS has reliably concluded that it is not in WB's hand (nor for that matter in Greene's either).[20] However, taking into account stylistic and contextual factors as well, the weight of opinion now favours Greene's claim to the authorship.[21]

♣

John Bland publishes *Anacreontic Songs for 1, 2, 3 & 4 Voices* composed and selected by Doct[R]. Arnold (1785).

Boyce's glee in three voices, 'Tis on earth the greatest blessing', a drinking song ideally suited to the musical tastes of such flourishing all-male societies as the Noblemen's and Gentlemen's Catch Club, appears on pp.13-15. It had first been published in 1763. A hand-written note at the foot of the title-page in a copy of this volume, (*Lbl*, H.1652.(1)), confirms the day of publication as 4 June 1785. Such pieces came to be associated with the worship of the muses, wine and love, characteristic of the odes of the Greek poet Anacreon.

♣

---

[18] Formerly in the possession of A.H. Mann, the MS is now in private hands in America (see Cooper(1969), 362-3).

[19] Williams *b*(1969).

[20] See Johnstone(1997), vii.

[21] For the case in favour of Boyce, see Cooper, op. cit., 363-6; for Greene, see Johnstone, op. cit. vii-viii, and for a view inclined towards Greene, see Williams(1969), i-ii.

From the *Liverpool General Advertiser*, 16 August 1787

The FESTIVAL of MUSIC, Will this Year be held at *LIVERPOOL* . . . also, on the MORNING of THURSDAY the 30th, and EVENING of FRIDAY the 31st, TWO GRAND MISCELLANEOUS CONCERTS. In the MORNING CONCERT will be introduced The SERENATA of SOLOMON Composed by Dr. BOYCE, And in the EVENING CONCERT, The MUSIC in the TEMPEST, & By PURCELL THE ORCHESTRA WILL CONSIST OF A VERY NUMEROUS AND SELECT BAND.[22] Principal Vocal Performers, Mr. HARRISON, Mr. MEREDITH, Mr. HINDLE, Mr. SALE, Miss HARWOOD, Miss PARKE, AND Mrs. BILLINGTON.

A word-book for *Solomon* printed for the morning concert survives entitled: '*Solomon: a Serenata composed by Dr. Boyce as it will be performed in the Music Hall, Liverpool, on Thursday morning, the 30th of August*'. [&c.] (*LVp*, H.783ORA) It reveals that a new text was adopted for the final chorus. The original words, 'In vain we trace the globe to try', are replaced by 'Proclaim it then thro' all the East'. The origin of this new version lies in a completely different and stylistically more progressive setting of the final duet and chorus that Boyce undertook in the late 1750s (autogr. at *Lcm*, MS2004).[23] Whether the impetus to do this came from Moore, the librettist, or Boyce himself is not known. However, the new text for the choral section not only draws on the same literary sources as the original in 1741, but also rounds off the work more convincingly perhaps than the earlier one did by returning to the theme of the opening chorus in praise of Solomon. A copy of WB's score for the new ending made by E.T. Warren, dated '1758' (*Lfom*, 1086), tends to confirm a time of origin shortly before then. The new duet, (but not the choral finale), was published by H. Wright with title-page: *Thou soft invader of my Soul | A favorite DUET | from D^R. Boyce's Solomon | (Never before Printed)* [*c*1789]. The MS, evidently used as the printer's copy (*Lbl*, Add.MS55337, ff. 51-57), was inscribed "Pres^d. by Sir J. Hawkins, 19 June, 1789", when it was deposited at the British Museum. The alternative finale was also adopted for the performances of *Solomon* for the Three Choirs Festivals at Worcester in 1794 and 1797.

---

[22] It is clear from the list of orchestral players printed later in the notice that at least 30 players were engaged for these concerts.

[23] Edition in Bartlett *b*(1996). No modern performance of *Solomon* using the alternative finale seems as yet to have taken place.

♣

A 2nd edition of Boyce's *Cathedral Music* is published (1788).

Title-page: Cathedral Music | BEING | A COLLECTION in SCORE | of the | Most Valuable and Useful Compositions | FOR THAT SERVICE, | BY THE Several English Masters | of the last Two Hundred Years. | The Whole Selected and Carefully Revis'd | By the late DR WILLIAM BOYCE. | Organist and Composer to the Royal Chapels, and Master of his MAJESTY'S Band of Musicians | London | Printed for John Ashley | M.DCC.LXXXVIII.

The great success of this enterprise of Ashley, a bassoonist and conductor, may be gauged by the degree of public support it gained. While Boyce's original edition had only 127 purchasers, this edition attracted 405. Clearly the significance and utility of WB's great work was now much more widely appreciated. Notable among the individual subscribers were Burney, and Joah Bates, the distinguished organist and conductor who had organised the great Handel Commemoration concerts at Westminster Abbey in 1784. Moreover, Ashley invited Sir John Hawkins to write his 'Memoirs of Dr. William Boyce' as a preface to the edition. This substantial biographical survey laid the foundations for all subsequent Boyce scholarship. Ashley also inserted into his edition a fine engraving of WB drawn from life in 1775 by J.K. Sherwin, then Engraver to the Prince of Wales, later George IV.

A further edition of Boyce's work was issued by Joseph Warren in 1849, thereby making his historical collection readily available to a new generation of church musicians. Warren not only took the opportunity to revise Boyce's biographies of the composers represented, but he also published the first substantial catalogue of Boyce's musical output including manuscript as well as printed sources.

♣

J. H. [John Hawkins] publishes 'Memoirs of Dr. William Boyce' in *Cathedral Music*, 2nd edn (1788).

[N.B. The author's footnotes are indicated by letters, and the editor's by numbers. The former are placed at the end of the document itself, and the latter after the commentary.]

Dr. WILLIAM BOYCE was born in the year 1710.[24] His father was a citizen of London and a mechanic, viz. a joiner and cabinet-maker, who, discovering in his son while an infant, a delight in musical sounds, placed him for tuition under Mr. *Charles King*, almoner or more properly master of the children in the cathedral church of *St. Paul*'s, into which, after a little instruction in the music-school, he was admitted a chorister.

Upon the breaking of his voice and his consequent dismission from the choir, he was taken as an apprentice by Dr. *Maurice Greene* then organist of that church, and by him taught the principles of music and the practice of choral service. At the expiration of his apprenticeship,[25] he became organist of the chapel in *Vere Street* near *Cavendish Square*, called *Oxford Chapel*;[26] when being arrived at an age when his proficiency in his art enabled him to become a teacher of the harpsichord, he betook himself to that profession, and taught chiefly at boarding schools, and among others at Mr. *Cavaller*'s in *Queen Square, Bloomsbury*, then deemed the best seminary for female tuition of any in the kingdom.

Greene, though an excellent organist and a fine composer, was but meanly skilled in the theory of music; *Boyce* was a studious young m[a]n and a lover of the science; he set himself to explore the principles of harmony, and to improve his natural genius by all the aids that learning could afford: to t[h]is end, as did also many young men of that time, *Travers, Keeble* and others, he took lectures under Dr. *Pepusch*, the greatest theorist then living; perusing with a most sedulous attention, as well the works of the Romish Church-musicians, such as *Palestrina, Orlando de Lasso, Stradella*, and *Carissimi*, as the no less excellent composers of our own church, namely, *Tallis, Bird, Purcell*, Dr. *Orlando Gibbons*, and others.

The fruits of his studies under this eminent tutor, were compositions to words, which to speak of them particularly, were at first only single songs, and were mere essays of a genius teeming with invention, but were well received. Many yet remember the elegant air to which he set the song of Lord *Chesterfield*'s addressed to Lady *Frances Shirley* 'When *Fanny*, blooming fair', and that it was a lullaby to many a celebrated toast now living, and kept time with the rocking of her cradle.

From exercises trivial as these, he proceeded to others of greater import: Lord *Lansdowne*'s masque of *Peleus* and *Thetis* having never been set, at least to any advantage, held out to him a temptation to emulate *Purcell, Weldon,* and others, who, though church-musicians, had suffered

---

[24] In 1711.
[25] In 1734.
[26] Also called the Marybone Chapel, and later St. Peter's, Vere Street.

themselves to be engaged in the service of the theatres, in an attempt at dramatic music. The masque above mentioned was of this kind; and though greatly inferior in the structure of it to the *Comus* of *Milton* and in the smoothness of its versification to the poetry of *Waller*, of whom Lord *Lansdowne* was an imitator, it had charms sufficient to attract the notice of *Boyce*; accordingly he set it in recitative, with airs and chorusses occasionally interspersed, and had it performed at the *Philharmonic Society*,[27] where it was received with the applause due to its merit.

Such a proficiency in his art as the above particulars imply, must astonish every one when it is related that before the expiration of his apprenticeship, *Boyce*'s organs of hearing were so sensibly affected that in a short time he became little less than deaf: a calamity like this, must in him who felt it, have damped the prosecution of a study which, exclusive of the understanding, tends to the gratification of a sense that in him was defective: Of musicians labouring under a deprivation of sight, history affords many instances; as *Salinas, Krumb[h]orn* and others;[28] but who ever heard of a deaf musician? This misfortune had however little effect on *Boyce* in diverting the course of his pursuits; it deprived him in some degree of a source of both delight and improvement, but he considered music as a mental and not a sensual pleasure, and secretly and with advantage contemplated that harmony which he could but just hear.

In the year 1736 he quitted his employment at *Oxford Chapel*, the salary whereof was but small, being chosen organist of the parish church of St. *Michael, Cornhill*, in the room of Mr. *Joseph Kelway* who had vacated that place by removing to the church of *St. Martin in the Fields.* Mr *Kelway* was the immediate successor of Mr. *Obadiah Shuttleworth*, a mere harpsichord player, who had the advantage of a good finger,[29] charmed his hearers with such music as was fit alone for that instrument, and drew after him greater numbers than came to hear the preacher.[a] *Boyce,* who well understood the nature and genius of the organ, on the contrary seldom played on any other stop than the stopped Diapason, and

---

[27] The Philharmonic Society, or Society of Gentlemen Performers, was a private music club that met at the Crown and Anchor Tavern in the Strand and whose members were largely amateur. Michael Festing, however, is known to have led the orchestra there from 1735-7 (see Busby(1825), I, 18). The reference by Hawkins to this performance is the only evidence we have for it.

[28] Francesco Salinas was a 16th-century Spanish organist and composer, and Caspar Krumbhorn an obscure Silesian composer and instrumentalist who died in 1621 (see *HawkinsH*, 2nd edn, 1875, vol. 1, 434).

[29] This word was erroneously transcribed as 'singer' in Beechey *b*(1971), 93.

on that in three and four parts, in a style suited both to the place and the occasion.

Upon the decease of Mr. *John Weldon* in the same year, he was, in his room, appointed one of the composers to his Majesty.[b] The duty of this office is to compose anthems for the service of the royal chapel: *Weldon* had held it for upwards of twenty years, during which time he had composed a communion service and sundry anthems, two of which 'In thee, O Lord, have I put my trust', and 'Hear my crying', inserted in the following collection, are remarkable for the sweetness of the melody in a very eminent degree.[30]

Having by his studies, and the many evidences of learning and invention exhibited in his compositions for the Chapel Royal, attained to great eminence in his faculty, he in the year 1749 set to music and published *Solomon*, a Serenata,[31] as it is styled, being a version of the Canticles, written by Mr. *Moore*, author of the fables for the female sex. This person had been a tradesman in the city, but for some time had quitted business, and addicted himself to poetical studies, and attaching himself to Mr. *Garrick,* was the author of sundry dramatic performances, which met with various success.[c]

The merits of *Boyce*'s *Solomon* are too well known to need any encomium, it may nevertheless be observed that the recitatives are to the greatest degree expressive of amorous sentiments. Of the airs that occur in it, one deserves particular notice 'Softly rise, O Southern breeze': besides violin parts, it has a solo accompanyment by the bassoon, and was never heard but with the utmost attention.

The publication and frequent performance of this drama, for so it may be called, had placed the composer in the foremost rank of his profession, and encouraged him to publish in the year 1747 twelve Sonatas for two violins and a bass: before this time the Sonatas of *Bassani* and of *Corelli* and the Balletti or airs of *Albinoni*, were the only practice for gentlemen-performers, and these having been composed at the latter end of the last century, were become so familiar to every musical ear, that a variety in these elegant amusements at the period above mentioned, was greatly wished for.

Besides the charm of novelty, these compositions of *Boyce* had every intrinsic excellence to recommend them. The fugues among them are conducted with great art, and the airs have an original and elegant cast. For near twenty years after their publication, they were performed between the

---

[30] These two anthems are edited in Boyce's *Cathedral Music*, vol. 2, 202-8 and 209-18 respectively.

[31] *Solomon* was composed in 1742 and published in 1743.

acts at the theatres; but at length gave way to the tumid extravaganzas of Lord *Kelly, Stamitz* and *Richter*, in which the monotonous clangor of French horns served to cover all defects both of skill and invention.

The success of these his essays in secular composition, was no temptation with *Boyce* to consider his employment in the Royal Chapel as a sinecure; he contributed largely to the increase of the stock of music there performed, by the composition of anthems at divers times, and on sundry occasions. The number of anthems in practise in the Chapel Royal was, until Dr. *Greene*'s time, but small, consisting chiefly of those of *Wise, Purcell, Blow*, and Dr. *Aldrich*. It is true that in the year 1724 Dr. *Croft*, who by the way was the first publisher of anthems in score, gave to the world a collection, to the amount of thirty; but the stock even thus increased was surely inadequate to the performance of divine service twice a day throughout the year. To these, *Greene* added at least fifty, in a stile less solemn it must be owned than those of his predecessors, but abounding in all the graces and elegancies which music had derived from the introduction of the Italian opera into this kingdom, and the subsequent improvements of *Handel* and *Bononcini*.

Forty anthems of *Greene*'s composition are happily in print,[32] and if any one should question the character here given of them, he is referred for the truth of it to the following, viz: 'I will sing of thy power', 'Lord let me know my end', and 'O Lord give ear unto my prayer'. *Boyce*'s addition to the stock of anthems above mentioned may be estimated at sixty.

Concerning this species of vocal harmony, it may be observed that in an age in which the love of music prevails even to affectation, its merits are but little known. The gay and fashionable flock in crouds [*sic*] to places of public entertainment, to the opera, to the theatres, and to concerts, and pretend to be charmed with what they hear. It was once as fashionable to be alike attracted by the charms of choral music, where the hearers were sure of enjoying all the delight that could result from the united powers of sublime poetry, and harmony the most exquisite.

That this is no longer a practice, is owing to certain prejudices, which it may be deemed a kindness to remove; the one is, that the style of the music appropriated to divine offices is suited to melancholy tempers, of which opinion was the late King of *Prussia*,[33] when he objected to certain compositions that had been shewn him, that they smelt of the church: the other no less idle cavil is, that our cathedral music is inferior to that of foreign countries. As to the former objection, every one is at liberty to

---

[32] Greene's *Forty Select Anthems* (1743).

[33] The reference is to 'Frederick the Great' of Prussia, the enlightened, keenly musical, but aggressive military leader, who died in 1786.

speak as he feels: In the opinion of some, divine service itself is but a dull employment: To the latter it may be answered that on good authority it is asserted, that from before the time of the reformation, the English have been celebrated for their skill in music, and it is well known that compositions of some of the most eminent of our church musicians are preserved in the *Vatican* library;[d] with truth it may also be said, that whether we consider it in point of learning, sublimity, or elegance, the music of our church will not suffer by a comparison with that of any other in *Europe*.

Soon after, *Boyce* employed himself to collect a variety of songs and cantatas which he had occasionally set to music: these he published at different periods, under the title of *Lyra Britannica*.[34]

In the year 1749, upon the erection of an organ in the church of the united parishes of *Allhallows* the Great and the Less, in *Thames Street*, in one of which *Joiners' Hall*, the dwelling of his father,[e] is situate, he was requested by the parishioners to become their organist, which employment, notwithstanding his various other engagements, he accepted.

In the same year, upon the decease of the Duke of Somerset, Chancellor of the University of *Cambridge*, the Duke of *Newcastle* was elected his successor. Upon this occasion an Ode written by Mr. *Mason*, was given to Mr. *Boyce* to set to music; and the same, and also an anthem suited to the solemnity,[35] was publicly performed in the church of St. *Mary* on the first day of *July* in the above year, being Commencement-Sunday.

This performance seems to have answered two purposes, viz. the celebration of the Duke's installation, and that of an exercise for a degree in music, which was an academical honor, Mr. *Boyce* was desirous of: he obtained it without any solicitation, and was permitted by the university to accumulate the degrees of bachelor and doctor in his faculty. Both the ode and the anthem were published by himself, the former with a dedication to the Duke of *Newcastle*.[36]

In the year 1749 he set to music a drama entitled *The Chaplet*, and in 1752[37] another, called *The Shepherd's Lottery*, both written by Mr. *Mendez*, and performed at *Drury Lane* Theatre.

Dr. *Boyce*, till about this time, had lived in apartments belonging to his father at *Joiner's Hall*, but being now arrived at great eminence in his

---

[34] Published in six vols. (1747-59).

[35] The ode, 'Here all thy active fires diffuse', and the anthem, 'O be joyful in God' (1749).

[36] In 1752.

[37] By Nov. 1751.

profession, he went to reside in *Quality Court, Chancery Lane*, and soon after married.[38]

Dr. *Greene*, who was living at this time, but advanced in years, considering the corrupted state of our cathedral music, which, by the multiplication of manuscript copies, and the ignorance of transcribers, was become so incorrect as that many of the services and anthems of which it consisted were scarce fit for practise, set himself to reform and secure it from future injury. It is true that, in the year 1641, a like attempt was made by the publication, under the patronage of King *Charles* the First, of a work entitled, 'The first book of selected church-music, consisting of services and anthems, such as are now used in the cathedral and collegiate churches of this kingdom, never before printed, whereby such books as were heretofore with much difficulty and charges transcribed for the use of the quire, are now, to the saving of much labour and expence, published for the general good of all such as shall desire them either for public or private exercise, collected out of divers approved authors, by *John Barnard*, one of the minor Canons of the cathedral church of St. *Paul, London*. But this being printed not in score, but in parts, single books were in a short time purloined, and when by public authority the liturgy was abolished, and the performance of choral service forbidden, the whole were considered as parts of a superstitious ritual, and seized as lawful plunder; and so general was the devastation, that Dr. *Boyce* himself has been heard to say that the library of the church of *Hereford* was the only one in the kingdom in which he was able to find a compleat set of *Barnard's* books.

To repair this loss, and to prevent any such calamity for the future, Dr. *Greene* undertook to collate the several manuscript copies of the most esteemed services and anthems, composed for the use of the reformed church from the final establishment of its liturgy to his own time. To this end, he some years before his death, set himself to collect all the written church music, either in score or in parts, that he could come at, together with a compleat set of the books published by *Barnard*. What progress he made in the collection is not known; but it is certain that, dying in the year 1755, he was disappointed in his hopes of giving to the world the work he had so long meditated, and remitted to Dr. *Boyce* the future conduct and publication thereof, by a bequest in his will of all his manuscript music.[39]

---

[38] Boyce moved to Quality Court in 1753, and married in 1759.

[39] It has been pointed out, contrary to the impression given by Hawkins here, that Greene did not formally request Boyce to undertake this task in his will (see Johnstone *b*(1975), 26).

In the same year he was, by the Duke of *Grafton*, then Lord Chamberlain of his Majesty's household, nominated to the office of master of the royal band of musicians, in the room of Dr. *Greene*,[f] upon whose decease the conduct of the annual performance at St. *Paul*'s, for the benefit of the sons of the clergy, had, almost of course, devolved on him. His office at this solemnity, was standing at a kind of desk among the performers, with a roll of paper in his right hand, to beat the time through every movement: this was the practice of his predecessor, and is continued to this day. Further to testify his regard for this institution, he composed instrumental parts to *Purcell*'s *Te Deum*,[40] and also two anthems 'Lord thou hast been our refuge' and 'Blessed is he that considereth the poor', which for their excellence have long been deemed an indispensable part of the performance.[41]

In the year 1758, Dr. *Boyce* was appointed one of the organists of the Royal Chapel, in the room of Mr. *John Travers*, then lately deceased, a person whose excellence as a musician is sufficiently known and universally acknowledged. Upon this occasion he resigned the two employments of organist of St. *Michael, Cornhill*, and *Allhallows, Thames Street*.[42]

Dr. *Boyce* was by this time nearly fifty years of age, and labouring still under the infirmity deafness, he quitted his house in town, and his practice of teaching, and took up his residence at *Kensington*, where with unwearied assiduity, he prosecuted his studies.[43] His employment, as master of the royal band, subjected him to the task of setting the new-year and birth-day odes, and his duty as composer to the chapel, required of him at times the production of a new anthem. Other of his hours were devoted to the instruction of organists and young musicians desirous of improvement in the theory of sounds, the laws of harmony, and the art of practical composition. This had been the employment of Dr. *Pepusch* after his retirement to the *Charterhouse*, and but for knowledge communicated in private lectures by those two persons, the character of a learned musician had probably, by this time, been unknown among us.

Amidst this variety of pursuits, he found leisure to revise many of his former publications, particularly the overtures to his *Solomon, The*

---

[40] The *Te Deum* and *Jubilate* of 1694.

[41] The first of these two anthems was indeed composed for the Sons of the Clergy in 1755; the second was not new, but was an adaptation of an orchestrally accompanied anthem originally written for, and performed in Dublin in 1741.

[42] Boyce did not relinquish his post at Allhallows until March 1764, when he was in fact dismissed, and he did not resign from St. Michael's until April 1768.

[43] The move to Kensington took place some time in 1763, or a little earlier.

Chaplet, and *Shepherd's Lottery*; to these he added an overture to an ode of *Pindar*, and a few others, as also one in D with the minor third, composed for a performance at *Worcester*, on occasion of the annual meeting of the three adjacent choirs which has long been admired by the lovers and judges of harmony, and is known by the name of the *Worcester* overture. These he published under the title of Eight Symphonies for violins and other instruments.[44]

In the year 1760, came abroad the first volume of that laborious work, the Cathedral Music, with a dedication to the King, and a list of subscribers, which, in respect to number, redounded little to the honor of those whose duty and interest it is to encourage choral service, and served only to shew to what a low ebb the love of it was sunk. The second and third volumes were published at different and remote periods, with little better encouragement, so that, but for the delight the employment afforded him, the editor of this noble work had been left to deplore having undertaken so arduous a task as he found it to be, and the loss of his time at a period of life when time becomes most valuable. And it cannot but excite the wonder, if not the indignation, of those who have encouraged the present edition of it, to be told that, after twelve years labor employed in it, and the expence of the engraving, the paper, and the printing, he did but little more than reimburse himself the cost of its publication.

Dr. *Boyce* had no sooner acquitted himself of his engagements to the public in the above instance, than he gave another direction to his studies. Mr. *Garrick* had, some years before, employed him to compose a Dirge for the funeral procession in *Romeo and Juliet*, another for the play of *Cymbeline*, and other songs for the theatre, and being now about to revive *The Winter's Tale*, he got him to contribute his aid to that performance by setting the songs: Dr. *Boyce* readily undertook the task, and succeeded very happily in it, particularly in that pleasant dialogue for three voices between *Autolycus* and his two sweethearts 'Get you hence for I must go', in which with singular ingenuity he has expressed the humour of *Shakespeare*, in a melody, the gayest and most natural that can be conceived.[45]

---

[44] The *8 Symphonys* were published in January 1760, i.e. about three years before WB settled in Kensington.

[45] This paragraph is rather loosely construed. Boyce continued to devote himself to the completion of *Cathedral Music* until the publication of the third volume in 1773. His dirge for *Cymbeline* was commissioned for Covent Garden in April 1746 by John Rich, not Garrick, while his music for Garrick's production of *The Winter's Tale* (*Florizel and Perdita*) dates from January 1756. At that time WB must have been fully occupied with his work on *Cathedral Music*, not to mention his numerous other on-going practical and creative musical commitments.

Before this time the instrumental music of the theatres, Vauxhall, and other places of public resort, had consisted chiefly of the concertos of *Corelli, Geminiani,* and *Martini*,[46] and the overtures of Mr. *Handel*: These last had, for many years, served for the first music or prelude to plays, and were grown so familiar, that the country-dance tunes, *Green sleeves,* and *Roger de Coverly* were not better known and more common with the vulgar than the gavot in *Otho*, the minuet in *Rodelinda*, and that in *Ariadne*. At this crisis, Dr. *Boyce* had lying by him, the new-years' and birth-day odes which he had composed during the time he had filled the station of master of the royal band. The overtures to these he thought would be well received, and, about the year 1770, he published twelve of them. They are very original and spirited compositions, and abound with elegant airs, and the evidences of deep skill and learned ingenuity.

The taste of the people at the time of the publication of these, was very unpropitious to their success: they had the misfortune to meet with the compositions of *Bach* and *Abel* which had already gotten possession of the public ear. Those two persons had the patronage of the late Duke of *York*, who himself was a proficient on the violoncello; the style they introduced was void of the chief excellencies of music, it was coarse and artless; their basses had no melody, but were tediously monotonous, and to the eye resembled a row of pins.

Bach and *Abel* were nevertheless eminent musicians, especially the former, who in the composition of the music to an oratorio of *Metastasio* entitled *Gioas*, performed at the *Haymarket* to a thin audience, gave proof of his great abilities; but like most of that profession who are to live by the favor of the public, both he and *Abel* had two styles of composition, the one for their own private delight, the other for the gratification of the many.

Yet these, too, had their fate; the multifarious productions of *Bach* and *Abel*, their *Trios, Quartettos,* and *Quintettos*, as they are called, together with their *Periodical Overtures*, were heard, and consigned to oblivion, but their style of writing in a great measure survives. We no more hear the solemn and pathetic Adagio, the artful and well-studied Fugue, or the sweet modulations of the keys with the minor third: all is *Allegro* and *Prestissimo*, and, if not discord, such harmony as the ear sickens at hearing. Such music Mr. *Handel* was used to listen to and laugh at, and comparing it to a game at cards, would exclaim 'Now D is trumps, now A', in allusion to those vulgar transitions from the key-note to its fifth,

---

[46] Hawkins almost certainly had in mind here the works of Giuseppe Sammartini rather than those of his younger brother, Giovanni Battista Sammartini.

with which such sort of music, especially when accompanied with French horns, abounds.

Having thus experienced the vitiated taste of the public, Dr. *Boyce* abandoned the thoughts of giving to the world any more of his works, and so deeply rooted in him was this resolution, that being once prest by the writer of these memoirs, to follow the example of *Croft* and *Greene*, who had each of them published a collection of anthems, the one of thirty, and the other of forty, his answer was, that he was contented his should remain in the church books, and that he would never solicit the aid of a subscription to enable him to publish what might fail of being well received.

The last exercise of his genius and invention was the setting to music [of] a few elegiac lines written by Sir *John Hawkins* and intended as a monumental inscription to the memory of the late Rev. *William Gostling* one of the minor Canons of the cathedral of *Canterbury*, who died in or about the year 1777, and left behind him a collection of music made by him and his father, the most curious and valuable of its kind in this kingdom.

As he advanced in years he became afflicted with the gout, which increased upon him, interrupted his studies, and at length put a period to his life, on the seventh day of *February, 1779.*[47] He left a widow, a son and a daughter.

His interment, which was in St. *Paul*'s Cathedral, on the sixteenth day of *February*, was honored with testimonies of affection and respect, not only suited to his profession and character, but such in degree as were never paid to the memory of any musician or other artist, unless perhaps to that of Sir *Christopher Wren*, the architect of the noble fabric that covers the remains of both. The procession began from *Kensington*, and the corpse was carried into the cathedral (attended by his son, a youth of about fifteen years of age, and several other mourners) and entering at the south door, proceeded down the south aisle to the west door, where being received by the Rev. Dr. *Wilson*, and the Rev. Dr. *Douglas*, Canons Residentiary of the church, the Minor Canons, Lay-Vicars, and choristers thereof, and also of *Westminster-Abbey*, and the priests in ordinary, gentlemen, and children of the King's Chapel and many other gentlemen,

---

[47] Thomas Busby later provided a fuller account of Boyce's illness: "As Dr. Boyce advanced in years, his constitution became subject to gout. The fits increasing both in their frequency and violence, at length the disorder attacked his stomach, and the affliction that for a while had only induced pain, and the interruption of his studies, on the 7th of February, 1779, terminated his existence" (Busby(1825), 3, 174).

professors and lovers of music, all in surplices, it was conducted up the nave of the church into the choir, the attendants walking two and two, singing the first part of the burial service, composed by *Purcell* and Dr. *Croft* 'I am the resurrection and the life', without the organ. When arrived at the choir, the body was rested upon tressels, and the attendants being seated, the Rev. Mr. Wight, senior Minor Canon of St. *Paul's*, began the daily service, in the course of which the 39th and 90th psalms were chanted to solemn music; the first lesson was read by Mr. *Hayes*, and the second by Mr. *Gibbons*. Before the prayer for the King, an anthem composed by the deceased, beginning 'If we believe that *Jesus* died', was sung by Mr. *Dyne* and Mr. *Soper*, and the chorus by them and the other singers. After this, the reader proceeded to the end of the morning service, which being concluded, the attendants rose and moved to the area under the dome, and placed themselves in a circle, the organ all the while playing as a kind of dead march, the air in *Elami* flat[48] in the fourth of his Sonatas. During this short procession and arrangement, the bearers were removing the body to the crypt or vaults under the pavement, where they deposited it. After this, the service at the grave, beginning 'Man that is born of a woman', was sung to the organ: Mr. *Wight* then recited the prayer on committing the body to the ground, while a person with a shovel scattered dust, through the perforations in the central plate, on the coffin, which lay immediately under it. Then was sung to the organ the verse 'I heard a voice from Heaven', which being done, the reader proceeded to the end of the burial service.

As a musician, Dr. *Boyce* was doubtless one of the first of his time, if we except Mr. Handel, whom the sublimity of his genius has placed above all comparison. Dr. *Boyce's* merit consisted in the union in his own person and character, of the various excellencies of former church musicians. In musical erudition, he emulated *Tallis* and *Bird*; in harmony and various modulation, *Orlando Gibbons*; and in the sweetness of their melody, *Purcell and Weldon*: In a word, it may be said, that in skill, and the powers of invention, he was not surpassed by the most celebrated of his predecessors or contemporaries. In the art of musical composition he had formed some rules which were the result of his own study and reflection, that served to guard him from the errors of others. One axiom of his in particular, is worthy of remembrance by all students in the science; it is this, that whereas it is the endeavour of most musicians, both in composition and extempore performance on the organ, to modulate from

---

[48] In modern terminology Eb major. Hawkins introduces here archaic terms derived from solmization.

key to key by all the various methods their invention can suggest, 'the skill of the artist is best shewn, not in departing from the original key, but in keeping within it', and producing, by the interchanges of its own consonances, all that variety of harmony of which it may be found capable.

A glimpse of this rule may be discerned in Dr. *Pepusch*'s short treatise on harmony, chap. II, and a curious observer may see it exemplified in the motets of *Palestrina*, the anthem 'Bow thine ear, O Lord' of *Bird*, and *Orlando Gibbons*'s service in F.

To the above account of his studies, a sketch of his moral character maybe thought not an improper adjunct. He possessed a great degree of that modesty peculiar to real artists, arising from a comparison of their works with their ideas, and the inferiority of the former to the latter, that rendered him ever indifferent to applause and even commendation. He declined composing an anthem on occasion of his present Majesty's coronation, to the words '*Zadok* the priest, &c.' alledging that it would be presumption in him to attempt it after Mr. *Handel*; his excuse was accepted, and he made one to other words, which was performed. He had composed a three-part song to the words, 'Tis on earth the greatest blessing,' printed in *Hale*'s Social Harmony with the foolish title of 'The Mystic Bower,' and adapted to a panegyric on Free-Masonry. This composition, a friend of his once took occasion to commend, saying it was nearly equal to *Blow*'s 'Go perjured man'. *Boyce* was offended with the comparison, said it deserved not to be named at the same time with that fine song, and accused his friend of insincerity and a design to flatter him. He was endowed with the qualities of truth, justice, and integrity, was mild and gentle in his deportment, above all resentment against such as envied his reputation, communicative of his knowledge, sedulous and punctual in the discharge of the duties of his several employments, particularly those that regarded the performance of divine service, and in every relation of life a worthy man.[49]

a   Of this class of organists, Mr. *Robinson,* St. *Lawrence Jewry*, was the first. In parish churches the voluntary between the psalms and the first lesson was anciently a slow solemn movement, tending like the Sanctus in choral service, to compose the minds of the hearers, and to excite sentiments of piety and devotion. Mr. *Robinson* introduced a different practice, calculated to display the agility of his fingers in

---

[49] In view of the commentary which follows, perhaps it should be observed here that Hawkins's attitude to Boyce throughout these memoirs is entirely positive.

Allegro movements on the Cornet, Trumpet, Sesquialtera, and other noisy stops degrading the instrument, and instead of the full and noble harmony with which it was designed to gratify the ear, tickling it with mere airs in two parts, in fact solos for a flute and a bass.

b   This establishment owes its rise to the zeal and bounty of Queen *Mary*, the consort of King *William*: the thought of it was suggested by Dr. *Tillotson*, when Dean of St. Paul's; it was intended by her Majesty that there should be two composers, and that *Blow* and *Purcell* should be the persons, who should each produce a new anthem on the first Sunday of his month of waiting: but the design was not carried into execution till 1699, when *Blow* alone was nominated with a salary of 40l. a year, *Purcell* then being dead. The nomination of a second composer slept till the year 1715, when *Weldon* was appointed, the other being Dr. *Croft*. At the same time an addition of persons was made to the gentlemen of the chapel, and a lutenist and violist also appointed. See Sir *John Hawkins*'s History of Music, Vol. IV. Page 487, Vol. V. 59.

c   Mr. *Moore* has been heard to confess that he was unacquainted with any other language than his own, and that all his abilities for writing were derived from the perusal of the poets of our own country.

d   Among which is the *Gloria Patri*, a canon of four parts in one, by Dr. *Blow* at the end of the *Jubilate* in his morning service in the key of G, and which is engraven on his monument in *Westminster Abbey*.

e   He was beadle of the Joiners' Company.

f   He was not sworn in until June 1757, when the Duke of Devonshire held that station, but he performed the functions of the office from the time of his nomination.

(Beechey *b*(1979) It has sometimes been held against Hawkins that, notwithstanding his evident long friendship and collaboration with Boyce, he snubbed him by failing to include him in his *History of Music* (1776), and subsequently wrote these memoirs in recompense. Such suggestions were, however, wide of the mark. The explanation for the omission was simply that Hawkins had "conscientiously excluded all living composers from his History" (see Davis(1973), 142-3). Confirmation of this may be found in the 'Conclusion' to *HawkinsH*, 2nd edn, 1875, 2, 917: "In the original plan of the foregoing work, it was for reasons, which have yet their weight with the author, determined to continue it no further than to that period at which it is made to end". The last composer whose work Hawkins did assess was in fact John Stanley, who had died in 1770.

John Ashley's 2nd edition of WB's *Cathedral Music* was a bold but evidently timely enterprise, for it attracted as many as 392 subscribers for 477 sets, whereas the original edition had been supported by a modest 126 subscribers for 212 copies. While Hawkins's 'Memoirs' suffers from its author's inclination towards prolixity and discursiveness, it was by far the most extensive and informative of the early accounts of Boyce's life.

♣

From Charles Burney's *General History of Music*, vol. 3 (1789)

Dr. WILLIAM BOYCE has been frequently mentioned in the course of this work, as a professor to whom our choral service is greatly indebted for the well selected, correct, and splendid collection of our cathedral Music which he published in three volumes large folio, upon the plan, and at the recommendation, of his master and predecessor Dr. Greene; and now, in gratitude for the care he has taken of the productions and fame of others, it becomes the duty of an historian of the musical art, to pay a just tribute to his own memory, as an artist.

In 1734, he was a candidate for the place of organist of St. Michael's church, Cornhill, with Froud, Young, James Worgan, and Kelway. But though he was unsuccessful in this application, Kelway having been elected, yet he was appointed, the same year, to the place of organist of Oxford Chapel; and in 1736, upon the death of Weldon, when Kelway being elected organist of St. Martin's in the Field's, resigned his place at St. Michael's Cornhill, Boyce was not only elected organist of that church, but organist and composer in the Chapel Royal.

The same year he set *David's Lamentation over Saul and Jonathan*, which was performed at the Apollo Society. About the year 1743, he produced his serenata of *Solomon*, which was not only long and justly admired, as a pleasing and elegant composition, but still affords great delight to the friends of English Music, whenever it is performed. His next publication was *Twelve Sonatas or Trios for two violins and a Base*, which were longer and more generally purchased, performed, and admired, than any productions of the kind in this Kingdom, except those of Corelli. They were not only in constant use, as chamber Music, in private concerts, for which they were originally designed, but in our theatres, as act-tunes, and public gardens, as favourite pieces, during many years.

In 1749, he set the ode written by the late Rev. Mr. Mason, for the installation of the late Duke of Newcastle, as chancellor of the University of Cambridge, at which time he was honoured with the degree of doctor in Music, by that university. Soon after this event, he set the *Chaplet*, a musical drama, written by the late Mr. Mendez, for Drury-lane theatre, which had a very favourable reception, and long run, and continued many years in use among the *stock* pieces for that theatre. Not long after the first performance of this drama, his friend Mr Beard brought on the same stage the secular ode,[50] written by Dryden, and originally set by Dr. Boyce for Hickford's room, or the Castle Concert, where it was first performed, in still life[51] This piece, though less successful than the *Chaplet*, by the animated performance and friendly zeal of Mr. Beard, was many times exhibited before it was wholly laid aside. These compositions, with occasional single songs for Vauxhall and Ranelagh, disseminated the fame of Dr. Boyce throughout the kingdom, as a dramatic and miscellaneous composer, while his choral compositions for the King's chapel, for the feast of the sons of the clergy at St. Paul's, and for the triennial meetings at the three cathedrals of Worcester, Hereford, and Gloucester at the performances at all which places he constantly presided till the time of his death, established his reputation as an ecclesiastical composer and able master of harmony.

Dr. Boyce, with all due reverence for the abilities of Handel, was one of the few of our church composers who neither pillaged nor servilely imitated him. There is an original and sterling merit in his productions, founded as much on the study of our own old masters, as on the best models of other countries, that gives to all his works a peculiar stamp and character of his own, for strength, clearness, and facility, without any mixture of styles, or extraneous and heterogeneous ornaments.

Dr. Boyce dying in 1779, was succeeded, in the Chapel Royal by Mr. Dupuis and, as master of his Majesty's band, by Mr. Stanley.

BurneyH, 3, 619-21. This account forms part of a chapter entitled 'Progress of Church Music in England after the Death of Purcell'. Burney's judicious assessments here of Boyce's *Solomon*, the *Twelve Sonatas* and his church music have been widely quoted in later writings on Boyce. Burney's description of him as "a dramatic and miscellaneous composer" is of some significance, for it counters the erroneous view which took hold in the late 19th century, namely that he was essentially a composer and editor of

---

[50] Burney is referring here to the *Secular Masque*.
[51] i.e. with scenery and costumes but without action.

anthems. Thirty years later Burney wrote another biography of the composer for Rees's *Cyclopedia* (1819), most of it taken from the above.

♣

Philip Hayes publishes a second volume of anthems by Boyce (1790).

Title-page: *A COLLECTION* |OF | Anthems | *And a Short Service in* | SCORE, | FOR *1, 2, 3, 4, 5, and 8* VOICES | *Compos'd for the Use of the* | Royal Chapels, | *By the late* WILLIAM BOYCE, *Mus. Doc.* | *Organist &* | *Composer to his* | MAJESTY, | *And Master of his Majesty's Band of* | *Musicians,* | London | *Printed for the Author's Widow.* | MDCCXC.

A copy of the preliminary notice for this edition advertising "Proposals for printing by subscription, A Collection of Anthems" is preserved at *SA*, (Finzi Collection, 304) along with a note from WB's son: "M^r. Boyce's compliments to M^r. Smith returns him his sincere thanks for the kind assistance he has afforded him in publishing his father's anthems, & begging his acceptance of a book", dated July 12 1790. 'Mr. Smith' would almost certainly have been the musical antiquarian John Stafford Smith, a former pupil of Boyce's, whose name appears in the list of subscribers to the edition. Among the other subscribers were Arnold, Ashley, Battishill and Callcott, all of them admirers of Boyce, along with the distinguished tenors, Beard and Incledon. Subject to its receiving a favourable reception, Hayes had anticipated in the preface to his earlier volume, *Fifteen Anthems* (1780), the possibility of publishing a second collection. The appearance of this volume suggests he was satisfied on that score. However, given that, apart from other considerations, the first collection was intended to raise funds on behalf of the composer's widow and family, in attracting only 59 subscribers for 94 copies (less than a third as many as before), this second enterprise was much less successful in this respect. The absence of a preface tends to confirm that it was indeed the sequel to the 1780 volume. The contents of this book are: *BC* 3, 12, 13, 23, 29, 42, 43, 44, 45, 51, 58, 63 and 70.

♣

From the Preface to Samuel Arnold's edition
of *Cathedral Music* (1790)

As the late DOCTOR BOYCE lived only to compleat Three Volumes of Cathedral Music, and as many of the Valuable Works of the English Composers, (who were so eminent in that stile of writing) which he had not room to insert in his work, appear to me to be worthy of preservation, I have undertaken a Supplement to it, trusting it will not be unacceptable to the remaining few, who have judgement to taste their sublimities, and liberality enough to encourage it.

Indeed I am well aware that the encouragement will not be great, as it is not the fashion to study Church, so much as secular Musick; and if the Cathedral[s] and Churches in England, Scotland, Ireland and Wales, where Choir Service is performed (and for whose use this work was principally intended) do not encourage it. The time may come, when this sublime, tho' much neglected state of composition (so well understood by our forefathers) will be totally lost in this Kingdom.

In order to render this work as useful and easy as the nature of it will admit, I have removed the C Cliff from the treble parts, and substituted the G Cliff,[52] and at the request of many Gentlemen in the profession, I have printed a separate part for the Organ to every Service and Anthem &c. the reason for which will appear too obvious to point out.

Doctor Boyce remarks in his Preface, "that no person employed to copy Church Musick can afford to provide good paper, and write what is here contained in a page at the price these pages are sold for, which is less than seven farthings each; this must undoubtedly be the cheapest, and most eligible way of purchasing Books for the above mentioned purpose', to which, I beg leave to remark, that the work I have undertaken, will be delivered to Subscribers at a trifle more than FOUR FARTHINGS[53] a page and, if (in the words of my worthy predecessor) there should arise to me any further benefit than the reputation of perpetuating those valuable remains of my ingenious countrymen, it will be more than I expect".

Novr 1.st 1790
N.° 480 Strand

S. Arnold

---

[52] The late 18th century saw a gradual move away from the traditional use of the soprano C clef for the notation of treble parts (as may be illustrated in Boyce's edition of *Cathedral Music*) towards the adoption of the modern G clef.
[53] Equal to about a third of a penny today.

Title-page: Cathedral Music: | BEING | *A COLLECTION in SCORE,* | of the | *Most valuable & useful Compositions* | *FOR THAT SERVICE* | BY THE | *Several English Masters* | Of the last two Hundred Years. | *The whole Selected, & carefully Revis'd* | By D^R. SAMUEL ARNOLD. | Organist & Composer | *To his Majesty's Royal Chapels.* [&c.] This substantial publication is in four volumes; the first three containing the vocal scores, and the last the organ parts. It appeared only two years after Ashley's highly successful 2nd edition of Boyce's *Cathedral Music.* In these circumstances it was inevitable perhaps that Arnold's would be no more economically viable than WB's original edition. Arnold's dedicatee, George III, acquired two sets, and another 117 were subscribed for by 98 others. Among these were leading musicians such as Alcock (who had in the early 1750s intended to publish a historical collection of anthems as Boyce eventually did), J.W. Callcott, Philip Hayes, the first editor of WB anthems, William Shield, and Charles Wesley, a former pupil of Boyce, as well as Boyce's son, William. The new names in Arnold's supplement are mainly 18th-century contemporaries of Boyce whose work could not be included in his essentially retrospective collection, plus Richard Patrick, an early 17th-century composer whom WB had omitted from his selection with some reluctance. Arnold also included seven items by Boyce himself. In doing so, Arnold played an important role in the wider dissemination of WB's church music, for none of his works published here in Vol. III had appeared in print before. They are *BC* 2, 14, 47, 50, 64, 67, and 74. Arnold's edition also exerted a long-term influence on English church music for Vincent Novello issued 1,500 copies of it in 1859, and a further 1,500 three years later.[54]

♣

A hymn by Boyce is published in 'The Psalms of David' (1791).

Edited by Samuel Arnold and W.J. Callcott. this volume includes WB's hymn, 'To Sion's hill I lift my eyes', on pp.142-3.

♣

---

[54] See Cooper(2003), 81.

From the *Second London Notebook* (1791-92) of Joseph Haydn

Covent-Garden is the National Theatre. I was there on 10th Dec. and saw an opera called *The Woodman*.[55] It was the very day on which the life story of Madam Billington both from the good as well as the bad sides, was announced; such impertinent enterprises are generally undertaken for [selfish] interests.[56] She sang rather timidly this evening, but very well all the same. The first tenor [space for name left blank][57] has a good voice and quite a good style, but he uses the falsetto to excess. He sang a trill on high C and ran up to G. The 2nd tenor[58] tries to imitate him, but could not make the change from falsetto to the natural voice, and apart from that he is most unmusical. He creates a new tempo for himself, now 3/4 then 2/4, makes cuts whenever it occurs to him. The leader is Herr Baumgartner[59] a German who, however, has almost forgotten his mother-tongue. The Theatre is very dark and dirty, and is almost as large as the Vienna Court Theatre. The common people in the galleries of all the theatres are very impertinent; they set the fashion with all their unrestrained impetuosity and whether some thing is repeated or not is determined by their yells. The parterre and all the boxes sometimes have to applaud a great deal to have something good repeated. That was just what happened this evening, with the Duet in the 3rd Act, which was very beautiful;[60] and the pro's and contra's went on for nearly a quarter of an hour, till finally the parterre and the boxes won, and they repeated the Duet. Both the performers stood on the stage quite terrified, first retiring, then again coming forward. THE ORCHESTRA IS SLEEPY.

---

[55] A comic opera mainly composed by William Shield to a libretto by Bate Dudley, first performed at CG on 26 Feb. 1791.

[56] Haydn must have got wind of the impending publication of a scurrilous and sexually explicit volume, *Memoirs of Mrs Billington* (1792), by an anonymous author purporting to be the singer herself. A refutation entitled, *An Answer to the Memoirs of Mrs Billington*, attributed to 'a gentleman', appeared later in the year.

[57] Charles Incledon, the leading tenor of his time.

[58] An Irish singer, John Johnstone.

[59] A violinist and composer who had settled in London *c*1768, and led the band at CG from 1780-94.

[60] Boyce's duet (see below) was published separately as late as 1820 when it was described as "A Favourite Duet introduced & Sung by M'r Incledon & Miss Poole at the Theatre Royal, Covent Garden in the Opera of the Woodman". While the piece itself was evidently still in favour, Elizabeth Billington had given way at some stage to Miss Poole in performances of this work.

(Landon(1959), 273-4) Haydn attended CG on 10 Dec. 1791 during his first visit to London from January of that year to June 1792. Elizabeth Billington, a brilliant and assertive coloratura soprano, often insisted on introducing music of her own choice into productions in which she was involved. She had already inserted Boyce's duet, 'Together let us range the fields' from *Solomon* (1742), into earlier performances of *The Woodman* that year.

♣

From E. L. Gerber's *Historisch-Biographisches Lexicon der Tonkünstler* (Leipzig, 1790-92)

Boyce (William) Doctor of Music, organist and composer of the Chapel Royal in London, was already celebrated as a composer from about the year 1730. He also enjoyed the honour of conducting the famous anthem [Ordnungsmotetto] accompanied by a large orchestra at the coronation of the contemporary king.[61] He did much work for the theatre and the chamber, but even more for the church. I can report the following of his works: David's Lamentation over Saul and Jonathan, an oratorio 1736: an Ode on the Feast of St. Cecilia, 1739[62] [and] a celebrated piece of funeral music, 1751.[63] He has had fugues for the organ published.[64] He also collected together with considerable care the best English church music which was published with great splendour in 1763[65] under the title: Cathedral-Music being a Collection in score of the most valuable and useful compositions for that service, by the several English Masters of the last two hundred years. The whole selected, and carefully revised by Dr. W. Boyce. He died about the year 1770.[66] [transl.]

Gerber(1790-92), 195. A revised entry on Boyce appeared later in *Neues Historish-Biographisches Lexicon der Tonkünstler* (Leipzig, 1812-14) and this has been reproduced in a modern edition, Wessely(1969), vol. 1, columns 491-2. In his later edition Gerber drew largely on material taken from Burney's *History,* vol. 3. The 'famous anthem' referred to must have

---

[61] Clearly that of George III in 1761.

[62] John Lockman's Ode 'See famed Apollo and the nine' (1739).

[63] The Burial Service (*BC* 7) composed for the funeral of Thomas Coram, the founder of the Foundling Hospital in London, on 3 April 1751.

[64] *Ten Voluntaries for the Organ or Harpsichord* (c1785).

[65] Actually, in 1760, 1768 and 1773.

[66] More accurately, 1779.

been Handel's 'Zadok the priest', originally written for the coronation of George II in 1727. This work was not only included in the 1761 coronation service (Boyce himself having declined to reset that text in the light of Handel's supreme achievement), but it has retained a place in every subsequent Royal Coronation to this day.

♣

An anthem by Boyce is sung at the funeral of Joshua Reynolds on 3 March 1792.

Never was a public solemnity conducted with more decorum and dignity. The procession set out half an hour after twelve o'clock. The hearse arrived at the great western gate of St. Paul's about a quarter after two, and was there met by the Dignitaries of the church, and the gentlemen of the choir, who chaunted the proper Psalms, while the procession moved to the entrance of the choir, where was performed, in a more than usual solemn manner, the full choir evening service, together with the famous anthem of Dr. Boyce; the body remaining during the whole time in the centre of the choir.

(Northcote(1819), 2, 295) The complete account of the great painter's funeral, from which this extract is taken, echoes in many respects those relating to the funeral of Boyce himself in 1779. It seems most likely that the unidentified anthem of WB was 'If we believe', chosen for performance at the composer's own funeral.

♣

From the *Public Advertiser*, 20 December 1792

COVENT GARDEN. AT the NEW THEATRE ROYAL in Covent Garden, This Day will be performed DOUGLAS.[67] . . . After which will be performed (1st time) a Pantomime Entertainment, called HARLEQUIN's MUSEUM, Or, MOTHER SHIPTON TRIUMPHANT. . . . The Music chiefly compiled from Pepuch [*sic*], Galliard, Arne, Vincent, Dibdin, Arnold, Fisher, and the rest by Mr Shield, &c.

This pantomime was a great success in its first season during which it was given 48 performances, but it was rarely performed subsequently. A vocal

---

[67] A popular melodrama by John Home first performed in 1757.

score was published by Longman and Broderip THE | OVERTURE, SONGS, DANCES &c. | *in the Pantomime Entertainment of* | Harlequin's Museum | or | Mother Shipton Triumphant | *The new Music Composed by* M*ʳ. Shield* | *the rest Compiled by T. Goodwin, from the Works of* | *PEPUSCH, GALLIARD, VINCENT, Dᴿ BOYCE, Dᴿ FISHER and Dᴿ ARNOLD* [&c.] [1793]. The song that appears on pp.12-13 is headed "Old England for ever' Sung by Mʳ Incledon", and its first verse begins 'Come cheer up my lads merry Christmas is here'. The tune attached to this text comes from Boyce's setting of David Garrick's patriotic song 'Heart of Oak': 'Come cheer up my lads 'tis to glory we steer', originally introduced into the latter's pantomime, *Harlequin's Invasion*, at Drury Lane on 31 Dec. 1759. A synopsis of *Harlequin's Museum* was also published in *A Correct Account of the Celebrated Pantomime Entertainment of Harlequin's Museum* [&c.] (*Lbl*, 11621e2(29)). One of the scenes takes place at Deptford Dock in London where a ship is launched: "After the firing of *cannon*, and every demonstration of joy, a *Lieutenant* enters, and sings the following Song, which, as it is undoubtedly the most popular ever produced on the Stage, we present the public with a copy: Tune — 'Hearts of Oak'" (p.4).[68]

♣

From *Jackson's Oxford Journal*, 30 August 1794

The Meeting of the three Choirs of WORCESTER, HEREFORD, and GLOUCESTER, will be held at Worcester on Wednesday the 10th of September next, and the two following Days. At the Cathedral, on Wednesday Morning . . . will be performed the Overture to the occasional Oratorio, Purcel's grand Te Deum and Jubilate; 'O, magnify the Lord,' Handel (to be sung by Miss Parke) 'Blessed is he that considereth the poor and needy,' Boyce;[69] — and Handel's Coronation anthem, 'Zadok the Priest.' . . . At the Cathedral, on Friday morning, The Messiah. In the Evening, at the College Hall, a Grand Miscellaneous Concert in two Acts, the first selected from Dr. Boyce's celebrated serenata of SOLOMON; the second to consist of capital Songs, Glees, and Instrumental Pieces, and to conclude with 'God save the King'. [&c.]

---

[68] The opening line of the song quoted here in the synopsis, 'Come cheer up my Lads, 'tis to Honor we steer', differs from that printed in the vocal score (see above).

[69] 'Blessed is he' (1741), (*BC* 11), had been performed at the Three Choirs Festival first in 1743.

♣

From Berrow's *Worcester Journal,* 7 August 1794

FRIDAY EVENING, at the COLLEGE HALL. From *Solomon* - Overture, Behold Jerusalem thy King - Tell me Lovely Shepherd, - Fairest of the Virgin Throng - Beneath his ample Shade - Balmy Sweetness - Ah simple Me - Fair and Comely - The cheerful Spring - Arise my Fair - Together let us range - Charming Source of endless Pleasure - Soft I adjure you - Ye blooming Virgins - Who is thy Love - On his Face the vernal Rose - Thou soft Invader - Proclaim it then thro' all the East.

It is clear from the selection of items provided here that this performance of *Solomon* was given with the final duet and chorus reset and with a new text, 'Proclaim it then', for the chorus section replacing the original 'In vain we trace the globe'. Composed by Boyce *c*1758, this alternative finale had also been performed at the Liverpool Festival in August 1787. The vocal and instrumental parts prepared for Worcester this year (and doubtless used again for the performance of *Solomon* there in 1797) are now preserved at *Ob*, MSSMus.d.127/128. The occurrence here of a text, 'Charming source of endless pleasure', that had not previously been part of *Solomon*, appears at first sight to be an anomaly. However, it is clearly a substitute text for the overtly sexual air beginning 'Let me, love, thy bole ascending, | On the swelling clusters feed'. Public sensibilities appear never to have been disturbed by this aspect of the work in the previous half-century of *Solomon*'s history, but public attitudes were evidently changing towards the end of the century.

It has been suggested that this performance was of Handel's *Solomon* rather than Boyce's (Shaw(1954), 118-19), even though Lysons(1895), 74, had clearly identified Boyce as the composer of *Solomon* at Worcester in 1794. These uncertainties were doubtless due to the fact that the issues of *BWJ* for the weeks preceding the Three Choirs Meeting in 1797 appear no longer to be extant, and that the evidence provided in *JOJ* in both years, and in *BWJ* on 7 Aug. 1794, was overlooked.

♣

Charles Wesley jnr. publishes *Six Hymns* (1795) with an additional hymn by Boyce.

Title-page: *Six Hymns* | *Respectfully Inscribed to* | *Mrs Tighe* Composed by | *Charles Wesley;* | With | A Hymn, | *By the late Dr. Boyce* [*c*1795].

Boyce's setting of 'Servant of God well done', pp.8-9, appears with the inscription "Written by the Rev[d]. Charles Wesley on the death of the Rev[d]. George Whitefield". Charles jnr. was the son of the great hymn writer, and a pupil of WB's.

♣

William Mason publishes *Essays, Historical and Critical, on English Church Music* (1795).

Mason was a man of remarkable talents and versatility who made his mark as a poet, writer, cleric, inventor and garden designer. Early in his career as a young, recently appointed Fellow of St. John's College Cambridge, he had been invited to write the ode set by Boyce for the installation of the Duke of Newcastle as Chancellor of the University in July 1749. He was eminently qualified both by experience and commitment to comment on church music, for as Precentor at York Minster from 1762 until his death in 1797 he was in charge of the music there. Mason developed strong opinions, taking the view that musical settings of services and anthems should above all be restrained. The music should be intimately related to the text, and should eschew elaborate counterpoint and highly decorated vocal parts. He regarded the church music of Henry Purcell in particular as a model for later composers to emulate. His second essay in particular, on 'Cathedral Music', received the approbation of Charles Burney when he described it as "a work in which there are many remarks that do honour to the refined taste of the author in all the polite arts; and are well worthy the attentions of our ecclesiastical composers" (*BurneyH*, 4, (1789), 191, n.).

In this essay Mason sometimes expresses reservations about the direction in which Boyce and his contemporaries were moving in this field: "It was the pleasing Melodies of Wise, the pathetic Airs of Clarke, the majestic Movements of Blow and the sublime Strains of Purcell, which at once proved the good sense, as well as genius, of these Masters; and at the same time the powers which Vocal Music might have upon the mind, when so managed, that sound might be subservient, or rather assistant to sense. Yet as this can never be the case, but when Melody, and consequently appropriated Air are principally attended to, it has led, as we have seen, Dr. Boyce and other professed Harmonists to think, that by the addition of too much Air, by which these Masters deprived Harmony of its absolute supremacy, they robbed Church Music of its ancient solemnity. The public ear however, will, I believe, generally allow, that Music in their hands, became more intelligible and expressive than it had been heretofore".[70] [&c.] (Mason(1795), 131-2)

Earlier in his essay, having praised the anthems of Purcell for their "clear articulation and verbal expression" (op. cit., 124), Mason invokes Boyce, himself an acknowledged admirer of the 'ancient masters',[71] to identify the distinctive qualities of Purcell and his best contemporaries in late 17th-century England: "A studious mind seems in general to acquire, by applying itself to what is ancient, so great a prejudice for it, that I do not wonder the late judicious Dr. Boyce, after having employed himself many years in giving a correct and elegant Score of the Services and Anthems of these older Masters came to a conclusion very different from this, and declared, in a preface to the last volume,[72] "that the early writers *were not wanting in musical expression* though not so particularly marked: but that their successors deviated from 'the gravity of their predecessors', and in compliance with the gay taste of Charles II. had adopted a lighter species of music: However, they still preserved a solemnity and *learning* in their compositions which have rendered them lasting monuments of *ingenuity* and expression" (ibid., 125).

Later, Mason presents his arguments against the adoption of florid, instrumentally influenced vocal writing in the setting of texts in church music: "A too great indulgence, or indeed any at all, to the performer in these instrumental tricks, must not only greatly diminish the gravity and solemnity of Church Music, but also render it, as a vehicle for words, much less intelligible"[73] (ibid., 137-8.). In a footnote Mason elaborates on this particular point and puts both Handel and Boyce under the spotlight: "The late Dr. Nares, whose memory both as a man and a Composer I greatly respect, in a short but judicious preface expresses the same sentiment concerning a collection of his own Anthems. "I have been very sparing" (says he) "of Divisions, thinking them too airy for the Church, and have rather endeavoured to inforce the sentiment of the words, than to

---

[70] Mason implies here, perhaps, that while the general public may feel this way, connoisseurs of fine church music may not concur.

[71] In this context, the leading composers of English church music in the 16th and early-17th century.

[72] Mason does not quote Boyce verbatim here, but freely extracts ideas from the second paragraph of his foreword to vol. 3 of *Cathedral Music* (1773).

[73] This is not a direct quotation form Nares but a summary of his views. The preface to which reference is made is from his *Twenty Anthems In Score For 1, 2, 3, 4, and 5 Voices Composed for the Use of His Majesty's Chapels Royal* [&c.] (1778). This publication, dedicated to George III, was well supported, attracting 144 subscribers for 279 copies.

display the *Art of Musical Composition*". It is certainly this fondness of Division, indulged for the purpose mentioned above, which Croft sometimes exhibited, and Green carried to much greater excess, that rendered many of their Anthems too light and theatrical: And as in several of their choral movements we find sentiment neglected, and the Art of Musical Composition solely attended to, it is not improbable the Author of the Preface had these two Composers principally in view; though he might with equal justice have included Dr. Boyce in his idea as to the latter foible, and the great Handel himself both in the former and the latter".[74]

Finally, Mason charges Boyce with being wrong in claiming that Tallis was the first composer to set the new service in English, translated from the Latin for the first time, in the *Book of Common Praier* (1549).[75] "The Service, which Thomas Tallis composed in the reign of Queen Elizabeth, was so very similar to Marbeck's, with respect to its plan, that Dr. Boyce was certainly in error when he gave to Tallis the merit of being the first Composer of the musical part of Divine Service in the English language" (ibid., 93-4). Modern musical scholarship, however, suggests that Boyce was almost certainly correct. While the first published settings of the new service appear in Marbeck's *The Books of Common Praier Noted* (1550), by that time Tallis had already started to compose settings of the new service, at least one of which, a 'Benedictus', was included in a set of Chapel Royal part books that have been dated 1547-8.[76]

♣

John Page publishes anthems and arrangements by Boyce in *Harmonia Sacra* (1800).

Title-page: Harmonia Sacra, | A | Collection of ANTHEMS *in Score* | Selected for | Cathedral and Parochial *Churches*; | *from the most* EMINENT MASTERS *of the* | *Sixteenth, Seventeenth, and Eighteenth Centuries,* | AND | *Humbly dedicated by Permission* | To her Royal Highness | *THE* | *Princess Augusta*[77] | by | JOHN PAGE | *of St Paul's Cathedral.* [&c.]

---

[74] If Mason expresses himself clearly here, he seems to be exonerating Boyce from over-indulging in divisions, but not from sometimes neglecting 'sentiment'. Nevertheless, being cited alongside Handel, Boyce is in good company.

[75] In the Preface to *Cathedral Music*, vol. I, vii.

[76] See Edward Ellinwood, ed.: EECM, 13, *Thomas Tallis: English Sacred Music*, II (1971), ix.

Page's work may be seen as a supplement both to Boyce's *Cathedral Music* itself and to Arnold's similarly entitled amplification of it (1790). In his 'Dedication', Page expresses his objective "to bring together works so gratifying to the ear of real taste, and so honorable to the talents and science of their ingenious Composers, that they might become more generally known". In his 'Advertisement' an acknowledgement is made to "*Mr William Boyce*, for a valuable accession to this compilation from the inestimable manuscripts of his late father Dr. Boyce". Page's compilation, in three substantial volumes, sold 195 sets to 165 subscribers, among them George III, Queen Charlotte and three of the Royal Princesses. The List of Subscribers also includes the prominent musicians Samuel Arnold, Thomas Attwood, Thomas Busby, J.W. Callcott, William Shield and Charles Wesley, as well as WB's son.

The works composed by Boyce selected for publication here were all previously unpublished. They are, in vol. 1 the anthem 'Let my complaint', pp.142-8, and the Burial Service, 173-86; and in vol. 3 the anthem 'I will magnify Thee, O God', 113-25. The Boyce arrangements in these volumes are based on music from anthems or oratorios by Handel: in vol. 2 the independent anthem, 'As pants the heart for cooling streams', 198-218, and in vol. 3 the eight-part anthem, 'Moses and the children of Israel' from the oratorio *Israel in Egypt*, 153-77. According to the title-pages these arrangements were "Adapted for Voices only, by Desire of his present Majesty". Finally in vol. 3, 178-225, Page includes WB's "Four Occasional Anthems, the Words selected from the Works of George Frederick Handel Esq. by his present Majesty, and by his Command adapted to Voices only". All four of these anthems are based on material from *Messiah* and are designed for performance on Christmas Day (178-90), Good Friday (191-9), Easter Day (200-11) and Whit-Sunday (212-25) respectively.

All of these admired pieces by Handel were originally written with orchestral accompaniment. It is clear that the purpose of these arrangements was to facilitate performances in the Chapel Royal and other places of worship where only an organ accompaniment was normally available. It has been suggested that the adaptation of 'As pants the hart' may have been "commanded and encouraged" by George II in the late 1750s (see Burrows(1985), 113), but bearing in mind the great enthusiasm of George III for Handel's music, it seems more likely that it was undertaken after his accession in 1760 and probably after 1763 when Boyce had "retired to Kensington". The extract from *Israel in Egypt* was probably arranged *c*1771 when Boyce subscribed to an edition of the work in full score.

As far as the *Messiah* arrangements are concerned, the placing of their organ parts in the Chapel Royal Organ Book (*Lbl*, R.M.27.d.8) immediately before an anthem by James Nares, known to have been first performed there in June 1769, suggests a dating shortly before that time. It would also tend to confirm that "his present Majesty" must refer to George III rather than II. Handel himself produced a number of different versions of 'As pants the hart'. Originally composed for the Chapel Royal *c*1712, it was revised for use at Cannons, the seat of the Duke of Chandos, in 1717-18, but the version adapted by Boyce was the one that Handel prepared for performances at the Chapel Royal in the mid 1720s, HWV, 251b (see Beekes *b*(1993), 49). In the absence of any 18th-century comments on these arrangements, a modern assessment may not be out of place: "We may today object to Boyce's tampering with Handel's proportions, textures and key schemes, yet still recognize his sincere and skillful effort to honor his distinguished predecessor as Composer to his Majesty's Chapel" (Beekes, ibid.).

♣

John Ashley publishes two of Boyce's orchestral anthems (1802).

The first, with title-page: ANTHEM. | *"Lord thou hast been our refuge"* | Composed by | WILL^M. BOYCE, | *M.D. Oxon* | *Organist & Composer of his Majesty's* | Chapel Royal. | *Conductor, & Master of his Majesty's Band of* | MUSICIANS. | *Dedicated by Permission to the* | STEWARDS *of the* | *Sons of the Clergy.*

A copy of this edition (*Lbl*, H.1081.c(1)) was formerly owned by Charles Wesley jnr. and is inscribed on the fly-leaf in his hand: "This anthem is a most excellent composition, I think not inferior to Handel or Purcel".[77]

The title-page of the second is: ANTHEM, | *Blessed is he that considereth the Poor* Composed by | *William Boyce,* | Mus. D. Cam. | *Organist & Composer of his Majesty's Chapel Royal* | *and Conductor & Master of his Majestys* | BAND OF MUSICIANS. [&c.]

Ashley was proprietor of the publishers, Bland and Weller. Neither of these important orchestrally accompanied works had been printed previously. The first was composed for the Sons of the Clergy's annual service at St. Paul's in 1755, and the second for Dublin in 1741. Of the ten

---

[77] Wesley had as a child been a pupil of Boyce.

anthems with orchestra that WB produced only 'O be joyful' (*BC* 56), written for his doctoral exercise at Cambridge in 1749, had previously been published.

♣

From a letter of Samuel Wesley to his brother Charles

Camden Town, 15 January 1807

. . . You speak of a movement in Handel's original MS. I have lately seen a very curious original of Marcello's Psalms, which become of course more valuable from their being almost impossible to read. — They were placed upon a desk before a young friend of ours, who was wholly puzzled, & *no marvel* (as J.W. would say)[78] for really they might have made *Argus*[79] stare to no purpose.

By the way I think very moderately of Marcello, as far as spirit & effect are concerned. — His writing is chaste; his style generally solemn & his harmony occasionally rich — but he wants the sweetness of Steffani the strength of Purcell & certainly the fire of Handel — If I am not mistaken, Boyce thought that Marcello has been over-rated. — Whoever thinks so, I am quite of his mind.

Mr, DDWF15/1. (Olleson(2001), 45) Samuel's brother was an ardent admirer of Handel. Olleson believes that Charles was probably referring to one of the autogr. MSS owned by Richard, Viscount Fitzwilliam, to which he had access. If Samuel is correct with regard to Marcello, Boyce's judgement was certainly based on familiarity with the Italian composer's music, for he had subscribed to the publication of his *First Fifty Psalms* in 1757, and owned two MSS of Marcello's vocal duets. The latter were eventually sold when WB's music collection was auctioned by Christie and Ansell in April 1779.[80]

♣

---

[78] The reference is to their uncleo, John Wesley, the founder of Methodism.

[79] A monster in Greek mythology with 100 eyes.

[80] See Sale catalogue, lots 199 and 207 respectively.

From a letter of Samuel Wesley to his brother Charles (1807)

Camden Town March 21 1807

I not only agree with Dr Boyce that chromatic subjects produce the worst melodies in *descant for the voice.* The *best* Italian melodies consist of diatonic intervals, & unless deep sorrow or acute pain are to be expressed, I cannot subscribe to the propriety of wire-drawing the chromatic scale, till your hair stands on end & then calling it *melody* — As Johnson said of another subject, "Sir, you had as well call it geometry"[81] and that *the deepest* sorrow may be completely expressed without one chromatic semitone, we need go no further than the air 'Behold & see', in the Messiah which I take to be the most finished specimen of the simple sublime in melody that ever was produced.

Mr, MA9787. (Olleson(2001), 52-3) Boyce's compositional style in general bears out the attitude to chromatic melody, and indeed to fugal subjects, that Wesley attributes to him here; see, for example, his *Ten Voluntaries.*

♣

From the *Cyclopedia; or, Universal Dictionary of Arts, Sciences, and Literature* (1819)

BOYCE, Dr. WILLIAM, organist and composer to his majesty, was a musician to whom our choral service is greatly indebted, not only for his own excellent choral works, but for the well selected, correct, and splendid edition of our choral music, which he published in three volumes, large folio, upon the plan, and at the recommendation of his master and predecessor, Dr. Greene, to whom he served an apprenticeship.

This eminent professor (Boyce) was born at Joyners' hall, in the city, of which his father was housekeeper, and with whom he resided during celibacy. When he became a family man, his residence was in Chancery-lane, to the end of the reign of his late Majesty George II, about which time he removed to Kensington Gore, where he ended his days in 1779.[82]

---

[81] None of the experts on Samuel Johnson consulted were able to authenticate this quotation. Wesley was clearly mistaken about it.
[82] Boyce moved to Quality Court in 1753, but did not marry until 1759. George II died in 1760, but WB did not move to Kensington until *c*1763.

He was educated at St. Paul's school, and began his musical career as a chorister in that cathedral. When he lost his treble voice, he was bound apprentice to Dr. Greene, then organist of the metropolitan church.[83] The master and scholar seemed worthy of each other, living in the utmost cordiality and friendship; the master loving the pupil, and the pupil honouring and respecting the master, to the end of their lives.

[Paragraphs 3, 4, 5, and 6 are omitted here]

On the decease of Dr. Greene in 1757, he was appointed master of the king's band, and, in 1758, on the death of Travers, organist of the chapel royal; of which he had succeeded Weldon in 1736, as composer; so that he enjoyed three honourable appointments at once, which used to be supplied by three several professors. The gout put an end to the existence of this worthy man, and excellent composer, at the age of 69. He was succeeded in the chapel royal by Mr. (afterwards Dr.) Dupuis and, as a master of his majesty's band, by Mr. Stanley.

Rees(1819), vol. 5. Burney had written an assessment of Boyce's career in *BurneyH*, 3, (1789). Rather than write a new article for Rees he decided to base his contribution on the earlier one. The first two paragraphs and the last are new (as above), but the others replicate the 2nd, 3rd, 4th and 5th paragraphs of his earlier account (see pp.266-7 above).

♣

Thomas Busby writes on Boyce in his *General History of Music*, vol. 2 (1819).

Busby later wrote a fairly substantial account of Boyce's life and works in his *Concert Room and Orchestra Anecdotes* (1825), and he had written an earlier, shorter article on the composer in the *Universal Dictionary of Music* (1783). Apart from sometimes being vague as to the chronology of events, Busby often relies on the ideas of other historians, Hawkins and Burney in particular, even to the point of sometimes adopting (without attribution) their phraseology. However, from time to time, he sometimes provides details lacking elsewhere. In a chapter on Boyce and Jonathan Battishill Busby throws particular light on WB's deafness and gout.

On his deafness he writes: "the fact, that at the time of its production [the masque *Peleus and Thetis* (*c*1740)], the composer from cold, or some

---

[83] i.e. St Paul's Cathedral.

other cause, was permanently, and almost totally, deprived of his hearing, will be learnt by every reader with astonishment. To a musician of ordinary capacity, such a misfortune would have been insurmountable. But Boyce's music was in his soul, rather than in his external sense: what his mind knew his sensibility could apply; and if he lost the gratification of listeners to the sounds of harmony, the page of instruction was open to his eye, and the scores he perused he inwardly heard"[84] (484-5). With regard to his gout he records: "As Dr. Boyce advanced in years, his constitution became subject to gout. The fits increasing both in their frequency and violence, at length the disorder attacked his stomach and the affliction that, for a while had only induced pain, and the interruption of his studies, on the 7th day of February, 1779, terminated his existence".

From time to time inaccuracies or lapses of memory occur in Busby's writings. In his 'Memoirs of the late Mr. Jonathan Battishill', prefacing the publication of the composer's *Six Anthems and Ten Chants* (1804), for example, he refers to the performance of a funeral anthem by WB, 'I am the Resurrection and the Life', during Battishill's funeral at St. Paul's Cathedral in 1801 No such anthem, however, is known to have been written by WB. What probably was performed was 'If we believe that Jesus died', an anthem sung at the composer's own funeral, when both Battishill and Busby are likely to have been present.

♣

From Thomas Busby's *Concert Room and Orchestra Anecdotes* (1825)

Dr. William Boyce, the son of a respectable citizen of London, and a man of considerable property,[85] was born in the year 1710.[86] A fine voice, and an early propensity to the study of music, induced his father to place him under the tuition of Mr. Charles King master of the children of St. Paul's cathedral into the choir of which, when prepared by the routine of the music school, he was admitted. At the usual age, he quitted the station of a singing-boy, and became an articled pupil of Dr. Greene then organist of that church. Endowed with a noble genius, and fortunate in the qualifications of his tutor, he made a rapid progress, both in theory and

---

[84] Busby's remarks would have been equally applicable to his contemporary, Beethoven.

[85] It is clear from Boyce's will that he was comfortably off, but his widow, Hannah, gave the impression that she was impoverished after his death.

[86] 1711.

practice; and at the expiration of his pupilage, was unanimously elected organist of Vere-street chapel, Cavendish-Square. To the emoluments of this place, his industry added those of teaching; and among the several schools which he attended, was the then highly distinguished seminary of Mrs. Cavaller, in Queen-square, Bloomsbury.

Not contented with his acquisitions under Dr. Greene, Mr. Boyce ardently proceeded in the prosecution of his studies, patiently explored the principles of harmony, and completed his theoretical accomplishments, under the profoundest harmonician of his time. Dr. Pepusch could boast of having under his tuition at the same moment, three very superiorly gifted pupils, — Travers, Keeble and Boyce. To these, his learning and judgement pointed out the excellencies of Palestrina, Orlando de Lasso, Stradella and Carissimi, Tallis, Bird, Purcell, and Orlando Gibbons. The mind of Boyce, teeming with invention, produced a variety of sacred and other effusions, upon which his view to greater things would not permit him to place any great value. However, a few single songs found their way from his study, and were favorably received.

The first dramatic effort of this great composer was his music to Lord Lansdowne's 'Peleus and Thetis'. If the language of that mask cannot compete with the poetry of 'Comus' neither, perhaps, can this early trial of Mr. Boyce claim equality with Arne's music to the latter drama; but, nevertheless, it was a noble production. If its airs wanted the limpid sweetness of those in 'Comus', the choruses presented a solidity and grandeur that transcended the conception of the composer of 'Artexerxes', and when performed at the Philharmonic Society the piece was heard with equal pleasure and surprise.[87] Under any circumstances, the force of genius, and scientific proficiency, evinced by the music of 'Peleus and Thetis', would have been worthy of eulogistic notice; but the fact that, at the time of its production, the composer, from cold or some other cause, was permanently and almost totally deprived of his hearing, will be learnt by every capacity, such a misfortune would have been insurmountable; but Boyce's music was in his soul, rather than in his external sense: what his mind knew, his sensibility could apply; and if he lost the gratification of listening to the *sounds* of harmony, the page of instruction was open to his eye, and the scores he perused he inwardly heard.

In 1736, he succeeded Mr. Joseph Kelway as organist of St. Michael's, Cornhill and upon the decease of Mr. John Weldon in the same year, was appointed one of the composers to his Majesty. In this latter situation,

---

[87] Busby follows a number of other writers, starting with Hawkins (1788), in referring here to an early performance of *Peleus* at the Philharmonic Society, but no documentary evidence for this has so far come to light.

Boyce was in his natural sphere. Of the secrets of church composition he was a perfect master; and deaf as he might be, no musician's genius was more constantly prompt than his own. His compositions for the *chapel* were so many evidences of his learning and invention; and gave him an undisputed eminence in his faculty, as a composer of ecclesiastical music.

In 1747,[88] appeared his serenata of 'Solomon'. In this production, the words of which are a version of the Canticles, by the author of 'Fables for the Female Sex', an originality of style, elegance of imagination, purity of harmony, and beauty of air, at once point out the genius, science, and refined feeling of the composer, and justify the rapturous applause with which it has ever been received. 'Solomon' was no sooner heard, than its merits placed Mr. Boyce in the foremost rank of his profession.[89] Finding the public eager to receive demonstrations of his powers in a different department of composition, he, in 1749,[90] printed twelve sonatas for two violins and a bass. Besides the novelty of fancy their style presented, the intrinsic beauty of the ideas, and masterly construction of the harmony, struck every tasteful hearer. Till the tumid extravagancies of Stamitz and Lord Kelly were adopted, the elegant airs and well-conducted fugues of these sonatas continued to contribute to the bill-of-fare of every public concert, and, as inter-act pieces, to be listened to with attention at the theatres.[91] Though Boyce (not one of those place-holders who convert their offices into sinecures) continued to regularly supply the chapel, he found leisure to pursue his secular studies; and collecting all his fugitive songs and cantatas, presented them to the public in a folio volume, under the general title of 'Lyra Britannica'.[92] In the same year,[93] he was elected to the place of organist, by the united parishes of Allhallows the Great and the Less in Thames-street; an appointment, partly complimentary to the respected character of his father, but more so to the extraordinary professional merits of the musician. And when the Duke of Newcastle succeeded his Grace of Somerset as Chancellor of the University of Cambridge, he was engaged to compose for the occasion an ode, written by Mason, and also an anthem which, on Commencement Sunday, was performed at St. Mary's Church.[94] These compositions, produced for the ordinary purpose of an installation, but ultimately employed as exercises

---

[88] *Solomon* dates from 1742/3.

[89] Busby's phraseology here is drawn from Hawkins *b*(1788).

[90] 1747.

[91] His comments on the *Sonatas* also derive from Hawkins.

[92] 1747.

[93] 1749.

[94] 'O be joyful in God', *BC* 56.

for procuring their illustrious author the highest degree of his faculty, were turned to a much more worthy account than that for which they were originally produced. His great merit induced the professor's request, that he would *accumulate* the degrees of *Bachelor* and *Doctor*: he did so; and the publication of his exercises justified, in the opinion of all qualified critics, the honors conferred upon his exalted talents and sound science.

The following winter produced the lively, novel, and characteristic music of his 'Chaplet', and that of his 'Shepherd's Lottery', two after-pieces written by the ingenious Mr. Mendez, and performed with great applause at Drury-lane Theatre. Soon after this, Dr. Boyce became the worthy successor of Dr. Greene in the office of master of the royal band of musicians the station afterwards occupied by Sir William Parsons, and William Shield, Esq. At the same time, he undertook the conduct of the annual performance at St. Paul's cathedral, established for the benefit of the Sons of the Clergy, and thereby served and honored an institution, in the benevolent purpose of which his heart took an interest. Not satisfied with the benefit rendered to the priesthood of his country, by his personal and mechanical skill, he contributed to its necessities the offerings of his genius, by super-adding instrumental parts to Purcell's 'Te Deum' and by composing two anthems, which still continue to be the admiration of the charitable auditors of the *Rehearsal at St. Paul's for the Benefit of the Sons of the Clergy.*

In the year 1758, Dr. Boyce was appointed one of the organists of the Royal Chapel, in the room of John Travers Esq. by whose decease, the lovers of ingenious and effective composition, whether sacred or secular, lost an able contributor to their gratification. This and his other superior appointments, together with his advancing age, induced the Doctor to resign his two *parochial* employments in the city, quit his town-house in Chancery-lane, and fix his residence at Kensington.[95] There his ardor, unchecked by years, and the continued and growing infirmity of deafness, continued to urge the prosecution of his studies. Following up the original design of Dr. Greene to collect and embody the most esteemed services and anthems, composed for the use of the reformed church, he compiled a volume of cathedral music. The time allowed him as organist and composer to the chapel, and the furnisher of music for the birth-day and new-year odes, was now chiefly devoted to the theoretical instruction of organists and young musicians; but, nevertheless, he found leisure to consult the stability of his fame, by revising many of his former

---

[95] Boyce was already living in Kensington when he was dismissed from Allhallows in 1764. He did not resign from St. Michael's Cornhill until 1768.

publications, among which were the overtures to his immortal *Serenata,* his pastoral operettas, 'The Chaplet', and 'The Shepherd's Lottery', his overture to an Ode of Pindar, an overture composed for the performance at Worcester, on occasion of the meeting there of the three adjacent choirs, and three others, all of which he published under the title of 'Eight Symphonies for Violins and other Instruments'.[96]

Two years after his retirement to Kensington, Dr. Boyce published the first volume of his cathedral music,[97] dedicated to the King; which was speedily succeeded by two other volumes and we wish it were in our power to say, that the munificent piety of his Majesty had, at least, so far counterbalanced the deficiency of the general subscription, as to have secured the industrious compiler and collator from eventual loss. This laborious and profitless undertaking completed, the Doctor again directed his studies to the drama. Mr. Garrick having, some years before, experienced the advantage of this master's services, in the production of a dirge for the procession in 'Romeo and Juliet',[98] and a similar composition for the play 'Cymbeline'[99] now applied to the same talents for music to the songs in 'The Winter's Tale'.[100] The task was undertaken, and executed in a style worthy of the composer's genius. About the year 1770, he resolved to select, and publish collectively, the overtures to his new-year and birth-day odes. The theatrical and garden orchestras, hitherto limited in their inter-act pieces, to the concertos of Corelli, Geminiani, Martini, and the overtures of Handel received with delight compositions that, while they relieved them from the monotony to which they had been so long confined, charmed every ear with their originality, beauty and spirit.

As Dr. Boyce advanced in years, his constitution became subject to gout. The fits increasing both in their frequency and violence, at length the disorder attacked his stomach; and the affliction that, for a while, had only induced pain, and the interruption of his studies, on the 7th of February, 1779, terminated his existence. Nine days afterwards, he was buried in the crypt of St. Paul's cathedral, with testimonies and honors suited to his extraordinary merits; and the funeral was attended with some ceremonies which had never before been observed to any distinguished character, except the illustrious architect of that magnificent edifice.

---

[96] In 1760.

[97] The 1st volume of *Cathedral Music* came out in 1760, but the 3rd and last not until 1773. WB had moved to Kensington in 1763.

[98] In 1750.

[99] Cymbeline (1746) had been commissioned not by Garrick, but by John Rich at Covent Garden.

[100] The music for the *Winter's Tale* was written in 1756.

Dr. Boyce, as one of the *glories* of his profession, demands the homage of his historian; as *a man conferring honor on his country,* flatters the pride of every Englishman. Gifted with a noble genius, he might boast both freedom and greatness of conception; deeply versed in the various excellencies of our church composers, he knew how to blend with the legitimate harmony and artful modulation of Orlando Gibbons, and the comprehensiveness of Bird, and elegance of Tallis the fire and mellifluous fancy of Purcell and Weldon, In all his anthems we find the happiest union of solid grandeur and fluid sweetness; in his secular music, a purity and originality of style, an independence of character, that marks his place among the inspired musicians of all times and countries. As his personal habits and manners were manly and polite, so the emanations of his genius were energetic and chaste. To peruse the melodies of his 'Chaplet' and 'Shepherd's Lottery' is to be struck with the inventive playfulness of the most regulated imagination; examining the score of his 'Solomon' we look into a mine of gold; but this allusion is not punctiliously complete; for all Boyce's gold is *refined.*

If this composer was not so completely alive to public applause as most men of science, or letters, we are to impute the comparative indifference of his sensations, to the degree in which his ideas of excellence transcended, in his own judgement, his powers of execution. It frequently happened that, while masters and amateurs were enjoying and extolling his compositions, he was oppressed with secret dissatisfaction with their merits, but never was a great mind more quickly sensible to the deserts of others. With such reverential feelings did he regard the powers of Handel, that when, to celebrate the coronation of George the Third he was supplicated to re-set the words 'Zadok the Priest, &c.' his modesty declined the task. Alleging the presumption, 'I cannot', said he, 'be guilty of a compliance which would bring my limited talents in competition with the genius of Mr. Handel'.

The moral character of Dr. Boyce comprised veracity, honor and justice; while his manners manifested the mildness and urbanity of his disposition. He was remarkably communicative of his knowledge; and, incapable of envying others, felt no resentment towards those who were jealous of his high and well-earned reputation. He left a widow, son, and daughter, to remember and relate his domestic virtues, and to be in some degree, consoled for the loss of a husband and father, by the world's admiration of the musician and the man.

(Busby(1825), 166-77) Busby took the opportunity here to write an even more extensive and detailed account of Boyce's career than he had previously done in the *Universal Dictionary of Music* (1783). Having been born in 1754, Busby's assessment here was the last to have been published by an author who had himself lived through the latter stages of the composer's life.

♣

John Smith publishes *Seventy of the Psalms of David* (*c*1830).

Amongst this collection of hymns "arranged and harmonised by Doctor John Smith" and printed in Dublin, is one attributed to Boyce but otherwise unknown: 'I'll celebrate thy praises', no. 10, a setting of verses from psalm 30.

♣

Alfred Novello publishes *W. Boyce: Services and Anthems*, 4 vols. (1846-9).

This timely collection served to make a great deal of Boyce's sacred music readily accessible to a new generation of musicians in cathedrals, chapels and churches throughout Britain in the later 19th century, and indeed, beyond. Novello had set up his highly successful and innovative music publishing house in 1829. Furthermore, in 1844 he founded the widely influential and still flourishing periodical, *The Musical Times.* These volumes were edited by Novello's father, Vincent, an Italian emigré who had achieved prominence in London as an organist, composer and publisher. The great majority of the works included had originally appeared in the last two decades of the 18th century in the collections of Philip Hayes (1780/90), Arnold (1790), Page (1800), and also by Ashley in 1802. However, Novello included seven anthems that had not previously been available in print, namely, 'Give unto the Lord', 'Hear my crying', 'How long wilt thou forget me', 'I cried unto the the Lord', 'I have set God always before me', 'I will also give thanks' and 'Like as the hart', most of these being early works. The distribution of the other anthems is as follows: in vol. 1, *BC* 8, 15, 18, 33, 46, 55, 59, 60, 61, 66, 68, 69, 72, 73 and 76; in vol. 2, *BC* 12, 13, 23, 29, 33, 42 ,43, 44, 45, 51, 58, 63 and 70, and in vol. 3, *BC* 14, 21, 27, 28, 31, 32, 37, 39, 49, 50, 64 and 74. The services, *BC* 1-7, are distributed among all three volumes. Vol. 4 is devoted to the organ parts for the anthems listed above, plus two originally orchestrally accompanied works, *BC* 11 and 48, which did not appear in vols. 1-3.

Additionally, in an Appendix Novello prints the two chants, *BC* 77 and 78, and the hymn, *BC* 79.

CATALOGUE OF WORKS

(Incorporating the index of works cited in the Documentary Biography. The locations of the manuscript sources of unpublished works are shown in brackets. An asterisk indicates an autograph.)

Services

Anthems

(The entries for the eight Coronation anthems show Boyce's timings for these works)

61	O sing unto the Lord a new song. S.B. verse, 243, 290
62	O sing unto the Lord a new song. A.T.B. verse. Lost
63	O where shall wisdom be found, 268, 290
64	Ponder my words, O Lord, 270, 290
65	Praise the Lord, O Jerusalem (*Ob**), 147, 149-50, 173 ($3^{1/2}$ mins.)
66	Praise the Lord, ye servants, 144, 243, 290
67	Save me, O God, 270
68	Sing, O heavens, 243, 290
69	Sing praises unto the Lord, 243, 290
70	Sing unto the Lord, 268, 290
71	The souls of the righteous, 139-40
72	Teach me, O Lord, the way of thy statutes, 243, 290
73	Turn Thee unto me. Full, 243, 290
74	Turn Thee unto me. A. verse, 270, 290
75	Unto Thee, O Lord. Lost
76	Wherewithal shall a young man cleanse his way, 243, 290

Chants and Hymns (Original Texts)

77	Double Psalm Chant in D, 291
78	Double Psalm Chant in F, 291
79	Faint is my head and sick my heart, 291
80	Hosanna to the King, 176
81	How long O my God shall I plead, 176
82	I'll celebrate thy praises, Lord, 290
83	Lord, how my bosom foes increase, 175
84	The Lord my pasture shall prepare, 93, 196
84a	The Lord does them support that fall, 196
85	The man is blest of God through Christ, 175
86	O God who dost for ever live (*Lbl; Lcm*)
87	Servant of God, well done, 275-6
88	To the call of pressing need, 175
89	Weigh the words of my profession, 175-6
90	When rising from the bed of death, 143
90a	To Sion's hill I lift my eyes, 270

Serenata

91	Solomon, 22, 30, 31-5, 37-8, 40-1, 43-4, 52-4, 59, 105, 107, 126-7, 131, 156, 172, 187-8, 244-5, 248, 251, 255, 266, 271-2, 274-5, 286, 289

Choral Works to Sacred Texts

92   David's lamentation over Saul and Jonathan (*Ob**), 9-10, 14, 18-
        21, 36-7, 266, 272
93   Lo! On the thorny bed of care (*US: Wc**), 203-5, 245
94   Noah: An oratorio. Lost
95   Vital spark of heavenly flame (*Ob*), 21-2
96   Hither, ye sons of harmony repair, 218-9, 227, 262
97   O how perverse is flesh and blood (*Lcm**)

Theatre Music

98   Agis (*Lcm**), 119-20
99   Amphitryon (*Drc*), 113-4, 122-3, 126
100   Boadicia. Lost, 90-1
101   The Chaplet, 36, 39, 67-9, 80, 94, 131, 154, 158, 182, 249, 257,
        267, 287, 289
102   The Conscious Lovers, 81-2, 126
103   Cymbeline (*Ob**), 43-4, 260, 288
104   Florizel and Perdita (*Ob**), 106-7, 109, 157, 260, 283, 288
105   The Gamester, 52, 87-8, 105, 110
106   Harlequin's invasion, 128-9, 157
107   Lethe, 36, 55-6, 93-4, 245
108   Peleus and Thetis (*Ob**), 18, 43, 48-51, 59, 253, 283
109   The Rehearsal, or Bays in petticoats (*Ob**), 72-3
110   The Roman father. Lost, 71-2
111   Romeo and Juliet (*Ob**), 75-6, 260, 288
112   Secular masque (*Lcm**), 42-3, 47-9, 59, 157, 177, 245, 267
113   The Shepherd's lottery, 36, 39, 79-80, 131, 154, 257, 287, 289
114   The Tempest (*Ob**), 117

Court Odes (All *Ob**)

115   Pierian sisters hail the morn. OKB 1755, 101-3, 229
116   Hail! hail! auspicious day. ONY 1756, 105, 131
117   When Caesar's natal day. OKB 1756, 113, 131
118   While Britain, in her monarch blest. ONY 1757, 115
119   Rejoice, ye Britons, hail the day! OKB 1757, 118
120   Behold the circle forms! prepare! ONY 1758, 118
121   When Othbert left the Italian plain. OKB 1758, 122
122   Ye guardian powers, to whose command. ONY 1759, 124

123   Begin the song - ye subject choirs. OKB 1759, 128
124   Again the sun's revolving sphere. ONY 1760, 131
125   Still must the muse, indignant, hear. ONY 1761, 143
126   'Twas at the nectared feast of Jove. OKB 1761, 143
127   God of slaughter, quit the scene. ONY 1762, 153
128   Go Flora, said the impatient queen. OKB 1762, 158
129   At length the imperious lord of war. ONY 1763, 159
130   Common births, like common things. OKB 1763, 165
131   To wedded love the song shall flow. OKB 1764, 172-3
132   Sacred to thee, O commerce. ONY 1765, 174
133   Hail to the rosy morn. OKB 1765, 226
134   Hail to the man, so sings the Hebrew bard. OKB 1766, 181
135   When first the rude o'erpeopled north. ONY 1767, 181
136   Friend to the poor! for sure, O king. OKB 1767, 183
137   Let the voice of music breathe. ONY 1768, 183
138   Prepare, prepare your songs of praise. OKB 1768, 186
139   Patron of Arts! at length by thee. OKB 1769, 187
140   Forward, Janus, turn thine eyes. ONY 1770, 189
141   Discord hence! the torch resign. OKB 1770, 192
142   Again returns the circling year. ONY 1771, 193
143   Long did the churlish East detain. OKB 1771, 195
144   At length the fleeting year is o'er. ONY 1772, 196
145   From scenes of death, and deep distress. OKB 1772, 196
146   Wrapt in stole of sable train. ONY 1773, 196
147   Born for millions are the kings. OKB 1773, 199
148   Pass but a few short fleeting years. ONY 1774, 200
149   Hark! or does the muse's ear. OKB 1774, 202
150   Ye powers, who rule o'er states and kings. OKB 1775, 211
151   On the white rocks which guard her coast. ONY 1776, 206-7, 213
152   Ye western gales, whose genial breath. OKB 1776, 216
153   Again imperial winter's sway. ONY 1777, 217
154   Driven out from heaven's ethereal domes. OKB 1777, 222
155   When rival nations great in arms. ONY 1778, 225
156   Armed with her native force, behold. OKB 1778, 229
157   To arms, to arms, ye sons of might. ONY 1779, 229

Other Odes

158   Another passing year is flown (*Ob**), 82
159   Arise, immortal Shakespeare (*Ob**), 112-3
160   Cetra de canti amica, 114-5

161	The charms of harmony display (*Ob**), 18, 21,

161 The charms of harmony display (*Ob**), 18, 21,
162 Degli amor la madre altera, 114-5
163 Gentle lyre begin the strain (*Ob**), 21, 37, 59, 131
164 Here all thy active fires diffuse, 58-9, 61, 65n, 80-1, 84-5, 257, 267, 286
165 In elder time. Lost
166 Let grief subside (*Ob**)
167 See fam'd Apollo and the Nine (*Ob**), 18-9, 22, 36-7, 131, 248, 272
168 See, white-robed peace (*Ob**), 162-3, 189
169 Strike, strike the lyre (*Ob**), 73
170 Titles and ermine fall behind (*Bu**), 111-2, 187

Cantatas, Dialogues and Two-Part Songs

171 Blate Jonny, 110
172 Blest in Maria's friendship, 52-3, 74-5
173 By Danae's progeny (*Ob**)
174 Did you not once, Lucinda, vow (*Ob**)
175 Gentle Zephyrs smoothly rove (*Lcm**)
176 Haste, haste every nymph, 47, 126
177 How hard is the fortune, 40
178 The inconstant swain. Lost
179 Let rakes for pleasure, 52-3, 94, 105, 110n, 157
180 Long with undistinguished flame, 47, 83, 87
181 Since nature mankind for society framed, 40, 52, 202
182 Tell me, ye brooks, 52
183 Thou rising sun, 126
184 Through flowery meads (*Lcm**)
185 Thus on a bed of dew bespangled flowers (*Ob**)
186 When ye celestial beauties strove (*Lcm**)
187 Young Damon, fired with amorous heat (*Lcm**)

Glees, Catches and Rounds

188 A blooming youth *a 3,* 163-4, 202
189 Genius of harmony *a 3,* 211
190 Glory be to God on high *a 3,* 163-4
191 Hallelujah *a 3,* 163-4
192 Here's to thee Dick *a 3,* (*Ob*)
193 John Cooper *a 3,* 163-4

Solo Songs

232   Love bids me go (*Lcm**), 83
233   Love's no irregular desire (*Lcm**)
234   The man that says Dick Leveridge stinks (*Lcm**)
235   My Florio, 87, 93, 157, 175n
236   Near Thames' green banks, 47, 157
237   Near to a silent shady grove (*Lcm**)
238   No more shall meads, 36, 41, 44
239   The nymph that I loved, 126
240   O nightingale, 5
241   Of all the torments all the cares, 9, 13, 15, 249
242   Of roses, while I wove, 93
243   Oft' am I by the women told, 47, 157
244   On a bank beside a willow, 29
245   On thy banks, gentle Stour, 48. 157, 202
246   One summer's morning (*Lcm**)
247   Parent of blooming flowers. Lost
248   Rail no more ye learned asses, 110, 157, 249
249   Saw you Phoebe pass this way, 109
250   She's blest with wit. (*Lcm**)
251   Silvia the fair, 7, 15
252   Since I with Chloe last was seen, 83, 110
253   The sun now darts fainter his rays, 9, 13
254   Tell me lovely loving pair (*Lcm**)
255   Tell me no more, 47
256   Tho' Chloe's out of fashion, 67, 94, 157
257   To Harriote all accomplished fair, 40, 65n, 87, 175n
258   To make the wife kind, 36, 52-3, 105
259   To sooth my heart, 42
260   'Twas summer time (*Lcm**)
261   Venus to sooth my heart, 44
262   What though you cannot move her, 7
263   When Chloe frowning bids me go (*Lcm**)
264   When Fanny/Cloe, blooming fair, 7, 12, 253
265   When first on her my eyes were thrown, 83
266   When I but dream of her (*Lcm**)
267   When mariners long wind-bound (*Lcm**)
268   When Orpheus went down, 30, 44, 94, 249
269   When the nymphs were contending, 93, 157, 245
270   When young and artless as the lamb, 40, 87, 93-4, 245
271   While on my Colin's knee I sit, 126
272   Who but remembers yesterday (*Ob**)

Instrumental Music

Twelve sonatas for two violins with a bass
for the violoncello or harpsichord, 44-7, 107, 255, 266, 286

Three sonatas for two violins and basso continuo (*Cfm*)

Ten voluntaries for the organ or harpsichord, 249-50, 272, 282

301	in g
302	in D
303	in C
304	in d
305	in C
306	in a, 250
307	in G, 250
308	Voluntary for organ in a, 250
309	Overture in C major. Keyboard score. (*Ob**)

Eight Symphonys in eight parts. Op. 2, 131-3, 259-60, 287-8

1	in Bb, 105, 131, 132n
2	in A, 113, 131
3	in C, 131-2
4	in F, 131-2
5	in D, 131-2
6	in F, 131
7	in Bb, 131-2
8	in d, 132, 245

Twelve Overtures in seven, nine, ten and twelve parts, 39, 189-90, 261, 288

1	in D, 158
2	in G, 175
3	in F, 159
4	in D, 163
5	in F, 153
6	in d, 49
7	in G, 174
8	in D, 143
9	in A, 183
10	in F, 173
11	in D, 181
12	in G, 181

Editions and Arrangements

Cathedral Music, being a collection in score of the most valuable and useful compositions for that service, by the several English masters of the last two hundred years. 3 vols. London, 1760, 1768, 1773; 5, 135-8, 156, 183-4, 197-9, 200-1, 207, 218, 228, 232, 248, 252, 258-60, 266, 269-70, 272, 288

Six arrangements from the works of Handel

As pants the hart, 279-80
Moses and the children of Israel, 192, 279-80
There were shepherds abiding, 279-80
Behold the lamb of God, 279-80
Behold I tell you a mystery, 279-80
Thou art gone up on high, 279-80

Matthew Locke: *The original songs, airs & choruses, which were introduced in the tragedy of Macbeth . . . composed by M. Locke . . . revised & corrected by Dr. Boyce,* 190-1

Henry Purcell: Te Deum and Jubilate in D [Z. 232], 98, 100, 121, 144, 173, 193, 259, 274, 287

Theoretical Work

Harmonics, or an attempt to explain the principles on which the Science of Music is founded (*Ob**), 224-5

Stage Works Interpolating Boyce Songs

The Disappointment, 181-2
Tom Jones, 186-7
Harlequin's museum, 273-4
Love in a village, 159
Midas, 153-4
The Royal Chace, 176-7
The Summer's tale, 177-8
The Temple of peace, 56-7

BOYCE BIBLIOGRAPHY

Articles

[Ayrton, William, ed.]: 'Memoir of William Boyce, Doctor in Music.' *The Harmonicon* 23 (1824), 193-5.

Bartlett, Ian: 'Boyce and Early English Oratorio - 1', *MT* 120 (1979), 293-97; and 2, 385-91.

—. 'Boyce's Homage to St. Cecilia.' *MT* 123 (1982), 758-61.

—. Preface to *William Boyce Solomon: A Serenata.* MB 68 (1996), xiv- xix.

—. 'Lambert, Finzi and the anatomy of the Boyce revival.' *MT* 144 (2003), 54-59.

—. 'Thomas Philips, Lord Chesterfield and the enigma of a popular 18th-century ballad by William Boyce: A new conspiracy theory.' *MT* 149 (2008), 26-38.

—. 'Was Boyce a Mason?' *MT* 153 (2012), 87-95.

Bartlett, Ian and Bruce, Robert J.: 'William Boyce's 'Solomon.'' *ML* 61 (1980), 28-49.

Beechey, Gwilym: 'Memoirs of Dr. William Boyce.' (With an Introduction and Notes by Gwilym Beechey). *MQ* 57 (1971), 87-106.

—. 'William Boyce, 1711-1779: A Bicentenary Tribute.' *MO* 102 (1978-9), 429-30 and 434.

Beeks, Graydon F.: 'William Boyce's Adaptations of Handel's Works for Use in the Chapel Royal.' *Handel-Jahrbuch* 39 (1993), 42-59.

Bruce, Robert J.: 'William Boyce: some Manuscript Recoveries.' *ML* 55 (1974), 437-43.

—. Intro. to *William Boyce*: *Lyra Britannica,* facs. edn (Tunbridge Wells, 1985).

—. Intro. to *William Boyce*: *Three Birthday Odes for Prince George 1749 or 1750, 1751, 1752,* facs. edn (Tunbridge Wells, 1989).

—. Intro. to *William Boyce*: *The Shepherd's Lottery,* facs. edn (Tunbridge Wells, 1990).—. 'William Boyce: Composer of the month.' *BBC Music Magazine* (November 1999), 45-9.

Bruce, Robert J. and Johnstone, H. Diack: 'A Catalogue of the Truly Valuable and Curious Library of Music Late in the Possession of Dr

William Boyce (1779): Transcription and Commentary.' *RMARC* 43 (2010), 111-171.

Colles, H. C.: 'The Chamber Music of William Boyce.' *MT* 51 (1910), 11-13.

—. 'William Boyce, 1710-1779.' *MT* 51 (1910), 697-700; see also 786.

Cudworth, C. L.: 'The Symphonys of Dr. William Boyce.' *Music* 2 (1953), 27-29.

—. 'Boyce and Arne: The Generation of 1710.' *ML* 41 (1960), 136-45.

Dawe, Donovan: 'New Light on William Boyce.' *MT* 109 (1968), 802-7.

E[dwards], F. G.: 'Dr. Boyce.' *MT* 42 (1901), 441-9; see also 529-30 and 805.

Finzi, Gerald ed.: Preface to *William Boyce*: *Overtures.* MB 13 (1957), xiii-xxii.

Fiske, Roger: 'Boyce's Operas.' *MT* 111 (1970), 1217-18.

Hadland, F. A.: 'Dr. William Boyce.' *MMR* 43 (1913), 284-85.

H[awkins], J[ohn]: 'Memoirs of Dr. William Boyce.' Prefixed to the 2nd (1788) edn of Boyce's *Cathedral Music,* i-xi.

Haywood, Charles: 'William Boyce's Solemn Dirge in Garrick's Romeo and Juliet Production of 1750.' *Shakespeare Quarterly* 11 (1960), 173-87.

Holman, Peter & Bartlett, Clifford eds.: Intro to *Boyce Trio Sonatas(1747),* facs. edn (1985).

Johnstone, H. Diack: 'The Genesis of Boyce's 'Cathedral Music.' *ML* 56 (1975), 26-40.

Kenyon, Nicholas: 'William Boyce (1711-1779).' *Music and Musicians* 27 (1979), 24-7.

Lambert, Constant: 'A half-forgotten composer,' *The Listener* (16 January 1929), 10.

Platt, Richard ed.: Preface to *Boyce Eight Symphonies Op. 2* (1994).

Range, Matthias: 'William Boyce's anthem for the wedding of King George III.' *MT* 147 (2006), 59-66.

Russell, John F.: 'The Instrumental Works of William Boyce.' *MO* 72 (1948-9), 635-37.

Sadie, Stanley: 'The Chamber Music of Boyce and Arne.' *MQ* 46 (1960), 425-36.

Smith, Fiona Eila: 'William Boyce and the orchestra: The original performing material of the court odes.' *Early Music Performer,* (18 May 2006), 4-17.

Taylor, Eric: 'William Boyce and the Theatre.' *MR* 14, (1953), 275-87.

Timms, Colin: 'Boyce's Ode to Shakespeare: The Missing Autograph Folio', *The Handel Institute Newsletter,* vol. 17, no. 1 (2006).

Van Nice, J.R.: Preface to 'William Boyce: Two Anthems for the Georgian Court. Part I The Souls of the Righteous. Part II The King Shall Rejoice.' *Recent Researches in the Music of the Baroque Era*, B 7, 8. (Middleton, Wisconsin, (1970)), 5-8.

Warren, Joseph ed.: Preface to *W. Boyce: Cathedral Music* (1849).

Westrup, J. A.: 'A minor English Master.' *Listener*, 24 (18 July1940), 105.

Williams, Peter ed.: Preface to *Twelve Voluntaries for Organ or Harpsichord by William Boyce or Maurice Greene* (New York, 1969).

University Dissertations

Bartlett, Ian: 'A critical study and transcription of William Boyce, Solomon (London, John Walsh, 1743), part III, together with London, RCM, MS.2004.' MMus London (King's) 1974.

Ford, Frederic H: 'The Court Odes of William Boyce (1711-1779).' PhD New York at Buffalo 1990.

Lee, Bostian R.: 'The Trio Sonatas of William Boyce.' MA North Carolina, Chapel Hill 1958.

Le Grove, Elizabeth A: 'The Anthems and Services of William Boyce.' MPhil North Wales, Bangor 1991.

Macintosh, Robert D: 'The Dramatic Music of William Boyce.' PhD Washington 1979.

Riches, Edgar: 'William Boyce, 'The Lord is full of compassion', anthem for two voices and chorus, edited with an introduction.' MMus London (Goldsmiths) 2001.

Sims, Phillip W: 'The Non-Orchestral Anthems of William Boyce: A Stylistic and Formal Study.' DMA Southwestern Baptist Theological Seminary 1970.

Stevenson, P. W: 'The collections of cathedral music of the 18th century by Thomas Tudway, Samuel Arnold and William Boyce.' MA Durham 1958.

Summers, Billy Wayne: 'The Coronation Anthems of William Boyce (1761). A Performing Edition.' DMA North Carolina 2001.

Tavinor, Michael E: "Titles and ermine fall behind', an Ode to Shakespeare, by William Boyce: A critical study and performing edition.' MMus London (King's) 1977.

Van Nice, John A.: 'The Larger Sacred Choral Works of William Boyce (1710-1779).' PhD Iowa 1956.

GENERAL BIBLIOGRAPHY

(Books listed without a place of publication were published in London)

Abraham, Gerald ed.: *Handel: A Symposium* (Oxford, 1954).

Academy of Ancient Music: *The Words of such Pieces, as are most usually performed by the Academy of Ancient Music*, 2nd edn, (1768).

Amberg, Anthony ed.: *The Foundling A Comedy and The Gamester A Tragedy, Edward Moore* (Newark & London, 1996).

Andrewes, Richard: *A Catalogue of Ascribed Music in pre 1800 Music MSS* (1982).

The Annual Register, or a View of the History, Politicks and Literature of the Year . . . [from 1758].

Argent, Mark, ed.: *Recollections of R.J.S. Stevens, an Organist in Georgian London* (1992).

Arnold, Denis: 'The Corellian Cult in England', *Quaderni della rivista italiana di musicologi a cura della Societa italiana di Musicologica*, no. 4 (1974), 81-89.

Ashby, Andrew & Harley, John eds.: *The Cheque Books of the Chapel Royal* (Aldershot, 2000).

Atkinson. Monte: *The Orchestral Anthem in Eighteenth-Century England*, PhD diss. (University of Illinois), 1989.

Baldwin, David: *The Chapel Royal ancient & modern* (1990).

Baldwin, David B.: *The Boyce-Hawkins 'Monumental Inscription to the Memory of Mr. Gostling', late Minor Canon of Canterbury Cathedral* (Princeton, NJ, 1973).

Baldwin, Olive & Wilson, Thelma, eds.: Introduction to *Richard Leveridge: Complete Songs (with the Music in 'Macbeth')*, MLE, A, 6 (1997).

Baker, Betty: *A History of the 1724 Chapel known as St Peter's, Vere Street* (n.d.).

Baker, David Erskine: *Biographia Dramatica; or, a Companion to the Playhouse: . . .* 2nd edn, 2 vols. (Dublin, 1782).

Bateson, F.W. ed. *The Cambridge Bibliography of English Literature*, vol. 2 (1940).

Bayley, Stephen: *The Albert Memorial* (1981).

Bell, A. Craig: *Handel Chronological Thematic Catalogue* (Darley, 1972).

Besant, Walter: *London in the Eighteenth Century* (1902).

Bibliothèque Britannique, ou Histoire des Ouvrages des Scavans de la Grande-Bretagne: Pour les Mois d'Avril, Mai et Juin, MDCCXI, XV/1 (The Hague, 1740).

Blakeney, Edward Henry ed.: *Horace on the Art of Poetry* (1928).

Boaden, James: *The Private Correspondence of David Garrick*, 2 vols. (1831-2).

Boden, Anthony: *Three Choirs: History of the Festival – Gloucester, Hereford, Worcester* (Bath, 1992).

Boswell, James: *An Account of Corsica: The Journal of a Tour . . .* (1768)

—. *The Life of Samuel Johnson . . .* , 2 vols. (1791).

Boyd, Malcolm: 'English secular Cantatas in the 18th Century', *MR* 30 (1969), 85-97.

Boydell, Barra: *Music at Christ Church before 1800* (Dublin, 1998).

Boydell, Brian: 'The Dublin Musical Scene 1749-50 and its Background', *PRMA* 105 (1978-9), 77-89.

Boydell, Brian: *A Dublin Musical Calendar 1700-1760* (Blackrock, 1988).

Bumpus, Francis T.: *Ancient London Churches* (1923).

Bumpus, John S.: *A History of English Church Music 1549-1889*, 2 vols. (1908); repr. with an introduction by Watkins Shaw (1972).

Burchell, Jenny: *Polite or Commercial Concerts? Concert Management and Orchestral Repertoire in Edinburgh, Bath, Oxford, Manchester, and Newcastle, 1730-1799* (New York & London, 1996).

Burney, Charles: *A General History of Music, from the Earliest Ages to the Present Period,* 4 vols. (1776-89); ed. F. Mercer, 2 vols. (1935; repr. New York, 1957).

—. *An Account of the Musical Performances in Westminster Abbey* (1785).

Burrows, Donald: 'Handel and the Foundling Hospital', *ML* 58 (1977), 269-84.

—. 'Handel and the 1727 Coronation', *MT* 118 (1977), 469-73.

—. 'Handel's 'As Pants the Hart', *MT* 126 (1985), 113-16.

—. *Handel* (1994).

—. *Handel and the English Chapel Royal* (Oxford, 2005).

—. 'Singing the 'Hallelujah' Chorus, still', *The Handel Institute Newsletter*, 18, no. 2 (Autumn 2007).

—. ed.: *Handel's Will: Facsimiles and Commentary* (2008).

Burrows, Donald and Dunhill, Rosemary, eds.: *Music and Theatre in Handel's World: The Family Papers of James Harris 1732-1780* (Oxford, 2002).

Busby, Thomas: 'Boyce' in *An Universal Dictionary of Music* (1783).

—. *Concert Room and Orchestra Anecdotes of Music and Musicians, Ancient and Modern,* vol. 3, (1825).

—. *A General History of Music, from the Earliest Times to the Present,* 2 vols. (1819).

Butt, J.: *Poems of Alexander Pope* (1963).

Caldwell, John: *The Oxford History of English Music from c. 1715 to the present day,* (Oxford, 1999).

—. *English Keyboard Music before the Nineteenth Century* (Oxford, 1973).

Campbell, Murray & Greated, Clive: *The Musician's Guide to Acoustics* (1987).

Caskey, John Homer: *The Life and Works of Edward Moore* (New Haven, (1927).

Cholij, Irena: *Music in Eighteenth-Century London Shakespeare Productions,* PhD diss. (University of London, King's, 1995).

A Collection of Anthems used in his Majesty's Chapels Royal [texts] (1736, 1749, 1769 & 1795).

Cibber, Colley: *An Apology for the Life of Mr. Colley Cibber, Comedian* (1740); ed. B.R.S. Fone (Ann Arbor, 1968).

Cobbett, R.S.: *Memorials of Twickenham: Parochial and Topographical* (1872).

Collier, Joel (pseud. for John Bicknell): *Musical Travels through England,* 2nd edn (1775).

Cook, Donald Frederick: *The Life and Work of Johann Christoph Pepusch (1667-1752), with special reference to the dramatic works and cantatas,* PhD diss. (University of London, King's, 1983).

Cooper, Barry: *English Solo Keyboard Music of the Middle and Late Baroque* (1974/1969).

Cotte, Roger: *La Musique Maconnique et ses Musiciens* (Baucens, 1975).

Cowgill, Rachel & Holman, Peter eds.: *Music in the British Provinces 1690-1914* (Aldershot, (2007).

Cradock, Joseph: *Literary and Miscellaneous Memoirs ,* 2nd edn, 4 vols. (1828).

Craig-McFeely, Julia: 'A Register of Theses on Eighteenth-Century British Music', in *A Handbook for Studies in 18th-Century British Music,* II, ed. M. Burden and I. Cholij (Edinburgh, 1989), 82-134.

Crosby, Brian: 'Private Concerts on Land and Water: The Musical Activities of the Sharp Family, *c.*1750?-*c.*1790', *RMARC* 34: 2001, [1]-119.

Cudworth, Charles: 'The Prospect before us', *The Decca Book of Ballet,* ed. D. Drew (1958), 84-6.

—. 'R.J.S. Stevens, 1757-1837', *MT* 103 (1962), 754-6, 834-5.

—. Intro. to *The Musical Entertainer* (1740), vol. 1, facs. edn (1965).

—. 'Masters of the Queen's Music', *MT* 107 (1966), 676-7.

D'Arblay, Frances Burney: *Memoirs of Doctor Burney*, 3 vols. (1832).

Dart, R. Thurston, ed.: 'An Eighteenth-Century Directory of London Musicians from Mortimer's London Universal Director (1763)', *The Galpin Society Journal* 2 (1949), 27-38.

Daub, Peggy E.: 'Music at the Court of George II (r. 1727-1760)', PhD diss. (University of Cornell, 1985).

Davies, Malcolm: 'The muse of Freemasonry: masonic songs, marches, odes, cantatas, oratorios and operas, 1730-1812', *The Canonbury Papers* 2, (2005), 85-103.

Davies, Thomas: *Memoirs of the Life of David Garrick*, 2 vols. 3rd edn (1781).

Davis, Bertram, H.: *A Proof of Eminence The Life of Sir John Hawkins* (Bloomington & London, 1973).

—. Introduction to *Monumental Inscription to the Memory of Mr. Gostling, late Minor Canon of the Cathedral of Canterbury* (Princeton, NJ, 1973).

Dawe, Donovan: *Organists of the City of London 1666-1850: a Record of one thousand Organists with an Annotated Index* (Author, n.p., (1983).

Dearnley, Christopher: *English Church Music in Royal Chapel, Cathedral and Parish Church* (1970).

Dean, Winton: *Handel's Dramatic Oratorios and Masques* (1959).

Deelman, C.: *The Great Shakespeare Jubilee* (1964).

Dent, E.J.: *Foundations of English Opera: a Study of Musical Drama in England during the Seventeenth Century* (Cambridge, 1928/R).

Devine, Patrick F. & White, Harry, *Irish Musical Studies* 4 (Dublin, 1996).

Dobree, Bonamy, ed.: *The Letters of Philip Dormer Stanhope 4th Earl of Chesterfield*, 6 vols. (1932).

Draper, John, W.: *William Mason: A Study in Eighteenth-Century Culture* (New York, 1924).

Drew, David ed.: *Decca Book of Ballet* (1958).

Dunhill, Rosemary: *Handel and the Harris Circle*, Hampshire Papers 8 (Hampshire, 1995).

Eddy, Donald D. ed.: *The Universal Visiter and Memorialist* (1756), facs. edn (New York, 1979).

Edwards, Owain: 'English String Concertos before 1800', *PRMA* 95 (1968-9), 1-13.

Encyclopaedia Britannica: A Dictionary of Arts, Sciences, Literature and General Information, 11th ed. (Cambridge, 1910).

England, N.W.: *Garrick's Jubilee* (1964).

Evans, Rosemary: 'Theatre Music in Nottingham, 1760-1800', *Trans. Thoroton Society* 88, (1984), 47-53.

—. *Music in Eighteenth-century Nottingham,* MA diss. (University of Loughborough, 1983).

Fawcett, Trevor: *Music in Eighteenth-Century Norwich and Norfolk* (Norwich, 1979).

Fellowes, Edmund H.: *English Cathedral Music from Edward VI to Edward VII* (1941); 5th edn, rev. J.A. Westrup (1969).

Ferrero, Bonnie: 'Samuel Johnson, Richard Rolt, and the *Universal Visiter*', *Review of English Studies,* new series, vol. XLIV, no. 174 (1993), 176-86.

Fiske, Roger: *English Theatre Music in the Eighteenth Century* (London, 1973; 2nd edn, Oxford, 1986).

—. 'The 'Macbeth' Music', *ML* 45 (1964), 114-25.

Franklin, Colin: *Lord Chesterfield: His Character and* Characters (Aldershot, 1993).

Gardiner, William: *Music and Friends; or Pleasant Recollections of a Dilettante*, 2 vols. (1838).

Garrett, K.I.: 'A List of some of St. Paul's Cathedral Choristers before 1873', *Guildhall Studies in London History*, vol. 1, no. 2, (April, 1974), 82-93.

Garrick, David: *Romeo and Juliet. A Tragedy. Written by Shakespeare.* (n.d.).

—. *The Collected Works* (1768).

Gefen, Gerard: *Les Musiciens et la Franc-maconnerie* (Fayard, 1993).

Gerber, Ernst Ludwig: *Historisch-biographisches Lexicon der Tonkünstler* (Leipzig, 1790-92).

—. *Neues historisch-biographisches Lexicon der Tonkünstler* (Leipzig, 1812-14).

Good, B.N.S. & Thatcher, D. eds.: *A Shakespeare Music Catalogue* (Oxford, 1991).

Goodall, J.R.: *Eighteenth-Century English Secular Cantatas* (New York & London, 1989).

Gower, Arthur F.G.L.: *St. Peter's, Vere Street (1722-1922)* (1922).

Gramenz, F.L.: *John Stafford Smith, 1750-1836: An early English Musicologist,* PhD diss. (University of Boston, 1987).

Graue, Jerald C. & Layng, Judith eds.: *Recent Researches in American Music*, vols. 3 & 4.

—. 'Andrew Barton *The Disappointment*' (Madison, 1976).

Gray, Thomas: *Poems and Letters* (1912).

Griffin, Ralph: *An Account of two Volumes of Manuscript Anthems once in the Barrett Collection* (privately printed,1929).

Grove, George ed.: *A Dictionary of Music and Musicians*, 3rd edn, ed. H.C. Colles, 5 vols. (1927).

Hartnell, Phillis ed.: *Shakespeare in Music* (1964).

Hawkesworth, John: Preface to *Amphitryon: Or, the Two Sosias. A Comedy, alter'd from Dryden* (1756).

[Hawkins, Sir John]: *An Account of the Institution and Progress of the Academy of Ancient Music. With a Comparative View of the Music of the Past and Present Times. By a Member . . .* (1770).

—. *A General History of the Science and Progress of Music*, 5 vols. (1776); facs. repr. of 2nd edn (1853/1875), with an introduction by C. Cudworth, 2 vols. (New York, 1963).

Hawkins, Laetitia-Matilda: *Anecdotes, Biographical Sketches and Memoirs* (1822).

—. *Memoirs, Anecdotes, Facts and Opinions*, 2 vols. (1824).

Herman, Arthur: *To Rule the Waves* (2005).

Highfill, Philip H., Burnim, Kalman A., and Langhans, Edward A.: *A Biographical Dictionary of Actors, Actresses, Musicians, Dancers, Managers & Other Stage Personnel in London, 1660-1800*, 16 vols. (Carbondale, Il., 1973-93).

Hogan, Charles Beecher: *Shakespeare in the Theatre 1701-1800* (Oxford, 1952).

Holland, Philip: *St Margaret's Westminster* (1993).

Home, John: *Agis: A Tragedy. As it is Acted at the Theatre-Royal in Drury-Lane* (Edinburgh, 1758).

Hume, Robert D.: 'The Economics of Culture in London, 1660-1740', *Huntingdon Library Quarterly*, 69 (2006), 487-553.

Humphries, Charles, and Smith, William C.: *Music Publishing in the British Isles from the beginning until the nineteenth century,* 2nd edn (Oxford, 1970).

Hunter, J. Paul, ed.: *The Plays of Edward Moore* (New York and London, 1983).

Jackson, Thomas, ed.: *Journal of the Rev. Charles* Wesley, 2 vols. (1849).

Jacobi, E.R.: 'Harmonic Theory in England after the Time of Rameau', *Journal of Music Theory* 1 (1957), 131-46.

Jenkins, John: *Mozart and the English Connection* (1998).

Jones, David Wyne, ed.: *Music in Eighteenth-Century Britain* (Aldershot, 2000).

Johnstone, H. Diack: 'English Solo Song *c*1710-1760', *PRMA* 95 (1968-9), 67-80.

—. ed.: *The Blackwell History of Music in Britain. The Eighteenth Century*, vol. 4, (Oxford, 1990).

—. Preface to *Maurice Greene Complete Organ Works* (Oxford, 1997).

Justamond, J.O., ed.: *Miscellaneous Works of the late Philip Dormer Stanhope, Earl of Chesterfield, to which are prefixed Memoirs of his Life by M. Maty,* 3 vols, (Dublin, 1777).

Kassler, Jamie Croy: *The Science of Music in Britain, 1714-1830 A Catalogue of Writings Lectures and Investigations*, 2 vols. (New York and London, 1979).

Kassler, Michael: *Music Entries at Stationers' Hall, 1710-1818* (Aldershot, 2004).

—. ed.: *The English Bach Awakening: Knowledge of J.S. Bach and his Music in England 1750-1830* (2004).

—. *A.F.C. Kollman's Quarterly Magazine Register (1812),* (Aldershot, 2009).

Kassler, Michael & Olleson, Philip: *Samuel Wesley (1766-1837) A Source Book* (Aldershot, 2001).

Kennedy, Josepha: 'An Index to the Songs in the *London Magazine* (1732-1783), *MR* 46 (1985), 83-91.

Kimbrough, S.T. Jr. and Beckerlegge, Oliver A., eds.: *The Unpublished Poetry of Charles Wesley*, 3 vols. (Nashville, Tennesse, 1988-92).

King, A. Hyatt: 'Portrait of a Bibliophile V. Frederick Nicolay, 1728/9-1809', *The Book Collector* 9 (1960), 401-13.

King, A. Hyatt: *Some British Collectors of Music c.*1600-1960 (Cambridge, 1963).

Knight, David S.: 'Resources for Musicologists in Lambeth Palace Library', *A Handbook for Studies in 18th-Century Music*, 14 (2003), 1-15.

Knight, Frida: *Cambridge Music from the Middle Ages to Modern Times* (Cambridge and New York, 1981).

Landon, H.C. Robbins, ed.: *The Collected Correspondence and London Notebooks of Joseph Haydn* (1959).

Langford, Paul: *A Polite and Commercial People: England 1727-1783* (Oxford, 1989).

Langwill, Lyndsay G.: 'Two Rare Eighteenth-Century London Directories', *ML* 30 (1949), 37-43.

Laurie, Margaret: 'The Chapel Royal Part Books', in *Music and Bibliography: Essays in Honour of Alec Hyatt King*, ed. O. Neighbour (1981), 28-50.

Lennhoff, Eugen and Posner, Oskar: *Internationales Freimaurer Lexicon* (Munich, 1932).

Lewis, W.S. ed.: *Horace Walpole's Correspondence*, 48 vols. (New Haven, Connecticut, 1937-1983).

Linley, William jnr. ed.: *Shakespeare's Dramatic Songs* (1816).

Linley, William jnr.: Preface to *Eight Glees* (1832).

Little, David M. and Kahrl, George M., eds.: *The Letters of David Garrick*, 3 vols. (Oxford, 1963).

The London Stage, 1660-1800, Part 3: 1729-1747, ed. A.H. Scouten, 2 vols. (Carbondale, 1961). *Part 4: 1747-1776*, ed. G.W. Stone, 3 vols. (Carbondale,1962). *Part 5: 1776-1800*, ed. C.B. Hogan, 3 vols. (Carbondale, 1968). *Index*, comp. B.R. Schneider (Carbondale, 1979).

Loewenberg, Alfred: *Annals of Opera 1597-1940*, (Cambridge, 1943), rev. 3rd edn. H. Rosenthal (1978).

Lonsdale, Roger: *Dr. Charles Burney, a Literary Biography*, (Oxford, 1965).

Lysons, Daniel: *History of the Origin and Progress of the Meeting of the Three Choirs of Gloucester,Worcester, and Hereford, and of the Charity connected with it* (Gloucester, 1812).

—. *The Environs of London*, vol. 2 (1795).

Macauly, John S., & Greaves, P.W., eds.: *The Autobiography of Thomas Secker* (Kansas, 1988).

McGuiness, Rosamund: *English Court Odes 1660-1820* (Oxford, 1971).

Mack, Robert L.: *Thomas Gray* (Yale, 2000).

McVeigh, Simon: 'Music and Lock Hospital in the 18th Century', *MT* 129 (1988), 235-40.

—. *Concert Life in London from Mozart to Haydn* (Cambridge, 1993).

—. 'Freemasonry and Musical Life in London in the Late Eighteenth Century', *Music in Eighteenth Century Britain*, ed. D.W. Jones (2000), 72-100.

Mclamore, Alyson: "By the will and order of Providence': The Wesley family concerts, 1779-1787', *RMARC* 37, 2004, [71]-220.

Marsh, John: Preface to *Six Anthems, in Four Parts . . .* op. 18 (1797).

Martin, Peter: *The Life of Boswell* (1999).

Mason, William, ed.: *Plays and Poems by William Whitehead, Esq. . . . . To which are prefixed, Memoirs of his Life and Writings* (York, 1788).

—. *Essays, Historical and Critical, on English Church Music* (York, 1795).

Matthew, H.C.G. & Harrison, Brian, eds.: *Oxford Dictionary of National Biography*, 60 vols. (Oxford, 2004).

Matthews, Betty: 'Handel and the Corfes', *MT* 112 (1971), 231-2.

—. *A History of the Royal Society of Musicians 1738-1988* (1988).

Maty, Matthew: *The Life of Lord Chesterfield: or the Man of the World,*

2 vols. (1774).

Malmsbury, first Earl of: *The Works of James Harris, Esq. With an Account of his Life and Character, by his Son, the Earl of Malmesbury* (1841).

Mays, David ed.: *'The Disappointment, or, the Force of Credulity' by Andrew Barton . . .* (Gainesville, 1976).

Mee, John H.: *The Oldest Music Room in Europe: A Record of Eighteenth -Century Enterprise at Oxford* (1911).

Monsey, Chris: *Christopher Smart* (Lewisburg, 2001).

Mortimer, [Thomas]: *The Universal Director, or, the Nobleman and Gentleman's True Guide to the Masters and Professors of the Liberal and Polite Arts and Sciences, . . .* (1763). Repr. in *GSJ* 2 (1949), 27-31.

Murphy, Arthur: *The Works of Arthur Murphy Esq.,* 7 vols. (1786).

Nash, Mary: *The Provoked Wife: The Life and Times of Susannah Cibber* (1977).

Nichols, R.H., and Wray, F.A.: *The History of the Foundling Hospital* (1935).

O'Keeffe, Eamonn J.: 'Sources of Church Music in Ireland in the Eighteenth Century: A Report', in Devine & White (1996) 111-18.

—. 'The Score-books of Christ Church Cathedral Dublin. A Catalogue', *FAM* 44 (1997), 42-104.

Olleson, Philip, and Kassler, Michael: *Samuel Wesley (1766-1837): A Sourcebook* (Aldershot, 2001).

Olleson, Philip, ed.: *The Letters of Samuel Wesley: Professional and Social Correspondence, 1797-1837* (Oxford, 2001).

—. *Samuel Wesley The Man and his Music* (Woodbridge, 2003).

O'Neill, Evelyn B.: *Music in Dublin 1700-1780*, MA diss. (University College Dublin, 1971).

Page, John ed.: 'Memoirs of the late Mr. Jonathan Battishill' from *Six Anthems and Ten Chants, Composed by the late Jonathan Battishill* (1804).

Parkinson, John A.: *An Index to the Vocal Works of Thomas Augustine Arne and Michael Arne* (Detroit, 1972).

Pearce, E.H. *The Sons of the Clergy*, 2nd edn (1928).

Pearmain, Andrew: 'Music and Masonry', *Ars Quatuor Coronatorum* 103 (1990), 150-4.

Pedicord, H.W. and Bergman, F.L. eds. *The Plays of David Garrick,* 7 vols. (Southern Illinois, 1980-82).

Pink, Andrew G.: *The Musical Culture of Freemasonry in early eighteenth-century London*, PhD diss. (University of London, Goldsmiths, 2007).

Pinsent, John; *Greek Mythology* (1969).

Piper, John (pseud. John Alcock): *The Life of Miss Fanny Brown* (Birmingham, 1760).

Poole, R.: 'The Oxford Music School & the Collection of Portraits formerly preserved there', *The Musical Antiquary*, 4 (1912-13), 143-59.

Pope, W.J.M.: *Theatre Royal Drury Lane* (1945).

Popkin, J.M.: *Musical Monuments* (1986).

Potter, John: *Observations on the Present State of Music in England* (1762).

Pritchard, Brian: 'Some Festival Programmes of the Eighteenth and Nineteenth Centuries, 3', *RMARC* 7, (1969), 1-25.

Pritchard, Brian, and Reid, Douglas J.: 'Some Festival Programmes of the Eighteenth and Nineteenth Centuries, 4', *RMARC* 4 (1970), 1-22.

Quennell, Peter, ed.: *Memoirs of William Hickey* (1960).

Rees, Abraham, ed.: *The Cyclopaedia; or, Universal Dictionary of Arts, Sciences, and Literature*, vol. 5, (1819).

Reid, Douglas J.: 'Some Festival Programmes of the Eighteenth and Nineteenth Centuries', 2, *RMARC* 6 (1966), 3-23.

Rhys, Ernest, ed.: *The Poems of Thomas Gray with a Selection of Letters & Essays* (1912).

Ribeiro, Alvaro, ed.: *The Letters of Dr. Charles Burney*, vol. 1, 1751-1784, (Oxford, 1991).

Rice, Paul F.: *The Solo Cantata in Eighteenth-Century Britain: A Thematic Catalogue* (Warren, Michigan, 2003).

Rimbault, E.F., ed.: *The Old Cheque–Book or Book of Remembrance of the Chapel Royal from 1561 to 1744*, Camden Society N. S. 3 (1872); facs. repr. with an introduction by Elwyn A. Wienandt (New York, 1966).

Rizzo, Betty, & Mahony, Robert: *The annotated Letters of Christopher Smart* (Carbondale and Edwardsville, 1991).

Roberts, W. Wright: 'The Trial of Midas the Second', *ML* 14 (1933) 303-12.

Robins, Brian: 'John Marsh and Provincial Music Making in Eighteenth-Century England', RMARC 29 (1996), 96-142.

—. ed.: *The John Marsh Journals: The Life and Times of a Gentleman Composer (1752-1828),* (Stuyvesant, NY, 1998).

Rodger, N.A.M.: *The insatiable Earl: A Life of John Montague, fourth Earl of Sandwich 1718-1792* (1993).

Rogers, Shef: 'The Use of Royal Licences for Printing in England, 1695-1760, a Bibliography, *The Library*, 7th series, vol. 1, no. 2 (June, 2000), [133]-192.

Routley, Erik: *The Musical Wesleys* (1968).

Rowden, Alfred W.: *The Primates of the Four Georges* (1916).

Sadie, Stanley: *British Chamber Music 1710-90*, PhD diss. (University of Cambridge, 1958).

—. 'Two British Worthies', *The Listener*, LXIII, 1610, 2 Jan. 1960, 241.

Sadie, Stanley ed.: *The New Grove Dictionary of Music and Musicians*, 1st edn, 20 vols. (1980).

Sadie, Stanley & Tyrell, John, eds.: *The New Grove Dictionary of Music and Musicians,* 2nd edn, 29 vols. (2001).

Sadler, Henry: *Masonic Reprints and Historical Revelations* (1898).

Schneider, Ben Ross ed.: *Index to the London Stage 1660-1800* (Carbondale, 1979).

Scholes, Percy A.: *The Life and Activities of Sir John Hawkins, Musician, Magistrate, and Friend of Johnson,* (1953).

Shaw, H. Watkins: *The Three Choirs Festival: The Official History of the Meetings of the Three Choirs of Gloucester, Hereford and Worcester, c1713-1953* (Worcester, 1954).

—. *The Succession of Organists of the Chapel Royal and the Cathedrals of England and Wales from c. 1538* (Oxford, 1991).

Sanders, L.D.G.: 'The Festival of the Sons of the Clergy, 1665-1955', *MT* 97 (1956), 133-5.

Sheppard, Edgar: *Memorials of St. James's Palace,* 2 vols. (1894).

Skrine, Francis Henry: *Gossip about Dr Johnson and Others being Characters from the Memoirs of Miss Laetitia Matilda Hawkins* (1926).

Smart Christopher: *Poems on Several Occasions* (1752).

—. *The Hilliard: An Epic Poem*, book 1 (1753).

—. *The Works of Horace, Translated into English Prose, . . .* 2 vols. (1756).

—. *A Translation of the Psalms of David with Hymns and Spirituals* (1765).

—. *The Poems of the late Christopher Smart* (1791).

Smith, John Stafford: Preface to *Musica Antiqua* [1812].

Smith, Robert: *Harmonics, or the Philosophy of Musical Sounds* (Cambridge, 1749); 2nd edn enlarged (1759); modern edn with intro. (New York, 1966).

Sonneck Oscar G.T.: *Early Opera in America* (New York, 1915).

Southey, Roz: *Music-Making in North-East England during the Eighteenth Century* (Aldershot, 2006).

Spector, Robert Donald: *Arthur Murphy* (Boston, 1979).

Steele, Sir Richard: *The Conscious Lovers. A Comedy* (1723).

Stein, Elizabeth P.: *Three Plays by David Garrick* (New York (1926).
—. *David Garrick, Dramatist* (New York, 1938).
Stevenson, George .J.: *Memorials of the Wesley Family* (1876).
Stewart, Trevor ed.: *Freemasonry in Literature,* Canonbury Papers, vol. 2 (2005).
Stockholm, Johanne M.: *Garrick's Folly The Stratford Jubilee of 1769* (1964).
Strype, J.: *A Survey of the cities of London and Westminster by John Stow, corrected and brought up to date by John Strype in 1720*, 2 vols., 6th edn (1755).
Temperley, Nicholas: 'William Mason: an Exhibition', *MT* 114 (1973), 894.
—. *Music in the English Parish Church*, 2 vols. (Cambridge, 1979)
—. *'The Lock Hospital and its Music'*, *JRMA* 118 (1993), 44-72.
—. *The Hymn Tune Index*, 4 vols. (Oxford, 1998).
Tollet, Elizabeth: *Poems on Several Occasions* (1755).
Trend, John B.: 'Jonathan Battishill: from the unpublished Recollections of R.J.S. Stevens', *ML* 13 (1932), 264-71.
Wagner, Gillian: *Thomas Coram, Gent. 1668-1751* (Woodbridge, 2004).
Walsh, T.J.: Opera in Dublin 1705-1797 The Social Scene (Dublin, 1973).
Watson, George, ed.: *The New Cambridge Bibliography of English Literature*, vol. 2, 1660-1800 (Cambridge, 1971).
Weber, William: *The Rise of Musical Classics in Eighteenth-Century England* (Oxford, 1992).
Wessely, Othmar ed.: *Neues Historisches-Biographisches-Lexikon der Tonkünstler* (Graz, 1969).
Wilkes, Thomas: *A Theatrical View of the Stage* (1759).
Williams, C. Lee, & Chance, H. Goodwin eds.: *Origins and Progress of the Meetings of the Three Choirs of Gloucester, Worcester, and Hereford, and of the Charity connected with it* (Gloucester, 1895).
Williamson, George C.: *John Russell, R.A.* (1894).
Williamson, Karina: 'Christopher Smart in the Songbooks', *The Review of English Studies*, New Series, vol. 25, no. 100 (1974), 410-21.
—. ed.: *The Poetical Works of Christopher Smart*, vol. 4, (Oxford, 1987).
Willson, Anthony Beckles: *Mr Pope & Others at Cross Deep Twickenham in the 18th Century* (Twickenham, 1996).
Winstanley, D.A.: *The University of Cambridge in the Eighteenth Century* (Cambridge, 1922).
Wollenberg, Susan: *Music at Oxford in the Eighteenth and Nineteenth Centuries* (Oxford, 2001).

Wilson, Ruth M.: *Anglican Chant and Chanting in England, Scotland, and America 1660 to 1820* (Oxford, 1996).

Yung, Philippe: *Guide d'Oxford* (Oxford, 1789).

SELECT DISCOGRAPHY

Sacred Music and Organ Voluntaries

Te Deum and Jubilate. Sung by the Cathedral Choirs of Rochester, Norwich, Hereford and Ripon. / B. Ferguson. Priory Records, PRCD 934, disc 1, 1992. Te Deum and Jubilate in C.

The Glory of New College. The Choir of New College, Oxford / E. Higginbottom. RRC2091, 2010. By the waters of Babylon.

William Boyce: Anthems and Voluntaries: Choir of Ely Cathedral / A. Wills. Saga, 5440, 1976. Anthems: O where shall wisdom be found; Turn unto me, O Lord; By the waters of Babylon; I have surely built Thee an house. Voluntaries: Nos. 1, 2, 4 and 10.

William Boyce: Select anthems: The Choir of New College, Oxford / E. Higginbottom. CRD 3483, 2000. O where shall wisdom be found; Wherewithal shall a young man; I have surely built thee an house; Voluntary IV; O praise the Lord; Turn thee unto me; O give thanks; Voluntary I; By the waters of Babylon; The Lord is King; Voluntary VII.

The Georgian Anthem. The choir of New College, Oxford / E. Higginbottom. Meridian CDE84151, 2010. Turn thee unto me; O where shall wisdom be found?

Coronation anthems: Academy of ancient music, Choir of New College, Oxford / E. Higginbottom. Decca, 470 226-2, 2002. The King shall rejoice; Come, Holy Ghost; Praise the Lord, O Jerusalem.

I was glad. The Choir of St Giles' Cathedral, Edinburgh / M. Harris. York Ambisonic YORK201, 2008. Turn Thee unto me, O Lord.

Music for St. Paul's. St. Paul's Cathedral Choir, The Parley of Instruments, J. Scott. Helios, CDA67009/CDH55359, 1998. Lord, thou hast been our refuge.

English Cathedral Classics. The Choir of New College Oxford / E. Higginbottom. CRD3507, 1999. The Lord is King.

David's Lamentation over Saul and Jonathan. The Choir of New College, Oxford, The Hanover Band / G. Lea-Cox. ASV CD GAU 208, 2000. With Ode on St. Cecilia's Day (Vidal); David's Lamentation (extracts from the London version, 1736).

Odes

Ode for St Cecilia's Day. The Choir of New College, Oxford, The Hanover Band / G. Lea-Cox. ASV CD GAU 200, 2000.

Pindar's Ode (Dublin version, 1741): New Year Ode 1774. The Choir of New College, Oxford, The Hanover Band / G. Lea-Cox. ASV CD GAU 232, 2001.

The Secular Masque. The Choir of New College, Oxford, The Hanover Band / G. Lea-Cox. ASV CD GAU 176, 1998. With the Ode for the New Year (1772) Overture; Ode for St. Cecilia's Day (Lockman) Overture; Birthday Ode for George III (1768) Overture.

David's Lamentation over Saul and Jonathan. The Choir of New College, Oxford, The Hanover Band / G. Lea-Cox. ASV CD GAU 208, 2000. With Ode on St. Cecilia's Day (Vidal); David's Lamentation (extracts from the London version, 1736).

Secular Choral Music and Song

Songs from the Pleasure Gardens. P. Langridge [et al]. Signum Classics SIGCD101, 2007. Orpheus and Euridice [*BC* 268], Spring Gardens [*BC* 217], The Non-Pareil [*BC* 256].

Classical Kirkby: Orpheus and Corinna. Bis Records, CD1435, 2002. When Orpheus went down to the Regions below; An answer to Orpheus and Euridice (the Words by a Lady) [*BC* 268].

William Boyce: Solomon, a Serenata: The Parley of Instruments / R. Goodman. Hyperion, CDA66378, 1990.

Theatre Music

Peleus and Thetis and other theatre music. Opera Restor'd / P. Holman. Hyperion, CDA66935, 1997. With Music for Florizel and Perdita; Corydon and Miranda; The Dirge from Romeo and Juliet.

The Secular Masque. The Choir of New College, Oxford, The Hanover Band / G. Lea-Cox. ASV CD GAU 176, 1998. With King's Ode for the New Year (1772) Overture; Ode for St. Cecilia's Day (Lockman) Overture; Birthday Ode for George III (1768) Overture.

Instrumental Music

William Boyce Eight Symphonies. New York Sinfonietta / M. Gobermann. Timely Recording, 1938.

The symphonies of William Boyce. Zimbler Sinfonietta, Decca, DX 105, 1950.

Eight Symphonies. I Solisti di Zagreb / A. Janigro. Vanguard Classics, 08.6115 or BG668/BGS70668, 1965.

The 8 Symphonies. Wurtenberg Chamber Orchestra, Heilbronn / J. Faeber. Carl 30371 0005-2 or Turnabout TV 341335, 1968.

Academy of Saint Martins-in-the-Fields / N. Marriner. Decca 444 523-2DM, 1978.

The English Concert / T. Pinnock. Archiv 419 631-2, Symphonies, Op.2. 1987.

William Boyce Symphonies, Op. 2. The Academy of Ancient Music / C. Hogwood. Decca Universal Classics, 473 081-2, 1993, 2002.

Eight Symphonies, Op.2. Aradia Ensemble / K. Mallon. Naxos, 8557278, 2005.

Boyce. Six Overtures [from Musica Britannica 13] Orchestre des Concerts Lamoureux / A. Lewis. L'Oiseau-Lyre, SOL 60041, 1962.

William Boyce: 12 Overtures ; Concerti grossi. Cantilena / A. Shepherd. Chandos, CHAN 6665(2), 1979, 2006.

The Baroque Concerto in England. Thames Chamber Orchestra London / M. Dobson. CRD3331, 2004. Concerti grossi in B minor and E minor.

Boyce: Complete trio sonatas. Collegium Musicum 90 / S. Standage. Chandos, CHAN 0648(2), 2006.

Boyce Trio Sonatas. The Parley of Instruments / P. Holman. Hyperion, CDA67151/2 CDD22063, 1996. [The 12 trio sonatas, plus the 3 in MS.]

Peleus and Thetis and other theatre music. Opera Restor'd / P. Holman. Hyperion, CDA66935, 1997. With Music for Florizel and Perdita; Corydon and Miranda (with the Overture from the *Ode for the King's Birthday* (1758); The Dirge from Romeo and Juliet.

Subject Index

Index of Names